한국어 학습 총서 02

Korean Vocabulary Practice for Foreigners

English Version

Intermediate Level

중급

외국인을 위한

한국어 어휘 연습

연세대학교 한국어학당 편

연세대학교 출판문화원

Preface

The Korean Language Institute of Yonsei University celebrated its 53rd anniversary this year. Throughout the years, the Korean Language Institute has published teaching materials for conversational Korean, practice workbooks, and much more. However, as the number of students that are learning Korean increases, their demands became more diverse. As a result of a rise in demands to practice Korean vocabulary, it became necessary to increase teaching materials for practicing vocabulary words.

'Korean Vocabulary Pratice for Foreigners' is divided into three books: Beginner, Intermediate, and Advanced. This book was published in order to build the vocabulary of Korean language students while increasing their proficiency in the language. Also, this book was written to prepare students for the various kinds of Korean Proficiency Examinations that currently exist. Vocabulary words that form part of the text book and that may appear on the Korean Proficiency Examinations have been carefully chosen and along with each word an explication of its meaning and example sentence have been provided. Also, a section of various practice problems is included so that students can make good use of the words they have learned.

'Korean Vocabulary Pratice for Foreigners' can be used as a complimentary textbook at the Korean Language Institute for learning vocabulary or can be used by students who are studying Korean on their own. We hope that 'Korean Vocabulary Pratice for Foreigners' can be used to efficiently teach vocabulary to students of the Korean language while improving their proficiency.

Yonsei University Language Research and Education Center
Korean Language Institute Compilation Committee

머리말

연세대학교 한국어학당은 올해로 창립 53주년을 맞이했습니다. 연세대학교 한국어학당은 그동안 회화 교재, 언어기능별 교재, 활용연습용 교재 등 많은 교재를 집필, 출간하였습니다. 그러나 한국어를 배우는 학습자들이 늘면서 그들의 요구도 다양해졌습니다. 특히 한국어 어휘 학습에 대한 학습자들의 요구가 높아져 어휘 학습용 교재가 필요하게 되었습니다.

'외국인을 위한 한국어 어휘 연습'은 초급, 중급, 고급의 3권으로 구성되었습니다. 이 책은 한국어를 공부하는 학습자들의 어휘력을 향상시켜 한국어 숙달도를 높이기 위해서 출간하게 되었습니다. 특히 '외국인을 위한 한국어 어휘 연습'은 현재 시행되고 있는 다양한 한국어능력 평가 시험에 대비하도록 구성되었습니다. 한국어 교재와 한국어능력 평가 시험에서 다루어지고 있는 어휘를 등급에 맞게 선정하여 각 어휘의 의미를 설명하고 예문을 제시하였습니다. 또한 다양한 문제를 통해 학습한 어휘를 활용할 수 있도록 구성하였습니다.

'외국인을 위한 한국어 어휘 연습'은 한국어교육기관에서 어휘 학습을 위한 부교재로 활용할 수 있으며 혼자서 공부하는 학습자는 자습용으로 활용할 수 있습니다. '외국인을 위한 한국어 어휘 연습'이 한국어 학습자들이 효율적으로 어휘를 학습하여 한국어능력을 향상할 수 있도록 하는 데 기여할 수 있기를 바랍니다.

연세대학교 언어연구교육원 한국어학당 교재편찬위원회

Introductory Remarks

01 'Korean Vocabulary Practice for Foreigners' is a compilation of vocabulary words deemed essential for foreign students learning Korean at the intermediate level.

02 This book is separated into 11 chapters based on topics.

03 This book is divided by topics in which around 70-90 words are presented and explained. The total number of vocabulary words, including the head words, synonyms, antonyms, related words, etc. reaches over 1800 entries.

04 The explanation of the vocabulary words include pronunciation, part of speech, translation, descriptions of the meaning when needed, usage, sentence structure, sample expressions, synonyms, antonyms, related words, example sentences, etc.

05 The part of speech will be written next to each word. If the word is a Noun(명사), it will expressed as N(Noun), a Verb(동사) as AV(Action Verb), and an Adjective(형용사) as DV(Descriptive Verb).

06 The example sentences are written using grammar that students at the intermediate level should be able to understand.

07 The vocabulary words are put into the alphabetical order of 가나다.

08 Each lesson is separated into two parts, an explanation of the vocabulary word and then practice questions. First, in the section where the term is explained, the students are provided with a description of the vocabulary word's definition when needed, sample phrases, synonyms, antonyms, related vocabulary words, and example sentences in order to ensure their complete understanding of the vocabulary word. The practice questions are used to check to see if the student has been able to accurately utilize the vocabulary words.

09 The vocabulary practice questions are presented in various forms. Taking into consideration students who are preparing for The Korean Language Test (TOPIK), the questions have been formatted to fit the style of the test.

10 Finally, in chapter 11, in order to facilitate the understanding of Korean culture, a wide variety of sayings, proverbs, expressions, and Chinese derived phrases that are commonly used in daily life have been divided into two sections, explanation of the term and practice questions, just as in the other chapters.

11 In the index of vocabulary words, the words considered to be most important, including the word's synonym, antonym, and related words are listed in alphabetical order. In the index, the pages and lessons in which the words appear are annotated as well. (Sayings, proverbs, Chinese derived expressions, and phrases, all are listed in alphabetical order)

일러두기

01 '외국인을 위한 한국어 어휘 연습(중급)'은 한국어를 배우는 외국인 학습자를 위한 어휘집으로 중급단계에서 필수적으로 알아야 할 어휘를 소개하였다.

02 이 책은 주제별 총 11과로 되어 있다.

03 이 책은 주제별로 약 70개~90개 정도의 어휘를 제시하여 설명하였다. 총 어휘 개수는 표제어, 유의어, 반의어, 관련어 등을 모두 포함하여 약 1800개 이상에 이른다.

04 각 어휘 설명에는 발음, 품사, 번역, 어휘 의미에 대한 상세설명, 활용 구문, 활용 표현, 유의어, 반의어, 관련어, 예문 등이 포함되어 있다.

05 활용 구문에서는 Noun(명사)는 'N(Noun)'으로, Verb(동사)는 'AV(Action Verb)'로, Adjective(형용사)는 'DV(Descript Verb)'로 표시했다.

06 예문은 중급 단계의 학습자가 이해할 만한 문법을 사용하여 제시하였다.

07 어휘 제시 순서는 대주제, 가나다순이다.

08 각 과는 크게 어휘설명과 연습문제 두 부분으로 구성되어 있다. 먼저 어휘 설명 부분에서는 어휘 정의에 대한 상세 설명, 활용 구문, 활용 표현, 유의어, 반의어, 관련 어휘, 예문을 통해 학습자들이 어휘에 대해 충분히 이해할 수 있도록 했고, 어휘 연습 문제 부분에서는 어휘문제들을 통해 앞서 배운 어휘를 정확하게 이해했는지 확인할 수 있도록 했다.

09 어휘 연습 문제는 다양한 유형으로 제시하였다. 특히, 한국어능력시험(TOPIK)을 준비하는 학습자들을 고려하여 한국어능력시험 시험 문제 유형과 같거나 유사한 문제들을 수록하였다.

10 마지막 11과에는 한국 문화의 이해를 돕기 위해 실생활에서 많이 쓰이는 다양한 속담과 격언, 한자성어, 관용어 등을 다른 과와 마찬가지로 어휘설명과 연습문제 두 부분으로 나누어 수록하였다.

11 단어색인에는 각 과에서 주요하게 다룬 표제어는 물론 표제어의 유의어, 반의어, 관련 어휘도 모두 포함하여 가나다순으로 제시하였다. 단어색인에는 단어가 제시된 페이지와 과도 같이 제시하였다. (속담, 격언, 한자성어, 관용어도 따로 가나다순으로 제시)

Subject Map

Chapter	Subject	Number of Vocabulary Words
1	People	73
2	Daily Life	73
3	Heath	90
4	Food	78
5	Family	74
6	Relationships	84
7	School and Class	66
8	Economy	79
9	Society	79
10	Culture	93
11	Proverbs, Idioms, Chinese character phrases, Mimetic words, Onomatopoeias	Proverbs 33, Idioms 25, Chinese character phrases 20, Mimetic words 10, Onomatopoeias 10

내용 구성

과	주제	단어 개수
1	사람	73
2	일상생활	73
3	건강	90
4	음식	78
5	가정	74
6	인간관계	84
7	학교와 수업	66
8	경제	79
9	사회	79
10	문화	93
11	속담, 관용어, 한자성어, 의태어, 의성어	속담 33, 관용어 25, 한자성어 20, 의태어 10, 의성어 10

차례 Contents

사람

01

Person

01 사람

01
가식적이다

[가식쩌기다] 형용사 to be false, to be fake

[Usage] 가식적인 N
가식적으로 AV

[Expression] 가식적인 웃음 fake smile

[Example] 사람들을 가식적인 태도로 대하지 마라.
Don't treat people with a fake attitude.

미선 씨는 항상 가식적으로 행동해서 아무도 좋아하지 않아요.
No one likes Mi Son because she always acts two-faced.

02
감정

[감정] 명사 feeling, emotion

[Expression] 감정이 상하다 to get one's feelings hurt
감정이 메마르다 to be cold hearted, emotionless
감정이 풍부하다 to be full of emotion
감정을 느끼다 to feel an emotion
감정을 표현하다 to express an emotion

[Example] 아까 한 말에 감정이 상했다면 내가 사과할게.
I will apologize to you if what I said a moment ago hurt your feelings.

예술가 중에는 감정이 풍부한 사람이 많다고 합니다.
It is said that there are many artists that are full of emotion.

03
개성적이다

[개성저기다] 형용사 to be unique, to be distinguished

[Usage] 개성적인 N

[Example] 요즘은 평범한 사람보다는 개성적인 사람이 더 인기가 있어요.
Nowadays, people with a sense of individuality are more popular than average people.

영수 씨는 얼굴이 매우 개성적이어서 누구나 한 번 보면 잊지 못한다.
Anyone who sees Youngsoo's face once can't forget it because it is so unique.

04
개인

[개인] 명사 individual

[Expression] 개인용 individual use, private use
개인택시 privately owned taxi
개인주의 individualism

개인 사업 privately owned business

[Example] 감옥 안에서는 개인의 자유가 없어요.
In prison, there is no freedom for any individual.

찌개 좀 덜어 먹게 개인 접시 좀 주세요.
Please give us individual plates so we can serve ourselves the stew.

05
겁

[겁] 명사 fear

[Expression] 겁쟁이 coward
겁이 나다 to be afraid
겁이 많다 to be frightened
겁을 먹다 to be afraid, to show one's fear
겁을 내다 to be fearful, to express one's fears

[Example] 밖이 너무 어두워서 혼자 집에 가기 겁이 난다.
I am afraid to go home alone because it is very dark outside.

동생은 겁이 많아서 놀이공원에서 롤러코스터를 절대 못 타요.
My younger sibling never rides the roller coaster at the amusement park because he is too afraid.

도움말

'N 쟁이' 와 'N '꾸러기
쟁이 Means a person who holds a certain unique characteristic.
꾸러기 Means a person who is overly expressive of a certain characteristic

N 쟁이	N 꾸러기
겁쟁이 coward	잠꾸러기 sleepyhead
멋쟁이 sharp dresser	말썽꾸러기 troublemaker
고집쟁이 stubborn person	장난꾸러기 jokester
욕심쟁이 greedy person	욕심꾸러기 miser
엄살쟁이 faker	엄살꾸러기 crybaby
말썽쟁이 troublemaker	심술쟁이 mean person
거짓말쟁이 liar	

06
고려하다

[고려하다] 동사 to consider

[Related Words] 생각하다 to think

[Example] 사장님께서 그 건의를 한번 더 고려해 보시겠대요.
The president of the company said he would consider the proposal one more time.

전공을 선택할 때는 자기 자신의 적성을 먼저 고려해야 합니다.
When choosing your major, you must first consider your own aptitude.

07
고민하다

[고민하다] 동사 to be troubled, to worry

[Expression] 고민스럽다 to be worrisome

[Related Words] 근심하다 to be uneasy, to be anxious
걱정하다 to worry

[Example] 진로 때문에 고민이라더니 무엇을 할 지 결정했어요?
I heard you were really worrying about your career. Have you decided what you are going to do?

공부도 하고 싶고 회사도 포기하고 싶지 않아 요즘 고민하고 있어요.
Nowadays, I'm struggling because I want to study but at the same time I also don't want to give up my job.

08
고집

[고집] 명사 stubbornness

[Expression] 고집쟁이 stubborn person
고집이 세다 to be very stubborn
고집이 있다 to be stubborn
고집이 없다 to lack resistance
고집을 부리다 to act stubborn

[Example] 네가 이렇게 고집을 부린다고 해결될 일이 아니야.
This isn't something that can be solved by acting so stubbornly.

제 여동생은 고집이 세서 늘 자기 생각대로만 하려고 해요.
My younger sister does everything the way she wants to because she is very stubborn person.

09
괴롭다

[괴롭따] 형용사 to be strenuous, to be painful

[Usage] AV 기가 괴롭다

[Synonym] 힘들다 to be hard

[Example] 괴로운 일이 있을 때마다 저는 등산을 가요.
I go mountain climbing whenever I have a strenuous day.

영수 씨는 여자 친구와 헤어진 후에 너무 괴로워서 매일 술을 마신다.
After Yongsoo broke up with his girlfriend, he had a difficult time and drank alcohol everyday.

10
급하다

[그파다] 형용사 to be urgent, to be impatient

[Usage] N 이/가 급하다

[Expression] 성격이 급하다 to have an impatient personality
마음이 급하다 to be in a rush

[Example] 마음이 급하다고 일을 대충하면 안 되지요.
Even though you are in a rush, you cannot make a hasty job out of it.

우리 아버지는 성격이 급해서 무슨 일이든지 서두르세요.
Since my father is very impatient, he rushes through everything.

11
긍정적이다

[긍정저기다] 형용사 to be affirmative, to be positive

[Usage] 긍정적인 N

[Expression] 긍정적인 생각 positive thought
긍정적인 반응 positive reaction
긍정적인 영향 positive influence

[Antonym] 부정적이다 negative

[Example] 이번 사업 계획에 대해 회장님께서 매우 긍정적으로 검토하고 계십니다.
The president is positively reviewing the upcoming business plan.

부정적인 생각은 마음을 어둡게 하고 긍정적인 생각은 마음을 밝게 만든다고 생각해요.
I think that negative thoughts make us feel gloomy while positive thoughts cheer us up.

12
까다롭다

[까다롭따] 형용사 1. to be picky, to be fussy 2. to be strict, to be harsh

1. to have tastes or likes that are not easy to please but rather strange and numerous.

[Usage] 까다로운 N
N 이/가 까다롭다

[Expression] 까다로운 손님 a customer that is difficult to please
성격이 까다롭다 to be a picky person

식성이 까다롭다 to be a picky eater

[Synonym] 까탈스럽다 to be disturbing, to be troublesome

[Example] 사장님 성격이 까다로워서 부하 직원들이 힘들어해요.
The office workers have a very hard time because the boss is very hard to please.

2. to be difficult and costly to fulfill a requirement or complete a task

[Usage] N 이/가 까다롭다

[Expression] 일이 까다롭다 A job is complicated.
조건이 까다롭다 Requirements are complex.
격식이 까다롭다 Formalities are strict.

[Example] 연세 주식회사에 지원하고 싶은데 조건이 너무 까다롭네요.
I want to apply to work in the Yonsei stock firm, but the application process is really complex.

13
꼼꼼하다

[꼼꼼하다] 형용사 to be precise, to be meticulous

[Usage] N 이/가 꼼꼼하다
꼼꼼하게 AV

[Antonym] 덜렁대다 to be forgetful
덜렁거리다 to be clumsy, to be absent-minded

[Example] 꼼꼼하게 일하는 사람은 실수가 적어요.
People who work very meticulously make few mistakes.

제 친구는 꼼꼼한 성격이라서 무슨 일을 하든 완벽하게 처리해요.
Since my friend is very meticulous, she handles all her work perfectly no matter what it is.

14
내성적이다

[내성저기다] 형용사 to be introverted

[Usage] 내성적인 N

[Expression] 내성적인 성격 an introverted personality
내성적인 태도 a reserved attitude

[Antonym] 외향적이다 extroverted

[Example] 은영 씨는 내성적이어서 사람을 쉽게 사귀지 못해요.
Since Eunyeong is introverted, she can't make friends easily.

사랑하는 사람이 생겨도 나는 내성적이라서 고백을 잘 못해.
Even if I start liking someone, I can't confess it to her since I'm very reserved.

15
너그럽다

[너그럽따] 형용사 to be tolerant, to be lenient, to be generous

[Usage] N 이/가 너그럽다
너그럽게 AV

[Example] 제발 제 잘못을 너그럽게 용서해 주세요.
Please, I beg you to generously forgive my mistake.

우리 선생님은 너그러우셔서 학생들이 잘못을 해도 좀처럼 화를 내지 않으세요.
Even though student make mistakes, my teacher barely gets angry because he is a very lenient person.

16
느끼다

[느끼다] 동사 to feel

[Usage] N 을/를 느끼다
AV / DV 는다고/ㄴ다고/다고 느끼다
AV / DV 는다는/ㄴ다는/다는 것을 느끼다

[Expression] 느낀 점 things one has learned
보람을 느끼다 to feel worth or value, to be worth while

[Example] 봉사활동을 한 후에 큰 보람을 느꼈어요.
It was very rewarding to work as a volunteer.

아르바이트를 하면서 돈 버는 것이 얼마나 힘든지 온 몸으로 느낄 수 있었어요.
Working a part-time job while making money was so difficult that I really felt it in my body.

17
단순하다

[단순하다] 형용사 1. to be naive, simple-minded 2. to be simple

1. natural and unaffected; innocent

[Usage] N 이/가 단순하다

[Expression] 단순한 성격 a naive personality
단순한 감정 a simple feeling

[Related Words] 순진하다 to be naive, to be innocent, to be pure

[Example] 민철 씨는 성격이 까다로워 보이지만 의외로 단순하고 솔직한 편이다.
Even though Minchol looks very fussy, he is surprisingly quite simple and honest.

2. Not complicated but simple.

[Usage] N 이/가 단순하다

[Antonym] 복잡하다 to be complicated

[Related Words] 간단하다 to be simple

[Example] 이 연습 문제는 단순해서 쉽게 풀 수 있을 거예요.
I can easily solve this practice question because it is very simple.

18
답답하다

[답따파다] 형용사 1. to feel stuffy or suffocated 2. to feel heavy with worry or burden

1. to be cramped to the point where one can't breath.

[Usage] AV 기가 답답하다

[Expression] 가슴이 답답하다 to feel cramped/ suffocated
숨쉬기가 답답하다 to feel suffocated or stuffy

[Example] 버스에 사람이 너무 많아서 가슴이 답답했어요.
I felt like I was suffocating because there were so many people in the bus.

2. To feel nervous or worried

[Usage] N 이/가 답답하다

[Expression] 마음이 답답하다 To feel fretted or frustrated

[Example] 말을 느리게 하는 사람과 대화를 하면 답답할 때가 많아요.
I feel very frustrated when I have a conversation with people that speak slowly.

19
당황하다

[당황하다] 동사 to be flustered or confused

[Usage] N 에 당황하다

[Related Words] 황당하다 to be absurd or ridiculous

[Example] 동생은 가끔 엉뚱한 질문으로 가족들을 당황하게 만들어요.
My younger sibling confuses our family at times with his random questions.

갑자기 큰 사고를 당하면 누구든지 당황해서 아무것도 할 수 없지요.
If you suddenly get into an accident, you become very flustered and are unable to do anything.

20
덜렁거리다

[덜렁거리다] 동사 to be absent-minded

[Usage] N 이/가 덜렁거리다

[Synonym] 덜렁대다 to be absent-minded

[Antonym] 꼼꼼하다 to be careful

[Example] 제 후배는 덜렁거려서 물건을 잘 잃어버려요.
My friend is very absent-minded and often loses things.

여동생이 어렸을 때는 자주 덜렁거렸지만 요즘은 실수를 거의 안 해요.
My younger sister was very careless when she was younger, but she doesn't really make mistakes anymore.

21
독립적이다

[동닙쩌기다] 형용사 to be independent

[Usage] 독립적인 N
독립적으로 AV

[Expression] 독립적인 생활 an independent life

[Antonym] 의존적이다 dependent

[Example] 더 이상 어린아이가 아니니까 독립적으로 생활해라.
Live independently because you are no longer a young child.

이 가게는 지점이 아닌 독립적으로 운영되는 가게입니다.
This store isn't part of a chain but rather is an independently run store.

22
떨리다

[떨리다] 동사 to tremble

[Usage] N 이/가 떨리다

[Expression] 몸이 떨리다 to tremble

[Related Words] 떨다 to shake

[Example] 몸살감기에 걸려서 열도 나고 몸도 떨려요.
I have both a fever and the shakes because my entire body is aching.

시험 볼 때 얼마나 떨리던지 문제가 제대로 보이지 않더군요.
When I was taking the test, I was so nervous that I couldn't read the questions properly.

23
뛰어나다

[뛰어나다] 형용사 to be excellent or outstanding

[Related Words] 훌륭하다 to be admirable

[Example] 좋은 곳에 취직하려면 영어 실력은 물론 일 처리 능력도 뛰어나야 해요.
If you want to get a job at a good office, you obviously need to speak English very well but also have very good work ethic.

영화배우 이지원 씨는 연기 실력이 좋을 뿐만 아니라 노래 실력도 아주 뛰어나요.
Lee Jiwon, the movie actor, not only has good acting skills but also amazing singing capabilities.

24
매력

[매력] 명사 charm

[Expression] 매력적이다 to be charming
매력이 있다 to have charm
매력을 느끼다 to feel another person's charm
매력에 빠지다 to fall for someone's charm

[Example] 영희 씨의 가장 큰 매력은 목소리가 예쁘다는 거예요.
They say that Younghui's biggest charm is that her voice is beautiful.

제 여동생은 얼굴은 별로 예쁘진 않지만 사람을 끄는 매력이 있어요.
My younger sister's face isn't all that pretty, but it has a charm that attracts people.

25
무뚝뚝하다

[무뚝뚜카다] 형용사 to be cold, to be abrupt

[Usage] N 이/가 무뚝뚝하다
무뚝뚝한 N

[Expression] 무뚝뚝한 말 cold or abrupt style of speaking
무뚝뚝한 표정 a cold expression

[Example] 지금 사귀는 남자 친구가 처음 만났을 때는 무뚝뚝했다면서요?
Is it true that the man you are dating now was very cold and unfriendly when you first met each other ?

저는 민수 씨가 너무 말이 없어서 무뚝뚝한 사람인 줄 알았어요.
I originally thought that Minsoo was an unfriendly person because he never really spoke.

26
밉다

[밉따] 형용사 1. to hate 2. to be ugly

1. To dislike someone or something.

[Synonym] 싫다 to hate

[Antonym] 좋다 to like

[Example] 항상 말썽만 일으키는 동생이 너무 미워요.
I really dislike that my brother always causes trouble.

2. to be ugly

[Antonym] 곱다 to be beautiful
예쁘다 to be pretty

[Example] 수학여행 때 찍은 사진이 모두 밉게 나와서 정말 속상해요.
I was very disappointed that all the pictures I took from the school trip turned out to be ugly.

27
바르다

[바르다] 형용사 to be proper, to be rightful

[Usage] N 이/가 바르다

[Expression] 생각이 바르다 to have proper thoughts
예의가 바르다 to have good manners

[Synonym] 올바르다 to be honest, to be correct

[Antonym] 그르다 to be wrong, to be improper

[Example] 현정 씨는 미모와 학식도 갖춘 데다가 예의도 바릅니다.
Not only is Hyunjeong beautiful and intelligent but also has proper etiquette.

만일 내가 선생님이라면 예의 바른 학생들을 좋아할 것 같다.
If I were a teacher, I would like to have well-mannered students.

28
버릇

[버른] 명사 habit, vice, manners

A habit or action that is frequently done. A negative quality- i.e. a vice. Manners or etiquette

[Usage] AV 는 버릇이 있다

[Expression] 버릇이 나쁘다 to have bad manners
버릇이 생기다 to make a habit
버릇을 고치다 to fix a bad habit
버릇을 버리다 to get rid of a habit

[Related Words] 습관 a habit

[Example] 나쁜 버릇은 가능한 빨리 고쳐야 해요.
You must fix your bad habits as soon as you can.

저는 주위 사람들로부터 다리를 떠는 버릇을 고치라는 충고를 자주 들어요.
I often hear from people that I should fix my habit of shaking my legs.

29
변덕스럽다

[변덕쓰럽따] 형용사 to be capricious, to be fickle

[Usage] N 이/가 변덕스럽다
변덕스러운 N

[Expression] 변덕스러운 날씨 unpredictable weather
변덕스러운 성격 a capricious personality

[Example] 변덕스러운 사람과 일할 때 정말 힘들어요.
It is very hard to work with people that often change their mind.

요즘 날씨가 변덕스러워서 옷을 어떻게 입고 나가야 할 지 모르겠다.
I don't know what to wear since the weather has been so capricious lately.

30
부끄럽다

[부끄럽따] 형용사 1. to be shy, to be embarrassed 2. to be ashamed

1. nervous or timid in the presence of others.

[Usage] 부끄러운 N

부끄럽게 AV

[Synonym] 수줍다 to be shy

[Example] 저는 사람들 앞에 서면 부끄러워서 아무 말도 못해요.
When I stand up in front of people, I am very shy and therefore am unable to say anything.

2. To be ashamed for having acted improperly or out of line.

[Usage] 부끄러운 N

[Synonym] 창피하다 to be humiliated

[Antonym] 자랑스럽다 to be proud

[Example] 부끄러운 일을 했다고 생각하면 빨리 사과해.
Apologize quickly if you think you did something shameful.

31
부럽다

[부럽따] 형용사 to be envious

[Usage] AV 는/은/ㄴ 것이 부럽다

[Example] 공부를 잘 하는 민수가 진짜 부럽네요.
I am really jealous of Minsoo since she does well in school.

형은 음치라서 노래 잘 하는 사람을 부러워해요.
My older brother is jealous of people who can sing well since he is tone-deaf.

32
불쌍하다

[불쌍하다] 형용사 to be pitiful, to be miserable

[Synonym] 가엾다 to feel sad and sorry for someone

[Example] 부모가 없는 아이들이 제일 불쌍해요.
I feel really sad for children without parents

우리 어머니는 정이 많으셔서 불쌍한 사람을 보면 꼭 도와주세요.
My mother always helps people who are down on their luck because she has a very loving heart.

33
불안하다

[불안하다] 형용사 to be anxious, to be uneasy

[Usage] 불안한 N

[Expression] 마음이 불안하다 to feel uneasy

[Antonym] 편안하다 to feel at ease

[Example] 시험 시간이 다가오니까 마음이 점점 불안해지네요.
I am starting to feel anxious as the time to take the test approaches.

밤늦게 빈 집에 혼자 있기가 불안해서 친구를 부르기로 했다.
I decided to call my friend over since I feel uneasy about being home alone late at night.

34
불행하다

[불행하다] 형용사 to be unhappy, to be misfortunate

[Usage] 불행한 N
불행하게도 AV

[Antonym] 행복하다 to be happy

[Example] 불행했던 과거는 잊고 행복하게 살 수 있도록 노력해 봐요.
Let's forget the unfortunate past and try to live happily.

어렸을 때는 불행한 삶을 살았지만 지금은 결혼해서 행복하게 산대요.
They say that when he was younger he lived an unhappy life, but now that he is married he lives happily.

35
비관적이다

[비관저기다] 형용사 to be pessimistic

[Usage] 비관적인 N
비관적으로 AV

[Expression] 비관적인 태도 a pessimistic attitude
비관적으로 생각하다 to think pessimistically

[Antonym] 낙관적이다 optimistic

[Example] 모든 일을 비관적으로만 보지 마라.
Don't only look at everything so pessimistically.

올해 하반기 경제 성장에 대해서 대부분 비관적으로 예상하고 있어요.
There are negative projections about the first half of this year's economic growth.

36
사랑스럽다

[사랑스럽따] 형용사 to be lovable

[Usage] 사랑스러운 N

[Example] 내 동생은 귀엽고 사랑스럽게 웃는다.
My sibling is cute and laughs very adorably.

나를 위해 아침 일찍 밥을 하는 아내의 모습이 매우 사랑스러워 보였어.
My wife seemed so lovable when she made me breakfast early in the morning.

도움말

'N스럽다' can be added on to nouns to convert them into adjectives displaying the qualities that they represent.

촌스럽다	to be tacky or country-like	변덕스럽다	to be capricious
걱정스럽다	to be worrisome	자연스럽다	to be natural
자랑스럽다	to be proud	고통스럽다	to be painful
사랑스럽다	to be lovable	부담스럽다	to be burdensome
조심스럽다	to be careful		

37
사생활

[사생활] 명사 private life

[Expression] 사생활 보호 protection of private life
사생활 침해 invasion of private life
사생활 폭로 exposure of private life

[Related Words] 단체생활 a group of people living together

[Example] 제 사생활에 관심 갖지 마세요.
Please don't take interest in my private life.

다른 사람과 한방에서 같이 살면 사생활이 너무 많이 알려져서 불편할 때가 많아요.
If you live with other people in one room, it can be very uncomfortable because too much of your private life can be revealed.

38
상상하다

[상상하다] 동사 to imagine

[Usage] N 을/를 상상하다

[Example] 가끔 내가 만약에 천재로 태어났다면 어땠을까 하고 상상하곤 한다.
I sometimes wonder what it would be like if I had been born a genius.

제 꿈은 멋진 피아니스트가 되는 것인데 그 때를 상상하면 기분이 좋아져요.
My dream is to become a loved pianist. I feel great whenever I think about it.

39
상하다[1]

[상하다] 동사 to feel bad or take offense to something

[Usage] N 이/가 상하다

[Expression] 속이 상하다 to feel bad
기분이 상하다 to take offense at something
마음이 상하다 to feel distressed
자존심이 상하다 to have one's pride hurt

[Example] 친구가 날 무시하는 것 같아서 자존심이 상했다.
My pride has been hurt because it seems like my friend has been ignoring me.

내 농담에 기분이 상했는지 계속 나하고 말을 안 해.
My friend isn't speaking to me because I think the joke I told hurt his feelings.

40
서운하다

[서운하다] 형용사 to feel sorry, to feel sad

[Usage] AV 기가 서운하다
서운하게 AV

[Expression] 서운한 마음 to feel hurt

[Example] 엄마는 나랑 동생이랑 싸우면 항상 동생 편만 드셔서 늘 서운했어요.
I always felt very sad that my mom took my younger sibling's side whenever we used to fight.

나는 친구의 생일에 선물까지 줬는데 친구는 내 생일이 언제인지도 몰라서 좀 서운했다.
I gave my friend a present for his birthday, but I felt a bit disappointed that my friend doesn't even know when my birthday is.

41
섭섭하다

[섭서파다] 형용사 to feel down and sad

[Usage] AV / DV 는/은/ㄴ 것이 섭섭하다

[Expression] 시원섭섭하다 to have mixed feelings, to be bitter-sweat

[Synonym] 서운하다 to feel sorry, to feel disappointed

[Example] 고향처럼 정든 한국을 떠난다고 생각하니 너무 섭섭해요.
I feel really disappointed when I think about leaving Korea, the country that I love like my own hometown.

친한 친구가 다음 달에 외국으로 이민을 가서 너무 섭섭해요.
I am very sad that my friend is going to immigrate to a foreign country next month.

42
소극적이다

[소극쩌기다] 형용사 to be passive, to be reserved

[Usage] 소극적인 N
소극적으로 AV

[Expression] 소극적인 자세 passive manner
소극적인 태도 passive attitude

[Antonym] 적극적이다 active

[Example] 내 친구는 모든 일에 매우 소극적이다.
My friend is very passive when it comes to most things.

동아리 활동을 소극적으로 하지 말고 좀 더 적극적으로 하면 좋겠어.
It would be nice if you took a more active role in your school club rather than a passive one.

43
소심하다

[소심하다] 형용사 to be timid, to be shy

[Usage] N 이/가 소심하다
소심한 N
소심하게 AV

[Expression] 소심한 성격 a shy personality
소심하게 굴다 to act shyly

[Related Words] 조심하다 to be careful

[Example] 그 남자는 몸집은 큰데 성격은 의외로 소심하다.
That man has a built physique but his personality is unexpectedly timid.

부모의 칭찬을 듣지 못하고 자란 아이들은 자신감이 없고 소심하여 친구 관계에서도 소극적이라고 합니다.
They say that children that grow up being unable to listen to their parents' compliments are later on timid and lack self confidence, which makes them very passive in relationships between friends

44
솔직하다

[솔지카다] 형용사 to be honest

[Usage] N 이/가 솔직하다
솔직한 N
솔직하게 AV

[Expression] 솔직한 성격 an honest personality

[Example] 변명하지 말고 솔직하게 말하세요.
Don't make any excuses and just tell me honestly.

그동안 하고 싶었던 말을 솔직하게 말하고 나니까 마음이 정말 시원해졌어요.
I really felt relieved after honestly saying what I wanted to say for a long time.

45
수수하다

[수수하다] 형용사 to be ordinary, to be plain

[Usage] 수수한 N

[Expression] 수수한 옷차림 modest outfit

[Antonym] 화려하다 to be extravagant

[Example] 할머니는 항상 수수한 옷을 즐겨 입으세요.
My grandmother always dresses in a modest manner.

수수한 평소의 모습과는 달리 화려한 옷차림을 한 내 모습에 사람들이 모두 놀라는 것 같았다.
It seemed like everyone was shocked when I dressed in a showy manner rather than my average plain look.

46
순수하다

[순수하다] 형용사 to be pure

[Usage] N 이/가 순수하다
순수한 N

[Expression] 순수한 마음 a pure heart
순수한 애정 a pure sentiment

[Example] 제 사촌 누나는 어린아이같이 마음이 순수해요.
My older cousin has the pure heart of a young child.

남편을 처음 만났을 때 정이 많고 자상하며 순수한 사람이라는 인상을 받았어요.
When I first met my husband, my impression was that he was very considerate, lovable and pure person.

47
심리

[심니] 명사 psychology, mentality

[Expression] 심리학 studies of psychology
심리학자 psychologist
심리 검사 psychological exam
심리 상태 psychological state

[Example] 심리학을 전공하면 인간의 심리를 잘 알 수 있나요?
Do you think you can understand mankind's psyche if you major in psychology?

심리학자가 되려면 무엇보다 사람을 잘 관찰하는 능력이 있어야 합니다.
If you want to become a psychologist, most importantly you need to have the capability of observing other humans very well.

48
심술궂다

[심술굳따] 형용사 to be ill-tempered, to be mean, to have a bad temper

[Usage] 심술궂은 N
심술궂게 AV

[Expression] 심술궂게 굴다 to act meanly

[Example] 얼굴은 심술궂게 생겼지만 마음은 따뜻하고 자상한 사람이야.
She looks like she has a bad-temper, but she has a warm heart and is a considerate person.

판소리 '흥부와 놀부'는 심술궂은 형 놀부와 따뜻한 마음을 가진 동생 흥부의 이야기를 감동적이고 재미있는 소리로 보여주고 있다.
The Pansori story of Hongbu and Nolbu, the tale of the ill-tempered older brother Nolbu and the warm hearted younger brother Hongbu, is very touching and entertaining.

49
쑥스럽다

[쑥쓰럽따] 형용사 to be shy, to be bashful

[Usage] AV 기가 쑥스럽다
AV 는 것이 쑥스럽다

[Related Words] 수줍다 to be shy
창피하다 to be embarrassed

[Example] 친구는 쑥스러워하는 표정으로 부탁을 했다.
My friend asked me a favor with an embarrassed look on his face.

사람들이 많은 곳에서 노래를 부르기가 쑥스럽지만 그래도 한번 불러 보겠습니다.
Even though I'm shy when singing at a place with a lot of people, I will give it a try this one time.

50
씩씩하다

[씩씨카다] 형용사 to be strong and healthy

[Usage] N 이/가 씩씩하다
씩씩하게 AV

[Example] 우리 아이가 씩씩하게 자랐으면 좋겠어요.
I hope my child grows up to be strong and healthy.

군인들이 씩씩하게 걷는 모습을 보면서 멋있다고 생각했다.
I thought that the soldiers look really cool as they were walking with such vigor.

51
얌전하다

[얌전하다] 형용사 to be well-behaved, to have manners

[Usage]
N 이/가 얌전하다
얌전한 N
얌전하게 AV

[Related Words]
조용하다 to be quiet
차분하다 to be calm, to be quiet

[Example]
우리 며느리는 얌전하고 착해서 아주 마음에 들어.
I really like my daughter-in-law because she has good manners and is very kind.

영수는 고등학교 때 얌전하고 말썽도 안 부리는 모범생이었다.
In high school, Yongsoo was the perfect student that was very well behaved and did not cause any trouble.

52
엄살

[엄살] 명사 a crybaby, a person who feigns a problem or sickness, a person who exaggerate one's problem

[Expression]
엄살쟁이 a crybaby
엄살꾸러기 a crybaby
엄살이 심하다 to exaggerate a problem
엄살을 떨다 to be a crybaby
엄살을 부리다 to fake pain or hardship

[Related Words]
꾀병 pretending to be sick

[Example]
남자와 여자 중에 누가 더 엄살이 심할까요?
Who tends to exaggerate more, men or women?

어린아이처럼 엄살 부리지 말고 빨리 일어나.
Stop being a crybaby and get up already.

53
염려하다

[염녀하다] 동사 to feel worry, to feel concern

[Usage]
AV / DV 는/은/ㄴ/을/ㄹ 것을 염려하다

[Synonym]
걱정하다 to worry

[Example]
제가 잘 처리할 테니까 아무 염려하지 마십시오.
Don't worry about anything since I'll take care of everything.

어머니는 항상 할아버지, 할머니의 건강을 염려하세요.
My mother always is concerned about the health of my grandparents.

54
오직

[오직] 부사 only, solely, exclusively

[Synonym] 단지 just

[Example] 제 남자친구는 오직 저만을 사랑한다고 말했어요.
My boyfriend said that he only loves me.

김 교수님은 최근 다른 일은 안 하시고 오직 전기차 기술 개발에만 몰두하고 계신다.
Recently, professor Kim does nothing else but focus on developing new technology for an electrically run car.

55
완벽하다

[완벼카다] 형용사 to be perfect

[Usage] N 이/가 완벽하다
완벽한 N

[Related Words] 완전하다 to be complete

[Example] 발표할 때 실수하지 않도록 완벽하게 준비하세요.
When you do your presentation, please prepare everything perfectly so you do not make any mistakes.

세상에는 단점이 하나도 없는 완벽한 사람은 없어요.
In this world, no one is flawless.

56
왠지

[왠지] 부사 for some reason, somehow

[Synonym] 어쩐지 for some reason

[Example] 매일 만나는 사람인데 오늘따라 왠지 멋있어 보인다.
He is someone I see everyday, but today for some reason he seems to be really handsome.

밤늦도록 멈추지 않고 주룩주룩 내리는 비를 보면서 왠지 모를 외로움을 느꼈다.
As I watched the rain that continuously fell all night long, I felt a strange sense of loneliness.

57
욕심

[욕씸] 명사 greed

[Expression] 욕심쟁이 a greedy person
욕심꾸러기 a greedy individual
욕심이 많다 to be very greedy
욕심이 나다 to show ones greed
욕심을 부리다 to be greedy

[Example] 세상에 돈에 욕심이 없는 사람이 어디 있겠어요?
Is there anyone in the world who is not greedy for money?

욕심 부리지 말고 나에게 꼭 필요한 것인지 다시 한번 생각하세요.
Stop being so greedy and decide if it is something that you really need.

58
용기

[용-기] 명사 bravery, courage

[Expression]
용기가 없다 to be timid
용기가 나다 to be brave
용기가 생기다 to become brave, to muster up courage
용기를 주다 to give someone courage, to give someone strength
용기를 얻다 to receive help or encouragement from someone

[Example] 민수 씨는 다른 사람을 잘 이해하고 용기를 주는 사람이에요.
Minsoo is the kind of person that understands others very well and gives them strength to carry on.

저도 봉사 활동을 한번 한다 한다하는 게 용기가 안 나서 아직 못하고 있어요.
I still haven't started doing any volunteer work because I am unable to gather up the courage to do so.

59
우울하다

[우울하다] 형용사 to be depressed

[Usage] N 이/가 우울하다

[Expression] 기분이 우울하다 to feel depressed

[Example] 명절인데도 회사 일을 해야 해서 기분이 우울해요.
I felt depressed that I had to work even though it was a holiday.

우울하다가도 여행 생각을 하면 기분이 좋아진다.
Even if I am depressed, once I think about traveling I feel good again.

60
이상하다

[이상하다] 형용사 to be strange

[Example] 세탁기가 고장이 났는지 세탁할 때마다 이상한 소리가 나요.
Since the washing machine is broken, whenever I do the laundry, it makes a strange sound.

지각 한 번 안 하시던 김 과장님이 결근을 하시다니 이상하네요.
It's quite strange that Mr. Kim is absent today seeing as he is never late.

61
자신

[자신] 명사 oneseIf, one's own

[Usage] 자신의 N

[Expression] 자기 자신 oneself
자신의 의견 your own opinion
자신의 생각 your own thought

[Synonym] 자기 self

[Example] 여러분에게 행복을 주는 것은 바로 지금 현재의 여러분 자신입니다.
The thing that is making you happy is nothing more than yourself.

아주머니는 자신처럼 돈이 없어 공부를 못한 사람을 돕고 싶어하셨다.
The woman wanted to help others without money like herself that were unable to study.

62
자유롭다

[자유롭따] 형용사 to be free

[Usage] N 이/가 자유롭다

[Synonym] 자유스럽다 to feel free

[Example] 네가 바라는 것처럼 자유롭게 일할 수 있는 직업은 많지 않아.
There aren't many jobs in which you can work freely like the one you are hoping for.

외국에서 살면 혼자 생활해서 자유롭긴 한데 외로울 때도 있어요.
When you live alone abroad, it is true that you are free, but there are times when you are lonely.

63
장점

[장쩜] 명사 a pro, a strength, a positive point

[Expression] 장단점 pro's and con's
장점이 있다 to have a positive point
장점이 없다 to have no strengths, no merit
장점이 되다 to become one's strength,
장점을 가지다 to hold a good quality or aspect

[Antonym] 단점 negative aspect

[Example] 언어 교환은 다양한 장점을 가지고 있다.
Language exchange has a diverse number of pros.

처음 보는 사람들과도 쉽게 가까워질 수 있고 곧 친한 친구가 될 수 있는 것이 제 성격의 장점입니다.
I believe that being able to become very close to people for the first time and quickly become their friend is my personality's strong point.

64
주장하다

[주장하다] 동사 to support, to advocate

[Usage] N 을/를 주장하다
AV / DV 는다고/ㄴ다고/다고 주장하다

[Example] 할머니가 돌아가신 후 아들들이 서로 재산권을 주장하며 소송을 했대요.
After the grandmother died, her sons all expressed their right to inherit her fortune, which ended in a lawsuit.

자신의 의견을 주장할 때는 그것을 뒷받침하기 위한 근거를 내놓아야 합니다.
When you support your opinion, you need to lay down a foundation to back it up.

65
짜증

[짜증] 명사 annoyance, irritation

[Usage] N 에게 짜증을 내다

[Expression] 짜증스럽다 to be bothersome
짜증이 나다 to be annoyed
짜증을 내다 to show one's anger or annoyance
짜증을 부리다 to get annoyed

[Example] 날씨가 너무 더워서 짜증이 나요.
I'm annoyed that the weather is so hot.

여자 친구가 자꾸 약속 시간에 늦어서 짜증을 내고 말았어요.
I got annoyed at my girlfriend because she kept showing up late to all our dates.

66
참을성

[차믈썽] 명사 patience, endurance, self-control

[Expression] 참을성이 있다 to be patient
참을성이 없다 to lack patience
참을성이 부족하다 to be lacking in patience
참을성을 기르다 to improve one's endurance

[Synonym] 인내심 patience

[Example] 저는 침착하고 참을성이 많아서 한번 시작한 일은 끝까지 하는 편입니다.
Since I am very calm and patient, once I start a job I tend to finish it.

명상을 하게 되면 마음을 안정시킬 수 있을 뿐만 아니라 참을성도 기를 수 있습니다.
If you meditate, you not only calm yourself down but you also improve your patience.

67
타다[1]

[타다] 동사 to be sensitive to, to become, to show signs of a physical or emotion change

[Usage] N 을/를 타다

[Expression] 간지럼을 타다 to be ticklish
부끄럼을 타다 to easily get embarrassed
수줍음을 타다 to be very shy
외로움을 타다 to be lonely

[Related Words] 느끼다 to feel

[Example] 외로움을 잘 타는 사람은 혼자 살기 힘들어요.
It is hard for people that feel lonely very quickly to live alone.

너는 어렸을 때부터 그렇게 수줍음을 잘 탔니?
Have you always been this shy since you were little?

68
태도

[태도] 명사 attitude, manner

[Expression] 태도가 바르다 to have a proper attitude
태도가 변하다 to change one's attitude
태도가 바뀌다 to have a change of attitude

[Example] 다른 사람에게 부탁할 때는 예의바른 태도로 해야 한다.
When you ask a favor of someone, it is best to do it with a polite attitude.

남을 배려하는 태도에 마음이 끌려 남편과 결혼하게 되었어요.
She ended up marrying her husband because she was attracted to his manner of being considerate to others.

69
특징

[특찡] 명사 characteristic, quality

[Expression] 특징이 있다 to be unique, peculiar, distinguished
특징이 없다 to have no unique quality, to be common or ordinary
특징이 나타나다 to show one's unique quality
특징을 나타내다 to present one's characteristic or quality

[Related Words] 특성 a quality

[Example] 이 핸드폰의 특징이 무엇인가요?
What are this cell phone's unique characteristics?

성공한 사람들의 특징은 항상 모든 일을 긍정적으로 본다는 것이다.
They say that the trait of a successful person is their ability to see everything positively.

70
판단하다

[판단하다] 동사 to judge

[Usage]
N 을/를 N 으로/로 판단하다
N 을/를 N 이라고/라고 판단하다
AV / DV 는다고/ㄴ다고/다고 판단하다

[Example]
한쪽 이야기만 듣지 말고 양쪽의 이야기를 다 들어보고 판단해야지요.
You need to listen to not just one side of the story but rather both sides and then make a judgment.

실력보다는 외모로 사람을 판단하는 외모 지상주의가 심해져서 무리하게 성형 수술을 하는 사례가 늘고 있습니다.
The number of examples of people undergoing extreme plastic surgery has increased because more and more people are judging others based on their appearance rather than their abilities.

71
평범하다

[평범하다] 형용사 to be average, to be normal

[Usage]
N 이/가 평범하다
평범한 N

[Antonym]
비범하다 to be extraordinary

[Example]
어제 본 연극 공연 내용은 평범한 남자와 여자의 사랑 이야기였다.
The content of the play I saw yesterday was a love story between an average man and woman.

평범한 주부로 생활하던 김영선 씨는 뒤늦게 작가의 길에 들어서게 되었다.
Ms. Kim Yongson, living as an average housewife, ended up going down the path of a writer later on.

72
표정

[표정] 명사 facial expression

[Expression]
무표정하다 to have no expression
표정이 없다 to have no expression
표정이 어둡다 to have a dark look
표정이 변하다 to change an expression
표정을 짓다 to make an expression

[Example]
표정이 어두운 걸 보니까 무슨 걱정거리가 있는 것 같다.
After seeing that he had a long face, it seems like something is bothering him.

두 사람의 표정이 안 좋은데다가 서로 말도 하지 않는 걸 보니 어제 싸운 게 틀림없어요.
After seeing that they not only had a bad look on their face but also weren't speaking to each other, now I am sure that they fought yesterday.

73
활발하다

[활발하다] 형용사 to be lively, to be active

[Usage]
N 이/가 활발하다
활발한 N
활발하게 AV

[Expression]
활발한 교류 lively exchange
활발한 움직임 swift movement

[Related Words]
활달하다 to be liberal, to be open

[Example]
우리 누나는 활발해서 동아리 회장으로 뽑혔어요.
My older sister was chosen as the president of the school club because she is very open and social.

미혼 여성들도 많지만 요즘은 기혼 여성들도 활발한 활동을 하고 있습니다.
Single women are active, but nowadays, married women also participate lively in a number of activities.

01 연습문제

[1-16] 다음 단어를 한국어로 바꿔 쓰십시오.
Change the following vocabulary words to Korean.

1. Exaggeration, Crybaby (　　　)
2. Individual (　　　)
3. Courage (　　　)
4. Facial Expresison (　　　)
5. Stubborn (　　　)
6. Patience, Endurance (　　　)
7. To be proper (　　　)
8. To be pure (　　　)
9. To be generous, lenient (　　　)
10. To be strong (　　　)
11. To be well-mannered (　　　)
12. To be average (　　　)
13. To be perfect (　　　)
14. To be simple (　　　)
15. Absence of facial expression (　　　)
16. To be pessimistic (　　　)

[17-28] [보기]에서 알맞은 단어를 골라 (　　) 안에 쓰십시오.
Choose the appropriate word from the box below and then fill in the parenthesis.

[보기]

겁	감정	짜증	밉다
느끼다	부럽다	떨리다	심술궂다
쑥스럽다	우울하다	이상하다	사랑스럽다

17. 평소에 언어 교환을 하면서 말하기 연습을 하면 외국인을 만났을 때 (　　　　　)는/은/ㄴ 두려움을 없앨 수 있다.

18. 이번 시험이 너무 중요한 시험이라서 많이 (　　　　　)고 긴장이 된다.

19. 제 친구 선아는 좋으면 좋다, 싫으면 싫다고 자신의 (　　　　　)을/를 숨기지 않고 솔직하게 말하는 편이에요.

20. 저는 (　　　　　　　)이/가 많아서 무서운 영화를 못 봐요.

21. 버스 정류장에서 30분이나 기다렸는데 버스가 안 와서 (　　　　　　　)이/가 났어요.

22. 아무리 예쁜 아기라도 자꾸 울면 (　　　　　　　)어요/아요/여요.

23. 나는 제주도에 한 번도 못 가 봤는데 친한 친구가 이번에 제주도로 가족 여행을 간다는 이야기를 듣고 아주 (　　　　　　　)었다/았다/였다.

24. 동성끼리 손을 잡고 다니면 사람들이 (　　　　　　　)게 생각할 수 있어요.

25. 얼굴도 예쁘고 웃는 모습도 귀여운 내 동생이 (　　　　　　　)어요/아요/여요.

26. 어렸을 때는 이유 없이 친구들에게 장난을 치고 때리기도 하는 등 (　　　　　　　)게 행동했어요.

27. 당연히 해야 할 일을 했는데 이렇게 칭찬을 받으니까 (　　　　　　　)습니다/ㅂ니다.

28. 날씨도 흐리고 슬픈 음악까지 들으니까 기분이 더 (　　　　　　　)어/아/여 지는 것 같다.

[29-35] **다음 밑줄 친 부분과 의미가 비슷한 것을 고르십시오.**

Choose the word that is similar in meaning to the underlined part of the sentence.

29. 처음 만나는 사람 앞에서는 수줍어서 얘기를 잘 못 해요.

❶ 부럽다　❷ 어색하다　❸ 당황하다　❹ 부끄럽다

30. 그 동안 정들었는데 이렇게 헤어지다니 정말 서운하네요.

❶ 아깝다　❷ 섭섭하다　❸ 염려하다　❹ 걱정하다

31. 10년 동안 사귄 여자 친구와 헤어진 후 너무 힘들었어요.

❶ 괴롭다　❷ 불행하다　❸ 편안하다　❹ 불안하다

32. 부모는 외국에서 혼자 생활하고 있는 자식을 항상 걱정한다.

❶ 고려하다　❷ 생각하다　❸ 판단하다　❹ 염려하다

33. 그 회사에서 월급을 더 준다고 하니까 회사 옮기는 것을 한번 생각해 보세요.

❶ 의논하다 ❷ 주장하다 ❸ 고려하다 ❹ 상상하다

34. 김 과장님은 영어 실력도 좋은 데다가 중국어 실력도 훌륭해서 회사에서 인정받고 있어요.

❶ 여전하다 ❷ 뛰어나다 ❸ 익숙하다 ❹ 매력적이다

35. 오늘 처음 만난 사람인데 왜 그런지 친근하게 느껴진다.

❶ 왠지 ❷ 뭔지 ❸ 언젠지 ❹ 누군지

[36-41] [보기]에서 알맞은 말을 찾아 빈칸에 넣으십시오.

Fill in the empty spaces with the appropriate word from the box below.

[보기]

소심하다	꼼꼼하다	솔직하다
무뚝뚝하다	변덕스럽다	성격이 급하다

36. 너무 조심하는 것이 많고 작은 일에도 걱정을 많이 해요.

( )

37. 다른 사람에게 말을 별로 하지 않아요. 말을 해도 친절하지 않아서 화가 난 사람 같아요.

( )

38. 무슨 일이든지 아주 빨리 하려고 해요. 다른 사람을 별로 기다려 주지 않아요.

( )

39. 이거 하고 싶어하다가 저거 하고 싶어해요. 마음이 금방 바뀌어요.

( )

40. 작은 일까지 신경을 많이 써서 실수가 별로 없어요.

( )

41. 좋으면 좋다, 싫으면 싫다고 말해요. 감정을 숨기지 않는 편이에요.

( )

[42-47] [보기]에서 알맞은 말을 찾아 대화를 완성하십시오.

Complete the conversation with the appropriate word from the box below.

[보기]

겁이 많다	고집이 세다	짜증이 나다
욕심이 많다	용기를 내다	엄살이 심하다

42. 가 : 이번 주에 놀이동산에 가는데 같이 가지 않을래?

나 : 미안해. 내가 ( )어서/아서/여서 놀이기구 타는 것을 좋아하지 않아.

43. 가 : 어제 눈길을 걷다가 넘어져서 무릎을 다쳤는데 너무 아파서 죽을 것 같아.

나 : 야, 너 정말 ( )구나. 아무리 무릎이 아프다고 어떻게 죽을 수 있니?

44. 가 : 내가 어제 약속 시간보다 2시간쯤 늦게 갔는데 남자친구가 화를 많이 냈어.

나 : 당연하지. 내가 남자친구여도 2시간 넘게 기다리면 ( )었을/았을/였을 것 같아. 남자친구한테 미안하다고 사과해.

45. 가 : 어제 어머니께서 케이크를 사 오셨는데 내 동생이 내 케이크까지 다 먹어버렸어.

나 : 네 동생이 먹을 것에 ( )는/은/ㄴ 것 같다.

46. 가 : 나는 외국에서 혼자 생활할 자신이 없어.

나 : 그게 무슨 말이야. 너는 잘 할 수 있어. ( )어/아/여.

47. 가 : 우리 아버지는 가족들의 의견을 별로 듣지 않고 늘 아버지 생각대로만 하시려고 해.

나 : 너도 네 아버님을 닮아서 그렇게 ( )구나.

[48-62] [보기]에서 알맞은 단어를 골라 ( ) 안에 쓰십시오.

Choose the apporiate word from the box below and then fill in the parenthesis.

[보기]

특징	자신	매력	태도	심리
버릇	오직	사생활	당황하다	상상하다
자유롭다	불쌍하다	판단하다	주장하다	고민하다

48. 수업시간에 잠깐 졸았는데 선생님이 갑자기 어려운 질문을 하셔서 ( )었어요/았어요/였어요.
49. 사람들은 왜 그렇게 연예인들의 ( )에 관심이 많은지 모르겠어요.
50. 인터넷상에서 다른 사람이 쓴 글을 읽고 ( )의 생각이나 느낌을 적은 글을 댓글이라고 한다.
51. 한국어의 ( ) 중에 하나는 다른 언어에 비해서 높임말이 많이 발달했다는 점이다.
52. 그 남자는 키도 작고 얼굴도 잘 생기지 않았지만 표현할 수 없는 그 사람만의 ( )을/를 가지고 있다.
53. 어려서 부모님을 잃고 힘들게 살아가는 ( )은/ㄴ 아이 때문에 그녀는 마음이 아팠다.
54. 대학교를 졸업하고 대학원에 갈지 회사에 취직할지 ( )고 있어요.
55. 우리 회사는 자기가 출퇴근하고 싶은 시간을 ( )게 정할 수 있어서 좋아요.
56. 50년 후의 한국의 모습이 어떻게 변할지 ( )어/아/여 봤어요.
57. 사람의 성격이 태어날 때부터 결정된다고 ( )는 사람들도 있습니다.
58. 학생들이 싸웠을 때는 한 학생의 말만 듣는 것보다 두 학생의 말을 모두 듣고 누가 더 잘못했는지 ( )는 것이 좋습니다.
59. 저는 긴장을 하면 손톱을 물어뜯는 나쁜 ( )이/가 있어요.
60. 대학교에서 사람의 마음을 연구하는 ( )학을 전공하는 것이 제 꿈이에요.
61. 학생들의 예의 없는 ( )에 선생님이 화를 내셨다.
62. 영수 씨는 일 년 동안 다른 일은 아무 것도 하지 않고 ( ) 한국어 공부만 했다.

[63-67] 다음 밑줄 친 부분과 반대되는 뜻을 가진 것을 고르십시오.

Choose the word that has an opposite meaning with the word underlined below.

63. 언어 교환의 가장 큰 <u>장점</u>은 무료로 언어를 배울 수 있다는 것이다.

❶ 맹점　　❷ 종점　　❸ 단점　　❹ 헛점

64. 중고등학교 시절의 독서는 평생 그 사람에게 <u>긍정적인</u> 영향을 미칠 것이다.

❶ 비판적이다　　❷ 부정적이다　　❸ 보수적이다　　❹ 소극적이다

65. 자신의 생활에 만족하지 못하고 항상 남과 비교하면서 사는 것은 <u>불행하게</u> 사는 것이다.

❶ 우수하다　　❷ 화창하다　　❸ 훌륭하다　　❹ 행복하다

66. 내 친구 경희는 화장하는 것도 좋아하지 않고 색깔이 있는 옷보다는 흰색이나 검은색 같은 <u>수수한</u> 옷차림을 좋아해요.

❶ 순수하다　　❷ 단순하다　　❸ 화려하다　　❹ 솔직하다

67. 혼자 있는 것을 좋아하고 자신의 성격을 사람들 앞에서 잘 표현하지 않는 사람을 <u>내성적인</u> 사람이라고 한다.

❶ 외향적이다　　❷ 개성적이다　　❸ 가식적이다　　❹ 긍정적이다

[68-73] 이야기를 읽고 밑줄 친 표현과 바꿔서 쓸 수 있는 단어를 [보기]에서 찾아 바꿔 쓰십시오.

Read the following story and change the underlined expressions with the word that you can use from the box below.

[보기]

활발하다	개성적이다	소극적이다
가식적이다	덜렁거리다	독립적이다

안녕하십니까? 저는 32살의 회사에 다니고 있는 남자입니다. 여자 친구가 없기 때문에 저와 어울리는 멋진 여성을 만나고 싶습니다. 저는 68. <u>보통 사람들과 좀 다른 생</u>

각과 행동을 하는 편이에요. 그리고 제 성격이 좀 69. 소심하고 내성적인 편이기 때문에 70. 밝고 적극적인 성격의 여성을 소개 받고 싶습니다. 또 사람들이 71. 있을 때와 없을 때의 행동이 다르거나 솔직하지 않은 성격을 가진 여성을 좋아하지 않습니다. 제가 꼼꼼한 성격이기 때문에 72. 실수가 많고 꼼꼼하지 못한 여성보다는 저처럼 꼼꼼한 사람이면 좋겠습니다. 또한 73. 자신의 일은 스스로 해결할 수 있는 여성이었으면 좋겠습니다. 이런 여성을 소개해 주시면 감사하겠습니다.

68. (   )

69. (   )

70. (   )

71. (   )

72. (   )

73. (   )

[74-76] **다음 (   )에 공통적으로 들어갈 단어의 기본형을 쓰십시오.**

Write the basic form of a word that can be used in both of the parenthesis.

74.
❶ 제가 말실수를 해서 부장님의 기분을 (   )하게 한 것 같아 죄송스럽네요.
❷ 아들이 공부도 안 하고 놀기만 해서 너무 속이 (   )어요/아요/여요.

(   )

75.
❶ (   )은/ㄴ 사람과 일하는 것은 쉬운 일은 아니지요.
❷ 아버지는 식성이 (   )으셔서/셔서 어머니가 힘들어하세요.
❸ 지난 번 사건 때문에 입국 수속이 더 (   )어졌어요/아졌어요/여졌어요.

(   )

76. ❶ 제 방은 지하에 있는데 햇빛도 안 들어오고 창문도 없어서 좀 (   )어요/아요/여요.

❷ 저는 영어를 못해서 외국인과 대화할 때 너무 (   )어요/아요/여요.

❸ 오늘 날씨도 좋은데 (   )게 실내에만 있지 말고 밖으로 나가서 산책할까요?

(   )

[77] 단어 설명을 읽고, 다음 [보기]에서 알맞은 말을 골라 빈칸에 쓰십시오.

Read the explanation of the vocabulary words and then choose a word from the box and fill in the empty spaces.

[보기]

감정	개인	고민	상상	심리
욕심	표정	참을성	개성적	내성적
부럽다	심하다	떨리다	고려하다	부끄럽다
불안하다	불행하다	소심하다	이상하다	

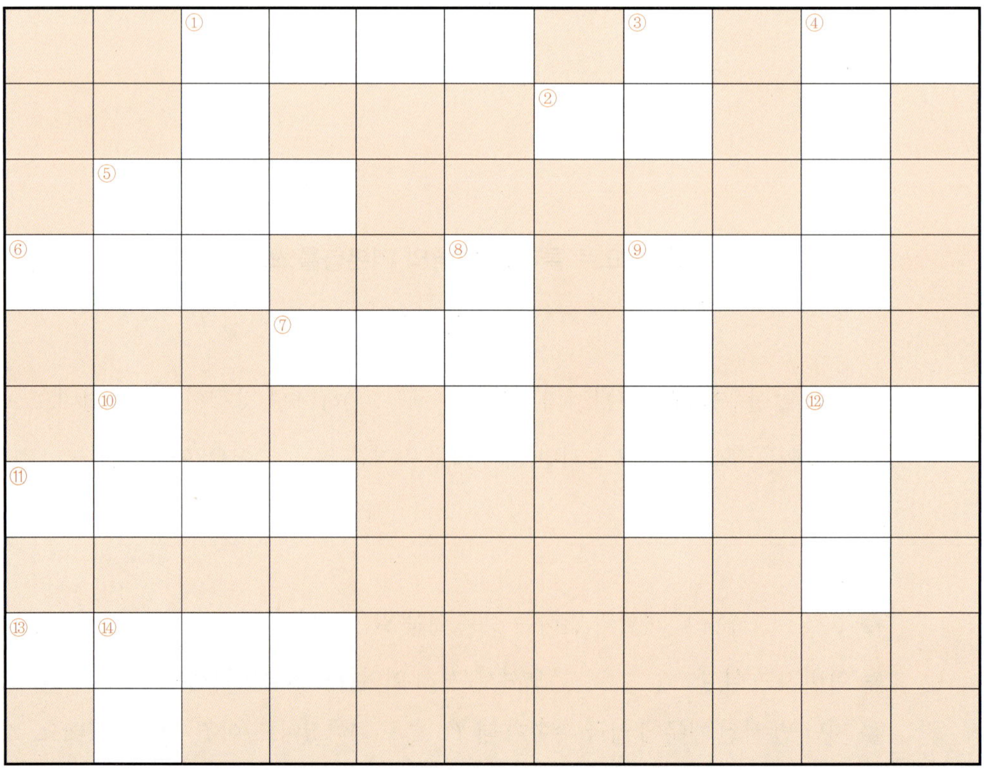

[가로]

① 마음이 편하지 않고 조마조마해요.

② 이것을 보면 그 사람의 기분, 느낌을 알 수 있어요.

④ 걱정이나 문제가 있어서 괴로워하는 것.

⑤ 약을 먹어도 감기가 낫지 않아요. 예) 감기가 ☐☐☐

⑥ 많이 추워하거나 두려워하다. 예) 시험 때문에 많이 ☐☐☐

⑦ 아프고 힘든 것을 잘 참는 성격.

⑨ 다른 사람에게 있는 좋은 일이나 물건을 보고 나도 그것을 가졌으면 좋겠다고 바라고 생각하다.

⑪ 작은 일에도 걱정을 많이 하고 모든 일을 할 때 조심스럽게 행동하다.

⑫ 국가나 사회, 단체 등을 구성하는 각각의 사람. 예) ☐☐ 택시, ☐☐ 적인 문제

⑬ 보통과 다르다.

[세로]

① 행복하지 않다.

③ 어떤 일에 대하여 일어나는 마음이나 느끼는 기분.

④ 어떤 일에 대해서 더 생각해 보다.

⑤ 인간의 마음 상태.

⑧ 다른 사람들에게 이야기를 하는 것을 좋아하지 않고 마음속으로 혼자 생각하는 성격을 나타내는 것.

⑨ 다른 사람들 앞에 서는 것을 싫어하고 수줍어하다.

⑩ 자기가 가지고 있는 것보다 더 많이 가지고 싶어하는 마음.

⑫ 다른 사람들과 구별되는 특별한 성격을 나타내는 것.

⑭ 실제로 경험하지 않은 일 또는 미래의 일을 생각해 보는 것.

일상생활

02

Daily life

02 일상생활

01
가까이

[가까이] 부사 1. nearby, close to 2. around (time) 3. close to someone

1. **[Expression]** 가까이 두다 to leave something or someone close by

[Example] 행사가 곧 시작될 테니까 멀리 가지 말고 가까이에서 기다리세요.
Don't go too far since the event is about to start.

2. **[Usage]** N 가까이

[Example] 두 시간 가까이 친구를 기다렸지만 만나지 못했다.
I waited for my friend around two hours but I wasn't able to meet him.

3. **[Expression]** 가까이 하다 (in terms of a relation, not distance)
to be close to someone

[Antonym] 멀리하다 to be distant from someone

[Example] 성호 씨는 좋은 사람이 아닌 것 같으니까 가능하면 가까이 하지 마세요.
If it's possible, don't get too close to Seongho because he doesn't look like a good person.

02
가득

[가득] 부사 full

[Expression]
가득하다 to be full
가득 담다 to fill up
가득 차다 to be full of
가득 따르다 to fill to the max (liquid in a cup)

[Example] 과일 가게 아주머니가 바구니에 과일을 가득 담아 주셨어요.
The fruit store lady filled the basket up with fruit.

꽤 오랫동안 청소를 안 했는지 방에는 먼지가 가득 쌓여 있었다.
My room is full of dust since I have not cleaned it in a very long time.

03
가만히

[가만히] 부사 1. still, motionlessly 2. secretly

1. **[Example]** 너무 더워서 가만히 있어도 땀이 줄줄 흘러요.
It is so hot that even though I am standing still, I am sweating profusely.

2. **[Example]** 영수는 주무시는 어머니가 깨시지 않도록 가만히 집을 나왔다.
Youngsoo came out of his house quietly in order to not wake up his mother who was sleeping.

04
결국

[결국] 부사 finally

[Synonym] 마침내 in the end

[Example] 그는 최선을 다해 노력했지만 결국 실패했어요.
Even though he tried his hardest, in the end he failed.

아이가 새로 나온 게임기를 사 달라고 계속 조르는 바람에 결국 사 주고 말았다.
The child got his way in the end after whining to his parents so that they would buy him the new game.

05
결심하다

[결씸하다] 동사 to determine, to make one's mind up

[Usage] N 을/를 결심하다

[Synonym] 마음먹다 to make a resolution

[Related Words] 결정하다 to decide

[Example] 영수는 열심히 공부해야겠다고 결심했다.
Youngsoo made up his mind to study much harder.

교수님의 말씀에 용기를 얻어 유학을 결심하게 되었어요.
After speaking with my professor, I mustered up the courage and made up my mind to go study abroad.

06
고치다

[고치다] 동사 1. to fix 2. to treat 3. to correct 4. to change

1. to repair an object that is broken

[Usage] N 을/를 고치다

[Expression] 기계를 고치다 to fix a machine
자동차를 고치다 to fix a car

[Synonym] 수리하다to repair

[Example] 집을 다 고치려면 돈이 많이 들 거예요.
If you want to fix your house, it is going to cost a lot of money.

2. to treat a disease

[Usage] N 을/를 고치다

[Expression] 병을 고치다 to treat a disease

[Synonym] 치료하다 to cure

[Example] 우울증은 환자의 의지만으로는 고치기 어려운 병이에요.
Depression is a difficult disease to treat, one that can not only be cured by the patient's willpower.

3. to correct something that is wrong

[Usage] N 을/를 고치다

[Expression] 답을 고치다 to fix an answer
버릇을 고치다 to fix a habit
틀린 문장을 고치다 to correct a sentence that is wrong.

[Synonym] 바로잡다 to correct, to rectify
수정하다 to revise

[Example] 잘못된 버릇은 고치기가 힘들어요.
It's hard to correct a bad habit.

4. to change something

[Usage] N 을/를 고치다

[Synonym] 바꾸다 to change

[Example] 이름이 너무 촌스러워서 다른 이름으로 고치고 싶어요.
I want to change my name to something else because it is very tacky.

07
괜히

[괜히] 부사 in vain

[Synonym] 공연히 for nothing, without purpose

[Example] 오늘은 괜히 기분이 나쁘군요.
I am in a bad mood today for no reason.

옷 가게 주인이 저에게 잘 어울린다고 해서 옷을 샀는데 괜히 산 것 같아요.
I bought a piece of clothing because the storeowner said it looked good on me, but I think it bought it in vain.

08
그냥

[그냥] 부사 1. as it is 2. just 3. nothing more than

1. As it is, without any change or alteration

[Synonym] 그대로 in the same way

[Example] 가게에 들어갔다가 그냥 나왔다.
I entered the store and then left.

2. just

[Example] 하루 종일 그냥 자기만 하면 어떻게 하니?
How can you just sleep all day long?

3. without any further conditions, nothing more than what something is.

[Example] 아까 그 말은 그냥 해 본 말이 아니야.
I didn't just say what I said before for no reason at all.

09
깜짝

[깜짝] 부사 in a state of shock or disbelief

[Expression] 깜짝 놀라다 To be very surprised

[Example] 민수 씨가 교통사고를 냈다면서요? 그 얘기를 듣고 깜짝 놀랐어요.
You said that Minsoo got into a car accident? I was shocked after hearing that.

20년 동안 떡볶이를 팔아서 번 돈을 모두 학교에 기부했다는 어느 할머니의 이야기를 듣고 깜짝 놀랐어.
I was shocked after hearing about the grandma that donated all the money she made by selling ttokpokki for twenty years to a school.

10
꺼내다

[꺼내다] 동사 1. to take out 2. to mention, to bring up a topic

1. **[Usage]** N 에서 N 을/를 꺼내다

[Expression] 물건을 꺼내다 to take an object out

[Example] 옷장에서 옷을 꺼내 입었어요.
I took the clothes out of the closet and wore them.

2. **[Usage]** N 을/를 꺼내다

[Expression] 말을 꺼내다 to bring something up
이야기를 꺼내다 to bring up a subject

[Example] 영수 씨 이야기라면 한마디도 꺼내지 마세요.
Don't bring up anything that has to do with Youngsoo.

11
꽤

[꽤] 부사 quite

[Synonym] 아주 Very

[Related Words] 제법 Pretty, fairly

[Example] 요즘 날씨가 꽤 쌀쌀해 졌어요.
Recently the weather has gotten much chillier.

꽤 큰 교통사고였는데도 다치지 않으셔서 다행이에요.
It's a relief that you didn't get hurt even though it was quite a big car accident.

12
낡다

[낙따] 형용사 To be worn out

[Usage] N 이/가 낡다

[Expression] 물건이 낡다 The object is worn out.

[Related Words] 오래되다 to be old

[Example] 집이 낡아서 수리해야겠어요.
I should repair my house since it is shabby.

내 자동차는 너무 낡아서 운전할 때 이상한 소리가 난다.
My car is so old that when I drive, it makes a strange sound.

13
낫다

[낟따] 형용사 to be good/ better

[Usage] N 이/가 낫다

[Antonym] 못하다 to be worse off

[Example] 감기에 걸리면 약을 먹는 것보다 쉬는 게 더 나아요.
When you catch a cold, resting is better than taking medicine.

우리 집의 경제 사정은 10년 전에 비해 나아진 것이 없어요.
The economic situation of our family hasn't gotten any better in comparison to that of ten years ago.

14
내내

[내내] 부사 continuously

[Synonym] 줄곧 constantly

[Related Words] 항상 always
언제나 all the time

[Example] 영화의 내용을 알고 봐서 그런지 보는 내내 지루했다.
I think that since I knew what the movie was about, I was bored the whole time while I was watching it.

설악산은 서울에서 고속버스로 3시간 정도면 갈 수 있어서 사계절 내내 인기가 많아요.
It is very popular to go to Seorak Mountain from Seoul by express bus throughout the four seasons since it takes about three hours to go there.

15
넘어지다

[너머지다] 동사 to fall over

[Usage] N 이/가 넘어지다
N 에서 넘어지다

[Example] 계단에서 넘어지는 바람에 다리를 다쳤어요.
I hurt my leg since I fell down the stairs.

길이 미끄러워서 넘어질까 봐 조심조심 걸어요.
I am walking very carefully because I am afraid that I might fall since the road is slippery.

16
다듬다

[다듬따] 동사 1. to trim 2. to prepare, to prune

1. [Usage] N 을/를 다듬다

[Expression] 머리를 다듬다 to trim one's hair
손톱을 다듬다 to cut one's nails

[Related Words] 손질하다 to repair, to mend
정리하다 to organize, to arrange

[Example] 머리를 많이 자르지 마시고 끝만 조금 다듬어 주세요.
Don't take a lot a lot off. Just trim the ends a bit.

2. [Usage] N 을/를 다듬다

[Expression] 양파를 다듬다 to clean onions
채소를 다듬다 to prepare vegetables (for cooking)

[Example] 나물 반찬은 채소를 하나하나 깨끗하게 다듬어야 해서 귀찮아요.
It's annoying that I have to clean and prepare the vegetable side dishes one by one.

17
당장

[당장] 명사 right now

[Example] 내일 당장 운동을 시작하겠어요.
I'm going to start working out from tomorrow.

저녁에는 시간이 없으니까 지금 당장 전화해 봅시다.
Let's call right now since I won't have time this evening.

18
더구나

[더구나] 부사 moreover

[Synonym] 게다가 besides
더군다나 in addition

[Example] 비가 오는데 더구나 전기까지 안 들어와서 무서운 밤을 보냈다.
It was a very scary night because not only was it raining but the electricity also went out.

어려운 집안 사정에 더구나 건강까지 좋지 않다니 너무 불쌍하다.
I feel really sorry for him after hearing that in addition to the fact his situation at home is very bad, he has poor health.

19
들르다

[들르다] 동사 to stop by

[Usage] N 에 들르다

[Related Words] 거치다 to go through

[Example] 퇴근하는 길에 술집에 들러 한잔했다.
On my way home from work, I stopped by the bar to grab a drink.

친구 집에 들렀다가 와서 좀 늦었어요.
I was a little late because I stopped by my friend's house first.

20
때때로

[때때로] 부사 occasionally

[Synonym] 가끔 once in a while
이따금 from time to time

[Example] 인생을 살다 보면 때때로 거짓말을 해야 할 때가 있다.
As you live your life, there are times when you have to lie.

나는 때때로 중학교 시절로 돌아가고 싶다는 생각이 든다.
From time to time I think that I would like to return to the days of middle school.

21
떠오르다

[떠오르다] 동사 1. to recollect 2. to rise, to float

1. [Usage] N 이/가 떠오르다

[Expression] 생각이 떠오르다 to remember a thought
아이디어가 떠오르다 to remember an idea

[Related Words] 생각나다 to remember

[Example] 고등학교 시절을 회상할 때 가장 먼저 떠오르는 선생님은 3학년 때 수학 선생님이다.
When I think back on the days of high schools, the first teacher that comes to mind is my senior year math teacher.

2. [Usage] N 이/가 떠오르다

[Expression] 해가 떠오르다 The sun rises.

[Synonym] 솟다 to rise, to soar

[Example] 새해 아침 바닷가에서 떠오르는 태양을 보기 위해 새벽에 출발했어요.
I departed at dawn in order to see the sun rise over the shore on the morning of the new year.

22
떨어뜨리다

[떠러뜨리다] 동사 to drop

[Usage] N 을/를 떨어뜨리다

[Expression] 물건을 떨어뜨리다 to drop an object

[Synonym] 떨어트리다 to let fall down

[Example] 밥을 먹다가 젓가락을 떨어뜨렸어요.
I dropped my chopsticks as I was eating.

필통을 어디에 떨어뜨렸는지 가방 안을 아무리 찾아도 없네요.
I dropped my pencil case somewhere and no matter how hard I looked through my bag it wasn't there.

23
또한

[또한] 부사 also

[Related Words] 역시 as well

[Example] 우리 하숙집은 교통이 아주 편리합니다. 또한 방마다 모든 가구가 구비되어 있어 따로 구입할 필요가 없습니다.
The transportation around my boarding house is very convenient. Also, since each room comes fully equipped with furniture, there is no need to purchase anything separately.

광고는 독자들에게 상품 및 시장에 대한 정보를 제공해 준다. 또한 기업인들에게는 그들의 상품을 일반인에게 알려주는 기능을 한다.
The advertisement provides the reader with information about the market and the product. Also, it has the function for big business leaders of informing the public about their products.

24
마침

[마침] 부사 just in time

[Antonym] 하필 why, of all times and places

[Example] 맛있는 만두가 먹고 싶었는데 마침 어머니께서 사 오셨다.
I really wanted to eat tasty dumpling. Luckily my mom brought some home.

친구한테 전화를 하려고 하는데 마침 그 친구한테서 전화가 왔다.
I was planning to call my friend, but he called me just in time.

25
만족하다

[만조카다] 동사 to be satisfied

[Usage] N 에 만족하다

[Antonym] 불만족하다 to be dissatisfied

[Example] 이번 시험 성적에 만족해요.
I'm satisfied with my grade from the exam.

지금의 상태에 만족하지 말고 더 나아지도록 노력하세요.
Don't be satisfied with your present state but try to improve yourself even more.

26
맞벌이

[맏뻐리] 명사 dual income, a couple in which both members work and provide an income

[Expression] 맞벌이 부부 a working couple

[Example] 민수와 영희는 맞벌이 부부여서 경제적으로 넉넉한 것 같았다.
It seemed that Minsoo and Younghui were economically well off since they both had an income.

저는 요즘 맞벌이 부부의 아이들에게 무료로 영어를 가르쳐 주고 있어요.
I teach English for free to the children of working couples.

27
모습

[모습] 명사 appearance

[Expression] 모습이 변하다 His appearance changes.
모습으로 돌아오다 to return to a certain appearance

[Related Words] 모양 shape

[Example] 한국은 철마다 다른 모습으로 바뀌어요.
Each one of the four seasons at Korea has a different appearance.

이번 전시회에는 화가들이 자신들의 모습을 그린 초상화가 많았다.
At this exhibition, there were many portraits that the artists drew of their appearances.

28
모으다

[모으다] 동사 to gather

[Usage] N 을/를 모으다

[Expression] 돈을 모으다 to gather money
우표를 모으다 to collect stamps

[Related Words] 모이다 to gather

[Example] 여기저기 돈을 쓰다가 보니 돈 모으기가 어렵네요.
After spending money on a lot of different things, I realized it's very hard to save money.

여러 나라를 여행하면서 동전을 모으는 것을 좋아해요.
I like to gather coins while traveling around various countries.

29
몰다

[몰다] 동사 to steer, to navigate

[Usage] N 을/를 몰다

[Expression] 차를 몰다 to steer a car, to drive a car

[Synonym] 운전하다 to drive

[Example] 요즘은 왜 차를 안 몰고 다니세요?
Why don't you take your car when you go around?

그 남자는 지난 토요일에 차를 몰고 나갔다가 사고를 냈다.
He caused an accident when he took out his car last Saturday.

30
몰래

[몰래] adverb secretly

[Related Words] 슬쩍 stealthily, furtively

[Example] 쓰레기를 몰래 버리는 행위는 철저하게 단속해야 합니다.
We need to thoroughly crack down on people who secretly throw garbage on the floor.

그 남자는 마약을 몰래 가지고 들어오다가 공항 경찰에 붙잡혔다.
The police caught the man after he entered the airport for attempting to secretly bring drugs.

31
무조건

[무조껀] 부사 unconditionally, no questions asked

[Example] 동생하고 내가 싸우면 엄마는 무조건 나만 혼내셔.
If I fight with my younger sibling, my mom will definitely only punish me.

저는 백화점에 가면 세일하는 물품들을 무조건 구매하는 습관이 있어요.
When I go to the department store, I have a habit of buying goods without a doubt.

32
묶다

[묵따] 동사 1. to make a knot, to tie 2. to bind, to tie down

1. **[Usage]** N 을/를 묶다

[Expression] 끈을 묶다 to tie a string

[Example] 신발 끈이 풀리지 않도록 꽉 묶어.
Tie your shoes so they don't become undone.

2. **[Usage]** N 을/를 N 으로/로 묶다

[Expression] 머리를 묶다 to tie your hair back

[Example] 아침마다 딸아이가 머리를 묶어 달라고 졸라요.
Every day my daughter asks me to bind her hair.

33
묻다

[묻따] 동사 1. to bury 2. to stain, to stick, to be covered

1. **[Usage]** N 을/를 N 에 묻다

[Expression] 땅에 묻다 To bury in the ground

[Example] 김치 항아리를 마당에 묻었어요.
I buried the Kimchi jar in the yard.

2. **[Usage]** N 이/가 묻다

[Expression] 때가 묻다 to get dirty, to be stained with dirt

[Example] 코트에 잉크가 묻어서 세탁소에 맡겼어요.
I got an ink spot on my jacket so I left it at the dry cleaners.

34
밀다

[밀다] 동사 to push

[Usage] N 을/를 밀다

[Antonym] 당기다 to pull

[Example] 교실 창문은 손잡이를 잡고 오른쪽으로 밀면 열려요.
The window in the classroom opens if you grab the handle and push it to the right.

만원 지하철 안에서는 본의 아니게 사람들이 서로 밀게 된다.
In a crowded bus, people end up pushing each other even though it isn't their intention.

35
밟다

[밥따] 동사 to step on

[Usage] N 을/를 밟다

[Expression] 발을 밟다 to step on one's foot

[Related Words] 디디다 to step on

[Example] 얼마 전에 지하철을 탔는데 옆에 있는 사람이 내 발을 밟았다.
Not too long ago, I was riding the subway and the person next to me stepped on my foot.

제가 조금만 늦게 브레이크를 밟았으면 큰 사고가 날 뻔했어요.
If I had stepped on the brake a little later, there could have been a big accident.

36
방금

[방금] 부사 just now (in the past)

[Synonym] 금방 in a little bit, not too long ago (either past or future meaning is possible)

[Example] 방금 점심을 먹었어요.
I ate lunch a moment ago.

오래 기다리기는요. 저도 방금 전에 왔는걸요.
What do you mean if I waited a long time? I just got here a moment ago.

37
방문하다

[방문하다] 동사 to visit (formally)

[Usage] N 을/를 방문하다

[Example] 서울을 방문하는 외국 관광객의 수가 점차 늘고 있다.
The number of tourists that are visiting Seoul has been gradually increasing.

택배기사에게서 오후 2시에 방문하겠다는 메시지를 받았다.
I received a message from the delivery service that they would arrive at 2 o'clock.

38
변경하다

[변경하다] 동사 to alter, to modify

[Usage] N 을/를 변경하다

[Expression] 계획을 변경하다 to alter plans

[Synonym] 바꾸다 to change

[Example] 병원에 예약 날짜를 변경하려고 전화 드렸습니다.
I called the hospital to change the date of the appointment.

갑자기 급한 일이 생겨서 약속 시간을 변경해야 할 것 같아요.
I think I am going to have to change the time of our meeting because something urgent has come up.

39
변하다

[변하다] 동사 to become different, to turn into

[Usage] N 이/가 변하다

[Expression] 색깔이 변하다 The colors change.
마음이 변하다 to have a change of heart or mind

[Related Words] 변화하다 to transform

[Example] 소나무는 잎 색깔이 변하지 않아요.
The color of pine tree leaves does not change colors.

외국 생활을 오래 하더니 많이 변했어요.
After living abroad for so long, he really changed.

40
봉사하다

[봉사하다] 동사 to volunteer

[Usage] N 에서 봉사하다

[Expression] 자원 봉사를 하다
to do volunteer work

[Related Words] 돕다 to help

[Example] 저는 서울 올림픽 때 통역 자원 봉사를 했어요.
During the Seoul Olympics, I worked as a volunteer interpreter.

외국에 가서 한국어를 가르치는 자원 봉사를 하셨다면서요?
I heard that you went abroad and worked as a volunteer Korean teacher?

41
비교하다

[비교하다] 동사 to compare

[Usage] N 을/를 비교하다

[Expression] 가격을 비교하다 to compare prices

[Example] 두 가게의 가격을 비교해 봤더니 별로 차이가 없었어요.
After comparing the two store's prices, I realized that there wasn't any difference.

하숙집과 기숙사 생활을 비교했을 때 어디가 더 좋습니까?
When comparing the daily life in a boarding house or in a dormitory, which place is better?

42
서늘하다

[서늘하다] 형용사 to be chilly

[Usage] N 이/가 서늘하다

[Expression] 바람이 서늘하다 The wind is chilly.

[Related Words] 시원하다 to be refreshing/cool
선선하다 to be cool
쌀쌀하다 to be a bit cold

[Example] 포도주는 서늘한 곳에 보관하세요.
You have to store wine in a cool place.

9월이 되면 서늘한 바람이 불기 시작한다.
In September, the wind becomes very cool.

43
슬슬

[슬슬] 부사 slowly

[Example] 이제 슬슬 정리들 하시지요.
Let's start organizing things little by little.

약속 시간이 되어 가는데 슬슬 출발할까요?
It's almost time to meet, shall very slowly depart?

44
아까

[아까] 부사 a moment ago, just before

[Example] 아까 친구한테서 전화가 왔었어.
My friend called me just a second ago.

아까 봤던 영화가 정말 감동적이지 않니?
The movie we saw before was really touching, right?

45
아무래도

[아무래도] 부사 no matter what, inevitably

[Example] 자동차가 또 고장 났어요. 아무래도 새 자동차를 사야겠어요.
My car broke down again. I have no choice but to buy a new one.

아무래도 다른 곳에 투자하기 보다는 은행에 저축하는 게 좋겠어요.
No matter what they say, rather than investing in other places, it is better to save money in the bank.

46
알리다

[알리다] 동사 to let know, to make know

[Usage] N 을/를 알리다

[Expression] 소식을 알리다 to inform someone about the news

[Related Words] 알다 to know

[Example] 신제품을 알리기 위해서 회사가 광고비를 얼마나 쓸 것 같아요?
How much money do you think the company will use to inform everyone about the new product?

우리 연극 동아리를 알리려고 점심시간마다 식당 근처에서 여러 번 공연을 했어요.
We did a number of performances close to the restaurant during lunchtime in order to let people know about our theater club.

47
약간

[약깐] 부사 somewhat, a few, a little

[Synonym] 다소 more or less, a little bit
조금 a little bit

[Example] 오늘 발표 준비 때문에 약간 긴장한 것 같아요.
I'm somewhat nervous because I am preparing for my presentation today.

이 옷은 제게 약간 크니까 좀 작은 사이즈로 바꿔 주세요.
Please give me a smaller size because this piece of clothing is a little big on me.

48
어쩌면

[어쩌면] 부사 1. perhaps 2. how, what

1. [Synonym] 어쩜 maybe

[Example] 우리는 어쩌면 다시는 못 볼 지도 몰라.
We might not see each other again.

2. [Expression] 어쩌면 그렇게 how can it be
어쩌면 이렇게 how can it be
어쩌면 저렇게 how can it be

[Example] 영희는 어쩌면 그렇게 바이올린을 잘 켜지?
How is it possible that Younghui plays the violin so well?

49
어쩐지

[어쩐지] 부사 for some reason

[Synonym] 왠지 without knowing why

[Example] 처음 보는 사람인데 어쩐지 낯이 익어요.
We are meeting for the first time but for some reason I feel like you have a very familiar face.

오늘은 어쩐지 좋은 일이 생길 것 같아요.
I can't explain it but today I feel like something good is going to happen.

50
외출하다

[외출하다] 동사 to go out

[Usage] N 이/가 외출하다

[Related Words] 나가다 to go out

[Example] 우리 언니는 외출하기 전에 꼭 화장을 해요.
My sister always puts on makeup before leaving the house.

봄에는 황사가 심하니까 외출할 때 마스크를 쓰세요.
In the spring, put on a mask when going out because the sand storms from the Gobi desert can be very intense.

51
우연히

[우연히] 부사 by chance, by forture

[Example] 우연히 옛 친구를 만나면 너무 반가울 것 같아요.
If I met an old friend by chance, I would be very happy.

사흘 전에 지하철 안에서 우연히 첫사랑을 만났는데 아는 척을 안 했어.
Three days ago I met my first love by chance in the subway, but I pretended like I didn't know him.

52
이르다[1]

[이르다] 형용사 to be early

[Usage] N 이/가 이르다

[Expression] 시간이 이르다 to be early on time

[Synonym] 빠르다 to be quick

[Antonym] 늦다 to be late

[Example] 아직 포기하기엔 이르니까 좀 더 노력해봐.
It's still too early to give up so try harder.

이른 아침이나 밤늦은 시간에는 꼭 필요한 일이 아니면 전화를 걸지 않는다.
I do not call late at night or early in the moring unless it is a very important issue.

53
이르다[2]

[이르다] 동사 to arrive, to reach

[Usage] N 에 이르다

[Example] 오후 3시쯤에야 산 정상에 이르렀어요.
I arrived at the peak of the mountain at three in the afternoon.

자정에 이르러서야 집에 돌아올 수 있었어요.
I barely was able to make it home at midnight.

54
이용하다

[이용하다] 동사 to use

To use people, means of transportation, immobile objects

[Usage] N 을/를 이용하다

[Related Words] 사용하다 to use (with one's hand)

[Example] 택배를 이용해서 물건을 보냈어요.
I used a package service to send the object.
출퇴근할 때 주로 지하철을 이용해요.
I tend to take the subway during rush hour.

55
자르다

[자르다] 동사 to cut

[Usage] N 을/를 자르다
N 으로/로 자르다

[Expression] 머리를 자르다 to cut one's hair
가위로 자르다 to cut with a scissor

[Related Words] 깎다 to cut

[Example] 냉면을 좀 잘라 주세요.
Please cut the naeng myeon.
머리를 잘랐는데 잘 안 어울리는 것 같아요.
I cut my hair but I don't think it looks very good.

56
잔뜩

[잔뜩] 부사 1. fully 2. seriously

1. [Expression] 잔뜩 먹다 to eat to one's maximum capacity
일이 잔뜩 밀리다 to be behind on a lot of work

[Example] 음식을 잔뜩 먹었더니 소화가 잘 안 되네요.
My stomach doesn't feel well after eating so much food before.

2. [Expression] 잔뜩 화가 나다 to be extremely angry
잔뜩 겁을 먹다 to be extremely afraid

[Example] 동생이 잔뜩 화가 나서 저하고 말도 안하려고 해요.
My younger sibling is extremely angry with me so he is trying to avoid speaking with me.

57
점점

[점점] 부사 little by little, gradually

[Synonym] 점차 steadily
차차 little by little
차츰 gradually

[Example] 오늘 아침 뉴스에서 이혼율이 점점 높아지고 있다고 했어요.
Today on the morning news, they said that the divorce rate was going up little by little.

초보자의 경우는 하루에 30분 정도 가벼운 운동을 하다가 점점 시간을 늘리는 것이 좋습니다.
In the case of beginners, it's best to do a light workout for about 30 minutes then go on increasing the time little by little.

58
정거장

[정거장] 명사 station, stop

bus, train, or other means of public transportation

[Expression] 정거장을 지나다 to pass a stop
정거장에 내리다 to get off at a stop
정거장에 도착하다 to arrive at the station

[Related Words] 역 station
공항 airport
정류장 bus stop

[Example] 버스 정거장이 여기에서 멀어요?
Is the bus stop far from here?

매일 정거장에서 친구를 만나서 같이 학교에 가요.
I meet my friend at the bus stop and then go to school with him everyday.

59
줍다

[줍따] 동사 to gather, to pick up

[Usage] N 을/를 줍다

[Expression] 쓰레기를 줍다 to pick up garbage

[Related Words] 버리다 to throw away

[Example] 어떤 사람은 쓰레기를 버리는가 하면 어떤 사람은 쓰레기를 줍는다.
There are people that throw away garbage, and there are also people that pick it up.

지하철에서 내리다가 볼펜을 떨어뜨렸는데 다시 탈 수도 없고 해서 줍지 못했어요.
As I was getting off the subway I dropped my pen, and since I couldn't get back on I was unable to pick it up.

60
즐기다

[즐기다] 동사 1. to enjoy one's time 2. to enjoy a sport 3. to enjoy food or drinks

1. [Usage] N 을/를 즐기다

[Expression] 여유를 즐기다 to enjoy free time
인생을 즐기다 to enjoy one's life
주말을 즐기다 to enjoy the weekend

[Example] 공원에는 공휴일을 즐기러 나온 사람들이 많았다.
There were a lot of people who came to the park in order to enjoy the public holiday.

2. [Usage] N 을/를 즐기다

[Expression] 축구를 즐기다 to enjoy soccer
낚시를 즐기다 to enjoy fishing

[Example] 겨울에는 스키를 즐기고 여름에는 수영을 즐겨요.
I enjoy skiing in the winter and swimming in the summer.

3. [Usage] N 을/를 즐기다
즐겨 AV

[Expression] 술을 즐기다 to enjoy alchohol
커피를 즐기다 to enjoy drinking coffee

[Example] 한국에서 10년 동안 살다 보니까 매운 음식을 즐겨먹게 됐어요.
After living in South Korea for 10 years, I came to enjoy spicy food.

61
진하다

[진하다] 형용사 1. to be dark, to be deep 2. to be strong

1. [Usage] N 이/가 진하다

[Expression] 색이 진하다 a dark color

[Antonym] 옅다 to be light
연하다 to be weak, light

[Example] 진한 색깔보다는 밝은 색으로 염색해 보세요.
Try dying your hair a bright color rather than a dark one.

2. [Usage] N 이/가 진하다

[Expression] 커피가 진하다 The coffee is strong.
향이 진하다 to give off a strong scent

[Antonym] 연하다 to be weak

[Example] 커피 향이 너무 진한 것 같아요.
The smell of the coffee seems to be too strong.

62
짜다

[짜다] 동사 1. to make a plan 2. to pop, to wring, to squeeze

1. [Usage] N 을/를 짜다

[Expression] 계획을 짜다 to make a plan
일정표를 짜다 to make a schedule

[Synonym] 세우다 to devise

[Example] 일주일 동안의 일정을 잘 짜두는 것이 좋을 거예요.
It is good if we plan out our schedule for the next week.

2. [Usage] N 을/를 짜다

[Expression] 빨래를 짜다 to wring the laundry
치약을 짜다 to push out the toothpaste from the tube
여드름을 짜다 to pop a pimple

[Example] 걸레에 물기가 없도록 꽉 짜서 닦으세요.
Please squeeze all the water out of the cloth and then use it to clean.

63
차례

[차례] 명사 order, turn

[Expression] 차례가 오다 It is my turn.
차례가 되다 to be one's turn
차례를 지키다 to keep order
차례를 기다리다 to wait in order

[Synonym] 순서 order

[Example] 이번은 내 차례야. Now it's my turn.
먼저 번호표를 뽑은 후에 차례가 되면 창구로 가세요.
First take a number and when it's your turn, please go to the counter.

64
충고하다

[충고하다] 동사 to advise

[Usage] N 을/를 N 에/에게 충고하다

[Related Words] 조언하다 to give advice

[Example] 자신의 성격을 고치려면 친구들의 충고에 귀 기울여야 한다.
If you want to change your personality, you need to lend an ear to your friend's advice.

제가 여러 번 충고를 했는데도 친구는 제 말을 무시하더라고요.
Even though I gave my friend a lot of advice, he ignored what I told him.

65
타다²

[타다] 동사 1. to burn 2. to get tanned, to burn one's skin

1. [Usage] N 이/가 타다

[Expression] 밥이 타다 The rice is burnt.
불에 타다 to burn in a fire

[Example] 산불이 나서 수천 그루의 나무가 불에 탔습니다.
Thousands of trees burned down in the forest fire.

2. [Usage] N 이/가 타다

[Expression] 피부가 타다 to get some color on one's skin.

[Example] 햇볕에 얼굴이 새까맣게 탔어요.
My skin got burnt in the sun.

66
특기

[특끼] 명사 specialty, talent

[Usage] 특기가 있다 to have a special talent
특기가 없다 to not have any unique talent
특기를 살리다 to use one's specialty

[Example] 제 특기는 태권도예요.
My specialty is taekwondo.

자신만의 특기가 있다면 한번 얘기해 보세요.
If you have a unique talent, please tell us about it.

67
펴다

[펴다] 동사 1. to straighten out, to open, to stretch 2. to open 3. to smooth out

1. [Usage] N 을/를 펴다

[Expression] 주먹을 펴다 to open one's fist
허리를 펴다 to straighten out one's waist
다리를 펴다 to stretch one's legs
어깨를 펴다 to widen one's shoulders

[Example] 허리를 펴고 똑바로 앉으세요. Sit up straight.

2. [Usage] N 을/를 펴다

[Expression] 책을 펴다 to open a book
우산을 펴다 to open an umbrella

[Antonym] 접다 to fold
개다 to fold

[Example] 교과서 26쪽을 펴세요.
Open your textbook to page 26.

3. [Usage] N 을/를 펴다

[Expression] 주름을 펴다 to smooth out a wrinkle

[Antonym] 말다 to roll up
구기다 to crumble, to crush

[Example] 머리가 곱슬거려서 스트레이트 파마로 머리를 펴고 싶어요.
My hair got curly, so I want to straighten it.

68
평소

[평소] 명사 on average

[Synonym] 평상시 normally

[Example] 평소에 수다스럽던 미선이가 오늘따라 말이 없네.
Normally, Miseon is very talkative but today she surprisingly has nothing to say.

쓰기 시험을 잘 보려면 평소에 숙제를 잘 해야지요.
If you want to do well on your written exam, you need to do your homework often.

69
푹

[푹] 부사 fully

[Expression] 푹 자다 to sleep well
푹 쉬다 to rest up

[Example] 이번 주말에는 푹 쉴 거예요.
I am going to get some rest this weekend.

요즘 인터넷 쇼핑에 푹 빠졌이요.
I am completely obsessed with online shopping nowadays.

70
향기

[향기] 명사 scent, fragrance

[Expression] 향기가 좋다 to have a good scent
향기가 나다 to give off a scent
향기가 진하다 to have a strong scent
향기를 맡다 to smell a fragrance

[Related Words] 냄새 smell

[Example] 장미꽃 향기가 참 좋네요.
The smell of the rose is quite nice.

방안에서 은은한 향기가 나네요.
A delicate fragrance is coming from the room.

71
혹은

[호근] 부사 or

[Synonym] 또는 or

[Example] 한국에서는 지방마다 혹은 가정마다 특별한 건강식이 있습니다.
In Korea, there are different health food diets per region and per household.

교실 혹은 여러분의 집 앞에 무인 감시 카메라가 있다면 어떨 것 같습니까?
If there were a hidden camera in front of your house or in your classroom, how would you react?

72
활용하다

[화룡하다] 동사 to use (for a good purpose)

[Usage] N 을/를 활용하다

[Expression] 시간을 활용하다 to use time (to do something)
문법을 활용하다 to use grammar

[Related Words] 이용하다 to use (transportation, another person)
사용하다 to use (by hand ex: a pen, a computer)

[Example] 시간을 효율적으로 활용하기 위해 계획을 세우는 편이다.
I tend to make plans in order to effectively use my time.

여가 활동이란 일을 하고 남는 시간을 활용하여 하는 활동을 말합니다.
Leisure activity is what you do during your free time after work.

73
흔히

[흔히] 부사 commonly

[Synonym] 보통 usually
자주 often

[Example] 봄이 되면 활짝 핀 개나리를 흔히 볼 수 있어요.
In the spring, you can easily see forsythia.

요즘은 인터넷이나 신문 등에서 호기심을 자극하는 광고나 기사를 흔히 볼 수 있다.
Nowadays, you can commonly see advertisements or articles that stimulate the reader's curiosity in newspapers or on the internet.

02 연습문제

[1-12] **다음 단어를 한국어로 바꿔 쓰십시오.**
Change the following vocabulary words to Korean.

1. Appearance ( )
2. Definitely, Without a doubt ( )
3. To tie ( )
4. To push ( )
5. Bus stop ( )
6. Order ( )
7. Specialty ( )
8. To open, to straighten out ( )
9. To use (time) ( )
10. Normally ( )
11. Perhaps ( )
12. To gather ( )

[13-23] **[보기]에서 알맞은 단어를 골라 ( ) 안에 쓰십시오.**
Choose the appropriate word from the box below and fill in the parenthesis.

[보기]

푹	괜히	깜짝	맞벌이	변하다	향기
만족하다	이용하다	충고하다	비교하다	외출하다	

13. 얼마 전에 산 중고차가 자주 고장이 나서 불편해요. ( ) 중고차를 샀어요.
14. 대부분의 젊은 부부들은 부부가 함께 직장 생활을 하는 ( )을/를 선호하는 것으로 나타났다.
15. 중국 사람들은 교통수단으로 자전거를 많이 ( )는다고/ㄴ다고/다고 합니다.
16. 새벽에 갑자기 천둥이 쳐서 ( ) 놀랐어요.
17. 자기 일을 즐겁게 하고 그 일에 ( )어/아/여 하는 사람이 가장 행복한 사람이라고 생각해요.
18. 10년 만에 고향에 가 보니 많이 ( )어/아/여 있었어요.
19. 친구가 돈을 너무 함부로 써서 아껴 쓰라고 ( )었어요/았어요/였어요.

20. 감기약을 드시고 (   ) 쉬시면 좀 괜찮아지실 거예요.

21. 장미는 아름다울 뿐만 아니라 (   )도 좋아요.

22. (   )기 전에 문을 잘 닫았는지 집안을 잘 살펴보고 나가세요.

23. 중국과 한국의 음식 문화를 직접 (   )어/아/여 보니까 다른 점이 많네요.

[24-30] 다음 밑줄 친 부분과 의미가 비슷한 것을 고르십시오.

Choose the word that is similar in meaning to the underlined part of the sentence.

24. 오늘 데이트가 있어서 동생 <u>모르게</u> 동생이 아끼는 원피스를 입고 나왔어요.

❶ 미리 ❷ 몰래 ❸ 바삐 ❹ 살짝

25. 구름이 잔뜩 끼어서 날씨가 흐리고 <u>게다가</u> 바람까지 분다.

❶ 더구나 ❷ 오히려 ❸ 다행히 ❹ 나날이

26. 선생님이 한국어를 잘한다고 칭찬해 주셔서 기분이 <u>아주</u> 좋았다.

❶ 곧 ❷ 늘 ❸ 덜 ❹ 꽤

27. 운동을 하겠다고 <u>마음을 먹었는데</u> 일주일도 안 돼서 그만두고 말았다.

❶ 변경하다 ❷ 비교하다 ❸ 결심하다 ❹ 활용하다

28. 회원카드가 있으면 할인이 된다고 하니까 지금 <u>바로</u> 카드를 신청해야 겠어요.

❶ 보통 ❷ 당장 ❸ 훨씬 ❹ 특히

29. 할아버지께서는 30년이 지난 <u>오래된</u> 책상에서 책을 읽고 계셨다.

❶ 늙다 ❷ 낳다 ❸ 늘다 ❹ 낡다

30. 트럭을 운전할 줄 아세요?

❶ 밀다　　❷ 묻다　　❸ 들다　　❹ 몰다

[31-40] [보기]에서 알맞은 단어를 골라 대화를 완성하십시오.

Complete the conversation with the appropriate word from the box below.

[보기]

방금	마침	자르다	또한	줍다
들르다	어쩐지	넘어지다	변경하다	아무래도

31. 가 : 계속 비가 오네요. 어떻게 하죠?
    나 : 그러게요. 여행 일정을 좀 (　　　　　)어야/아야/여야 할 것 같아요.

32. 가 : 여행을 자주 하시나 봐요.
    나 : 여행을 하면 새로운 경험을 할 수 있어요. (　　　　　) 휴식도 취할 수 있고요.

33. 가 : 왜 그렇게 기분이 좋으세요?
    나 : 학교에 오는 길에 횡단보도 앞에서 오만 원짜리를 (　　　　　)었어요/았어요/였어요.

34. 가 : 오늘 미선 씨가 데이트가 있대요.
    나 : 아, (　　　　　) 그래서 미선 씨가 오늘 원피스를 입고 왔군요.

35. 가 : 어쩌다가 다리를 다치셨어요?
    나 : 계단에서 급하게 내려오다가 (　　　　　)어서/아서/여서 다리를 다쳤어요.

36. 가 : 왜 이렇게 늦었어요?
    나 : 집에 오는 길에 잠깐 서점에 (　　　　　)어서/아서/여서 오느라고요.

37. 가 : 오늘 제가 점심을 살게요.
    나 : 이를 어쩌죠? (　　　　　) 전에 점심을 먹었는데요.

38. 가 : 죄송해요. 차가 너무 밀려서 (   ) 약속시간까지 못 갈 것 같아서요.

나 : 괜찮아요. 천천히 오세요.

39. 가 : 저녁을 먹으러 가는데 같이 갈래요?

나 : (   ) 잘 됐군요. 저도 저녁을 먹으러 가려던 참이었어요.

40. 가 : 날씨가 너무 더워서 긴 머리를 짧게 (   )고 갈색으로 염색도 했어요.

나 : 아주 예쁜데요.

[41-47] 다음 밑줄 친 부분과 의미가 비슷한 것을 고르십시오.

Choose the word that is similar in meaning to the underlined part of the sentence.

41. 머리가 <u>조금</u> 아프네요. 약을 먹는 게 좋겠어요.

❶ 약간 ❷ 아까 ❸ 슬슬 ❹ 설마

42. 요즘 외국인과 결혼하는 사람들이 많아지면서 다문화 가정도 <u>점차</u> 늘고 있다.

❶ 마침 ❷ 점점 ❸ 깜짝 ❹ 흔히

43. 저는 고등학교 3년 동안 <u>계속</u> 우등생이었어요.

❶ 미리 ❷ 혹은 ❸ 내내 ❹ 그냥

44. 회사 일이 힘들 때는 <u>가끔</u> 대학교 시절로 돌아가고 싶을 때가 있다.

❶ 때때로 ❷ 더구나 ❸ 단순히 ❹ 다행히

45. <u>조금 전에</u> 점심을 먹었는데 이상하게도 또 배가 고프네요.

❶ 또한 ❷ 설마 ❸ 살짝 ❹ 아까

46. 자, 식사들 다 하셨으면 이제 천천히 일어날까요?

❶ 아까 ❷ 슬슬 ❸ 약간 ❹ 얼른

47. 여러분은 한국에서 또는 여러분 나라에서 이사한 경험이 있습니까?

❶ 혹은 ❷ 흔히 ❸ 훨씬 ❹ 한참

[48-51] 다음 (   )에 공통적으로 들어갈 단어를 쓰십시오.

Write one word that can commonly fit into the parenthesis below.

48.
❶ 수업 중이어서 (   ) 문을 열고 교실에 들어갔다.
❷ 모임에 가서 아무 말도 안 하고 (   ) 앉아 있다가 왔어.

(   )

49.
❶ 한국에서 생활한 지가 3년 (   ) 된 것 같아요.
❷ 텔레비전을 그렇게 (   )에서 보면 눈이 나빠져.
❸ 영철 씨는 소문이 안 좋으니까 (   ) 하지 마세요.

(   )

50.
❶ 회사 일이 (   ) 쌓여 있어요.
❷ 어제 늦게 들어와서 아내가 (   ) 화가 났어요.
❸ 주말에 친구 생일 파티에서 음식을 (   ) 먹고 배탈이 났어요.

(   )

51.
❶ 숙제도 안 하고 (   ) 놀기만 했어요
❷ 국이 싱거웠지만 소금을 넣지 않고 (   ) 먹었어요.
❸ 화장품 가게에서 물건을 사지 않아도 팩을 (   ) 주던데요.

(   )

[52-62] [보기]에서 알맞은 단어를 골라 (　　　) 안에 쓰십시오.

Chooes the appropriate word from the box below and then fill in the parenthesis.

[보기]

가득	결국	평소	밟다	모으다	알리다
우연히	방문하다	봉사하다	서늘하다	떨어뜨리다	

52. 두 사람은 서로 사랑했지만 부모님의 반대로 (　　　　　　) 헤어졌대요.

53. 가게에서 거스름돈을 받다가 잘못해서 동전을 바닥에 (　　　　　　)었어요/았어요/였어요.

54. 오늘 식당에서 어떤 사람이 제 발을 (　　　　　　)고도 사과를 하지 않았어요.

55. 다른 사람의 집을 (　　　　　　)을/ㄹ 때는 미리 전화를 걸어보고 가는 것이 예의예요.

56. 매달 고아원이나 양로원에 가서 아이들과 노인들을 돌보며 (　　　　　　)고 있어요.

57. 얼마 전까지 날씨가 더웠는데 비가 온 후에 날씨가 좀 (　　　　　　)어진/아진/여진 것 같아요.

58. 대학교 합격 소식을 부모님께 첫 번째로 (　　　　　　)어/아/여 드리고 싶어서 고향에 전화했어요.

59. 어제 명동에서 쇼핑할 때 (　　　　　　) 중학교 동창을 만났는데 너무 반가웠어요.

60. 아버지께서 제 술잔에 맥주를 (　　　　　　) 따라 주셨어요.

61. 친구가 유럽 여행을 하기 위해서 아르바이트를 하면서 돈을 (　　　　　　)고 있어요.

62. 백화점에 들어갔는데 세일기간이어서 그런지 (　　　　　　)보다 사람이 많았다.

[63-73] 다음 (　　　)에 공통적으로 들어갈 단어의 기본형을 쓰십시오.

Write the basic form of a word that can be used in both of the parenthasis.

63. ❶ 길이 막히지 않아서 생각보다 빨리 목적지에 (　　　　　　)었어요/았어요/였어요.
❷ 16살에 결혼을 하셨다면 정말 (　　　　　　)는/은/ㄴ 나이에 결혼을 하셨네요.

(　　　　　　　　　　)

64. ❶ 음식이 좀 (　　　　　　)네요. 소금을 너무 많이 넣었나 봐요.

❷ 다음 주에 여행을 가신다던데 여행 일정은 다 (　　　　　　)었어요/았어요/였어요?

(　　　　　　　　　　)

65. ❶ 미선이가 어렵게 이야기를 (　　　　　　)었다/았다/였다.

❷ 학생들이 학교에 도착하자마자 가방에서 책을 (　　　　　　)었다/았다/였다.

(　　　　　　　　　　)

66. ❶ 주말에 감기약을 먹고 푹 쉬었더니 감기가 다 (　　　　　　)었어요/았어요/였어요.

❷ 예전에 쓰던 휴대전화의 디자인이 새로 나온 휴대전화보다 더 (　　　　　　)는/은/ㄴ 것 같아요.

(　　　　　　　　　　)

67. ❶ 너무 (　　　　　　)는/은/ㄴ 화장을 하면 자연스러워 보이지 않아요.

❷ 커피가 너무 (　　　　　　)는/은/ㄴ 것 같으면 물을 조금 넣으세요.

(　　　　　　　　　　)

68. ❶ 머리를 조금 (　　　　　　)으니까/니까 훨씬 깔끔해 보이네요.

❷ 바쁜 현대인들을 위해 마트에서 채소를 깨끗하게 (　　　　　　)어서/아서/여서 팔기도 해요.

(　　　　　　　　　　)

69. ❶ 휴대전화가 고장 나서 (　　　　　　)어야겠어요/아야겠어요/여야겠어요.

❷ 그 병은 쉽게 (　　　　　　)을/ㄹ 수 없다고 의사 선생님이 말씀하셨어요.

❸ 선생님께서 제 숙제 공책에 있는 틀린 문장을 맞게 (　　　　　　)어/아/여 주셨어요.

(　　　　　　　　　　)

70.

❶ 키우던 고양이가 죽어서 근처 산에 (   )어/아/여 주었어요.

❷ 가끔 한국 사람들이 외국 사람인 저에게 길을 (   )기도 해요.

❸ 옷에 기름이 (   )어서/아서/여서 세탁소에 맡겼어요.

(   )

71.

❶ 서울역에 가려면 몇 번 버스를 (   )어야/아야/여야 해요?

❷ 오랫동안 햇볕 아래에서 일을 했더니 피부가 많이 (   )었어요/았어요/였어요.

❸ 김치찌개를 가스레인지에 올려놓고는 정신없이 드라마를 보는 바람에 김치찌개가 다 (   )어/아/여 버렸어요.

(   )

72.

❶ 영화를 보면서 주말을 (   )는/은/ㄴ 연인들이 많네요.

❷ 어머니는 빨간색을 좋아하셔서 빨간색 옷을 (   )어/아/여 입으세요.

❸ 한국인이 여가 활동으로 가장 (   )어/아/여 하는 취미는 등산이래요.

(   )

73.

❶ 저에게 아주 좋은 아이디어가 (   )었어요/았어요/였어요.

❷ 아침 해가 (   )는/은/ㄴ 모습을 보면서 하루를 시작했어요.

❸ 한국 전통 음식하면 머릿 속에 제일 먼저 (   )는/은/ㄴ 음식이 김치예요.

(   )

건강

03

Health

03 건강

01
간

[간] 명사 liver

[Expression] 간염 hepatitis
간암 liver cancer

[Example] 술을 많이 마시면 간이 나빠져요.
Your liver gets bad if you drink a lot of alcohol.

간이 나빠지면 눈동자와 얼굴이 유난히 다른 사람들에 비해 노랗습니다
If your liver gets bad, your face and pupils are unusually more yellow compared to others.

02
건강식

[건강식] 명사 healthy food

[Expression] 건강식을 먹다 to eat healthily

[Example] 김치라든가 된장 같은 음식은 대표적인 건강식이죠.
Foods like kimchi or duinjang are most representative of health foods.

신선한 야채를 넣어서 만든 샐러드는 좋은 건강식이에요.
Salad made using in fresh vegetables is a kind of healthy food.

03
고통

[고통] 명사 pain (physical or emotional)

[Expression] 고통스럽다 to be painful
고통이 심하다 to have a serious pain
고통을 견디다 to bear a pain
고통을 나누다 to share one's pain
고통을 느끼다 to feel pain

[Related Words] 아픔 pain
통증 pain (physical pain)

[Example] 환자는 고통이 심해서 소리를 지르고 말았다.
The patient screamed because the pain was very intense.

고통 없이 10분 만에 끝나는 간단한 수술이니까 걱정하지 마세요.
Don't worry at all because this is a simple, painless, surgery that ends within ten minutes.

04
과로사

[과로사] 명사 overworking oneself to death

[Expression] 과로사하다
to overwork oneself to death

[Example] 직장에서의 과도한 업무로 점점 과로사가 증가하고 있습니다.
Due to excessive office work, the number of deaths resulting from overworking is increasing.

우리나라 40대 직장인의 과로사 비율이 OECD국가 중 가장 높은 것으로 나타났다.
The percent of workers in their forties that die from overworking in our country appears as the highest among all OECD countries.

05
과식

[과식] 명사 overeating

[Expression] 과식을 하다 to overeat

[Antonym] 소식 eating very little

[Related Words] 폭식 binge eating

[Example] 연말에는 모임이 많아서 자주 과식을 하게 돼요.
Since there are a lot of meetings at the end of the year, I often end up overeating.

과식이나 폭식 같은 식습관은 건강에 해롭습니다.
Eating habits like overeating or binge eating are very damaging to our health.

도움말

과음 drinking excessively　　과로 overworking

06
구급차

[구급차] 명사 ambulance

[Expression] 구급차를 부르다 to call an ambulance
구급차에 실려 가다 to be transported in an ambulance

[Example] 교통사고가 난 곳에 구급차가 여러 대 왔어요.
Many ambulances came to the scene of the accident.

주말 교통 정체로 구급차가 1시간 후에 도착하는 바람에 아이의 부상 상태가 심해져서 수술까지 하게 되었다.
The child that was in a critical state had to get surgery after his condition worsened because the ambulance arrived one hour late due to weekend traffic.

07
규칙적이다

[규칙쩌기다] 형용사 to be regular

[Usage] 규칙적인 N
규칙적으로 N

[Expression] 규칙적인 운동 regular exercise
규칙적인 훈련 regular training
규칙적인 생활습관 regular daily living habits

[Antonym] 불규칙적이다 being irregular

[Example] 평소에 규칙적으로 일정한 시간에 주무십니까?
Do you normally sleep at a set time?

아주 가벼운 운동이라도 오랫동안 규칙적으로 하면 효과적으로 체중을 줄일 수 있습니다.
You can effectively lower your weight if you regularly work out a little bit over a long time.

08
근육

[그뉵] 명사 muscle

[Expression] 근육이 생기다 to get muscles
근육을 풀다 to relax/loosen a muscle
근육을 움직이다 to move your muscles

[Related Words] 살 flesh, fat
뼈 bones
지방 fat

[Example] 어떤 운동을 하면 근육이 생길까요?
What kind of exercise should I do if I want to get muscles?

매일 아침 한 시간씩 달리기를 하니까 다리에 근육이 생겼다.
I got muscles on my legs since I ran every morning for an hour.

09
기운

[기운] 명사 energy

[Expression] 기운이 나다 to have energy
기운이 없다 to have no energy
기운을 얻다 to get energy
기운을 차리다 to regain one's energy

[Synonym] 힘 energy

[Example] 더운 여름날 기운이 없을 때 한국 사람들은 삼계탕을 먹습니다.
Korean people eat samgketang on hot summer days when they have no energy.

친구의 부탁을 거절하자 친구는 기운이 없는 목소리로 짧게 인사를 하고는 전화를 끊었다.
After I rejected my friend's request, he said a quick goodbye with a weak voice and hung up the phone.

10
긴급

[긴급] 명사 emergency

[Expression] 긴급 구조 emergency rescue
긴급 뉴스 emergency news
긴급 출동 emergency dispatch
긴급 지원 emergency aid

[Related Words] 위급 crisis, emergency

[Example] 가스 폭발 사고로 주민들이 긴급 대피했다.
The citizens were evacuated due to the gas explosion.

119 신고를 받은 구조대원들은 사고 지역으로 긴급 출동하였다.
After the rescue team received the 911 notice, they were dispatched to the scene of the accident.

11
낳다

[나타] 동사 1. to give birth 2. to lead to, to bring forth

1. [Usage] N 을/를 낳다

[Expression] 알을 낳다 lay an egg
아이를 낳다 to give birth to a child
새끼를 낳다 to give birth to a baby
자식을 낳다 to give birth to a child

[Synonym] 출산하다 to give birth

[Example] 아이를 12명이나 낳았다니 정말 대단하네요.
It's amazing that she gave birth to twelve children.

2. [Usage] N 을/를 낳다

[Expression] 결과를 낳다 to bring about good results
문제를 낳다 to lead to problems
부작용을 낳다 to lead to side effects

[Example] 미움은 미움을 낳고 사랑은 사랑을 낳는다.
Hate creates hate and love creates love.

12
뇌

[뇌] 명사 brain

[Related Words] 뇌혈관 blood vessels in the brain
뇌졸중 brain hemorrhage that leads to an unconscious state of being
뇌종양 brain tumor
뇌신경 brain nerves
뇌출혈 brain hemorrhage

[Example] 천재의 뇌는 보통 사람의 뇌와 다를까요?
Is the brain of a genius really different from the brain of a regular person?

머리가 계속 아프면 한번 뇌 사진을 찍어 보세요.
If your heads keeps hurting, take an x-ray of your brain.

13
눈곱

[눈꼽] 명사 gunk/sleep

substance left in one's eyes after sleeping

[Expression] 눈곱이 끼다 to have gunk in one's eye
눈곱을 떼다 to take out sleep from one's eye

[Example] 남편은 항상 아침에 일어나서 눈곱을 떼요.
My husband wakes up every morning and takes the gunk out of his eyes.

자다 일어났는지 눈에 눈곱이 가득 끼어 있었다.
His eyes were full of gunk because he probably has just woken up.

14
눈썹

[눈썹] 명사 eyebrow

[Expression] 속눈썹 eyelash
짙은 눈썹 thick eyebrows
눈썹이 짙다 to have thick eyebrows
눈썹이 하얗게 세다 to have very white eyebrows

[Example] 속눈썹이 자꾸 눈을 찔러서 아파요.
My eyes hurt because my eyelashes keep on poking them.

영화배우 송승원은 눈썹이 참 진해요.
The actor Song Seungwon's eyebrows are very thick.

15
늙다

[늑따] 동사 to be old

[Usage] N 이/가 늙다
늙은 N

[Antonym] 젊다 to be young

[Example] 젊었을 때 건강관리를 잘 해야 늙어서 고생을 안 해요.
You need to take care of yourself when you are young so that when you are old, you don't have to suffer.

오랜만에 고등학교 때 선생님을 만났는데 많이 늙으셨더군요.
It was a long time since I met my high school teacher, and he really looks much older now.

16
당뇨병

[당뇨뼝] 명사 diabetes

[Expression] 당뇨병에 걸리다 to have diabetes

[Related Words] 인슐린 insulin

[Example] 당뇨병 환자들은 인슐린 치료를 받아야 한다.
Diabetes patients need to take insulin treatments.

당뇨병에 걸린 사람들은 항상 음식을 조심해서 먹어야 해요.
Patients that have diabetes need to be very careful when eating food.

17
동맥경화

[동맥꼉화] 명사 arteriosclerosis

[Expression] 동맥경화증 hardening of the arteries

[Example] 고혈압, 당뇨병은 동맥경화의 주요 원인이다.
High blood pressure or diabetes can be the main cause of arteriosclerosis.

아버지께서 갑자기 동맥경화로 쓰러지셨어요.
My father suddenly fainted due to arteriosclerosis.

18
떨다

[떨다] 동사 to shake, to shiver

[Usage] N 을/를 떨다

[Expression] 몸을 떨다 to shake one's body
다리를 떨다 to shake one's leg
덜덜 떨다 to tremble all over

[Example] 어린 고양이가 추워서 밖에서 떨고 있어요.
The young cat was cold and was trembling outside.

몸살이 나서 온몸이 떨리고 식은땀이 나요.
After getting sick, my entire body was shivering and I broke out into a cold sweat.

19
뚱뚱하다

[뚱뚱하다] 형용사 to be fat

[Usage] N 이/가 뚱뚱하다
뚱뚱한 N

[Expression] 뚱뚱한 몸매 overweight
뚱뚱한 몸집 fat body
몸이 뚱뚱하다 to be fat

[Antonym] 마르다 to be skinny

[Related Words] 살찌다 to gain weight

통통하다 to be chubby
날씬하다 to be slim

[Example] 제 누나는 고등학교 때는 뚱뚱했는데 지금은 날씬해졌어요.
My older sister was fat in high school but now she has become skinny.
아주 옛날에는 뚱뚱한 여자가 미인이었지만 현대 사회에서는 날씬한 여자가 미인이다.
A long time ago, a fat woman was considered to be beautiful but in modern day society, a skinny woman is beautiful.

20
뜨다

[뜨다] 동사 to open one's eyes

[Usage] N 을/를 뜨다

[Expression] 눈을 뜨다 to open one's eyes

[Antonym] 감다 to close one's eyes

[Example] 눈을 뜨니까 벌써 9시였다.
I realized it was 9 o'clock after I opened my eyes.
아침에 눈을 뜨면 물부터 한 잔 마신다.
I first have a glass of water when I wake up in the morning.

21
막

[막] 부사 1. suddenly or unexpectedly 2. thoughtlessly or without paying attention 3. right now

1. [Synonym] 마구 severely

[Example] 갑자기 코피가 막 나서 너무 당황했어요.
I was very flustered after I suddenly had a nosebleed.

2. [Synonym] 함부로 thoughtlessly

[Example] 아무거나 막 사지 말고 필요한 것만 사라.
Don't just buy anything but only buy whatever you need.

3. [Example] 수술이 조금 전에 막 시작됐어요.
The surgery quickly started not too long ago.

22
몸무게

[몸무게] 명사 weight

[Expression] 몸무게가 늘다 to go up in weight
몸무게가 줄다 to go down in weight
몸무게가 많이 나가다 to go past one's weight
몸무게가 적게 나가다 to be under one's weight
몸무게를 재다 to weight oneself

[Synonym] 체중 weight

[Example] 요즘 몸무게가 자꾸 늘어서 고민이에요.
I'm worried nowadays because I keep gaining weight.

키에 비해서 몸무게가 너무 많이 나갑니다.
You weigh too much for your height.

23
민간요법

[민간뇨뻡] 명사 folk remedy- home style or traditional ways to treat a disease or sickness

[Related Words] 식이요법 dietary treatment

[Example] 시골에서는 벌에 쏘이면 민간요법으로 된장을 발랐어요.
In the countryside, when a bee stings you, people apply fermented bean paste as a folk remedy.

여러분 나라에서는 감기에 걸렸을 때 하는 민간요법이 있나요?
In your country, when you catch a cold, what kind of traditional remedies exist?

24
배꼽

[배꼽] 명사 belly button

[Related Words] 배 stomach
복부 abdomen

[Example] 짧은 티셔츠를 입어서 배꼽이 다 보여요.
You can see her belly button because she is wearing a short shirt.

배보다 배꼽이 크다는 말을 들어본 적이 있어요?
Have you ever heard the expression, "Your belly button is bigger than your stomach?" (this is an expression that means the cost to repair an object cost more than the original value of the object in question.)

25
병들다

[병들다] 동사 to catch a disease

[Usage] N 이/가 병들다

[Expression] 몸이 병들다 My body is sick.

[Example] 아이는 병든 할머니와 같이 살고 있었다.
The child was living with the sick grandmother.

전쟁이 끝난 길거리는 병들고 굶주린 사람으로 가득했다.
After the war, the streets were full of diseased and hunger-stricken people.

26
보약

[보약] 명사 herbal medicine

[Expression] 보약을 먹다 to take herbal medicine

보약을 짓다 to prepare herbal medicine

[Related Words] 한약 traditional Korean medicine

한의원 traditional Korean medical center

한의사 Korean herbal medicine doctor

[Example] 뭐니 뭐니 해도 밥이 보약이에요.

In the end, a good meal will keep you healthy.

몸이 약한 아이들에게는 몸을 보호하고 튼튼하게 하는 보약을 먹이는 것이 좋습니다.

It is good to give herbal remedies to children whose bodies are weak so that it may protect and strengthen them.

27
부상

[부상] 명사 Injury

[Expression] 부상자 injured person

심한 부상 serious injury

부상이 가볍다 It is a very minor injury.

부상을 입다 to receive an injury

부상을 당하다 to be injured

[Related Words] 경상 light injury

중상 serious injury

[Example] 이번 태풍으로 인해 30명이 숨지고 100여명이 부상을 입었다.

On account of the typhoon, thirty people passed away and over one hundred were injured.

교통사고가 났지만 다행히 안전벨트를 매고 있어서 큰 부상은 당하지 않았다.

I wasn't seriously injusted even though there was an accident because fortunately I had fastened my seatbelt.

28
부작용

[부자공] 명사 side effect

[Expression] 부작용이 있다 to have a side effect

부작용이 없다 to have no side effect

부작용이 생기다 A side effect occurs.

부작용이 나타나다 A side effect develops.

부작용을 낳다 to lead to a side effect

[Related Words] 합병증 complications

[Example] 부작용이 있을 수 있으니까 약을 먹을 때 설명서를 잘 읽어 보세요.

Please read the instructions when taking the medicine since there is a possibility that there may be side effects.

성형수술은 수술 후 부작용이 있을 수 있으니까 안 하는 것이 좋다고 생각해요.
After getting plastic surgery, there is a risk of side effects, I think it's better that you don't undergo any.

29
부족하다

[부조카다] 형용사 to lack, to be deficient

[Usage] N 이/가 부족하다

[Expression] 영양이 부족하다 I am deficient in nutrients.
운동이 부족하다 to be lacking in exercise

[Antonym] 충분하다 to be full of, to be plenty

[Example] 평소 운동이 부족하여 집에서 운동하려고 운동 기구를 샀어요.
Since I don't exercise frequently, I bought some work out machines to do it at home.

회사의 육아 시설이 부족해 맞벌이 부부들이 어린 자녀를 키우는 데 어려움이 많아요.
Working couples that are raising children face many difficulties because the nursery at their work place isn't good enough.

30
불면증

[불면쯩] 명사 insomnia

[Expression] 불면증 환자 insomniac
불면증이 생기다 to start having insomnia
불면증이 심하다 to have serious insomnia
불면증으로 고생하다 to suffer from insomnia

[Example] 요즘 불면증 때문에 수면제를 먹고 있어요.
Nowadays, I've been taking sleeping pills because of my insomnia.

불면증이 심하면 어떻게 하는 것이 좋아요?
What should I do if I have serious insomnia?

31
붓다

[붇따] 동사 to swell

[Usage] N 이/가 붓다

[Expression] 붓기 swelling
눈이 붓다 My eyes are swollen.
퉁퉁 붓다 to be fully swollen

[Related Words] 부풀다 expand (balloon)

[Example] 오래 서 있어서 다리가 부었어요.
My leg swelled after standing up for a long time.

목이 부었을 때는 소금물 양치가 제일 빠르고 효과적인 방법입니다.
When your throat is swollen, gargling with salt water is the fastest and most effective way to get better.

32
비결

[비결] 명사 secret method

[Expression] 비결을 묻다 to ask abat one's secret method

[Related Words] 비밀 secret

[Example] 이 마을 노인들의 장수 비결이 무엇이라고 생각하세요?
What do you think is the secret of the old people's longevity in this village?

영수야, 학교 친구들한테서 인기가 많던데 그 비결 좀 가르쳐 줘.
Hey Youngsoo, you seem to be very popular in school. Please teach me your secret.

33
비만

[비만] 명사 obesity

[Expression] 비만 아동 child obesity
비만을 치료하다. to treat obesity

[Example] 요즘 비만 아동들이 많아지고 있어요.
They say that more children are becoming obese nowadays.

무릎이 아픈 이유는 바로 운동 부족과 비만 때문입니다.
The reason your knee is hurting is you don't exercise enough and you are overweight.

34
비상약

[비상약] 명사 emergency medicine

[Expression] 비상약을 준비하다 to prepare emergency medicine
비상약을 구비하다 to be prepared with emergency medicine

[Synonym] 구급약 emergency medicine

[Example] 만일을 대비하여 비상약을 챙기도록 하세요.
Just in case, please prepare the emergency medicine.

아이가 다쳐서 그런데 비상약 상자를 어디에 두셨어요?
The child is hurt. Where did you put the first aid kit?

도움말

비상구 emergency exit
비상용 emergency use
비상계단 emergency stairs
비상벨 emergency bell
비상금 emergency fee

35
비위생적이다 [비위생저기다] 형용사 to be unhygienic, to be unsanitary

[Usage] 비위생적인 N
비위생적으로 AV

[Antonym] 위생적이다 to be hygienic

[Example] 한 그릇에 있는 찌개를 같이 먹는 것이 비위생적이라고 생각했어요.
I thought it was unhygienic for us to eat the stew from the same bowl.

어제 친구와 같이 간 음식점은 더럽고 비위생적이서 다시는 가고 싶지 않아요.
I don't want to go again to the restaurant that I went to yesterday with my friend because it was dirty and unsanitary.

36
뺨 [뺨] 명사 cheek

[Expression] 뺨따귀 cheeks
뺨이 빨개지다 My cheeks are getting red.
뺨을 맞다 to get hit on the cheek
뺨을 치다 to hit someone's chek
뺨을 때리다 to hit one's cheek

[Synonym] 볼 cheek

[Example] 부끄러워서 뺨이 빨개졌어요.
I blushed because I was embarrassed.

제 친구는 웃을 때 양쪽 뺨에 보조개가 생겨요.
When my friend laughts, he gets dimples on both cheeks.

37
사망 [사망] 명사 death

[Expression] 사망률 death rate
사망자 a dead person
사망 소식 news of someone's death
사망 확인 to check to see if someone is dead
사망하다 to die

[Synonym] 죽음 death

[Example] 한국인의 사망 원인 1위는 암이라고 한다.
They say that the number one cause of death in Korea is cancer.

아들의 사망 소식을 듣고 어머니는 충격으로 쓰러지셨다.
After hearing the death of her son, the mother fainted from shock.

38
성인병

[성인뼝] 명사 diseases that affect middle aged people (adults)

[Expression] 성인병 예방 prevention of mid-life diseases
성인병에 걸리다 to catch a disease that affects an adult

[Example] 나이가 들면 여러 가지 성인병으로 고생할 가능성이 커진다.
As you get older, there is a greater possibility that you suffer from various diseases.

불규칙한 식생활과 스트레스로 인해 당뇨병, 고혈압 등 성인병에 걸릴 위험이 있습니다.
Due to irregular eating patterns and stress, there is a danger in catching diseases like high blood pressure or diabetes.

도움말
성인 adult
성인남성 male adult
성인여성 female adult
성인영화 adult movie

39
세다[1]

[세다] 형용사 to be strong

[Usage] N 이/가 세다

[Expression] 힘이 세다 to be full of energy
기운이 세다 to be strong (energetic)

[Antonym] 약하다 to be weak

[Example] 우리 큰형은 키도 크고 힘도 세요.
My older brother is tall and strong.

힘이 세다고 항상 싸움에서 이길 수 있는 것은 아니에요.
Just because you are strong doesn't mean you are always going to win in fights.

40
소모하다

[소모하다] 동사 to consume, use up, burn

[Usage] N 을/를 소모하다

[Expression] 열량을 소모하다 to burn calories

[Example] 똑같은 운동을 해도 사람마다 열량을 소모하는 정도는 차이가 있어요.
There is a difference in the amount of calories that each person burns even when doing the same exercise.

공부를 하면 열량이 빨리 소모되니까 가능하면 아침 식사를 하는 것이 좋다.
It's good to eat in the morning if possible when studying because calories are used up very quickly.

41
소화불량

[소화불량] 명사 upset stomach, indigestion

[Expression] 소화불량을 일으키다 to cause indigestion

[Example] 긴장된 분위기에서 식사를 했더니 소화불량이 되었다.
I got indigestion after eating food in a tense environment.

밀가루 음식을 많이 먹으면 소화불량이 되기 쉽습니다.
It's very common to get indigestion if you eat food with a lot of flour.

42
손등

[손뜽] 명사 back of the hand

[Related Words] 발등 back of the foot
손바닥 palm of the hand
발바닥 bottom of the foot

[Example] 제 손등에는 작은 흉터가 있어요.
I have a small scar on the back of my hand.

아이가 손등으로 이마에 흐르는 땀을 닦았다.
The kid wiped the sweat off his forehead with the back of his hand.

43
손목

[손목] 명사 wrist

[Expression] 손목시계 wrist watch
손목에 차다 to wear on one's wrist

[Related Words] 발목 ankle

[Example] 컴퓨터를 오래 해서 손목이 아파요.
My wrist hurts after using the computer for a long time.

손목에 비싼 시계를 찬 걸 보니까 부자인가 봐요.
He seems rich to me after I saw that he was wearing an expensive watch on his wrist.

44
수염

[수염] 명사 beard/mustache

hair that mature men have on their chin or that grows in on their cheeks and around their mouth.

[Expression] 콧수염 mustache
턱수염 beard
수염이 나다 to have a beard
수염을 깎다 to cut one's facial hair
수염을 기르다 to grow out a beard

[Example] 전기면도기로 수염을 깎아요.
Cut your facial hair with the electric shaver.

요즘은 수염을 기르는 사람들이 부쩍 늘었어요.
Recently, there have been a lot more people that are growing beards.

45
숙면

[숭면] 명사 deep sleep

[Expression] 숙면하다 to have a deep sleep
숙면을 취하다 to sleep well

[Example] 너무 환하게 불을 켜고 자면 숙면할 수 없다고 합니다.
They say you can't get a night of good sleep if you leave the lights on.

자기 전에 따뜻한 물로 샤워하거나 따뜻한 우유를 마시면 숙면을 취할 수 있어요.
I sleep really well if I drink warm milk or take a hot shower before going to bed.

46
숨

[숨] 명사 breath

[Expression] 한숨 a sigh
숨이 차다 to be out of breath
숨이 막히다 to be short of breath
숨을 쉬다 to take a breath
숨을 헐떡이다 to pant

[Example] 오늘은 정말 숨이 막힐 정도로 더웠다.
Today the weather was stifling hot.

그 아이는 너무 빨리 뛰어와서 숨을 헐떡였다.
That child ran so fast that he was panting to catch his breath.

47
식사량

[식싸량] 명사 amount or serving size of food

[Expression] 규칙적인 식사량 a regular serving size
식사량이 많다 serving size is large
식사량이 적다 serving size is small
식사량을 줄이다 to lessen a serving size
식사량을 조절하다 to control the size of one's meal

[Example] 장수와 식사량에는 어떤 관계가 있습니까?
Is there a relationship between longevity and the amount of food we eat?

살을 빼려면 운동뿐만 아니라 과식하지 않고 늘 정해진 식사량을 지키는 것도 중요합니다.
If you want to lose weight, it is important to not only work out and not overeat but also to adhere to set serving sizes.

48
식습관

[식씁꽌] 명사 eating habits

[Expression]
건강한 식습관 healthy eating habits
잘못된 식습관 improper eating habits
식습관이 불규칙하다 My eating habits are irregular.
식습관을 고치다 to fix one's eating habits
식습관을 바꾸다 to change one's eating habits

[Example]
건강을 위한 식습관으로는 어떤 것이 있을까요?
What kind of dietary habits are there in terms of leading a healthy lifestyle?

건강한 사람들은 대체로 매일 정해진 시간에 밥을 꼭 챙겨 먹는 식습관이 있다.
Healthy people generally have the habit of eating food at a set hour every day.

49
식욕

[시굑] 명사 appetite

[Expression]
식욕이 있다 to have an appetite
식욕이 없다 to not have an appetite
식욕이 생기다 to get an appetite
식욕이 왕성하다 to have a voracious appetite
식욕을 잃다 to lose one's appetite

[Example]
아침마다 운동을 했더니 기분도 상쾌하고 식욕도 생기네요.
After working out every morning, I now feel great and have an appetite.

회사일 때문에 신경을 많이 쓰니까 머리도 아프고 식욕도 없어요.
I have no appetite and my head hurts because I'm exerting myself a lot at the office.

50
신장

[신장] 명사 1. kidney 2. height, stature

1. [Expression]
신장염 inflammation of the kidneys
신장결석 a kidney stone
신장 기능 kidney function
신장이 나쁘다 to have a bad kidney

[Synonym]
콩팥 kidney

[Example]
신장이 나쁜 사람은 아침에 몸이 많이 부어요.
The body of people who have bad kidneys often swells up in the morning.

2. [Expression]
신장이 크다 to be tall
신장을 늘이다 to increase one's height

[Synonym]
키 height

[Example] 진료를 받기 전에 여기에 본인의 신장과 체중을 적으세요.
Before seeing the doctor, please write down your height and weight here.

51
심장병

[심장뼝] 명사 heart disease

[Example] 성격이 급하면 심장병에 더 잘 걸릴까요?
Do you think that if you are hot-tempered, you will be more likely to suffer from heart disease?

운동이 부족하면 비만이 되거나 고혈압, 심장병 등 여러 가지 질병에 걸리기 쉽습니다.
If you don't exercise enough, you may become obese or easily catch a number of other diseases like high blood pressure or heart disease.

도움말

인공심장 artificial heart
심장 마비 heart attack
심장이 약하다 to have a weak heart
심장 질환 heart disease
심장이 뛰다 My heart beats
심장이 떨리다 I am nervous

52
앓다

[알타] 동사 to be ill, sick

[Usage] N 을/를 앓다

[Expression]
병을 앓다 to be sick
감기를 앓다 to have a cold
몸살을 앓다 to have body aches
끙끙 앓다 to moan with pain

[Synonym] 아프다 to be sick

[Example] 몸살감기로 일주일 동안 앓았어요.
I was ill for a week with body aches.

아버지는 자주 사고를 치는 동생 때문에 두통을 앓고 계신다.
My father worries himself because my younger brother often causes a lot of trouble.

53
암

[암] 명사 cancer

[Expression]
암이 낫다 to recover from cancer
암을 고치다 to cure cancer
암을 치료하다 to treat cancer

암에 걸리다 to get cancer

[Example] 폐암에 걸린 사람이 많아졌다면서요?
I heard that a lot more people now suffer from lung cancer?

암이 생기는 가장 큰 원인 중 하나가 스트레스라고 합니다.
They say that stress is one of the biggest causes of cancer.

도움말

위암 stomach cancer
간암 liver cancer
폐암 lung cancer
피부암 skin cancer
대장암 colon cancer

54
약하다

[야카다] 형용사 to be weak

[Usage] N 이/가 약하다

[Expression] 몸이 약하다 to have a weak body
위가 약하다 to have a weak stomach

[Antonym] 튼튼하다 to be strong

[Example] 몸이 약해서 감기에 잘 걸려요.
I catch colds very often because my body is weak.

어렸을 때 몸이 약해서 자주 아팠어요.
When I was younger, I got sick very often because my body was weak.

55
어리다

[어리다] 형용사 to be young

[Usage] N 이/가 어리다
어린 N

[Expression] 어렸을 때 when I was younger
어릴 적 in my youth

[Example] 그 아이는 나이는 어리지만 생각이 깊어요.
Even though that child is young, he has deep thoughts.

어린 나이에 저런 연주를 하다니 놀랍네요.
I am shocked that he can perform so well at such a young age.

56
염증

[염쯩] 명사 infection

[Expression] 염증이 심하다 to have a serious infection
염증이 생기다 to get an infection

염증을 일으키다 to cause an infection

[Related Words] 고름 puss

[Example] 다친 손을 치료하지 않았더니 염증이 생겼다.
My hand got infected because I didn't treat it.

자극적인 음식과 불규칙한 식사로 인해 위에 염증이 생겼다.
I got a stomach infection from strong-tasting food and my irregular eating habits.

57
영양

[영양] 명사 nutrient

[Expression]
영양가 nutritional value
영양제 nutritional supplements
영양실조 malnutrition
영양 부족 undernourishment
영양이 풍부하다 to be nutritious

[Example] 비빔밥에는 다양한 나물과 고기 등이 들어 있어서 영양 면에서도 매우 좋다고 합니다.
It is said that because there are diverse greens and meat in bibimbap, nutritionally, it is very good for you.

평소 인스턴트 음식을 자주 먹는 편이라서 부족한 영양을 보충하기 위해 매일 영양제를 복용해요.
Since I eat a lot of instant food, I take nutritional supplements everyday in order to make up for undernourishment.

58
예방하다

[예방하다] 동사 to prevent

[Usage] N 을/를 예방하다

[Example] 병은 치료보다 예방하는 것이 더 중요하다.
It is more important to prevent a disease than to treat it.

양치질만으로는 충치를 완전히 예방할 수 없어요.
Only brushing your teeth cannot completely prevent cavities.

59
옮다

[옴따] 동사 to catch, to get infected

[Usage]
N 이/가 옮다
N 한테서 N 이/가 옮다
N 에서 N 이/가 옮다

[Expression]
병이 옮다 to catch a disease
감기가 옮다 to catch a cold

[Synonym] 전염되다 to be contagious

[Example] 대중목욕탕에서 피부병이 옮을 수 있으니 조심해야 합니다.
You need to be careful because you can catch skin diseases at the public bathhouse.

큰아버지 병문안을 갔을 때 병원에서 감기가 옮은 것 같아요.
I thought I caught a cold when I went to the hospital to visit my sick uncle.

60
우울증

[우울쯩] 명사 depression

[Expression] 우울증이 심하다 to have severe depression
우울증에 걸리다 to suffer from depression

[Example] 조사 결과 그 사람의 죽음은 우울증으로 인한 자살로 밝혀졌다.
The results revealed that the person's death was a result of suicide caused by depression.

회사에서 심하게 경쟁을 하다 보니까 항상 스트레스가 쌓이고 심한 경우에는 우울증에 걸리기도 한다.
After experiencing harsh competition at a company, many people end up stressed out and in severe cases even suffer from depression.

61
움직이다

[움지기다] 동사 to move

[Usage] N 이/가 움직이다
N 을/를 움직이다

[Example] 저는 시간이 있을 때마다 몸을 가볍게 움직입니다.
I lightly move my body around whenever I have time.

지하철에 사람들이 어찌나 많은지 움직일 수가 없었어요.
I couldn't move inside of the subway because there were so many people.

62
위

[위] 명사 stomach

[Expression] 위염 stomach infection
위경련 stomach cramps
위가 약하다 to have a weak stomach
위가 거북하다 to have an upset stomach
위가 튼튼하다 to have a strong stomach

[Example] 저는 위가 튼튼해서 무슨 음식이든지 잘 소화시켜요.
I can digest almost any kind of food well since I have a strong stomach.

술이나 커피 같은 자극적인 음식을 많이 먹으면 위가 아플 수 있어요.
If you eat a lot of strong-tasting foods like coffee or alchohol, your stomach can hurt.

63
응급실

[응급씰] 명사 emergency room

[Expression] 응급실에 가다 to go to the emergency room
응급실에 실려 가다 to be rushed to the emergency room

[Related Words] 진료실 doctor's office
주사실 shot room
입원실 hospital room

[Example] 새벽에 갑자기 배가 아파서 응급실에 갔어요.
I went to the emergency room because my stomach suddenly started to hurt at dawn.

환자의 건강 상태가 좋지 않아서 응급실로 옮겼습니다.
The patient was taken to the emergency room because his health was in a bad state.

도움말
응급 환자 emergency patient
응급 치료 emergency treatment
응급 상황 emergency situation

64
장

[장] 명사 intestines

[Expression] 소장 small intestines
대장 large intestines
장염 intestinal infection
장이 나쁘다 to have bad intestines
장이 약하다 to have weak intestines

[Example] 갑자기 장이 꼬여서 병원 응급실에 갔어요.
I went to the emergency room because my intestines were hurting.

장에 가스가 가득 찼는지 자꾸 이상한 소리가 나요.
My intestines kept making strange sounds because they might have been full of gas.

65
전염병

[저념뼝] 명사 infectious disease

[Expression] 전염병이 돌다 An infectious disease is spreading.
전염병이 발생하다 to have an infectious disease
전염병이 유행하다 An infectious disease is spreading.
전염병을 예방하다 to prevent a disease

전염병에 걸리다 to catch an infectious disease

[Example] 여름은 습하고 더워서 전염병이 발병하기 쉽다.
Since the summers are hot and humid, it is very easy for diseases to spread.
전염병을 예방하기 위해서는 자주 손을 씻는 게 좋아요.
It's good to frequently wash your hands to prevent infectious diseases.

66
주먹

[주먹] 명사 fist

[Expression] 주먹이 세다 to have a powerful fist
주먹을 쥐다 to clench one's fist
주먹을 펴다 to open one's fist
주먹으로 맞다 to be hit with a punch
주먹으로 치다 to hit someone with a fist

[Example] 얼굴이 주먹만 해요. His face is as big as his fist.
어린 아이의 주먹이 너무 작아서 귀여웠다.
The young child's fist is cute because it is small.

67
줄다

[줄다] 동사 to decrease, to diminish

[Usage] N 이/가 줄다

[Expression] 옷이 줄다 My clothes become smaller.
길이가 줄다 The length is lessened.
체중이 줄다 to weigh less

[Antonym] 늘다 to increase

[Example] 빨래를 잘못해서 옷이 줄었어요.
I messed up the laundry and the clothes shrunk.
오랫동안 운동과 식이요법을 같이 해서 체중이 많이 줄었다.
I lost a lot of weight after dieting and working out for a long time.

68
증상

[증상] 명사 symptoms

[Expression] 증상이 가볍다 to have light symptoms
증상이 생기다 to show symptoms
증상이 나타나다 to have symptoms
증상이 발생하다 to have symptoms

[Synonym] 증세 symptom

[Example] 위암에 걸리면 보통 어떤 증상이 나타납니까?
What kind of symptoms does one show if one suffers from a stomach infection?

증상이 가벼우니까 입원하실 필요는 없을 것 같습니다.
You don't have any serious symptoms, so I think there is no need for you to be hospitalized.

69
지치다

[지치다] 동사 to suffer from, to be exhausted from a sickness or hard situation

[Usage] N 이/가 지치다
N 에 지치다

[Expression] 몸이 지치다 to be exhausted

[Related Words] 힘들다 to be hard
피로하다 to be tired

[Example] 오늘 이사하느라고 많이 지쳤을 텐데 푹 쉬어.
You must be exhausted today after moving. Rest up.

지금 몸이 너무 지쳐서 아무 것도 하고 싶지 않아.
I don't feel like doing anything since by body is tired.

70
참다

[참따] 동사 to hold back

[Usage] N 을/를 참다

[Expression] 눈물을 참다 to hold back one's tears
아픔을 참다 to deal with pain
웃음을 참다 to hold back laughter
꾹 참다 to bite one's lips and hold on

[Synonym] 견디다 to withstand

[Example] 친구가 심한 말을 해서 화가 났지만 꾹 참았어요.
I remained calm even though my friend said some harsh words that got me angry.

상처가 심해서 많이 아팠을 텐데 아이가 잘 참네요.
The wound was pretty serious and must have hurt a lot. The child really seems to be dealing with the pain very well.

71
채식

[채식] 명사 vegetarian diet

[Expression] 채식주의자 vegetarian
채식을 하다 to eat vegetables

[Related Words] 육식 to eat meat

[Example] 장수하는 사람들은 보통 채식을 많이 한다고 합니다.
People who live long lives often are vegetarians.

앞으로는 운동을 규칙적으로 하고 육식보다는 비타민이 풍부한 채식 중심의 식사를 해야겠다.
From now on, I'm going to regularly work out and rather than eating meat, I'm going to follow a vegetable heavy diet full of vitamins.

72
취하다

[취하다] 동사 1. to be intoxicated, enebriated 2. to be lost or absorbed by something 3. to take

1. [Usage] N 에 취하다

[Expression]
술에 취하다 to be drunk
약에 취하다 to be drunk on medicine
잠에 취하다 to be drunk on sleep

[Example] 저는 소주 한 잔만 마셔도 금방 취해요.
I quickly get drunk just after one glass of soju.

2. [Usage] N 에 취하다

[Expression]
흥에 취하다 to be lost in red
음악에 취하다 to be lost in music
분위기에 취하다 to be absorbed by the mood/environment

[Example] 그는 노래에 취해서 다른 사람들의 말이 들리지 않았다.
He was so into his music that he couldn't hear what others were telling him.

3. [Usage] N 을/를 취하다

[Expression]
휴식을 취하다 to take a rest
숙면을 취하다 to get a full night of sleep

[Example] 매일 8시간 이상 자니까 수면을 충분히 취하는 편이다.
I get sufficient sleep since I sleep over 8 hours a day.

73
치과

[치꽈] 명사 the dentist

[Expression]
치과 대학 school of dentistry
치과 치료 dental treatment
치과에 다니다 to go to the dentist

[Related Words]
잇몸 gum
충치 cavity
치아 tooth
틀니 dentures

[Example] 치과에 가서 충치를 치료했어요.
I went to the dentist to treat my cavity.

우리 아이는 치과 가는 것을 제일 무서워해요.
My child is most afraid of going to the dentist.

도움말

외과 surgical department
안과 eye doctor
소아과 pediatrics
정형외과 orthopedics
이비인후과 ear, nose, and throat doctor
내과 internal medicine
피부과 dermatology
성형외과 plastic surgerical unit
산부인과 ob/gyn, obstetrics

74
치료하다

[치료하다] 동사 to treat

[Usage] N 을/를 치료하다

[Expression] 병을 치료하다 to treat a disease
상처를 치료하다 to treat a wound

[Synonym] 고치다 to fix

[Antonym] 치료받다 to get a treatment

[Related Words] 진료하다 to see a patient

[Example] 암은 치료하기 힘든 병 중에 하나이다.
Cancer is one of the diseases that is hard to treat.

과학의 발달로 고통없이 치료하는 방법이 개발되고 있다.
Thanks to scientific advances, the ways to treat diseases without pain are improving.

75
치매

[치매] 명사 demensia

[Expression] 치매 환자 dementia patient
치매 치료 dementia treatment
치매에 걸리다 to suffer from dementia

[Synonym] 중풍 stroke

[Example] 치매 예방에 좋은 음식이 있으면 좀 알려 주세요.
Please let me know if there are any foods that are good to help prevent dementia.

가족 중에 한 명이 치매에 걸리면 환자는 물론 가족들도 모두 힘든 생활을 하게 된다.
If one member of the family suffers from Alzheimer's disease, both the patient and the family end up leading difficult lives.

76
턱

[턱] 명사 chin

[Expression] 턱선 chin line
턱이 뾰족하다 to have a pointy chin
턱에 수염이 나다 to have hair on one's chin

[Example] 그녀는 얼굴이 아주 작고 턱이 뾰족했다.
She had a small face and a sharp chin.

그 사람은 며칠 동안 면도를 하지 않았는지 턱에 수염이 거칠게 나 있었다.
He had rough hairs on his chin because he probably hadn't shaved during the past few days.

77
털

[털] 명사 hair (body hair)

[Expression] 깃털 feather
털보 hairy person
털이 나다 to have hair come out
털을 깎다 to cut one's hair
털을 기르다 to grow one's hair

[Example] 우리 아빠는 다리에 털이 많이 났어요.
My dad has a lot of hair on his legs.

그 개의 하얀색 털이 길고 부드러웠다.
That dog's white fur is long and soft.

78
통

[통] 부사 any, at all

Usually comes after words that negate, such as to not have, to not know, to not be able to do, and has a meaning similar to that of 전혀, 도저히, 도무지

[Synonym] 전혀 at all
도무지 completely

[Example] 감기에 걸려서 그런지 통 입맛이 없네요.
I don't have any appetite at all since I have a cold.

너 무슨 일이 있니? 오늘은 통 말이 없구나.
What's wrong with you? Why are you so quiet today?

79
편식

[편식] 명사 eating only what one wants, to have an unbalanced diet

[Expression] 편식을 하다 to eat only what one wants or enjoys

[Example] 요즘 편식을 하는 아이들이 많던데 따님은 어때요?
Nowadays, there are a lot of children that only eat what they want, how about your daughter?

편식이 심하면 잘 자랄 수 없으니까 여러 가지 음식을 골고루 먹어야 한다.
If someone only eats what they want, they are going to have problems while growing up. Therefore, one must eat all kinds of food.

80
폐

[폐] 명사 lung

[Expression] 폐암 lung cancer
폐렴 lung infection

[Synonym] 허파 lung

[Example] 폐에 물이 들어가면 매우 위험하다.
It is very dangerous if water enters your lung.

담배를 많이 피워서 폐에 염증이 생겼습니다.
You have an infection in your lung from smoking too much.

81
피로

[피로] 명사 fatigue

[Expression] 만성피로 chronic fatigue syndrome
피로가 심하다 to be very tired
피로가 쌓이다 to have a build-up of exhaustion
피로가 풀리다 to no longer be tired/exhausted
피로를 풀다 to get rid of one's tiredness

[Related Words] 피곤 being tired

[Example] 피로 회복에는 충분한 휴식이 최고다.
The best way to recover from exhaustion is resting.

충분한 휴식을 취하지 않으면 피로가 쌓여 건강을 해칠 수 있어요.
If you do not get enough rest, you will get more and more tired and possibly damage your health.

82
하품

[하품] 명사 yawn

[Expression] 하품이 나오다 to yawn
하품을 하다 to yawn

[Example] 하품을 하면 왜 눈물이 나올까요?
Why is it that I cry when I yawn?

죄송합니다. 어젯밤에 잠을 잘 못 잤더니 자꾸 하품이 나오네요.
I'm sorry. Last night I didn't sleep well and I can't stop yawning today.

도움말

트림을 하다 to burp　방귀를 뀌다 to fart　재채기를 하다 to sneeze

83
합병증

[합뼝쯩] 명사 complications

[Expression] 합병증이 생기다 to have complications
합병증을 예방하다 to prevent complications

[Related Words] 부작용 side effect

[Example] 그 사람은 당뇨병에 합병증까지 겹쳐서 목숨을 잃었다.
He died because of diabetes and the complications from diabetes.
할아버지께서 수술 후 합병증으로 아직도 고생을 하고 계세요.
My grandfather is still suffering from the complications caused by the surgery.

84
항암제

[항암제] 명사 anti-cancer drugs/medicine

[Expression] 항암제 부작용 side effects from cancer medication
항암제를 맞다 to take anti-cancer medicine
항암제를 투여하다 to administer anticancer medicine

[Related Words] 암세포 cancer cell

[Example] 항암제 부작용으로 자꾸 머리카락이 빠져서 고민이에요.
I'm worried that my hair keeps falling out due to the cancer treatment.
여러 번의 실험 끝에 드디어 새로운 항암제가 개발되었다.
After numerous experiments, a new cancer medicine was finally developed.

도움말

소화제 digestive medicine　진통제 painkillers
영양제 nutritional supplement　마취제 anestetic

85
혀

[혀] 명사 tongue

[Expression] 혀를 차다 to click one's tongue
혀를 내밀다 to stick out one's tongue
혀를 깨물다 to bite one's tongue

[Related Words] 혓바닥 bottom of the tongue

[Example] 밥을 먹다가 혀를 깨물었어요. I bit my tongue while eating food.
사람들이 언제 혀를 내밉니까? When do people stick out their tongue?

86
혈관

[혈관] 명사 blood vessel

[Expression] 뇌혈관 brain blood vessel
혈관 질환 blood vessel disease
혈관 주사 blood vessel shot

[Related Words] 혈액 blood

[Example] 피는 혈관을 통해 몸의 이곳저곳을 다닙니다.
Blood travels around our body through the blood vessels.

스트레스를 많이 받는 직업을 가진 사람들이 혈관 질환의 위험이 더 높다고 해요.
People that have jobs that are very stressful suffer a greater risk of getting a blood vessel disease.

87
혈압

[혀랍] 명사 blood pressure

[Expression] 혈압이 낮다 to have low blood pressure
혈압이 높다 to have high blood pressure
혈압이 올라가다 to have an increase in blood pressure
혈압이 정상이다 normal blood pressure
혈압을 재다 to take one's blood pressure

[Related Words] 고혈압 high blood pressure
저혈압 low blood pressure
정상혈압 normal blood pressure

[Example] 혈압이 높은 사람은 짜게 먹으면 안 돼요.
People who have high blood pressure can't eat salty food.

건강 검진 결과 어머니의 혈압이 높다고 나왔습니다.
My mother's health result showed that she had high blood pressure.

88
회복하다

[회보카다] 동사 to recover

[Usage] N 을/를 회복하다

[Expression] 건강을 회복하다 to recover one's health, to have good health again

[Synonym] 낫다 to get better

[Example] 한 달 전에 수술하신 할아버지께서 이제 거의 회복하셨어요.
My grandfather that got surgery one month ago is now almost fully recovered.

건강식이란 건강을 유지하거나 회복하기 위하여 만든 식사를 말합니다.
Health foods refer to food that is made to help you maintain or recover your health.

89
효과

[효꽈] 명사 effect

[Expression] 효과적이다 effetive
효과가 있다 to have an effect
효과가 없다 to have no effect
효과가 나타나다 to show an effect
효과가 떨어지다 to have less of an effect

[Example] 그 약은 한 알만 먹어도 효과가 있어요.
Even if you take only one pill, it has an effect on you.

산소 운동이든 근력 운동이든 꾸준히 30분 이상 하시는 게 가장 효과적이에요.
Whether it's aerobic exercise or weight training, it's most effective when steadily done for over thirty minutes.

90
흡연

[흐번] 명사 smoking

[Expression] 흡연실 smoking room
간접흡연 second hand smoke
흡연 구역 smoking zone
흡연 금지 no smoking
흡연 습관 smoking habit

[Antonym] 금연 no smoking allowed

[Example] 담배 값을 올리면 흡연율이 낮아질 거라고 봐요.
I believe that if we raise the price of cigarettes, the rate number of smokers will drop.

지나친 흡연은 본인뿐만 아니라 주위 사람에게도 피해를 주게 됩니다.
Excessive smoking not only hurts you but also those around you.

03 연습문제

[1~9] **그림을 보고 신체부위를 나타내는 단어를 한국어로 쓰십시오.**

Look at the pictures and write the words to Korean that indicate the part of the body.

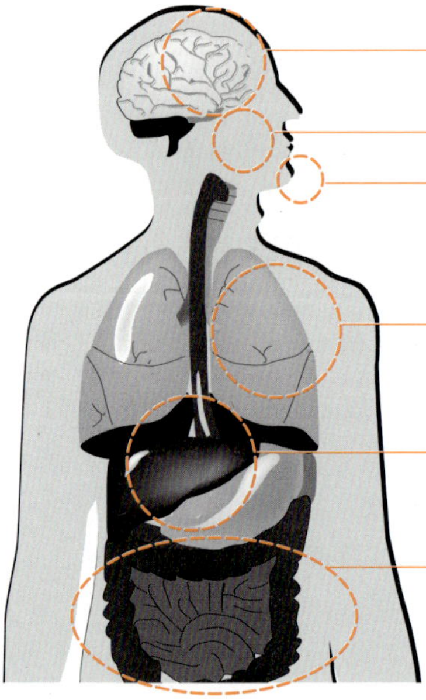

1. (　　　　　)
2. (　　　　　)
3. (　　　　　)
4. (　　　　　)
5. (　　　　　)
6. (　　　　　)

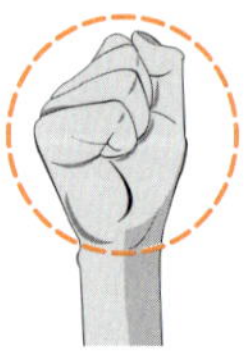

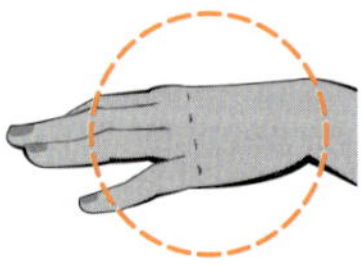

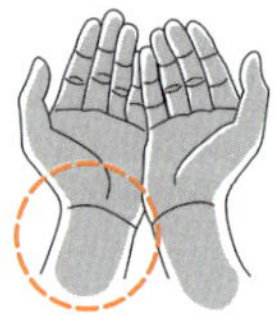

7. (　　　　　)　8. (　　　　　)　9. (　　　　　)

[10-22] **다음 단어를 한국어로 바꿔 쓰십시오.**

Change the following vocabulary words to Korean

10. Muscle (　　　　　)
11. Emergency (　　　　　)
12. Sleep (in the eyes) (　　　　　)
13. Eyebrows (　　　　　)
14. To be old (　　　　　)
15. To open (eyes) (　　　　　)
16. To catch a disease (　　　　　)
17. Breath (　　　　　)
18. Intestine (　　　　　)
19. Hair (　　　　　)
20. Tongue (　　　　　)
21. Blood vessel (　　　　　)

22. Blood pressure (　　　　　　)

[23-34] [보기]에서 알맞은 단어를 골라 (　　　　) 안에 쓰십시오.
Choose the appropriate word from the box below and then fill in the sentence.

[보기]

보약	비결	기운	숙면	식사량	민간요법
떨다	약하다	규칙적이다	비위생적이다	소모하다	움직이다

23. 날씨도 쌀쌀하고 비도 많이 오는데 밖에서 강아지 한 마리가 추워서 (　　　　　　)고 있어요.

24. 중국에서는 감기에 걸렸을 때 (　　　　　　)으로/로 파, 생강, 흑설탕을 함께 끓여서 마신다고 해요.

25. 수술한 곳이 아프다고 침대에 계속 누워 계시기만 하면 회복이 느리니까 조금씩이라도 (　　　　) 으셔야/셔야 해요.

26. (　　　　　　)인 생활을 해야 건강해질 수 있습니다.

27. 독감에 걸려서 입맛이 없었는데 하숙집 아주머니께서 끓여주신 죽을 먹으니까 (　　　　　　) 이/가 좀 나는 것 같아요.

28. 요즘 부모님 건강이 안 좋아지신 것 같아서 한의원에서 (　　　　　　)을/를 지어 드렸어요.

29. 미선 씨는 항상 날씬한 몸을 유지하는데 그 (　　　　　　)이/가 뭐예요?

30. 파리나 바퀴벌레가 많은 (　　　　　　)인 환경에서 전염병이 생길 위험이 커요.

31. 다이어트를 하고 싶다면 운동으로 열량을 많이 (　　　　　　)어야/아야/여야 한다.

32. 깨끗한 피부를 유지하기 위해서는 물을 많이 마시고, (　　　　　　)을/를 취하고, 일찍 자야 합니다.

33. 살을 빼고 싶다면 무조건 운동만 하기보다는 (　　　　　　)도 같이 조절하면 더 효과적이다.

34. 제가 어렸을 때 자주 아프고 몸이 (　　　　　　)어서/아서/여서 부모님이 항상 걱정하셨어요.

[35-40] [보기]에서 알맞은 말을 찾아 빈칸에 넣으십시오.

Fill in the empty spaces with hte approriate word from the box below.

[보기]

건강식	과식	소식	채식	편식	육식

35. 음식을 적게 먹어요. (　　　　　　)	38. 음식을 지나치게 많이 먹어요. (　　　　　　)
36. 건강을 유지하거나 회복하기 위하여 먹어요. (　　　　　　)	39. 고기는 전혀 먹지 않고 채소나 과일만 먹어요. (　　　　　　)
37. 채소나 과일은 먹지 않고 고기만 먹어요. (　　　　　　)	40. 음식을 골고루 먹지 않고 좋아하는 음식만 먹어요. (　　　　　　)

[41-44] 다음 밑줄 친 부분과 반대되는 뜻을 가진 것을 고르십시오.

Choose the word that has an opposite meaning with the word underlined below.

41. 매일 하루 1시간 씩, 한 달 동안 운동을 했더니 살이 2kg이나 줄었어요.

❶ 많다　❷ 빼다　❸ 늘다　❹ 마르다

42. 저는 고등학교 때 체중이 100kg으로 아주 뚱뚱했었어요.

❶ 살찌다　❷ 마르다　❸ 튼튼하다　❹ 통통하다

43. 소고기나 닭고기 같은 육식을 즐기면 비타민이 부족하니까 채소와 과일도 드셔야 해요.

❶ 충분하다　❷ 모자라다　❸ 만족하다　❹ 분명하다

44. 건강을 위해서 오늘부터 금연하기로 결심했어요.

❶ 연기 ❷ 흡연 ❸ 흡수 ❹ 연장

[45-55] **[보기]에서 알맞은 단어를 골라 (   ) 안에 쓰십시오.**

Coose the appropriate word from the box below and then fill in the parenthesis.

[보기]

부상	치과	식욕	피로	영양	당뇨병
부작용	식습관	구급차	참다	지치다	

45. 키가 작아서 걱정인 아이들에게는 우유나 계란같이 (   )이/가 풍부한 음식이 좋을 것 같아요.

46. 채소와 과일은 먹지 않고 소고기, 닭고기 같은 육류만 먹는 (   )은/는 건강에 좋지 않다.

47. 다이어트 중이었는데 갈비 굽는 냄새 때문에 (   )을/를 참지 못하고 결국 먹고 말았어요.

48. 푹 자고 일어나니까 이제 좀 (   )이/가 풀린 것 같아요.

49. 여기요, 사람이 쓰러졌어요. 빨리 (   ) 좀 불러 주세요.

50. 발목의 통증이 (   )기 힘들 정도로 심해서 걸을 수가 없어요.

51. 지난번 경기에서 박지섭 선수가 무릎 (   )을/를 당하는 바람에 이번 경기는 뛰지 못할 것 같아요.

52. 지난주에 이가 아프다고 했는데 (   )에 갔다 왔어요?

53. 아버님이 (   )에 걸리셔서 특히 케이크, 초콜릿, 아이스크림 등 설탕이 많이 들어 있는 음식을 조심해야 해요.

54. 이 약은 효과는 좋지만 가끔 설사 또는 소화가 안 되는 (   )이/가 있을 수 있어요.

55. 날씨도 더운데 밖에서 계속 일을 해서 너무 (   )었어요/았어요/였어요.

[56-65] [보기]에서 알맞은 말을 찾아 빈칸에 넣으십시오.

Fill in the empty spaces with hte approriate word from the box below.

[보기]

암	염증	불면증	성인병	심장병
우울증	전염병	합병증	소화불량	동맥경화

56. 동맥이 딱딱해져서 문제가 생기는 병

( )

57. 우리 몸에 나쁜 세포가 계속 자라서 종양이 되는 병

( )

58. 심장에 생기는 여러 가지 병

( )

59. 당뇨, 비만, 고혈압 등 성인들에게 자주 생기는 병

( )

60. 다른 사람에게 옮길 수 있는 병

( )

61. 밤에 잠을 자지 못하는 증상

( )

62. 이유가 없이 기분이 좋지 않고 우울해지는 증상

( )

63. 어떤 병에 함께 생기는 또 다른 병

( )

64. 음식을 먹으면 소화가 안 되고 속이 편하지 않은 증상

( )

65. 다치거나 상처가 난 곳을 잘 치료하지 않아서 생기는 증상

( )

[66-71] **다음 밑줄 친 부분과 의미가 비슷한 것을 고르십시오.**

Choose the word that is similar in meaning to the underlined part of the sentence.

66. 요즘 항암 치료를 받고 있어서 고통이 심할 거예요.

❶ 부담 ❷ 수고 ❸ 사정 ❹ 통증

67. 요즘 날마다 야식을 먹었더니 몸무게가 많이 늘었어요.

❶ 신장 ❷ 비만 ❸ 체중 ❹ 영양

68. 식중독에 걸렸을 때는 복통이나 설사 증상이 있어요.

❶ 염증 ❷ 증세 ❸ 짜증 ❹ 불면증

69. 이번에 연세 제약회사에서 암을 치료할 수 있는 약을 만들었어요.

❶ 그치다 ❷ 지치다 ❸ 고치다 ❹ 수리하다

70. 어머니께서 이제 거의 회복하셔서 다음 주에는 퇴원하실 거예요.

❶ 낫다 ❷ 옮다 ❸ 앓다 ❹ 붓다

71. 약을 먹어도 감기가 전혀 낫질 않아요.

❶ 덜 ❷ 약 ❸ 좀 ❹ 통

[72-73] 다음 ( )에 공통적으로 들어갈 단어를 쓰십시오.

Write one word that can commoly fit into the parenthesis below.

72. ❶ 저는 ( )이/가 안 좋아서 조금만 피곤해도 몸도 붓고 다리도 많이 부어요.

❷ 그 농구 선수는 178cm로 다른 선수들에 비해 ( )이/가 작은데도 실력은 뛰어나요.

( )

73. ❷ 밖으로 나오자마자 갑자기 비가 ( ) 쏟아졌어요.

❷ 버스 정류장에 도착하니까 버스가 ( ) 떠나고 있었어요.

❸ 쓰레기는 아무 데나 ( ) 버리지 말고 꼭 쓰레기통에 버리세요.

( )

[74-76] 다음 ( )에 공통적으로 들어갈 단어의 기본형을 쓰십시오.

Write the basic form of one word that can be used in the parenthesis.

74. ❶ 그 남자는 라디오에서 흘러나오는 흥겨운 음악에 ( )어서/아서/여서 춤을 추고 있었다.

❷ 저녁도 먹지 않고 술을 마셔서 그런지 빨리 ( )네요.

❸ 건강을 위해서 과로하지 마시고 충분한 휴식을 ( )으시는/시는 게 좋을 것 같아요.

( )

75. ❶ 컵라면에 뜨거운 물을 좀 ( )어/아/여 주세요.

❷ 축구를 하다가 다친 발목이 퉁퉁 ( )었어요/았어요/였어요.

❸ 슬픈 영화를 보고 울었더니 눈이 많이 ( )었어요/았어요/였어요.

( )

76. ❶ 우리 집 강아지가 새끼를 다섯 마리나 (　　　　　)었어요/았어요/였어요.
❷ 김 선생님 사모님이 지난주에 따님을 (　　　　　)으셨대요/셨대요.
❸ 좀 더 깊이 생각하지 않고 너무 급하게 결정했던 것이 이런 결과를 (　　　　　)은/ㄴ 것 같다.

(　　　　　　　　　　)

[77-87] **다음 [보기]에서 알맞은 단어를 골라 (　　　) 안에 쓰십시오.**
Choose the appropriate word from the box below and fill in the parenthesis.

[보기]

비만	치매	하품	효과	항암제	
비상약	응급실	앓다	옮다	어리다	사망하다

77. 눈이 빨갛게 됐어요. 아마 어제 수영장에서 눈병이 (　　　　　)은/ㄴ 것 같아요.

78. 이렇게 계속 살이 찌면 (　　　　　)이/가 될 수 있으니까 식사량을 조절하도록 하세요.

79. 우리 전통 음식들이 암을 예방하는데 (　　　　　)이/가 있다고 뉴스에서 들었어요.

80. 여행을 갈 때는 혹시 아플지도 모르니까 (　　　　　)을/를 가지고 가는 게 좋아요.

81. 일주일 동안 독감을 (　　　　　)았더니/었더니/였더니 기운도 없고 입맛도 없어요.

82. 어제 새벽에 갑자기 배가 아파서 병원 (　　　　　)에서 치료를 받았어요.

83. 이번 지진으로 8,000명 이상이 부상을 당하고 400명 이상이 (　　　　　)었습니다/았습니다/였습니다.

84. 할머니께서 (　　　　　)에 걸리셔서 가족들을 못 알아보세요.

85. 제 조카인 유리는 초등학교 2학년인데 나이는 (　　　　　)지만 생각이 깊어요.

86. 김 부장님은 암 치료 때문에 요즘 (　　　　　)을/를 맞고 계신데 부작용으로 머리카락이 많이 빠져서 고민이시래요.

87. 어제 한 시간밖에 못 잤더니 졸려서 계속 (　　　　　)이/가 나오네요.

음식

04

Food

04 음식

01
가지

[가지] 명사 eggplant

[Expression] 가지 나물 eggplant vegetables

[Example] 나물 중에서 가지 나물을 제일 좋아해요.
I like eggplant the most out of all vegetables.

가지를 너무 오래 삶으면 맛이 없으니까 삶을 때 조심하세요.
Be careful when boiling an eggplant because it loses its taste if you boil it for too long.

02
갈다[1]

[갈다] 동사 to sharpen, to grind

to sharpen an edge or smoothen out a surface of an object by rubbing it against or between another hard object.

[Usage] N 을/를 갈다
N 에 갈다

[Expression] 이를 갈다 to grind one's teeth
칼을 갈다 to sharpen a knife

[Example] 잘 때 이를 갈아서 아침엔 이가 아파요.
My teeth hurt in the morning because I grind my teeth while I sleep.

날씨가 더운 여름에는 콩을 믹서에 갈아서 콩국수를 만들어 먹어요.
On hot summer days, I make bean soup by grinding beans in a mixer.

03
고구마

[고구마] 명사 sweet potato

[Expression] 고구마 밭 sweet potato field
고구마를 깎다 to peel a sweet potato
고구마를 찌다 to steam sweet potatoes

[Related Words] 감자 potato

[Example] 저는 아침밥으로 고구마를 먹어요.
I eat sweet potatoes for breakfast.

어렸을 때 시골에 가면 할머니께서 고구마를 쪄 주시곤 했어요.
When I was younger, my grandmother would give me steamed sweet potatoes.

04
고소하다

[고소하다] 형용사 to be savory, to be sweet

a smell or taste similar to that of fried sesame or sesame oil

[Synonym] 구수하다 to be sweet

[Example] 나물에 참기름을 넣으면 고소해져요.
Vegetables become sweeter if you add sesame oil.

이번에 새로 나온 과자는 씹으면 씹을수록 고소한 맛이 나요.
These new cookies taste sweeter the more you chew on them.

05
고춧가루

[고추까루], [고춛까루] 명사 powdered red pepper

flour made from red ripe ground peppers

[Expression] 고춧가루가 끼다 to have powdered red pepper stuck in your teeth
고춧가루를 넣다 to add red pepper

[Related Words] 고추 pepper
고추장 red pepper paste

[Example] 김치를 먹은 후에는 이에 고춧가루가 끼었는지 확인하는 것이 좋아요.
It's good to check if you have any red pepper stuck in your teeth after eating kimchi.

설렁탕에 고춧가루를 조금 넣어 드시면 매콤한 맛을 느끼실 수 있습니다.
If you put in a little powdered red pepper into your solleungtang, you can really feel the somewhat spicy flavor.

도움말

후춧가루 pepper powder　　미숫가루 grain powder

06
곡류

[공뉴] 명사 types of grains

a word used to describe raw rice, barley, flour and other kinds of grains

[Related Words] 쌀 rice
밀 flour
보리 barley
곡식 grains

[Example] 시골 시장에서는 곡류를 가지고 나와서 파는 노인들을 쉽게 볼 수 있다.
You can commonly see old people selling grains in the countryside marketplace.

큰 대형마트에서는 곡류, 육류, 생선류, 주류 코너가 각각 나누어져 있다.
In big super markets, grain, meat, fish, and drink corners are divided into separate areas.

도움말

육류 meats　　주류 drinks　　생선류 fish

07
국물

[궁물] 명사 broth

the liquid inside of soups or stews

[Expression]
국물 맛 the taste of the broth
국물 한 모금 one sip of the broth
국물이 뜨겁다 The broth is hot.
국물을 흘리다 to spill the broth
국물에 말다 to soak in the broth

[Example]
옷에 국물을 흘려서 얼룩이 생겼어요.
I got a stain on my shirt after I spilled soup on it.

어머니는 입맛이 없을 때마다 국물에 밥을 말아서 드시곤 했어요.
My mother used to dip her rice into her soup broth whenever she didn't have an appetite.

08
기름

[기름] 명사 oil

a substance that is light and catches fire very easily

[Expression]
참기름 sesame oil
기름 덩어리 lumps of hardened oil or fat
기름지다 to be greasy
기름에 볶다 to roast in oil
기름에 튀기다 to fry in oil

[Synonym]
식용유 Cooking oil

[Example]
물과 기름은 절대로 섞이지 않는다.
Water and oil never mix.

기름을 너무 많이 먹으면 비만이 되기 쉽습니다.
It is easy to become fat if one eats too much oil.

09
김장

[김장] 명사 the act of making a lot of kimchi at once in order to eat it later on

[Expression]
김장독 kimchi jar
김장철 kimchi making season
김장 김치 kmichi made during the kimjang season

김장하다 to make a lot of kimchi

[Example] 김장철에는 배추 값이 많이 올라가요.
The price of napa cabbage goes up a lot during kimchi making season.

보통 11월 말부터 12월 초 사이에 김장을 해요.
Kimjang is usually done between the end of November and the start of December.

10
깎다

[깍따] 동사 1. to shave 2. to cut off

1. to shave or to pare the outside of something

[Usage] N 을/를 깎다

[Expression] 과일을 깎다 to peel a fruit
연필을 깎다 to sharpen a pencil

[Example] 연필을 깎다가 손가락을 베었어요.
I cut my finger while sharpening my pencil.

2. to cut off the useless parts of an object

[Usage] N 을/를 깎다

[Expression] 머리를 깎다 to cut one's hair
손톱을 깎다 to cut one's nails
수염을 깎다 to cut one's beard off

[Related Words] 자르다 to cut

[Example] 날씨가 더워져서 머리를 짧게 깎았어요.
I cut my hair short because the weather got really hot.

11
껌

[껌] 명사 gum

[Usage] 껌이 N 에 붙다

[Expression] 풍선껌 bubble gum
껌 한 통 one pack of gum
껌을 뱉다 to spit out gum
껌을 씹다 to chew gum

[Example] 수업시간에는 껌을 씹지 않도록 하세요.
Please don't chew gum during class.

껌을 다 씹은 후에는 종이에 싸서 버려야 합니다.
You need to wrap your gum up in a piece of paper and throw it out after you finish chewing it.

12
껍질

[껍질] 명사 peel, bark

[Expression] 껍질을 까다 to peel the skin
껍질을 벗기다 to peel the skin off

[Synonym] 껍데기 peel

[Example] 과일 껍질은 음식물 쓰레기로 분리해서 버려야 해요.
You need to separate the peels of fruits into the garbage for food waste and then throw it away.

사과 껍질에는 좋은 영양소가 많으니까 가능하면 깎지 말고 그냥 드세요.
It is better to just eat the skin of an apple and not peel it off if possible because it has a lot of good nutrients.

13
꿀

[꿀] 명사 honey

[Expression] 꿀물 honey water
꿀을 넣다 to add honey into something

[Related Words] 벌 bee
벌집 beehive

[Example] 기침할 때는 배와 꿀을 먹으면 좋아요.
It is good to eat honey and pears when you have a cough.

설탕보다는 꿀을 사용해서 단맛을 내는 것이 몸에 더 좋다고 한다.
They say that using honey rather than sugar to sweeten food is better for your body.

14
나물

[나물] 명사 herbs, greens

any word related to the leaves or plants that people can eat

[Expression] 나물을 무치다 to prepare vegetables in spices

[Example] 손으로 직접 나물을 무쳐야 제 맛이 나요.
Vegetables taste the best when prepared by hand.

나물에는 참기름이 들어가야 고소한 맛이 나고 좋다.
You need to put sesame oil in your vegetables for them to taste sweet and good.

15
남다

[남따] 동사 to be leftover, to remain

[Usage] N 이/가 남다

[Expression] 음식이 남다 There is leftover food.

[Example] 남은 음식은 싸 가지고 가세요.
Please take the leftover food with you.

이번 달 용돈을 하나도 남기지 않고 다 써 버렸어요.
I used all my allowance this month and didn't keep any of it.

16
넘치다

[넘치다] 동사 to overflow

to flow out because something is too full

[Usage] N 이/가 넘치다

[Example] 국이 넘쳐서 가스레인지가 더러워졌어요.
The stovetop became dirty after the soup spilt.

정보가 넘쳐 나는 사회에서 바쁜 현대인들이 모든 신문과 뉴스를 다 볼 수는 없지요.
In a society teeming with information, it is impossible for the modern man to read all the news.

17
느끼하다

[느끼하다] 형용사 to be greasy

the feeling of having eaten food that has too much oil in it and as a result not feeling pleased

[Usage] N 이/가 느끼하다

[Related Words] 담백하다 to be clean and light in taste

[Example] 저는 느끼한 음식보다는 담백한 음식을 더 좋아합니다.
I like clean tasting food more than greasy food.

기름진 음식을 많이 먹어서 그런지 속이 느끼하고 편하지 않아요.
My insides feel very uncomfortable and heavy after eating a lot of oily food.

18
달콤하다

[달콤하다] 형용사 to be somewhat sweet

[Usage] N 이/가 달콤하다

[Related Words] 매콤하다 to be semi-spicy
새콤하다 to be semi-sour

[Example] 오늘은 후식으로 달콤한 케이크를 준비해 봤어요.
I have prepared a sweet cake for today's dessert.

초콜릿의 달콤함보다는 사탕의 달콤함을 더 좋아해요.
I like the sweetness of candy more than that of chocolate.

19
담그다

[담그다] 동사 1. to prepare 2. to soak, to immerse in

1. to store food in a bowl or other container in order to let it ripen or mature

[Usage] N 을/를 담그다

[Expression] 술을 담그다 to prepare alcohol
김치를 담그다 to prepare kimchi

[Example] 어머니는 아버지를 위해 매년 술을 담그세요.
My mom prepares alcohol for my father every year.

2. to put something inside of a substance

[Usage] N 에 N 을/를 담그다

[Example] 여름에 계곡 물에 발을 담그면 너무 시원해요.
In the summer, it is refreshing to put your feet inside of valley water.

20
담다

[담따] 동사 to put in, to fill

to put something into a plate, a container, bag etc.

[Usage] N 을/를 담다
N 에 담다

[Example] 먹을 만큼 그릇에 담아서 드세요.
Please put as much as you are going to eat onto the bowl and enjoy.

등산하면서 마실 물을 물병에 가득 담았다.
I filled up my water bottle with water I was going to drink later on while hiking.

21
데치다

[데치다] 동사 to parboil, to blanch

to quickly place something into boiling water and then take it out

[Usage] N 을/를 데치다

[Expression] 시금치를 데치다 to place spinach into boiling water
오징어를 데치다 to put squid into boiling water

[Related Words] 삶다 to boil something and pour out the water
끓이다 to boil water, or to boil something

[Example] 오징어를 너무 오래 삶으면 질겨서 먹을 수 없으니까 살짝만 데치세요.
If you boil squid too long it becomes tough and you can't eat it so just make sure to put it in the water for a little bit.

시금치를 데쳐서 물기를 없앤 후에 양념을 넣어서 무치면 시금치 나물이 됩니다.

After boiling the spinach in water, remove the water, add the spice, mix it around, and then the spinach dish is complete.

22
도시락

[도시락] 명사 lunch box

a plate or bowl in which food is placed or a bowl that contains side dishes full of rice

[Expression] 도시락을 먹다 to eat a meal prepared in a lunch box

도시락을 싸다 to prepare a lunch box

[Example] 도시락을 싸 가지고 가까운 공원으로 소풍을 갑시다.

Let's prepare lunch box and go have a picnic at the park nearby.

학창 시절에 친구들과 같이 먹던 도시락이 너무 그립다.

I really miss the lunch boxes I would eat with my friends when I was in school.

23
뒤집다

[뒤집따] 동사 to turn over, to turn out, to turn around

[Usage] N 을/를 뒤집다

[Expression] 전을 뒤집다 to flip a pancake

[Example] 빈대떡을 뒤집는 일이 생각보다 쉽지 않네요.

Flipping a mung bean pancake is harder than I expected.

문제를 다 푼 학생은 시험지를 뒤집어 놓으세요.

The students that have solved the questions please turn over the test paper.

24
땅콩

[땅콩] 명사 peanut

[Expression] 땅콩이 고소하다 The peanut is sweet.

땅콩을 까먹다 to shell and eat a peanut

[Example] 맥주 안주로 땅콩이 좋아요.

Peanuts serve as good snacks when drinking beer.

오빠는 영화를 볼 때 땅콩을 까먹는 버릇이 있어요.

My older brother has the habit of shelling and eating peanuts when he watches movies.

25
떫다

[떨따] 형용사 to be bitter, to be sour

a strong and unpleasant taste like that of an unripe persimmon

[Expression] 떫은맛 a sour-bitter taste

[Example] 과일이 덜 익으면 떫은맛이 난다.

If a fruit isn't fully ripe it has a bitter taste.

감이 너무 떫어서 한 입도 먹을 수 없어요.
I can't even take a bite of this persimmon because it isn't fully ripe yet and tastes bitter.

26
레몬

[레몬] 명사 lemon

a yellow fruit that has a strong smell and a sour flavor

[Expression] 레몬차 lemon tea
레몬즙 lemon juice (essence that comes from the lemon)
레몬주스 lemon juice

[Example] 식초대신 레몬을 넣는 것도 좋아요.
It's good to put in lemon instead of vinegar.

샤워 후에 레몬차를 마시면 피로가 잘 풀리는 것 같아요.
I think that if you drink lemon tea after taking a shower you don't feel as tired.

27
막걸리

[막껄리] 명사 makkoli

one of the unique alcohols of Korea that is white in color and has a very bland taste

[Expression] 막걸리 한 사발 a bowl of makkoli
막걸리를 마시다 to drink makkoli

[Synonym] 탁주 raw rice wine

[Related Words] 소주 distilled rice wine
동동주 suspended rice wine

[Example] 막걸리는 한국의 대표적인 전통술 중에 하나이다.
Makkoli is one of the representative traditional alcohols of Korea.

요즘 막걸리가 세계적으로 주목을 받으며 높은 인기를 얻고 있습니다.
Recently makkoli is receiving attention and has gained a lot of popularity around the world.

28
맛보다

[맏뽀다] 동사 to taste

to have just a little food into order to check the taste

[Usage] N 을/를 맛보다

[Expression] 음식을 맛보다 to taste food

[Synonym] 시식하다 to sample food

[Example] 맛을 본 후에 간을 맞추세요.
Season the food with salt to your liking after tasting it.

제가 만든 음식이에요. 한번 맛보세요.
This is the food I made. Try tasting it.

29
맡다[1]

[맏따] 동사 to smell

to feel a smell through one's nose

[Usage] N 을/를 맡다

[Expression] 냄새를 맡다 to smell (a smell)

[Example] 꽃향기를 맡으면서 화원을 구경했어요.
I looked at the flower garden while smelling the fragrance of the flowers.

코가 막혀서 음식 냄새를 맡을 수 없어요.
I can't smell the food because my nose if clogged.

30
무

[무] 명사 radish

[Expression] 무를 뽑다 to pick a radish

[Related Words] 당근 carrot

[Example] 깍두기는 무로 만들어요.
Kkakdugi, cubed kimchi, is made from radish.

무를 뽑는 일이 쉬워 보였는데 직접 해 보니 생각보다 쉽지 않네요.
It looked like picking radishes was easy but after trying it, it turned out to be much harder than I thought.

31
무농약

[무농약] 명사 pesticide-free

[Expression] 무농약 식품
food products that have not been treated with pesticides

[Related Words] 유기농 organic
친환경 식품 environmentally friendly food products

[Example] 무농약 식품은 보통 다른 것들보다 값이 좀 비싸다.
Pesticide free products tend to be more expensive than other regular products.

요즘엔 많은 사람들이 건강을 위해 무농약 식품을 많이 찾는다.
Nowadays many people turn to pesticide free products for their health.

32
미지근하다

[미지근하다] 형용사 to be lukewarm, to be tepid

a somewhat warm temperature

[Related Words] 뜨겁다 to be hot
따뜻하다 to be warm

[Example] 국이 식어서 미지근해졌어요.
The soup was lukewarm after it cooled off.
상처 부위에 자극을 주면 안 되니까 미지근한 물로 씻으세요.
It's not good to aggravate the wound so you should wash it with lukewarm water.

33
밀가루

[밀까루] 명사 flour

[Expression] 밀가루 반죽 dough made from flour
밀가루로 반죽하다 to knead dough

[Example] 식빵의 재료는 밀가루와 우유, 달걀입니다.
The ingredients of table bread are flour, eggs, and milk.
나는 밀가루 음식을 먹으면 소화가 안 된다.
My stomach bothers me if I eat food with flour.

도움말
빵가루 bread crumbs 부침가루 pancake mix 튀김가루 frying mix

34
밥맛

[밤맏] 명사 appetite
the feeling of wanting to eat when thinking about the taste of food

[Expression] 밥맛이 있다 to have an appetite
밥맛이 없다 to have no appetite
밥맛이 좋다 to have a good appetite
밥맛이 떨어지다 to have less of an appetite
밥맛을 잃다 to lose one's appetite

[Related Words] 입맛 appetite

[Example] 감기에 걸려서 밥맛이 별로 없어요.
I don't have an appetite because I have a cold.
청정지역에서 나온 쌀로 만든 밥은 밥맛이 좋다.
Rice made from rice harvested in clean areas tastes very good.

35
배추

[배추] 명사 napa cabbage
main vegetable used when making kimchi

[Expression] 양배추 cabbage
배추김치 cabbage kimchi

배추를 절이다 to pickle kimchi

[Example] 배추뿐만 아니라 무로도 김치를 만들 수 있어요.
You can make kimchi with not only cabbage but also with radish.
김치 만들 때 가장 어려운 것이 배추를 알맞게 절이는 거예요.
The hardest part about making kimchi is pickling the cabbage properly.

36
버섯

[버섣] 명사 mushroom

[Expression] 독버섯 poisonous mushroom
송이버섯 matsutake mushroom
목이버섯 black mushroom
표고버섯 shiitake mushroom
버섯을 따다 to pick a mushroom

[Example] 삼촌 댁에서 버섯을 재배하고 계세요.
My uncle is cultivating mushrooms in his house.
보통 예쁜 버섯 중에 독버섯이 많아요.
There are many poisonous mushroom among the pretty ones.

37
버터

[버터] 명사 butter

[Expression] 버터를 바르다 to spread butter

[Related Words] 크림 cream
마가린 margarine

[Example] 빵에 버터와 잼을 발라서 먹으면 맛있어요.
It's tasty if you spread butter and jam onto bread and then eat it.
버터가 많이 들어간 음식을 먹으면 쉽게 뚱뚱해질 거예요.
It's easy to become fat if you eat food that has a lot of butter in it.

38
번거롭다

[번거롭따] 형용사 to be complicated, to be cumbersome

[Usage] N 이/가 번거롭다
AV 기가 번거롭다

[Related Words] 복잡하다 to be complicated

[Example] 번거로운 일을 부탁드려서 죄송합니다.
I'm sorry I've given you such a complicated job.
한국 요리는 만들기가 좀 번거로운 것 같아요.
I think that making Korean food can be quite tricky.

39
벗기다

[벋끼다] 동사 to take off, to peel off

to rip off or take off in order to expose the inside of something

[Usage] N 으로/로 N 을/를 벗기다

[Synonym] 까다 to peel

[Example] 먼저 칼로 감자 껍질을 벗기세요.
Please peel the skin of the potato first with a knife.

바나나 껍질을 벗긴 후에 아무데나 버리면 안 됩니다.
You can't just throw out the skin of a banana anywhere after you peel it.

40
보관하다

[보관하다] 동사 to store

to leave an object somewhere and watch over it

[Usage] N 을/를 보관하다
N 에 보관하다

[Example] 많은 문화재들이 박물관에 잘 보관되어 있습니다.
A lot of cultural assets are stored in museums.

고기는 냉동실에 보관하고 채소는 냉장실에 보관하세요.
Please store the meat in the freezer and the vegetables in the refrigerator.

41
부드럽다

[부드럽따] 형용사 to be soft

not rough or hard

[Usage] N 이/가 부드럽다

[Expression] 고기가 부드럽다 The meat is soft.
피부가 부드럽다 Her skin is soft.

[Example] 아기의 피부는 하얗고 부드러워요.
A baby's skin is soft and white.

이 고기는 연하고 부드러워서 이가 약한 노인들도 쉽게 드실 수 있을 거예요.
Elderly with weak teeth can easily eat this meat because it is soft and tender.

42
비리다

[비리다] 형용사 to smell fishy

the smell that the skin of fish or fresh beans give off

[Usage] N 이/가 비리다

[Expression] 생선이 비리다 The fish smells fishy.

[Example] 저는 비린 음식을 잘 먹지 못해요.
I can't eat foods that smell fishy.

신선하지 않은 생선에서는 비린 냄새가 심하게 나요.
Rotten fish gives off a very strong fishy smell.

43
빈대떡

[빈대떡] 명사 bindaetteok, mung bean pancake

a pancake that is made with peeled mung beans that have been grinded up in a stone bowl, that may include beef, pork, or other vegetables.

[Expression] 빈대떡을 부치다 to fry bindeatteok

[Related Words] 전 pancake

[Example] 한국에서는 명절 때 빈대떡을 만들어서 먹어요.
Koreans make bindaettoek during the holidays.

비가 올 때는 빈대떡에 막걸리를 같이 먹으면 좋아요.
It's good to eat bindaettoek on rainy days along with makkoli.

44
상하다[2]

[상하다] 동사 to go bad

to have spoiled food

[Usage] N 이/가 상하다

[Expression] 음식이 상하다 The food went bad.

[Synonym] 부패하다 to decay, to spoil

[Example] 냄새를 맡으면 음식이 상했는지 알 수 있지요.
You can tell if the food has gone bad by smelling it.

상한 음식을 먹으면 식중독에 걸릴 수 있으니까 빨리 버리세요.
Throw out that food right away because you can catch food poisoning if it has gone bad.

45
생강

[생강] 명사 ginger

[Expression] 생강차 ginger tea

[Related Words] 마늘 garlic

[Example] 감기에 걸렸을 때 생강차를 한번 드셔 보세요.
Try drinking some ginger tea when you catch a cold.

김치를 만들 때는 양념으로 마늘과 생강이 기본으로 들어가요.
When making kimchi, both garlic and ginger are used in the sauce.

46
섞다

[석따] 동사 to mix

[Usage] N 과/와 N 을/를 섞다

[Synonym] 혼합하다 to mix, to blend

[Example] 건강을 위해 쌀에 여러 가지 잡곡을 섞어서 밥을 지었어요.
I made the rice by mixing in various grains into the uncooked rice so it would be better for my health.

마지막으로 고기에 준비한 양념을 잘 섞어서 구우면 맛있는 불고기가 완성됩니다.
Lastly, cook the meat after mixing in the prepared sauces and you will have completed the bulgogi.

47
소시지

[소시지] 명사 sausage

[Related Words] 햄 ham

[Example] 길거리에서 소시지 구이를 파는 모습을 많이 봤어요.
I saw a lot of places that sell sausage in the street.

도시락 반찬 중에서 저는 소시지 반찬을 제일 좋아해요.
I like the sausage side dish the most out of all the side dishes that go into a lunchbox set.

48
솜씨

[솜씨] 명사 skill, ability

a talent or ability involved with making something by using your hands

[Expression] 말솜씨 ability to speak
요리 솜씨 ability to cook
솜씨가 있다 to have skill
솜씨가 없다 to have no skill
솜씨가 좋다 to have good skills

[Synonym] 소질 aptitude
재주 talent

[Example] 저는 말솜씨가 없어서 제 의견을 정확하게 전달하지 못할 때도 있어요.
I can't clearly express my opinion because I don't have very good speaking skills.

제 아내는 요리 솜씨가 뛰어나서 다양한 요리를 맛있게 만들 수 있어요.
My wife can make a lot of different kind of dishes because she has good cooking skills.

49
송편

[송편] 명사 songpyeon, half moon shaped rice cakes

rice cakes often eaten on the harvest festival of chuseok that can be filled with red beans, chestnuts, juju beans, or sesame.

[Expression] 송편을 빚다 to make songpyeon dumplings

[Related Words] 떡국 rice cake soup

오곡밥 five-grain rice

[Example] 추석 때는 송편을 먹고 설날에는 떡국을 먹어요.
On chuseok, we eat songpyeon and on new year's day we eat rice cake soup.

송편을 예쁘게 빚으면 예쁜 딸을 낳는다는 얘기를 할머니께 들은 적이 있어요.
I have heard from my grandmother that if you make pretty shaped half moon rice cakes you will give birth to a pretty daughter.

50
식다

[식따] 동사 to cool off

either the cooling of warm temperature or the passion/heat of anger or love

[Usage] N 이/가 식다

[Expression] 음식이 식다 The food gets cold.
사랑이 식다 Our love fades.

[Example] 식기 전에 드세요. Please eat it before it gets cold.

두 사람은 서로에 대한 사랑이 식어버렸는지 더 이상 연락도 하지 않아요.
It seems that their love has faded away, so the two of them don't contact each other anymore.

51
식료품

[싱뇨품] 명사 groceries, food

any food that form part the meat, fish, vegetables, food etc products at a market

[Expression] 식료품 가게 grocery store
식료품을 사다 to buy groceries

[Example] 식료품을 싸게 사려면 대형마트에 가세요.
Please go to a big market if you would like to buy cheap groceries.

유통 기한이 지난 식료품은 버리도록 하세요.
Make sure to throw away food whose expiration date has passed.

52
식빵

[식빵] 명사 plainbread

[Expression] 식빵을 굽다 to bake plain bread
식빵에 바르다 to spead something onto plain bread

[Related Words] 곰보빵 crumbly topping bread
단팥빵 red bean bread
토스트 toast

[Example] 아침마다 식빵에 딸기잼을 발라서 우유와 함께 먹어요.
Every morning I put strawberry jam on my plain bread and eat it with milk.

식빵 종류가 너무 많아서 무엇을 사야 할지 모르겠더군요.
I didn't know what kind of plain bread to buy because there were so many different kinds.

53
식초

[식초] 명사 vinegar

[Expression] 식초를 치다 to add vinegar
식초를 뿌리다 to sprinkle vinegar

[Example] 새콤한 맛을 좋아하는 분들은 식초를 넣어서 드셔 보세요.
People who like sour tasting food should put vinegar on their food.
초고추장은 고추장에 식초, 설탕, 마늘을 넣어서 만든 것이다.
Chogochujang is made by adding in vinegar, sugar, and garlic to red pepper paste.

54
식품

[식품] 명사 food products

[Expression] 가공식품 processed foods
발효식품 fermented foods
천연식품 natural foods
건강보조식품 health supplement
인스턴트식품 instant foods

[Example] 김치는 한국의 대표적인 발효식품이지요.
Kimchi is Korea's representative fermented food.
인스턴트식품은 몸에 안 좋으니까 자주 드시지는 마세요.
Don't eat too much instant food because it is bad for your body.

55
싸다

[싸다] 동사 1. to prepare food 2. to wrap 3. to pack

1. to prepare something so can it can be taken somewhere else

[Usage] N 을/를 싸다

[Expression] 김밥을 싸다 to make kimbab
도시락을 싸다 to prepare a lunch box

[Example] 소풍갈 때는 보통 김밥을 싸 가지고 가요.
People often prepare kimbab when they go on picnics.

2. to put an object into a paper or box so that it can no longer be seen

[Usage] N 을/를 N 에 싸다
N 을/를 N 으로/로 싸다

[Synonym] 포장하다 to wrap

[Example] 집에 가지고 갈 거니까 비닐봉지에 싸 주세요.
Please put it in a plastic bag because I am going to take it home.

3. to put into a box and prepare to be transported from one place to another

[Usage] N 을/를 싸다

[Expression] 책가방을 싸다 to pack a schoolbag
이삿짐을 싸다 to prepare to move

[Antonym] 풀다 to unpack

[Example] 주말에 이사를 가야 하니까 오늘부터 이삿짐을 싸야 해요.
I need to start packing my luggage today because I am moving this weekend.

56
썩다

[썩따] 동사 to rot, to go bad

the original state of an organic substance rots or decomposes

[Usage] N 이/가 썩다

[Expression] 이가 썩다 My teeth are rotting.
음식이 썩다 The food is rotting.

[Related Words] 상하다 to go bad

[Example] 흐르는 물은 썩지 않는다.
Moving water does not rot.

음식이 썩지 않도록 남은 음식은 꼭 냉장고에 보관하세요.
Please store the leftover food in the refrigerator so it doesn't rot.

57
쏟다

[쏟따] 동사 1. to spill 2. to devote oneself or concentrate on something

1. to spill the contents of a bowl out all at once.

[Usage] N 에 N 을/를 쏟다

[Expression] 커피를 쏟다 to spill coffee

[Related Words] 흘리다 to spill

[Example] 실수로 그만 친구 옷에 커피를 쏟고 말았어요.
I spilt coffee on my friend's clothes by accident.

2. to devote oneself or concentrate on something

[Usage] N 에 N 을/를 쏟다
N 에게 N 을/를 쏟다

[Expression] 신경을 쏟다 to focus on something
관심을 쏟다 to concentrate one's interest on something
정성을 쏟다 to try one's best

[Example] 음식을 만들 때는 모든 정성을 쏟도록 하세요.
Make sure to try your best when cooking.

58
씹다

[씹따] 동사 to chew

[Usage] N 을/를 씹다

[Expression] 껌을 씹다 to chew gum

[Related Words] 물다 to bite

[Example] 껌을 자주 씹으면 치아에 좋지 않은 영향을 줍니다.
When you chew a lot of gum, you are producing a lot of negative effects on your teeth.

이가 약해서 고기같이 질긴 음식은 잘 씹어 먹을 수 없어요.
I can't chew and eat rough meat very well because my teeth are weak.

59
안주

[안주] 명사 snacks served with alcoholic drinks

[Expression] 술안주 snacks served with alcohol
안주거리 kinds of anju
안주를 시키다 to order anju

[Example] 맥주가 남았으니까 안주를 더 시킵시다.
Let's order more food because we still have some beer left over.

밥과 같이 먹는 부식은 '반찬'이라고 하지만 같은 음식이라도 술과 같이 먹으면 '안주'라고 해요.
Even though some food eaten with rice is called banchan, the same food eaten with alcohol is called anju.

60
양념

[양념] 명사 marinade, condiments
the ingredients put into food to give it a certain flavor or taste

[Expression] 양념장 marinade
양념하다 to add marinade

[Example] 갈비 양념에 어떤 재료가 들어가나요?
What kind of ingredients go into making kalbi marinade?

나라마다 음식에 사용하는 양념이 달라요.
The condiments used in making food are different in every country.

61
억지로

[억찌로] 부사 against one's will or desire

[Example] 맛이 없으면 억지로 드시지 마세요.
Don't force yourself to eat it if it doesn't taste good.

술을 마시고 싶어하지 않는 사람에게 술을 억지로 권하는 것은 좋지 않다.
It is not good to force people to drink alcohol against their will.

62
연하다

[연하다] 형용사 1. to be soft 2. to be light

1. to be soft and durable in texture

[Usage] N 이/가 연하다

[Expression] 고기가 연하다 The meat is very soft.

[Synonym] 부드럽다 to be soft

[Example] 이 레스토랑의 고기는 연하고 부드럽네요.
This restaurant's meat is soft and tender.

2. a light color

[Usage] N 이/가 연하다

[Expression] 색이 연하다 The color is light.

[Synonym] 옅다 to be light

[Example] 연한 분홍색 원피스를 입고 데이트 장소에 나갔어요.
I went to on my date wearing a light pink one piece dress.

63
옥수수

[옥쑤수] 명사 corn

[Expression] 옥수수 알 corn kernel
옥수수를 찌다 to steam corn

[Example] 버터에 구운 옥수수가 너무 먹음직스러워 보였다.
The corn roasted in butter seemed very appetizing.

언니는 너무 배가 고팠는지 옥수수를 한 알도 남김없이 모두 먹어버렸다.
My older sister ate up every last corn kernel because she must have been very hungry.

64
인삼

[인삼] 명사 ginseng

[Expression] 인삼차 ginseng tea
인삼 한 뿌리 a ginseng root
인삼을 말리다 to dry ginseng

[Related Words] 산삼 wild ginseng
홍삼 red ginseng

[Example] 외국에서 한국의 인삼차가 유명하다고 하던데 정말인가요?
I heard that Korean ginseng tea is famous abroad. Is that really true?

삼계탕에는 인삼 이외에도 여러 가지 몸에 좋은 재료가 들어 있어서 건강에 좋다.
Samgyetang, chicken stew with ginseng, is good for your health because a number of ingredients that good for your body, including not just ginseng, are put into the soup.

65
재료

[재료] 명사 ingredients

[Expression] 음식 재료 food ingredients
재료를 준비하다 to prepare ingredients

[Example] 아침 일찍 시장에 가면 좋은 재료를 고를 수 있다.
You can choose good ingredients if you go to the market place early in the morning.

요리하기 전에 필요한 재료를 미리 준비해 두세요.
Please prepare the ingredients you will need before cooking.

66
전혀

[전혀] 부사 at all

often a word that negates a meaning and is used like '도무지', '아주', '완전히

[Related Words] 완전히 completely, at all
도무지 in the least bit

[Example] 우리 아이는 채소나 과일을 전혀 입에 안 대요.
My son barely eats any vegetables or fruits at all.

요즘은 너무 바빠서 집에서 요리할 시간이 전혀 없어요.
I've been so busy lately that I don't have any time to cook at home.

67
집다

[집따] 동사 to pick up

to grab and pick something up using your hands or any other instrument

[Usage] N 을/를 N 으로/로 집다

[Example] 손으로 집어 먹지 마!
Don't pick it up and eat it with your fingers.

튀김이 뜨거우니까 나무젓가락으로 집어 드세요.
Please eat the fried food with a wooden chopstick because it is very hot.

68
차갑다

[차갑따] 형용사 to be cold

to be cool and chilly to the touch

[Usage] N 이/가 차갑다

[Expression] 물이 차갑다 The water is cold.

[Synonym] 차다 to be cold

[Example] 감기가 낫기 전까지는 차가운 물은 가능하면 마시지 마세요.
Don't drink any cold water until you get over your cold.

여름에 차가운 아이스크림을 너무 많이 먹으면 쉽게 배탈이 납니다.
It is easy to get a stomachache in the summer if you eat too much cold ice cream.

69
차리다

[차리다] 동사 to prepare, to lay out

[Usage] N 을/를 차리다

[Expression] 상을 차리다 to set the dinner table
음식을 차리다 to prepare and lay out food on the table

[Example] 별로 차린 건 없지만 많이 드세요.
I'm sorry it's not much but help yourself.

저녁에 집에 도착했을 때 어머니는 나를 위해 벌써 저녁상을 차려 놓으셨어요.
My mom already had left the dinner table prepared for me when I got home at night.

70
충분하다

[충분하다] 형용사 to be enough

[Usage] N 에/에게 충분하다
AV 기에 충분하다
N 으로/로 충분하다

[Synonym] 넉넉하다 to be sufficient

[Antonym] 부족하다 to be lacking
모자라다 to not have enough

[Example] 충분한 휴식이 건강한 몸을 만든다.
Sufficient rest makes a healthy body.

오늘 손님이 10분 정도 오시는데 음식을 이 정도 준비하면 충분하겠지요?
Today about ten guests are coming. It should be enough if I prepare this much food, right?

71
콩나물

[콩나물] 명사 bean sprout

[Expression] 콩나물국 bean sprout soup
콩나물을 기르다 to grow bean sprouts
콩나물을 무치다 to prepare bean sprouts

[Example] 숙취 해소에는 콩나물국이 정말 좋아요.
Bean sprouts are very good in reducing hangovers.

키가 크고 마른 사람을 콩나물 같다고 표현하기도 해요.
It is often say that tall, skinny people look like bean sprouts.

72
탄산음료

[탄사늠뇨] 명사 carbonated drink

[Related Words] 콜라 coca cola
사이다 cider

[Example] 자판기에는 다양한 탄산음료들이 진열되어 있었다.
Various carbonated drinks were displayed in the vending machine.

탄산음료를 많이 마시면 이가 상할 수 있으니까 적당히 마시도록 해라.
Just drink reasonable amounts of carbonated drinks because too much can rot your teeth.

73
특별히

[특뼐히] 부사 especially

[Related Words] 특별하게 especially

[Example] 특별히 어디가 아픈 건 아니지만 기운이 없어요.
Nothing really hurts in particular. It's just that I don't have energy.

여러분은 건강을 위해 특별히 먹는 건강식이 있어요?
What kind of health products do you especially eat to improve your health?

74
팥

[팓] 명사 red bean

[Expression] 팥죽 red bean porridge
팥빙수 shaved ice with red beans

[Example] 여름에는 팥빙수가 최고예요.
Shaved ice with red beans is best in the summer.

아기 백일에 팥떡을 해서 이웃들에게 돌렸어요.
I gave the neighbors red bean rice cake on our child's 100th day celebration.

75
포도주

[포도주] 명사 wine

[Expression] 포도주를 따다 to open a bottle of wine

포도주를 마시다 to drink wine

[Synonym] 와인 wine

[Example] 포도주는 서늘한 곳에 보관하세요.
Please store the wine in a cool environment.

맥주라든가 포도주처럼 독하지 않은 술로 마시겠어요.
I would rather drink a weaker alcoholic beverage like wine or beer.

76
화학조미료

[화학조미료] 명사 MSG- artificial flavor enhancer

[Expression] 화학조미료를 넣다 to put in MSG

[Synonym] 인공조미료 artificial flavor enhancer
인공감미료 artificial sweetener

[Example] 가능하면 화학조미료보다는 천연조미료를 직접 만들어 드세요.
If possible, it is better to make your own natural spices than using artificially flavored ones.

음식을 할 때 화학조미료를 너무 많이 쓰는 것은 건강에 좋지 않습니다.
It is bad for your health to use a lot of artificial flavoring when cooking.

77
후추

[후추] 명사 pepper

[Expression] 통후추 black peppercorn
후춧가루를 치다 to put in powdered pepper

[Example] 후춧가루가 코에 들어가서 재채기를 했어요.
I sneezed after I got pepper into my nose.

불고기에 후추를 넣으면 고기 특유의 누린내가 없어져요.
The burnt smell of meat unique to beef disappears if you put marinated pepper onto it.

78
흘리다

[흘리다] 동사 to spill

[Usage] N 에 N 을/를 흘리다

[Synonym] 쏟다 to spill

[Example] 밥을 먹을 때 음식을 흘리지 않도록 조심해.
Try not to spill food while eating.

콜라를 마실 때 옆 사람이 치는 바람에 치마에 모두 흘렸어요.
I spilled the soda I was drinking all over myself after the person next to me ran into me.

04 연습문제

[1-23] **다음 음식을 나타내는 단어를 한국어로 바꿔 쓰십시오.**

Change the following food vocabulary words to Korean.

1.	honey	(　　　)	2.	radish	(　　　)
3.	red bean	(　　　)	4.	gum	(　　　)
5.	lemon	(　　　)	6.	cabbage	(　　　)
7.	mushroom	(　　　)	8.	ginger	(　　　)
9.	butter	(　　　)	10.	eggs	(　　　)
11.	peanut	(　　　)	12.	gingseng	(　　　)
13.	bread	(　　　)	14.	eggplant	(　　　)
15.	pepper	(　　　)	16.	vinegar	(　　　)
17.	sausage	(　　　)	18.	bean sprout	(　　　)
19.	corn	(　　　)	20.	sweet potato	(　　　)
21.	mung bean pancake	(　　　)	22.	cooking oil	(　　　)
23.	wine	(　　　)			

[24-31] **다음 (　　)에 가장 알맞은 것을 고르십시오.**

Choose the word that best fits into the parenthesis.

24. 많은 식당들이 맛을 내기 위해서 몸에 해로운 (　　　　)을/를 사용하고 있다고 한다.

❶ 설탕　　❷ 마늘　　❸ 참기름　　❹ 화학조미료

25. 맥주를 마실 때 (　　　　)으로/로 마른 오징어나 땅콩을 자주 먹어요.

❶ 양주　　❷ 반찬　　❸ 안주　　❹ 주류

26. 불고기는 잘게 썬 쇠고기에 간장, 설탕, 파, 마늘, 후춧가루 등 여러 가지 (   )을/를 넣어서 만든 요리이다.

❶ 양념 ❷ 양파 ❸ 생강 ❹ 고춧가루

27. 콜라라든가 사이다 같은 (   )은/는 심장이 약한 사람은 자주 마시지 않는 것이 좋습니다.

❶ 우유 ❷ 탄산음료 ❸ 아이스크림 ❹ 오렌지 주스

28. 비빔밥이란 여러 가지 (   )과/와 계란, 고기 등의 음식을 넣어 고추장에 비벼먹는 음식으로 한국 전통 음식 중 하나이다.

❶ 육류 ❷ 곡류 ❸ 나물 ❹ 소스

29. 된장과 요구르트 같은 발효 (   )은/는 건강에 좋다고 알려져 있다.

❶ 재료 ❷ 음료 ❸ 식품 ❹ 유제품

30. 한국에서는 감기가 심하거나 기침이 날 때 뜨거운 (   )을/를 마셔요.

❶ 맥주 ❷ 콜라 ❸ 커피 ❹ 생강차

31. 대형마트에는 쌀, 찹쌀, 옥수수, 보리, 밀 등과 같은 (   )을/를 파는 코너가 따로 있다.

❶ 식품 ❷ 곡류 ❸ 식료품 ❹ 밀가루

[32-45] [보기]에서 알맞은 단어를 골라 (   ) 안에 쓰십시오.
Choose the appropriate word from the box below and fill in the parenthesis.

[보기]

재료	껍질	송편	전혀	특별히	도시락	씹다
식다	집다	차리다	흘리다	김장하다	미지근하다	번거롭다

32. 내일 (   )으려고/려고 배추를 샀는데 지난주에 비해 값이 많이 올랐던데요.

33. 추석날 아침에 음식을 (   )어/아/여 놓고 조상님께 감사하는 마음으로 차례를 지냈다.

34. 삶은 달걀의 (   )을/를 잘 벗기려면 계란을 삶은 즉시 찬물에 담그면 된다.

35. 저는 집에서는 (　　　　　) 요리를 하지 않고 항상 식당에서 사 먹어요.

36. 목이 아플 때 뜨거운 물보다는 (　　　　　)는/은/ㄴ 소금물로 양치를 하면 좋아요.

37. 아이가 여기저기 지저분하게 밥을 (　　　　　)고 먹어도 너무 혼내지 마세요.

38. 이 뜨거운 커피가 차갑게 (　　　　　)기 전에 회의가 끝나면 좋겠다.

39. 일본에서는 자기 젓가락으로 음식을 (　　　　　)어서/아서/여서 다른 사람에게 주는 것은 실례예요.

40. 음식을 많이 (　　　　　)어서/아서/여서 먹으면 소화가 잘 되기 때문에 건강에 좋다.

41. 삼계탕을 만들 때는 닭, 인삼, 찹쌀, 마늘, 파, 소금, 후추 등 여러 가지 (　　　　　)들이 필요합니다.

42. (　　　　　)을/를 싸 가지고 근처 공원으로 소풍을 갑시다.

43. 저는 (　　　　　) 싫어하는 음식은 없어요. 음식을 가리지 않고 다 좋아하는 편이에요.

44. (　　　　　)은/는 추석에 가족들이 모여서 만들어 먹는 한국의 전통 음식이에요.

45. 김치를 담그는 일이 이렇게 힘들고 (　　　　　)는/은/ㄴ 일인 줄 몰랐어요.

[46-54] 다음 (　　　)에 공통적으로 들어갈 단어의 기본형을 쓰십시오.

Write the basic form of a word that can be used in the parenthesis.

46.
❶ 영수 씨는 표정도 밝고 항상 자신감이 (　　　　　)어서/아서/여서 보기 좋아요.
❷ 잠깐 텔레비전을 보는 사이에 된장찌개가 끓어서 (　　　　　)었어요/았어요/였어요.

(　　　　　　　)

47.
❶ 사과 한 박스를 샀는데 거의 다 (　　　　　)어서/아서/여서 먹지 못하고 버렸어요.
❷ 사탕과 초콜릿을 많이 먹으면 이가 쉽게 (　　　　　)어요/아요/여요.

(　　　　　　　)

48. ❶ 아직 할 일이 (　　　　　　)어서/아서/여서 집에 못 가요.
❷ 쓰고 (　　　　　　)는/은/ㄴ 돈은 은행에 저축했다.
❸ 음식이 너무 많이 (　　　　　　)어서/아서/여서 친구들한테 싸 주었어요.

(　　　　　　　　)

49. ❶ 사과를 예쁘게 (　　　　　　)어서/아서/여서 접시에 담았어요.
❷ 현금으로 지불하시면 10% (　　　　　　)어/아/여 드립니다.
❸ 손톱이 길어서 (　　　　　　)어야/아야/여야 하는데 손톱깎이가 어디에 있는지 못 찾겠어요.

(　　　　　　　　)

50. ❶ 어머니께서는 간장과 된장을 사 드시지 않으시고 항상 직접 (　　　　　　)어서/아서/여서 드십니다.
❷ 시냇물에 발을 (　　　　　　)으니까/니까 정말 시원하네요.
❷ 빨래가 너무 더러우면 물에 푹 (　　　　　　)어/아/여 놓으세요.

(　　　　　　　　)

51. ❶ 이 아이스크림은 입에서 살살 녹을 정도로 정말 (　　　　　　)네요.
❷ 미선 씨의 피부는 마치 아기 피부처럼 (　　　　　　)어요/아요/여요.
❸ 아이에게 큰소리로 말하지 말고 (　　　　　　)게 이야기해 보세요.

(　　　　　　　　)

52. ❶ 아까까지는 날씨가 화창했는데 갑자기 비가 (　　　　　　)어진다/아진다/여진다.
❷ 급하게 우유를 마시다가 새로 산 티셔츠에 그만 (　　　　　　)고 말았다.
❸ 아이들에게 부모님이 더 많은 관심과 애정을 (　　　　　　)는/은/ㄴ 것이 좋다.

(　　　　　　　　)

53. ❶ 백화점보다는 남대문 시장의 물건 값이 더 (　　　　　)어요/아요/여요.
❷ 내일 이사 간다면서 이삿짐은 다 (　　　　　)었어요/았어요/였어요?
❸ 점심은 사 먹지 말고 도시락을 (　　　　　)어/아/여 가지고 가서 먹읍시다.

(　　　　　　　　)

54. ❶ 우유를 냉장고에 넣어두지 않아서 상했을 수도 있으니까 뚜껑을 열고 냄새를 (　　　　　)어/아/여 보세요.
❷ 배우 이미영 씨는 이번 공연에서 주인공 역을 (　　　　　)었다/았다/였다.
❸ 김 과장님은 아무리 어려운 일을 (　　　　　)어도/아도/여도 모두 해결하세요.

(　　　　　　　　)

[55-66] [보기]에서 알맞은 단어를 골라 (　　　) 안에 쓰십시오.

Choose the appropriate word from the box below and then fill in the parenthesis.

[보기]

솜씨	밥맛	국물	밀가루	포도주	억지로
담다	갈다	섞다	뒤집다	벗기다	데치다

55. 사과 만 원 어치만 이 비닐봉지에 (　　　　　)어/아/여 주세요.

56. 어머니께서는 아침마다 사과와 당근을 함께 (　　　　　)어서/아서/여서 주스를 만들어 주십니다.

57. 여러 가지 채소에 소스를 뿌리고 잘 (　　　　　)으면/면 샐러드가 완성됩니다.

58. 잡채가 너무 맛있어요. 음식 (　　　　　)이/가 정말 좋으시네요.

59. 점심시간 전에 배가 고파서 빵이랑 과자를 좀 먹었더니 (　　　　　)이/가 없네요.

60. 김치부침개의 한 쪽 면이 잘 익으면 (　　　　　)어/아/여 주세요.

61. 감자는 깨끗이 씻은 후 껍질을 (　　　　　)어/아/여 놓으세요.

62. 시금치를 끓는 물에 1~2분간 살짝 (　　　　　)으세요/세요.

63. 배탈이 났을 때는 빵이나 라면 같은 (   ) 음식을 먹지 않는 것이 좋아요.

64. 쌀쌀한 겨울에는 우동이나 칼국수같이 따뜻한 (   )이/가 있는 음식이 먹고 싶어요.

65. 아이가 감기에 걸렸는데 약을 안 먹겠다고 해서 (   ) 약을 먹였어요.

66. 과음을 하는 것은 좋지 않지만 (   ) 한 잔 정도는 심장병 예방에 좋다고 합니다.

[67-70] 다음 밑줄 친 부분과 바꿔서 쓸 수 있는 것을 고르십시오.

Choose the word that can be used in place of the underlined word.

67. 집 근처에 <u>고기, 생선, 채소, 과일</u> 등을 파는 가게가 있어서 편해요.

❶ 제품　❷ 식료품　❸ 가공품　❹ 유제품

68. 혼자서 손님을 초대할 때는 만들기가 <u>복잡하고 어려운</u> 음식보다는 간단한 것을 준비하는 것이 좋아요.

❶ 지루하다　❷ 어지럽다　❸ 불편하다　❹ 번거롭다

69. 술잔에 맥주를 너무 많이 따라서 컵 밖으로 조금 <u>흘렀어요</u>.

❶ 차갑다　❷ 마시다　❸ 넘치다　❹ 닦다

70. 이 사과는 <u>무농약</u> 과일이니까 껍질까지 드셔도 괜찮아요.

❶ 유기농　❷ 통조림　❸ 냉동　❹ 식물성

[71-73] 다음 밑줄 친 부분과 반대되는 뜻을 가진 것을 고르십시오.

Choose the word that has the opposite meaning from the underlined word.

71. <u>차가운</u> 음료수가 있으면 한 잔만 주세요.

❶ 뜨겁다　❷ 미지근하다　❸ 식다　❹ 끓이다

72. 한우는 가격이 조금 비싸긴 하지만 아주 연하고 맛있어요.

❶ 진하다 ❷ 질기다 ❸ 고소하다 ❹ 부드럽다

73. 여름에는 음식을 냉장고에 넣지 않으면 음식이 상할 수 있으니까 꼭 냉장고에 넣어서 보관하세요.

❶ 썩다 ❷ 변하다 ❸ 신선하다 ❹ 부패하다

[74-78] 다음 [보기]에서 알맞은 단어를 골라 이야기를 완성하십시오.

Choose the appropriate word from the box to complete the story.

[보기]

떫다	비리다	고소하다	느끼하다	달콤하다

어제는 친구의 생일이어서 친구 생일 파티에 갔다. 친구는 정말 여러 가지 음식들을 준비했다. 그 중에 닭고기와 생선 조림이 있었는데 닭은 오븐에 구워서 그런지 기름기가 많지 않아서 담백하고 74.(　　　　　　)지 않았다. 또 생선 조림에는 생강과 마늘을 넣어서 생선의 75.(　　　　　　)은/ㄴ 맛이 전혀 나지 않았다. 친구는 정말 요리 솜씨가 좋은 것 같았다.

후식으로는 녹차와 호두 우유, 케이크가 준비되어 있었다. 나는 녹차를 마셨는데 녹차의 약간 76.(　　　　　　)은/ㄴ 맛이 입을 깔끔하게 해 주는 것 같았다. 녹차와 함께 케이크도 먹었는데 정말 부드럽고 77.(　　　　　　)어서/아서/여서 녹차와 잘 어울렸다.

호두 우유를 먹은 친구는 호두 맛이 아주 78.(　　　　　　)다고 했다. 오늘은 너무 과식을 한 것 같다. 내일은 시간을 내서 운동을 좀 해야겠다.

가정

05

Home

05 가정

01
가구

[가구] 명사 household, family

an expression related to the number of people that live with you

[Expression] 가구 수 number of family members

가구 소득 an increase in the number of family members

[Related Words] 다가구 many families living together

[Example] 내가 사는 빌라에는 여섯 가구가 살고 있다.

There are six families in the villa that I live in.

요즘 조부모를 모시고 사는 가구가 점점 줄고 있다고 한다.

They say that the number of families that take care and live with their grandparents is increasing.

02
가스

[가스] [가쓰] [까스] 명사 gas

[Expression] 가스밸브 gas valve

가스요금 gas bill

가스레인지 gas stove

가스가 새다 The gas leaks.

가스를 끄다 to turn off the gas

[Example] 가스 폭발로 인근 주민 10명이 중상을 입었다.

Ten citizens living nearby suffered serious damage due to the gas explosion.

외출하기 전에 반드시 가스를 잠갔는지 꼭 확인하시기 바랍니다.

It is urged that you check whether you have turned off the gas before leaving the house.

도움말

독가스 poisonous gas　　도시가스 city gas　　배기가스 exhaust gas

03
갈다²

[갈다] 동사 to replace, to change

to change an object that already exists with a new one

[Usage] N 을/를 갈다

N 으로/로 갈다

[Expression] 굽을 갈다 to change the heel of a shoe

전구를 갈다 to change a light bulb

[Example] 구두 굽이 너무 닳아서 새것으로 갈아야겠어요.

I need to change the heel of my shoe because it is worn out.

전구가 깜빡이는 걸 보니까 갈아야 할 때가 된 것 같아요.

I think it's time to change the light bulb because it is flickering.

04
공과금

[공꽈금] 명사 utility bills

a monetary responsibility of services provided by the state to the citizens

[Expression] 공과금 고지서 utilities bill
공과금 청구서 utilities bill
공과금을 내다 to pay the utilities

[Related Words] 세금 tax
관리비 maintenance fees

[Example] 이번 달 공과금 고지서를 아직 못 받았어요.
I still haven't gotten the utility bills for this month.
요즘은 인터넷 뱅킹으로 공과금을 내는 사람이 많아요.
Nowadays there are a lot of people that pay their bills using internet banking.

05
깨다

[깨다] 동사 1. to break 2. to wake up

1. to cause that a part of an object breaks off

[Usage] N 을/를 깨다

[Expression] 컵을 깨다 to break a cup
유리를 깨다 to break a glass

[Related Words] 부수다 to smash, to destroy
깨뜨리다 to break apart

[Example] 남편은 설거지를 할 때 가끔 그릇을 깨요.
My husband sometimes breaks a dish when washing the dishes.

2. to awake someone or bring them out of a certain state (sleep, alcoholic)

[Usage] N 이/가 깨다
N 에서 깨다

[Expression] 술이 깨다 to get out of a state of being drunk, to sober up
잠이 깨다 to wake up

[Example] 시끄러운 소리에 잠이 깼어요. I woke up from the loud noise.

06
꾸미다

[꾸미다] 동사 to decorate

[Usage] N 을/를 꾸미다

[Expression] 집을 꾸미다 to decorate one's house

[Related Words] 가꾸다 to adorn

[Example] 봄이 되었으니까 집을 좀 화려하게 꾸미고 싶어요.
I want to decorate my house more fancily now that spring is here.
오늘 데이트가 있어서 평소 때보다 좀 더 화려하게 꾸몄어요.
I spruced myself up today because I have a date.

07
남매

[남매] 명사 male-female siblings

[Synonym] 오누이 brother and sister

[Related Words] 자매 Sisters
형제 siblings

[Example] 그 남매는 사이가 참 좋아.
The brother and sister got along very well together.
우리 집은 아들 하나, 딸 둘로 모두 삼 남매입니다.
There are three siblings in total in our house, one boy and two girls.

08
달다

[달다] 동사 to attach, to hoist
to stick something on somewhere

[Usage] N 을/를 달다
N 에 달다

[Expression] 국기를 달다 to hoist a flag
단추를 달다 to attach a button
이름표를 달다 to put on a name tag

[Related Words] 걸다 to hang up

[Example] 학교에 등교할 때는 모두 가슴에 이름표를 달아야 해요.
When going to school, we all have to put on nametags on our chest.
어머니께서 제 옷의 단추가 떨어진 것을 보고는 다시 달아주셨어요.
When my mom saw that a button fell of my shirt, she attached it for me again.

09
닮다

[담따] 동사 to look like, to resemble
to be similar to someone or something else's appearance

[Usage] N 과/와 닮다

[Related Words] 비슷하다 to be similar to

[Example] 아드님이 아버님을 많이 닮았네요.
The son looks a lot like his father.
저는 어머니와 얼굴이 많이 닮았어요.
My mom and I have very similar faces.

10
담요

[담뇨] 명사 blanket

[Expression] 담요 한 장 a blanket
담요를 깔다 to lay down a blanket
담요를 덮다 to cover oneself with a blanket

[Example] 추우시면 담요를 드릴까요?
If you are cold, I can give you a blanket.

이번 겨울은 많이 추워서 예년에 비해 담요의 판매량이 증가했다고 한다.
They say that the sales rate of blankets went up this year compared to other years because this winter was much colder.

11
당신

[당신] 명사 1. you 2. you 3. you

1. a honorific 2nd person you that is used between couples

[Related Words] 자기 sweetie
여보 honey

[Example] 저녁에 당신이 좋아하는 김치찌개 해 놓을 테니까 일찍 들어오세요.
Come home early because I am going to make the kimchi stew that you really like.

2. 2nd person you often used in advertisements or hypothetical situations

[Example] 길을 가다가 5만원이 바닥에 떨어져 있다면 당신은 어떻게 하겠습니까?
What would you do if you found 50,000 won on the floor while walking?

3. a word used to mean you between two people that are fighting or arguing.

[Example] 당신이 왜 이곳에 온 거야?
Why did you come here?

12
대문

[대문] 명사 gate

the main gate of one's house

[Expression] 대문 밖 outside of the main gate
대문을 나서다 to come out of the main gate

[Example] 대문이 열려 있는 틈을 타서 개가 도망쳤어요.
The dog escaped through the slight opening in the main gate.

어머니께서 대문 밖까지 나와서 출근하시는 아버지를 배웅했다.
The mother saw the father out of the house to the main door while he was on his way to work.

13
도구

[도구] 명사 1. tool, kit, instrument 2. means, tool

1. an object used when working for a specific function

[Expression] 세면도구 toiletries
청소 도구 cleaning tools
촬영 도구 film instruments
도구를 쓰다 to use a tool
도구를 이용하다 to use a tool

[Example] 오실 때는 세면도구와 개인이 쓸 용돈 정도만 준비하시면 됩니다.
When coming, all you need to prepare are your toiletries and the money you will be using here.

2. a means or manner to help achieve a goal

[Expression] 도구로 이용하다 to use something as a tool

[Synonym] 수단 means

[Example] 자신의 성공을 위해 다른 사람을 도구로 이용하지 마세요.
Don't use other people as a means to achieve your own success.

14
동네

[동네] 명사 neighborhood

[Expression] 동네가 깨끗하다 The neighborhood is clean.
동네가 시끄럽다 The neighborhood is loud.

[Synonym] 마을 village

[Example] 우리 동네는 비교적 깨끗한 편이에요.
Our neighborhood is relatively clean.

두 사람이 싸우는 소리로 동네가 시끄러웠다.
The neighborhood got loud because of the sound of the two people's fighting.

15
들다

[들다] 동사 1. to cost, to need, to require 2. to join, to enter

1. to become necessary, to be used (related to money, energy, effort)

[Usage] N 에 N 이/가 들다
N 는 데에 N 이/가 들다

[Synonym] 소요되다 to be required

[Related Words] 필요하다 to need

[Example] 물가가 올라서 그런지 요즘 생활비가 많이 드는 것 같아요.
It seems that daily life is getting really expensive lately because the commodity prices have gone up.

2. to join a club, group, or event

[Usage] N 을/를 들다
N 에 들다

[Synonym] 가입하다 to become a member

[Example] 이번에 남편과 같이 배드민턴 동호회에 들었다.
I became a member of the badminton club with my husband.

16
라이터

[라이터] 명사 lighter

[Expression] 라이터를 끄다 to turn off a lighter
라이터를 켜다 to turn on a lighter
라이터에 가스를 충전하다 to refill the gas in a lighter

[Related Words] 성냥 matches

[Example] 옆 사람에게 라이터를 빌려서 담배에 불을 붙였다.
I lit my cigarette using the lighter I borrowed from the person next to me.

이 라이터는 뚜껑을 닫으면 자동으로 불이 꺼집니다.
If you close the top of this lighter, the light turns off by itself.

17
렌즈

[렌즈] 명사 contact lens

[Expression] 렌즈를 끼다 to put on contact lenses
렌즈를 빼다 to take off contact lenses
렌즈를 맞추다 to get fitted for contact lenses
렌즈를 착용하다 to wear contact lenses

[Related Words] 안경 glasses
식염수 saline solution
세척제 cleaning solution

[Example] 저는 눈이 나빠서 렌즈를 껴요.
I wear contacts because my eyes are bad.

반드시 손을 깨끗하게 씻은 후에 렌즈를 빼세요.
Take off your contacts only after washing your hands.

18
막내

[망내] 명사 youngest sibling

[Expression] 막내딸 youngest daughter
막내아들 youngest son
막내 동생 youngest sibling

[Antonym] 맏이 eldest child

[Example] 지난달에 막내딸이 결혼을 했어요.
Last month, my youngest daughter got married.

저는 막내라서 식구들의 귀여움을 많이 받으면서 자랐어요.
I grew up as the baby of the family since I am the youngest sibling.

19
먼지

[먼지] 명사 dust

[Expression] 먼지가 나다 to be dusty
먼지가 묻다 to become dusty
먼지가 쌓이다 The dust piles up.
먼지가 가득하다 to be full of dust
먼지를 닦다 to wipe off dust

[Related Words] 티끌 dirt, dust

[Example] 오랫동안 집을 비워 두었는지 가구 위에 먼지가 가득 쌓여 있네요.
There's a lot of dirt built up on furniture because the house has been vacant for a long time.

뚜껑을 열어 두면 먼지가 들어갈 수 있으니까 꼭 뚜껑을 덮어 놓으세요.
Make sure to put on the cap so that dust doesn't go in.

20
며느리

[며느리] 명사 daughter-in-law

[Expression] 맏며느리 wife of the eldest son
며느리를 보다 to get a wife for one's son

[Related Words] 사위 son-in-law

[Example] 며느리와 시어머니 사이를 '고부간'이라고 한다.
They say that the relationship between a mother-in-law and a daughter-in-law is called "go bu gan" in Korea.

우리 맏며느리는 안부 전화를 자주 하는 편이에요.
My eldest daughter-in-law calls from time to time to see how we are.

21
모시다

[모시다] 동사 to take one's parents in and take care of them, to take someone older to a certain location

[Usage] N 을/를 모시다
N 을/를 모셔다 드리다
N 에 모시고 가다

[Example] 한국에서는 보통 장남이 부모님을 모십니다.
In Korea, it is usually the first-born son that takes care of the parents.

제가 선생님을 터미널까지 모셔다 드리겠습니다.
I will take the teacher to the terminal.

22
모자라다

[모자라다] 동사 to not be enough

[Usage] N 이/가 모자라다

[Synonym] 부족하다 to be insufficient

[Antonym] 충분하다 to be sufficient
넉넉하다 to be enough

[Related Words] 남다 to be leftover, to remain

[Example] 한국말을 통역하기에는 아직 실력이 모자란 것 같아요.
I don't think I know enough Korean to be an interpreter yet.

집을 살 때 모자라는 돈은 시어머니께서 좀 도와주시기로 했어요.
My mother-in-law is going to give me the money I don't have when I buy my house.

23
목욕탕

[모굑탕] 명사 bathhouse

[Expression] 대중목욕탕 public bathhouse
목욕탕 때밀이 a professional scrubber that works at bathhouses
목욕탕을 다녀오다 to go to the bathhouse

[Synonym] 욕실 bathroom
욕탕 bathhouse

[Related Words] 목욕물 bath water

[Example] 저는 가끔 대중목욕탕에 가서 목욕해요.
I go to the public baths sometimes to take a bath.

우리 집 목욕탕을 신식으로 고치고 싶어요.
I want to remodel the bathtub in our house.

24
바구니

[바구니] 명사 basket

[Expression] 꽃바구니 flower basket
장바구니 shopping basket
과일바구니 fruit basket
바구니에 담다 to fill a basket

[Example] 쇼핑할 때 장바구니를 가져가면 50원을 할인해 줘요.
They give you a 50 won discount if you bring your own shopping bag when going shopping.

빨래할 옷은 세탁기 옆에 있는 바구니에 넣어 놓으세요.
Please leave the clothes that are going to be washed in the basket next to the washing machine.

25
바늘

[바늘] 명사 needle

[Expression] 바늘구멍 the eye of a needle
바늘에 찔리다 to be pricked by a needle
바늘에 실을 꿰다 to thread a needle

[Related Words] 실 thread
바느질 needlework, sewing

[Example] 바느질을 하다가 실수로 바늘로 손끝을 찔렀어요.
I pricked my finger with a needle by mistake while sewing.

큰 이불을 꿰매려면 더 굵은 바늘이 필요할 것 같아요.
I think you are going to need a thicker needle if you want to sew a bigger blanket.

26
바닥

[바닥] 명사 floor

[Expression] 바닥이 미끄럽다 The floor is slippery.
바닥에 떨어뜨리다 to drop on the floor

[Related Words] 천장 ceiling

[Example] 바닥이 미끄러우니까 조심하세요.
Please be careful because the floor is slippery.

유리컵이 바닥에 떨어져서 깨졌어요.
The glass cup fell to the floor and then broke.

도움말

땅바닥 ground floor
방바닥 floor of a room
손바닥 palm
온돌바닥 heated floor
마룻바닥 wooden floor

27
밥솥

[밥쏟] 명사 rice cooker

[Expression] 전기밥솥 electric rice cooker
압력 밥솥 pressure cooker

[Related Words] 밥통 rice bowl

[Example] 전기밥솥에 밥을 하니까 정말 편해요.
It's really convenient to make rice using the electric rice cooker.

압력 밥솥에 밥을 하면 더 맛있는 것 같아요.
I think the rice tastes better if you cook it using the pressure cooker.

28
배우자

[배우자] 명사 spouse

[Expression] 배우자를 만나다 to meet a spouse
배우자를 선택하다 to choose a spouse

[Related Words] 부부 couple

[Example] 좋은 배우자를 만나는 것은 쉬운 일이 아닌 것 같아요.
I don't think it's easy to meet a good spouse.

결혼은 일생일대의 아주 중요한 일이니까 배우자 선택에 신중해야 합니다.
You must really take time to think when choosing a spouse because marriage is a once in a lifetime important event.

29
배터리

[배터리] 명사 battery

[Expression] 배터리를 갈다 to change a battery
배터리를 끼우다 to put in a battery

[Synonym] 건전지 battery

[Example] 여기에 빨간 불이 들어오면 배터리를 충전하셔야 합니다.
You need to recharge the battery when the red light goes on.

카메라가 안 켜질 때는 배터리를 뺐다가 다시 잘 끼워 보십시오.
When the camera doesn't turn on, try taking out the battery and putting it back in again.

30
베개

[베개] 명사 pillow

[Expression] 팔베개 to sleep with one's head in one's arms
베개를 베다 to lay down on a pillow

[Related Words] 요 Korean style mattress used as a bed on the floor
이불 blanket

[Example] 베개가 너무 높아서 목이 아파요.
My neck hurts because the pillow is too high.

어머니께서 팔베개를 해 주셨어요.
My mom let me rest my head on her arms.

31
벨트

[벨트] 명사 belt

[Expression]
안전벨트 seat belt
벨트를 매다 to fasten your seat belt
벨트를 하다 to wear a belt

[Related Words]
허리띠 belt

[Example]
바지가 흘러내려서 허리에 벨트를 맸어요.
I put on a belt because my pants kept falling down.

백화점 잡화 코너 진열대에는 벨트와 모자, 목도리, 넥타이 등이 예쁘게 진열되어 있다.
In the window of the miscellaneous corner at the department store, there were belts, hats, scarves, ties, and other things prettily set out on display.

32
보증금

[보증금] 명사 monetary deposit

[Expression]
보증금을 내다 to pay a deposit
보증금을 받다 to receive a deposit

[Related Words]
월세 monthly payment
전세 one time payment for a set period of time
보증 deposit
보증인 depositor

[Example]
지금 살고 있는 집은 보증금 5,000만 원에 월세 50만 원이에요.
The house I am living in now has a one time deposit of 50,000,000 won and a monthly payment of 500,000 won.

집 주인이 이번 달부터 보증금을 300만 원 올려 달라고 해서 걱정이에요.
I am worried because the owner of the house asked to raise my deposit to 3,000,000 starting next month.

33
비닐봉지

[비닐봉지] 명사 plastic bag

[Expression]
비닐봉지 한 장 one plastic bag

[Example]
가게 주인은 내가 산 물건을 비닐봉지에 담아 줬다.
The store owner put the things I bought into a plastic bag.

얼마 전까지는 물건을 사면 비닐봉지를 공짜로 줬지만 지금은 돈을 주고 사야 합니다.
Until not too long ago they used to give you free plastic bags for the things you bought, but now you have to give money to use them.

34
빗

[빋] 명사 comb

[Expression] 빗으로 빗다 to comb one's hair with a comb

[Related Words] 머리끈 hairband

머리핀 hair pin

[Example] 어렸을 때는 혼자 빗으로 머리를 못 빗었어요.

When I was younger, I couldn't comb my hair with a comb by myself.

머리가 너무 지저분하니까 빗으로 좀 빗으세요.

Please comb your hair with a comb because it is very messy.

35
산더미

[산떠미] 명사 pile, stack

[Expression] 산더미같이 쌓이다 to be stacked up like a mountain

산더미처럼 쌓이다 to be piled up like a mountain

[Example] 빨래가 산더미처럼 쌓여 있어요.

My clothes are piled up.

해야 할 일이 산더미같이 쌓여서 오늘은 야근을 해야 할 것 같아요.

I am going to have to stay up all night because I have a lot of things to do.

도움말

돈더미 heap of money

잿더미 heap of ashes

눈 더미 pile of snow

빚더미 huge debt

흙더미 heap of mud

36
서랍

[서랍] 명사 drawer

[Expression] 서랍장 dresser

서랍 정리 to organize a drawer

서랍을 뒤지다 to go through a drawer

서랍을 잠그다 to lock a drawer

[Related Words] 장롱 dresser

화장대 vanity

[Example] 양말은 첫 번째 서랍 안에 있어요.

My socks are in the first drawer.

중요한 물건은 서랍 속에 잘 넣어 두었습니다.

I put all the important objects inside of the drawer.

37
석유

[서규] 명사 petroleum

natural oil from the earth

[Expression] 석유화학 petrochemistry
석유가 나다 to have oil
석유가 나오다 to have oil

[Related Words] 경유 diesel
등유 kerosene (oil used for lighting lamps)
석탄 coal
휘발유 gasoline

[Example] 석유 값이 올라서 차량 유지비도 많이 늘었어요.
The cost of maintaining a car has gone up because the price of oil has risen.

우리나라는 석유가 한 방울도 안 나오는 나라니까 아껴 써야 한다.
We need to use our oil sparingly because we don't have any natural oil sources in our country.

38
설치하다

[설치하다] 동사 to install

[Usage] N 을/를 설치하다
N 에 설치하다

[Expression] 에어컨을 설치하다 to install an air conditioner

[Synonym] 달다 to hang up

[Example] 보통 정수기를 사면 무료로 설치해 줍니다.
Normally, when you buy a water purifier, they install it for free.

새로 이사하는 집에 에어컨을 설치하려면 설치비를 내야 합니다.
You need to pay installation fees when putting an air conditioner into the new house you are moving into.

39
세입자

[세입짜] 명사 tenant

[Expression] 세입자를 들이다 to let a tenant in

[Example] 세입자에게 월세를 빨리 내라고 여러 번 말했지만 아직도 주지 않았어요.
Even though I told the tenant to pay the month's rent a number of times, he hasn't given it to me yet.

어느 날 갑자기 건물 주인이 건물에 있는 세입자들에게 모두 나가라고 말했다.
One day, the owner of the building suddenly told all the tenants to get out.

40
세탁하다

[세타카다] 동사 to do the wash

to wash dirty clothes

[Usage] N 을/를 세탁하다

[Synonym] 빨래하다 to do the laundry

[Example] 커피 얼룩은 아무리 세탁해도 잘 빠지지 않아요.
The coffee stain doesn't come out no matter how much I wash it.

저 분홍색 치마는 손세탁을 해야 하는 옷이니까 세탁기에 돌리지 마세요.
Don't put that pink skirt in the washing machine because it needs to be washed by hand.

41
손윗사람

[소뉘싸람] [소뉜싸람] 명사 one's elder member of an earlier generation

[Antonym] 손아랫사람 one's junior member of a later generation

[Example] 손아랫사람은 손윗사람에게 높임말을 써야 합니다.
Juniors must speak to their seniors in honorific form.

손윗사람을 봤을 때는 먼저 인사를 하는 것이 예의예요.
It is etiquette to first greet a senior when you see them.

42
손자

[손자] 명사 grandson

[Expression] 손자를 보다 to have grandson

[Related Words] 손녀 granddaughter
손주 grandchild

[Example] 아침 식사 후에 할아버지는 항상 손자를 데리고 산책을 가신다.
After eating breakfast, the grandfather always takes his grandson for a walk.

손자가 아무리 말썽을 부려도 할머니는 절대 화를 내지 않으세요.
No matter how much trouble the grandson causes, his grandmother never gets angry.

43
손잡이

[손자비] 명사 handle

[Expression] 손잡이가 망가지다 The handle is broken.
손잡이를 잡다 to grab the handle
손잡이를 돌리다 to turn the handle

[Example] 커피 잔의 손잡이가 깨져서 버렸어.
I threw away the coffee cup because the handle broke off.

손잡이를 오른쪽으로 돌리면 문이 열릴 거예요.
If you turn the handle to the right, the door will open.

44
수도

[수도] 명사 water works, water supply

system of pipes that brings water from one place to another

[Expression] 수도세 water fees
하수도 sewage system
수도를 틀다 to turn on the faucet
수도를 잠그다 to turn off the faucet

[Related Words] 수돗물 tap water
파이프 pipe

[Example] 수도를 틀어놓고 양치질을 하지 마세요.
Don't leave the water running while brushing your teeth.

이번 달에 물을 많이 써서 수도요금이 많이 나왔어요.
The water bill was very high this month because I used too much water.

45
수리

[수리] 명사 a repair

to fix something that is broken

[Expression] 수리 기사 repairman
수리비용 repair fees
수리하다 to repair
수리를 받다 to be repaired
수리를 맡기다 to assign a repair to someone

[Example] 자전거 수리비용으로 10만원이나 들었어요.
It cost me 100,000 won to repair my bicycle.

핸드폰이 고장이 나서 서비스 센터에 수리를 맡겼어요.
My phone broke so I left it at the service center to be repaired.

46
시부모

[시부모] 명사 parents of the husband

[Expression] 시부모를 모시다 to take care of one's parents in-laws

[Related Words] 시어른 elderly in-laws one the side of the husband

[Example] 이웃집 며느리는 시부모님 모시는 데에 모든 정성을 쏟았다.
The daughter-in-law that lives next door did her best in taking care of parents her in-laws.

요즘엔 시부모님을 안 모시고 사는 사람들이 점점 늘고 있다.
Nowadays, the number of people that are not living with their parents in-laws is increasing.

47
식구

[식꾸] 명사 family member

the number of members of a family that eat meals together

[Expression]

식구가 늘다 The number of members in my family has increased.
식구가 되다 to become part of someone's family
식구가 많다 to have a lot of mouths to feed
식구가 모이다 The family comes together.

[Related Words] 가족 family

[Example]

오랜만에 식구가 모두 모여서 식사를 하니 너무 좋구나.
It is great that the whole family is gathering after a long time to have a meal together.

오늘부터 식구가 한 명 더 늘었습니다. 서로 사이좋게 지내세요.
From now on, there will be another member in our family. Please get along well together.

48
신랑

[실랑] 명사 groom

[Expression] 신랑감 a suitable or likely bridegroom

[Related Words] 신부 bride

[Example]

지금부터 신랑 입장이 있겠습니다. 신랑 입장!
Now there will be the entrance of the groom. May the groom enter!

결혼식이 끝난 후에 신랑과 신부는 부모님들께 폐백을 드립니다.
After the marriage ceremony, the bride and groom pay respect to the parents in-laws.

49
신문지

[신문지] 명사 newspaper

Paper used when printing a newspaper

[Expression]

신문지를 깔다 to lay out a newspaper
신문지에 말다 to roll up in a newspaper
신문지로 덮다 o cover with a newspaper
신문지로 싸다 to wrap in a newspaper

[Example]

할머니는 집에 가는 길에 먹으라며 감자를 신문지에 싸 주셨다.
My grandmother told me to eat a potato on the way home so she wrapped one up for me in a newspaper.

한강 공원 잔디밭에 신문지를 깔고 앉아서 멋진 야경을 구경했다.
I layed down a newspaper on the grass in the Han River park and looked at the city at night.

50
신혼부부

[신혼부부] 명사 newlyweds

[Expression] 신혼부부 한 쌍 a pair of newlyweds

[Related Words] 신혼집 house of the newlyweds

신혼살림 household goods that newlyweds prepare

신혼여행 honeymoon

[Example] 두 사람은 결혼한 지 한 달밖에 안 된 신혼부부예요.

They are newlyweds that have only been married for one month.

요즘 신혼부부들은 국내보다는 해외로 신혼여행을 가는 경우가 많아요.

Nowadays, there are more cases of newlyweds that go on their honeymoon abroad than domestically.

51
심부름

[심부름] 명사 errand

[Expression] 심부름꾼 errand boy

심부름센터 detective agency

심부름을 가다 to go on an errand

심부름을 하다 to do an errand

심부름을 시키다 to order someone to go on an errand

[Example] 김 선생님은 학생들에게 가끔 심부름을 시키세요.

Mr. Kim sometimes orders his students to run errands for him.

엄마 심부름으로 슈퍼에 가서 콩나물을 사 왔어요.

My mom sent me on an errand to the supermarket to buy bean sprouts.

52
쓰레기통

[쓰레기통] 명사 garbage can

[Expression] 쓰레기통이 차다 The garbage can is full.

쓰레기통을 비우다 to empty the garbage can

쓰레기통에 버리다 to throw out into the garbage can

[Synonym] 휴지통 waste basket

[Example] 쓰레기통이 쓰레기로 가득 차 있어서 아침에 비웠어요.

I emptied the garbage can in the morning because it was full.

쓰레기는 바닥에 버리지 마시고 반드시 쓰레기통에 버리세요.

Don't throw the garbage on the floor. Throw it in the garbage can.

53
아끼다

[아끼다] 동사 to save, to use sparingly

[Usage] N 을/를 아끼다

[Expression] 물을 아끼다 to save money
돈을 아끼다 to be frugal with money
에너지를 아끼다 to save energy

[Synonym] 절약하다 to conserve

[Antonym] 낭비하다 to waste

[Example] 돈을 막 쓰지 말고 아껴서 쓰세요.
Don't waste your money on just anything. Try to be more frugal when spending.

교통비를 아끼면 생활비를 좀 줄일 수 있을 거예요.
If I use less money on transportation, I can lessen the total amount of money I use daily.

54
아버님

[아버님] 명사 1. father 2. father-in-law 3. one's wife's father

1. the honorific form of father

[Synonym] 아버지 father

[Related Words] 어머님 mother (honorific form)
어머니 mother

[Example] 어머님과 아버님 모두 살아 계십니다.
Both my father and mother are alive.

2. a word used to call one's father-in-law

[Synonym] 시아버지 father-in-law

[Related Words] 어머님 mother-in-law (honorific)
시어머니 mother-in-law

[Example] 오늘 아버님께서 몸이 편찮으시다고 해서 병원에 좀 다녀왔어요.
My father-in-law said he wasn't feeling good today, so we went to the hospital.

3. one's wife's father

[Synonym] 장인어른 father-in-law(the word that wife uses to call his wife's father)

[Related Words] 어머님 mother-in-law(the word that wife uses to call her husband's mother)
장모님 mother-in-law(the word that husband uses to call his wife's mother)

[Example] 아버님, 술 한 잔 받으시죠. 제가 따라드리겠습니다.
Father-in-law, have a glass of alcohol. I will pour it for you.

55
안방

[안빵] 명사 main room of a house

[Expression] 안방 문 the door to the main room

[Related Words] 건넌방 the opposite room

[Example] 보통 안방은 부모님께서 쓰세요.
The parents usually live in the main bedroom.

보통 아버지와 어머니가 쓰시는 방을 '안방'이라고 하고 안방의 맞은편에 있는 방을 '건넌방'이라고 해요.
Usually, the room that the parents sleep in is called the "anbang" and the room across from it is called the "konnonbang."

56
알뜰하다

[알뜰하다] 형용사 to be frugal

[Usage] N 이/가 알뜰하다
알뜰한 N
알뜰하게 AV

[Example] 우리 며느리는 살림을 알뜰하게 하는 편이에요.
My daughter-in-law tends to run the household in a very frugal manner.

출근 시간을 알뜰하게 쓰기 위해서 지하철 안에서 책을 봐요.
In order to prudently use my time while on the subway on my way to work, I read a book.

57
오븐

[오븐] 명사 oven

[Expression] 오븐에 넣다 to put in the oven
오븐에서 굽다 to roast in the oven
오븐으로 익히다 to cook in the oven

[Related Words] 가스레인지 stovetop
전자레인지 microwave

[Example] 오븐은 전기 오븐과 가스 오븐 두 종류가 있어요.
The two kinds of ovens are gas and electric.

제가 집에서 오븐으로 구운 과자예요. 한번 드셔 보세요.
There are the cookies I made in the oven at home. Try some.

58
외동딸

[외동딸] 명사 only daughter

[Related Words] 외(동)아들 only son
무남독녀 only daughter

[Example] 저는 동생도 오빠도 언니도 없는 외동딸이에요.
I am an only daughter without any siblings.

저는 외동딸이어서 형제가 많은 집이 부러워요.
I am jealous of houses with a lot of kids because I am an only daughter.

59
용돈

[용똔] 명사 allowance, pocket money

[Expression]

용돈이 떨어지다 to be out of money
용돈을 타다 to get an allowance
용돈을 모으다 to save one's pocket money
용돈을 절약하다 to economize one's spending of money

[Example]

지난주에 용돈을 줬는데 벌써 다 썼어?
I gave you money last week and you already used it all?

나는 대학교 때 아르바이트를 해서 용돈과 학비를 벌었다.
In college, I had a part-time job so I made some pocket money and money used for school.

60
유리

[유리] 명사 glass

[Expression]

유리 그릇 glass bowl
유리 제품 glass product
유리 조각 piece of glass
유리가 깨지다 The glass is broken.
유리를 갈다 to change glass

[Example]

야구를 하다가 옆집 유리를 깼어요.
I broke a neighbor's glass window while playing baseball.

유리 조각에 손을 베어서 피가 많이 났어요.
I bled a lot when I cut my hand on a piece of glass.

61
자식

[자식] 명사 children (son and daughter)

[Expression]

자식 걱정 worrying about one's children
자식 사랑 love for one's children
자식을 낳다 to give birth to children
자식을 기르다 to raise one's children

[Synonym]

자녀 children
자제 somebody's child

[Example]

자식을 길러봐야 부모님의 마음을 안다는 말이 있다.
They say that the only way to understand what a parent feels is to try raising kids.

부모님께서는 자식들이 잘 자라는 것을 최고의 행복으로 여긴다.
Parents believe raising children well to be the greatest happiness.

62
장남

[장남] 명사 the first born son

[Synonym] 맏아들 the first born son

큰아들 the eldest son

[Related Words] 차남 second son

장녀 oldest daughter

차녀 second daughter

[Example] 민수는 삼 형제 중 장남이다.

Minsoo is the eldest of his three brothers.

보통 장남은 결혼 후에 부모님을 모시고 삽니다.

Usually the oldest son takes care of the parents after he gets married.

63
전기

[전기] 명사 electricity

[Expression] 전기세 electricity fee

전기 요금 electricity bill

전기가 나가다 The power goes out.

전기를 절약하다 to conserve electricity

[Related Words] 전류 current

전선 electrical lines, wire

[Example] 가끔 전기 불을 끄지 않고 외출할 때가 있어요.

There are times when I go out without turning off the lights.

기름 없이 전기로만 달리는 자동차가 곧 일반화된다고 합니다.

They say that cars that run on electricity without oil will soon become the norm.

64
지붕

[지붕] 명사 roof

[Expression] 지붕이 낮다 The roof is low.

지붕을 고치다 to fix the roof

지붕에서 비가 새다 Rain is leaking from the roof.

[Example] 집이 너무 낡아서 비가 오면 지붕에서 비가 새요.

The house is so old that when it rains, water leaks from the roof.

막내 아들이 지붕에 올라갔다가 떨어져서 크게 다쳤어요.

The youngest son got very hurt when he went up to the roof and then fell off.

65
치우다

[치우다] 동사 1. to clean up 2. to move an object

1. to clean up something dirty

[Usage] N 을/를 치우다

[Related Words] 청소하다 to clean

[Example] 지저분한 방을 치우느라고 고생했어요.
I was very tired after cleaning up my messy room.

2. to move an object from one place to another

[Usage] N 을/를 치우다
N 에 치우다

[Synonym] 옮기다 to move

[Example] 위험한 물건들은 아이들의 손이 닿지 않는 곳에 치워 두세요.
Make sure to place any objects that can be harmful to children in a place that they cannot reach them.

66
침실

[침실] 명사 bedroom

[Expression] 침실을 꾸미다 to decorate one's bedroom

[Related Words] 거실 living room
부엌 kitchen
침대 bed
화장실 bathroom

[Example] 위층에는 화장실과 침실이 있어요.
On the upper floor, there is a bathroom and a bedroom.

저희 집 침실에서는 멋진 야경을 볼 수 있어요.
You have a great view at night from the bedroom in our house.

67
키우다

[키우다] 동사 to raise, to bring up

[Usage] N 을/를 키우다

[Expression] 아이를 키우다 to raise children
화초를 키우다 to raise plants
강아지를 키우다 to raise a puppy

[Synonym] 기르다 to grow

[Related Words] 가꾸다 to cultivate, to raise

[Example] 어렸을 때 강아지를 키운 적이 있어요.
When I was younger, I used to raise a dog.

부모님은 자녀를 키우기 위해서 많은 고생을 하세요.
Parents do through a lot of troubles to raise their children.

68
털다

[털다] 동사 to shake off, to dust off, to brush off

[Usage] N 을/를 털다

[Expression] 눈을 털다 to knock off snow
먼지를 털다 to shake off dust

[Related Words] 묻다 to have a stain, to get dirty

[Example] 어깨에 눈이 많이 쌓여서 손으로 털어 냈어요.
There was a lot of snow on my shoulder, so I knocked it off.

대청소를 하면서 텔레비전 위에 쌓인 먼지를 털었어요.
I dusted off the dirt that was on top of the television as I did my spring cleaning.

69
테이프

[테이프] 명사 1. tape 2. tape

1. used to stick something against another surface

[Synonym] 스카치테이프 scotch tape

[Example] 서랍이 볼펜, 지우개, 포스트잇, 테이프 등과 같은 문구류로 가득 차 있네요.
The drawer is full of stationary like pens, erasers, post-its, and scotch tape.

2. a tape used for recording

[Expression] 녹음 테이프 recording tape
비디오 테이프 video tape
테이프에 녹음하다 to record on a tape

[Example] 나는 영화를 좋아해서 집에 영화 비디오 테이프가 많다.
I have a lot of movie video tapes at home because I like watching movies.

70
플라스틱

[플라스틱] 명사 plastic

[Expression] 플라스틱 컵 plastic cup
플라스틱 그릇 plastic bowl
플라스틱 용기 plastic container
플라스틱 제품 plastic product

[Example] 플라스틱 제품은 가볍고 잘 깨지지 않아요.
Plastic products are very light and don't break easily.

플라스틱 제품들은 재활용이 가능하니까 버릴 때는 재활용 수거함에 넣으세요.
Since plastic products are recyclable, make sure to throw them out in the recyclables bin.

71
현관

[현관] 명사 front door

[Expression] 현관문 main door

현관을 나서다 to go out the front door

[Example] 현관에 있는 신발들을 정리했어요.

I organized the shoes at the front door.

아침마다 아내는 출근하는 남편을 현관까지 배웅한다.

Every morning the wife sees her husband off to work to the main door.

72
형님

[형님] 명사 1. older brother of one's wife 2. a word used to call one's older sister-in-law 3. honorific form of older brother

1. a word used to call the older brothers of one's wife

[Related Words] 처남 one's wife's brother

[Example] 형님들께 막내 사위가 인사를 드립니다.

The youngest son-in-law greets the older brothers of his wife.

2. a word used to call one's older sister-in-law

[Synonym] 동서 sister-in-law(a word used to call one's younger sister-in-law)

[Related Words] 올케 sister-in-law

시누이 sister-in-law

시동생 brother-in-law

시아주버니 elder brother of one's husband

[Example] 명절 때마다 형님들과 함께 음식을 장만해야 해요.

During holidays, you need to prepare food with your in-laws.

3. honorific form of older brother

[Expression] 형님 댁 the house of my older brother

형님이 계시다 My older brother is here.

[Synonym] 형 older brother

[Related Words] 형수님 older brother's wife

[Example] 부모님이 일찍 돌아가셔서 형님과 형수님이 저를 키우셨어요.

Since my parents died very early, my older brother and his wife raised me.

73
형부

[형부] 명사 the husband of one's older sister

[Related Words] 처제 one's wife's younger sister

[Example] 형부와 언니가 사이가 좋아서 보기 좋네요.
It's great to see that your older sister and her husband get along so well together.

내 조카는 언니보다는 형부를 더 많이 닮아서 키도 크고 눈도 크다.
My nephew looks a lot like my brother-in-law. He is tall and has big eyes.

74
화분

[화분] 명사 flower pot, plant

[Expression] 화분에 꽃을 심다 to plant a flower in a pot
화분에 물을 주다 to water a flower

[Related Words] 씨 seed
화초 plant

[Example] 화분이 너무 커서 혼자 옮기기 힘들 것 같아요.
The flower pot is too big for me to move alone.

아침마다 엄마는 저에게 화분에 물을 주라고 시키세요.
My mother orders me to water the plant in the flower pot every morning.

05 연습문제

[1-18] **다음 단어를 한국어로 바꿔 쓰십시오.**

Change the following vocabulary words to Korean

1. comb ( )
2. household ( )
3. oven ( )
4. roof ( )
5. bedroom ( )
6. pillow ( )
7. tool ( )
8. needle ( )
9. gate ( )
10. rice cooker ( )
11. contacts ( )
12. blanket ( )
13. glass ( )
14. belt ( )
15. gas ( )
16. newspaper ( )
17. lighter ( )
18. tape ( )

[19-30] **[보기]에서 알맞은 단어를 골라 ( ) 안에 쓰십시오.**

Choose the appropriate word from the box below and then fill in the parenthesis.

[보기]

동네	용돈	자식	공과금	외동딸	배터리
심부름	손윗사람	비닐봉지	닮다	치우다	알뜰하다

19. 한국에서는 나보다 나이가 많은 ( )에게 존댓말을 쓰고 예의 바르게 행동해야 해요.

20. 아내는 ( )어서/아서/여서 물건을 한 번 사면 오랫동안 아껴 써요.

21. 부부가 같이 오래 살다가 보면 외모도, 성격도 서로 ( )어/아/여 가는 것 같아요.

22. 나는 형제자매 없이 (   )으로/로 자라서 어린 시절에 조금 외로웠다.

23. 회사 근처에 우리 (   )까지 운행하는 마을버스가 있어서 아주 편해요.

24. 취직하기 전에는 부모님이 한 달에 10만원 씩 (   )을/를 주셨어요.

25. 부모들은 (   )을/를 위해서라면 무슨 일이든지 할 수 있을 것이다.

26. 어머니는 내게 우유를 사 오라고 (   )을/를 시키셨다.

27. 오늘 손님들이 오시니까 방을 (   ) 어야겠어요/아야겠어요/여야겠어요.

28. 휴대전화가 켜지지 않으면 (   )을/를 다시 한번 잘 끼워 보십시오.

29. 사과 만 원어치만 이 (   )에 좀 담아 주세요.

30. 전기세, 수도세, 전화세 등 각종 (   )을/를 기한 내에 내지 않으면 연체료를 내야 해요.

[31-42] 다음은 가족 관계를 나타내는 단어의 설명입니다. 단어의 설명과 단어의 첫소리를 보고 알맞은 단어를 [보기]와 같이 쓰십시오.

The following is an explanation of words that express relationships within the family. Look at the word's explanation and the first sound of each word and then fill in blanks with the missing letters as done in the example below.

[보기]

딸의 남편

ㅅ	ㅇ	➡	사	위

31. 남자와 여자 형제.

ㄴ	ㅁ	➡		

32. 아들의 아내.

ㅁ	ㄴ	ㄹ	➡			

33. 부부 관계에 있는 상대방, 남편이나 아내.

ㅂ ㅇ ㅈ → □ □ □

34. 아들의 아들 또는 딸의 아들.

ㅅ ㅈ → □ □

35. 시아버지와 시어머니.

ㅅ ㅂ ㅁ → □ □ □

36. 결혼하는 남자.

ㅅ ㄹ → □ □

37. 결혼한 지 얼마 안 된 부부.

ㅅ ㅎ ㅂ ㅂ → □ □ □ □

38. 둘 이상의 아들 중의 큰아들.

ㅈ ㄴ → □ □

39. 여러 형제, 자매 중에서 맨 마지막에 태어난 사람.

ㅁ ㄴ → □ □

40. 남자인 나보다 나이가 많은 남자 또는 아내의 오빠.

ㅎ ㄴ → □ □

41. 언니의 남편.

ㅎ ㅂ → □ □

42. 다른 사람의 아버지를 높이는 말.

ㅇ	ㅂ	ㄴ	➡			

[43-55] 다음 [보기]에서 알맞은 단어를 골라 (   ) 안에 쓰십시오.

Choose the appropriate word from the box below and then fill in the parenthesis.

[보기]

식구	서랍	안방	전기	화분	바구니	설치하다
보증금	손잡이	세입자	목욕탕	플라스틱	꾸미다	

43. (   )은/는 주인이 월세를 올려 달라고 할까 봐 걱정했다.

44. 지금 살고 있는 집은 (   ) 오천만 원에 매달 월세로 50만 원을 내고 있다.

45. 연세 이삿짐센터를 이용하시는 분들께는 에어컨, 정수기를 무료로 (   )어/아/여 드립니다.

46. 봄이 됐으니까 베란다에 놓을 작은 (   )을/를 한두 개 사야겠어요.

47. 재활용 쓰레기인 종이와 병과 (   )은/는 따로따로 분리해서 버려야 한다.

48. 바닥은 흰색으로, 벽과 가구는 핑크색으로 신혼집을 (   )었어요/았어요/였어요.

49. 지금 동생은 (   )에서 샤워를 하고 있어서 전화를 받을 수 없어요.

50. 여름에는 에어컨을 많이 사용해서 (   ) 요금이 많이 나와요.

51. (   )에 일주일 동안 빨래를 모아서 한꺼번에 세탁해요.

52. 양말은 옷장 왼쪽에 있는 첫 번째 (   ) 안에 들어 있어요.

53. 흔들리는 버스 안에서는 넘어지지 않게 (   )을/를 꽉 잡으십시오.

54. 저희 아버지는 혈압도 높으시고 성격도 급하셔서 가끔 화를 내시면 쓰러지실까 봐 (   )들이 걱정하곤 해요.

55. 보통 ( )의 맞은편에 있는 방을 건넌방이라고 해요.

[56-57] 다음 밑줄 친 부분과 반대되는 뜻을 가진 것을 고르십시오.

Choose the word that has the opposite meaning from the underlined word.

56. 돈을 아무 데나 쓰지 않고 꼭 필요한 데만 아껴서 써요.

❶ 절약하다 ❷ 낭비하다 ❸ 한턱내다 ❹ 계산하다

57. 생각보다 손님이 적게 와서 음식이 많이 남았다.

❶ 넉넉하다 ❷ 충분하다 ❸ 모자라다 ❹ 부유하다

[58-62] 다음 밑줄 친 부분과 의미가 비슷한 것을 고르십시오.

Choose a word that is similar in meaning to the underlined part of the sentence.

58. 우리 하숙집 아저씨는 모든 전자 제품을 수리하실 수 있어서 뭐든 고장이 날 때마다 아저씨께 부탁해요.

❶ 챙기다 ❷ 고치다 ❸ 수선하다 ❹ 서비스하다

59. 영미 씨는 유명한 가수 김소라와 비슷하게 생긴 것 같아요.

❶ 닮다 ❷ 낯익다 ❸ 똑같다 ❹ 익숙하다

60. 어린 아이들을 돌볼 수 있는 시설이 부족해 맞벌이 부부들이 어린 자녀를 키우는 데에 어려움이 많다.

❶ 낳다 ❷ 자라다 ❸ 가꾸다 ❹ 기르다

61. 한국에서는 석유가 나지 않아서 100% 수입을 해야 해요.

❶ 기름 ❷ 우유 ❸ 석탄 ❹ 식용유

62. 두꺼운 카펫이나 커튼같이 집에서 <u>세탁하기</u> 힘든 것은 세탁소에 맡긴다.

❶ 청소하기　　❷ 쇼핑하기　　❸ 빨래하기　　❹ 교환하기

[63-64] 다음 (　　　)에 공통적으로 들어갈 단어를 쓰십시오.

Write one word that can commonly fit into the parenthesis below.

63.
❶ "여보, 내가 제일 사랑하는 사랑은 바로 (　　　　)이야/야."
❷ (　　　　)은/는 건강을 위해서 무슨 운동을 하십니까?
❸ (　　　　)이/가 뭔데 남의 일에 참견이야?

(　　　　　　)

64.
❶ 대한민국의 (　　　　)은/는 서울이에요.
❷ 날씨가 너무 추워서 (　　　　)이/가 얼었어요.
❸ 이번 달에 물을 많이 써서 (　　　　) 요금이 많이 나왔어요.

(　　　　　　)

[65-69] 다음 (　　　)에 공통적으로 들어갈 단어의 기본형을 쓰십시오.

Write the basic form of one word that can be used in the parenthesis.

65.
❶ 수업이 끝나면 교실 바닥에 버린 쓰레기 좀 (　　　　)어/아/여 주세요.
❷ 어머니께서 방이 더럽다고 꾸중하시기 전에 방을 (　　　　)어야겠어요/아야겠어요/여야겠어요.

(　　　　　　)

66.
❶ 지난주 토요일에 장인어른을 (　　　　)고 식사를 했어요.
❷ 오늘은 김 박사님을 (　　　　)고 한국의 가족 관계에 대해 알아보겠습니다.
❸ 옛날에 한국에서는 보통 장남이 부모님을 (　　　　)고 살았는데 요즘은 꼭 그렇지는 않다.

(   )

67. ❶ 설거지를 하다가 잘못해서 유리컵을 (   )었어요/았어요/였어요.

❷ 어제 마신 술이 아직도 안 (   )는/은/ㄴ 것 같아요.

❸ 밖에서 시끄러운 소리가 나서 자다가 (   )었어요/았어요/였어요.

(   )

68. ❶ 아이스크림에는 설탕이 많이 들어 있어서 너무 (   )어요/아요/ 여요.

❷ 게시판의 글을 읽고 댓글을 (   )었어요/았어요/였어요.

❸ 햇빛이 많이 들어와서 창문에 커튼을 (   )었어요/았어요/였어요.

(   )

69. ❶ 친구가 생일 때 준 선물이 너무 마음에 (   )어요/아요/여요.

❷ 컴퓨터 동아리에 (   )으려면/려면 어떻게 해야 해요?

❸ 우리 집 목욕탕을 고치고 싶은데 돈이 너무 많이 (   )어서/아서/여서 망설이고 있어요.

(   )

[70-76] 다음 [보기]에서 알맞은 단어를 골라 이야기를 완성하십시오.

Choose the right word from the box below and complete the story.

[보기]

먼지	바닥	현관	산더미	쓰레기통	쓸다	털다

오랜만에 집에 일찍 들어와 보니 해야 할 일이 70.(   )처럼 쌓여 있었다. 문을 열고 들어서자 71.(   ) 앞에는 구두와 운동화가 잔뜩 나와 있었고 오랫동안 청소를 못해서 방 여기저기에 72.(   )이/가 가득 쌓여 있었다. 방 73.(   )에는 벗어 놓은 옷들과 먹다 버린 과자 봉

지가 놓여 있었다. 나는 바로 청소를 시작했다. 그런데 텔레비전 위에 쌓인 먼지를 74.(   )다가 잘못해서 TV 위에 있던 액자를 깼다. 깨진 액자 조각을 조심히 75.(   )에 버렸다. 그리고 방을 빗자루로 76.(   )고 물걸레로 닦았다. 조금 힘들었지만 깨끗하게 청소를 끝내니까 기분이 좋았다.

인간관계

06

Relationships

06 인간관계

01 개인적이다

[개인저기다] 형용사 to be personal or to be individual

anything related to or belong to the individual

[Usage] 개인적인 N

개인적으로 AV

[Example] 개인적인 문제로 회사를 그만두게 되었어요.

I ended up quitting my job at the office because of personal problems.

너무 개인적인 질문을 하면 대답하기가 참 곤란해요.

It's quite tough for me to answer your questions if they are very personal.

02 거절하다

[거절하다] 동사 to reject, to deny

to not accept and decline another party's demand, suggestion, present, or request.

[Usage] N 을/를 거절하다

AV 기를 거절하다

[Expression] 부탁을 거절하다 to reject a request

요구를 거절하다 to reject a demand

[Antonym] 승낙하다 to approve

허락하다 to permit

[Example] 저는 사람들의 부탁을 잘 거절하지 못해요.

I don't reject other people's requests too often.

친구가 제 부탁을 거절했지만 그렇게 기분이 나쁘지 않았어요.

My friend rejected my request but I didn't feel too bad.

03 거짓말

[거진말] 명사 lie

passing something that isn't true as the truth

[Expression] 거짓말쟁이 a liar

새빨간 거짓말 obvious lie

거짓말을 하다 to tell a lie

[Antonym] 진짜 true

[Example] 지은 씨는 거짓말을 자주 해서 믿을 수가 없어요.

I can't believe Jieun because she often lies.

어렸을 때부터 어머니는 제가 거짓말하는 것을 제일 싫어하셨어요.

From the time I was young, my mother most hated that I tell lies.

04
겸손하다

[겸손하다] 형용사 to be humble

[Usage] N 이/가 겸손하다
겸손한 N
겸손하게 AV

[Expression] 겸손한 태도 a humble attitude

[Antonym] 교만하다 to be arrogant

[Example] 높은 자리에 올라갈수록 겸손해야 해요.
You need to be humble as you go up in rank.

잘난 척하는 사람보다 겸손한 사람을 좋아하는 것은 당연하죠.
It's natural to like people that are humble more than people that are obnoxious.

05
고백하다

[고배카다] 동사 to confess

to say what you are thinking inside of your mind or something you have hidden inside in a truthful manner

[Usage] N 에게 N 을/를 고백하다
N 에게 AV 다고 고백하다

[Example] 미선 씨에게 좋아한다고 고백하고 싶지만 용기가 안 나요.
I want to confess to Miseon that I like her but I don't have the courage to do it.

민수 씨가 현정 씨에게 좋아한다고 고백했는데 거절당했대요.
They say that Minsoo confessed to Hyeonjeong that he liked her but that he was rejected.

06
공경하다

[공경하다] 동사 to be respectful

to politely respect someone

[Usage] N 을/를 공경하다

[Expression] 노인을 공경하다 to respect a old person
어른을 공경하다 to respect an adult

[Related Words] 존경하다 to respect

[Example] 웃어른을 공경해야 해요.
You need to respect your elders.

어른을 공경하고 부모에게 효도하는 젊은이들이 많아졌으면 좋겠어요.
It would be nice if there were more young people that were pious to their parents and respected their elders.

07
궁금하다

[궁금하다] 형용사 to wonder

to feel anxious or impatient to know something

[Usage] N 이/가 궁금하다
AV / DV 는지/은지/ㄴ지/을지/ㄹ지 궁금하다

[Example] 친구가 울기만 하는데 무슨 일인지 궁금해요.
My friend just keeps crying. I wonder what is wrong.

민철 씨도 나를 좋아하는지 그의 속마음이 궁금해요.
I wonder if Mincheol likes me deep down inside.

08
권하다

[권하다] 동사 to encourage, to recommend

to recommend someone to do something

[Usage] N 에/에게 N 을/를 권하다
N 에/에게 AV 으라고/라고 권하다

[Expression] 차를 권하다 to offer a cup of tea

[Example] 친구가 나에게 요가를 배워보라고 권했다.
My friend suggested that I try learning yoga.

술을 마시고 싶지 않은데 자꾸 권하면 어떻게 하시겠어요?
What would you do if someone keeps encouraging you to drink even though you don't want to?

09
그립다

[그립따] 형용사 to miss

to long for or miss something

[Usage] N 이/가 그립다

[Expression] 가족이 그립다 I miss my family.
고향이 그립다 I miss my hometown.

[Synonym] 생각나다 to think about

[Example] 사회생활을 하고 보니 학교생활이 그립네요.
After working and being a member of society, I miss being a student.

고향을 떠난 지 10년 됐는데 고향이 무척 그립습니다.
It's been over ten years since I have left my hometown, and I greatly miss it.

10
기대하다

[기대하다] 동사 to anticipate, to expect

to wait and hope that something will happen

[Usage] N 을/를 기대하다

AV / DV 기를 기대하다

[Example] 친구들과 처음으로 가는 여행이라서 정말 많이 기대하고 있어요.
Since it is the first time I am going on vacation with my friends, I'm really looking forward to it.

이번 시험에서 좋은 결과를 기대했었는데 결과가 안 좋아서 실망했어요.
I was really anticipating good test results this time, but I was disappointed when they turned out to be bad.

11
기억 [기억] 명사 memory

holding onto past impressions or experiences in one's mind and remembering them

[Expression] 기억력 capacity to remember
기억나다 to come to remembrance
기억하다 to remember
기억에 남다 to remain in one's memory

[Example] 중학교 때 친구였는데 그 친구 이름이 기억나지 않아요.
We were friends in middle school but I don't remember his name.

제가 오늘 휴대전화를 안 가져왔는데 혹시 미선 씨 전화번호를 기억하세요?
I didn't bring my cell phone today. By any chance, do you remember Miseon's cell phone number?

12
끄덕이다 [끄더기다] 동사 to nod

to move lightly from up to down (usually referring to one's head)

[Expression] 고개를 끄덕이다 to nod one's head

[Related Words] 젓다 to shake, to wave

[Example] 보통 고개를 끄덕이는 것은 허락을 의미해요.
Normally, nodding your head means that you permit something.

부모님께서는 대답 대신에 고개를 끄덕이셨어요.
My parents nodded their heads instead of answering.

13
끊어지다 [끄너지다] 동사 to end ties or to get cut off

to no longer have a connection to something

[Usage] N 이/가 끊어지다

[Expression] 교류가 끊어지다 The exchange is cut off.
소식이 끊어지다 There is no more news from him.

연락이 끊어지다 to lose contact.

[Synonym] 끊기다 to break off

[Example] 받자마자 전화가 끊어졌어요.
As soon as I answered the call, the line got cut off.

연락이 끊어졌던 고등학교 동창한테서 어제 이메일을 받았어요.
I got an email yesterday from a high school classmate with whom I had lost contact.

14
끼치다

[끼치다] 동사 to cause, to bring about

to cause others to undergo damage or influence

[Usage] N 을/를 끼치다

[Expression] 폐를 끼치다 to bother, to trouble someone
걱정을 끼치다 to make someone worry
불편을 끼치다 to cause an inconvenience
영향을 끼치다 to have an influence on someone

[Example] 선생님, 이번 일로 걱정을 끼쳐드려서 죄송합니다.
Teacher, I'm sorry I made you worry because of what happened.

일회용품 사용은 환경오염에 심각한 영향을 끼칩니다.
The use of single-use products has a very serious influence on environmental pollution.

15
나누다

[나누다] 동사 1. to exchange 2. to share

1. to have an exchange of words, greetings, or stories

[Usage] N 과/와 N 을/를 나누다

[Expression] 악수를 나누다 to shake hands
인사를 나누다 to greet one another
의견을 나누다 to share an opinion
이야기를 나누다 to have a conversation

[Example] 저는 낯을 가려서 친한 사람하고만 대화를 잘 나누는 편이에요.
I only tend to converse with people I am close to because I am bashful.

2. to eat food together or to split portions to eat together

[Usage] N 과/와 N 을/를 나누다

[Expression] 차를 나누다 to have a cup of tea together
음식을 나누다 to share food

[Example] 옛날 사람들은 음식을 만들면 자주 이웃 사람들과 나누어 먹었어요.
In the old days, people would make food and often share it with their neighbors.

16
낯설다

[낟썰다] 형용사 to be unknown, to be unfamiliar

to be awkward and unfamiliar because of not knowing someone or something

[Usage] N 이/가 낯설다
낯선 N

[Expression] 낯선 사람 unfamiliar person

[Antonym] 낯익다 to be familiar

[Example] 낯선 사람이 오면 문 열어 주지 마라.
Don't open the door if a stranger comes.

처음 한국에 왔을 때는 한국 사람들이 낯설고 이상했는데 요즘은 괜찮아졌어요.
When I first came to Korea, Korean people were unfamiliar and strange, but now things are better.

17
농담하다

[농담하다] 동사 to tell a joke

[Usage] N 에게 농담하다

[Related Words] 장난하다 to play around

[Example] 나는 심각하게 이야기했는데 친구들은 농담으로 받아들였어요.
I said something serious, but my friends took it as a joke.

영수는 자주 농담을 해서 사람들을 즐겁게 해 주기 때문에 인기가 많아요.
Youngsoo is very popular because he makes people enjoy themselves by telling jokes.

18
대하다

[대하다] 동사 to treat

to treat someone with a certain attitude

[Usage] N 으로/로 대하다
N 처럼 대하다
DV 게 대하다

[Expression] 가족처럼 대하다 to treat like family
자식처럼 대하다 to treat as one's child
친구처럼 대하다 to treat as a friend

[Example] 저희 시어머니가 저를 딸처럼 대해 주세요.
My mother-in-law treats me like a daughter.

요즘 미선이가 왜 나에게 쌀쌀하게 대하는지 모르겠어.
I don't understand why Miseon treats me so coldly nowadays.

19
대화하다

[대화하다] 동사 to converse, to have a dialogue

to exchange words with someone

[Usage] N 과/와 대화하다

[Synonym] 이야기하다 to talk

[Example] 처음에는 한국말을 하나도 몰랐는데 1년 만에 이렇게 한국말로 자유롭게 대화할 수 있다니 정말 신기해요.
At first, you didn't know any Korean, but it's really cool that after only one year you can converse so freely now in it.

인터넷으로 가족들하고 자주 영상채팅을 하다 보니 마치 마주보고 대화하는 것 같아요.
After speaking with my family very often through video chatting, it feels as if we were looking at each other and having a conversation.

20
데려가다

[데려가다] 동사 to take

to take someone and go

[Usage] N 을/를 데려가다
N 에 데려가다

[Expression] 아이를 데려가다 to take a child
강아지를 데려가다 to take a puppy

[Antonym] 데려오다 to bring

[Related Words] 가져가다 to take (objects)
모셔가다 to take (adults, honorific form)

[Example] 어제 연극을 보셨다면서요? 다음에는 저도 데려가 주세요.
I heard that yesterday you saw a play? Next time take me along with you.

그 공연은 9살이 넘어야 볼 수 있으니까 5살짜리 우리 아들은 데려갈 수가 없어요
I can't take my five year old son to see the performance because he needs to be over nine to see it.

21
도움

[도움] 명사 help

[Expression] 도움이 되다 to be helpful

도움이 필요하다 to need help
도움을 받다 to receive help
도움을 주다 to give help
도움을 구하다 to seek help

[Example] 김 선생님은 제가 힘들고 외로울 때마다 큰 도움을 주셨던 분이에요.
Mr. Kim was the person that gave me the most help whenever I had a hard time or felt lonely.

날마다 한국어로 일기를 쓰는 것은 좀 번거롭기는 하지만 한국어 공부에 큰 도움이 돼요.
Even though writing a diary in Korean everyday can be a little troublesome, it has really helped my Korean.

22
돌려주다

[돌려주다] 동사 to give back, to return something to someone

to return something borrowed, taken, or received to the owner

[Usage] N 에/에게 N 을/를 돌려주다

[Expression] 돈을 돌려주다 to return money
물건을 돌려주다 to give back an object

[Synonym] 반납하다 to return

[Antonym] 돌려받다 to receive back

[Example] 접수시키신 입사원서는 돌려드리지 않습니다.
We do not return the employment application form that you submitted.

친구한테서 빌린 물건을 돌려주는 것을 잊어버렸다.
I forgot to give what my friend lent me back to him.

23
돌보다

[돌보다] 동사 to take care of, to watch out for

[Usage] N 을/를 돌보다

[Expression] 가사를 돌보다 to take care of the household
건강을 돌보다 to take care of one's health
아기를 돌보다 to watch after a child
환자를 돌보다 to take care of a patient

[Synonym] 보살피다 to look after

[Example] 요즘 치매 환자를 돌보는 병원이 많이 생겼어요.
Nowadays, they have opened a lot more hospitals that take care of dementia patients.

매일 아이들을 돌보고 집안일을 하느라 내 시간이 없어요.
I have no time for myself because I have to take care of the kids everyday and finish the housework.

24
마중

[마중] 명사 going out to meet a person

to go out and greet someone that is coming

[Expression] 마중하다 to go and meet a person
마중을 나가다 to go out to meet someone
마중을 나오다 to come out to meet someone

[Antonym] 배웅 to see someone off

[Example] 친구가 우리 집을 못 찾을까 봐 마중을 나갔다.
I went out to meet my friend because I was afraid that he wouldn't be able to find my house.

바쁘실 텐데 이렇게 마중을 나와 주셔서 고맙습니다.
You must be busy. Thank you for coming out to meet me.

25
말다툼하다

[말다툼하다] 동사 to quarrel, to have an dispute

[Usage] N 과/와 말다툼하다

[Expression] 친구와 말다툼하다 to have a quarrel with a friend

[Related Words] 말싸움하다 to have a wordy conflict

[Example] 어제 친구와 말다툼하고 헤어져서 마음이 편하지 않네요.
I feel uncomfortable that I got into a quarrel with my friend yesterday.

어렸을 때는 형과 자주 말다툼했지만 지금은 전혀 싸우지 않아요.
When I was younger, I would get into a lot of arguments with my older brother, but now we don't fight at all.

26
맞서다

[맏써다] 동사 to stand face to face, to stand against

[Usage] N 과/와 맞서다
N 에/에게 맞서다

[Expression] 죽음과 맞서다 to stand face to face with death

[Example] 좌담회에서 찬성과 반대 의견이 팽팽하게 맞섰다.
In the debate, the opinions of the for and against team intensely faced off.

두 기업이 서로 맞서게 되면 한국 경제 전체에 악영향을 미칠 겁니다.
If the two businesses end up opposing each other, it will have an overall negative effect on the Korean economy.

27
모이다

[모이다] 동사 to gather, to come together

for many people to come together to one place

[Usage] N 이/가 모이다
N 에 모이다
N 으로/로 모이다

[Synonym] 집합하다 to assemble

[Example] 가족들이 오랜만에 모두 모여서 사진을 찍었다.
The family gathered together after long time and took a picture.

곧 행사가 시작되오니 모두 강당으로 모여 주시기 바랍니다.
The event will begin shortly. Please gather in the main hall.

28
몰라보다

[몰라보다] 동사 to fail to recognize

to be unable to know or recognize a fact or person that one should know

[Usage] N 을/를 몰라보다
몰라보게 AV

[Expression] 몰라보게 자라다
to grow to the point where one cannot recognize you anymore

몰라보게 달라지다
to change so much that one isn't recognizable anymore

몰라보게 예뻐지다
to become pretty so people fail to recognize you

[Antonym] 알아보다 to recognize

[Example] 한국어 실력이 몰라보게 늘었는데 비결이 뭐예요?
Your Korean skills have gotten outstandingly better, what is your secret?

10년 만에 만난 친구가 너무 예뻐져서 처음에는 몰라봤어요.
My friend that I hadn't met in ten years became so beautiful that I didn't recognize her at first.

29
무시하다

[무시하다] 동사 to ignore

to not pay attention to or recognize someone's existence or worth

[Usage] N 을/를 무시하다

[Expression] 사람을 무시하다 to ignore a person
의견을 무시하다 to ignore an opinion

[Example] 상대방의 의견을 무시하면 점점 불만이 쌓이게 됩니다.
If you ignore another person's opinion, their discontent will continue to build up little by little.

다수의 의견도 중요하지만 소수의 의견을 무시하면 안 된다.
Though the opinion of the majority is important, you cannot ignore the opinion of the minority.

30
미소

[미소] 명사 smile

[Expression] 미소를 잃다 to lose a smile
미소를 짓다 to make a smile

[Related Words] 웃음 laughter

[Example] 선생님은 화사한 미소로 나를 반겨 주셨다.
My teacher greeted me with a beautiful smile.

행복한 미소를 지으며 일하는 아들의 모습을 보고 감동을 받았다.
I was touched to see my son making a happy smile while working.

31
미팅

[미팅] 명사 group blind date

A word usually used by students, it refers to a meeting held between male and female students whose main goal is to promote social interaction.

[Expression] 미팅을 하다 to go on a blind date

[Synonym] 모임 meeting

[Related Words] 소개팅 an arranged blind date

[Example] 저는 미팅에서 남자 친구를 만났어요.
I met my boyfriend on a blind date.

대학에 입학해서 처음 하는 미팅이라서 많이 기대가 돼요.
I am very excited because this is the first blind date I am doing since I entered college.

32
바라보다

[바라보다] 동사 to look at

to direct one's eyes to an object

[Related Words] 쳐다보다 to stare

[Example] 신랑은 신부를 사랑스러운 눈빛으로 바라보고 있었어요.
The groom was looking at his bride with a loving look in his eyes.

그 사람은 아무 말 없이 몇 분 동안 제 얼굴만 바라보았어요.
That person just looked at my face for a few minutes without saying anything.

33
반하다

[반하다] 동사 to fall in love

[Usage] N 에/에게 반하다

[Expression] 매력에 반하다 to be taken by someone's charm
첫눈에 반하다 to fall in love at first sight

[Related Words] 빠지다 to fall in (love)

[Example] 옆 반 여학생에게 첫눈에 반했어요.
It was love at first sight with the female student in the classroom next door.

설악산의 아름다운 가을 풍경에 반해 버렸어요.
I was enamored with the beautiful fall landscape of Seorak mountain.

34
변명하다

[변명하다] 동사 to make up an excuse

to make an excuse about a mistake or error and explain the reason behind it

[Usage] N 을/를 변명하다
N 에 대해서 변명하다

[Example] 자기의 잘못은 인정하지 않고 변명하기만 해요.
He doesn't admit his mistakes and just keeps making excuses.

너무 당황해서 사장님께 전혀 변명하지 못했어요.
I was so flustered that I couldn't give the boss any excuses.

35
볼일

[볼릴] 명사 something one has to do

[Expression] 급한 볼일 an urgent matter
볼일이 있다 to have something to attend to
볼일이 생기다 Something has come up.
볼일을 보다 to take care of business

[Synonym] 용건 business
용무 business

[Example] 볼일도 있고 해서 이쪽에 왔다가 잠깐 들렀어요.
I stopped by here for a bit because I had some business to attend to.

영수 씨는 볼일이 있어서 오늘 모임에 좀 늦게 온대요.
Youngsoo has something to do so he says he is coming to the meeting a little late today.

36
분위기

[부니기] 명사 atmosphere, mood, ambience

what is felt by someone in a certain place

[Expression]

분위기가 있다 It has ambience.
분위기가 좋다 The atmosphere is nice.
분위기가 나쁘다 The atmosphere is bad.
분위기를 바꾸다 to change the atmosphere

[Example]

분위기가 좋은 커피숍에서 차나 한잔 할까요?
Do you want to have a cup of tea in a coffee shop that has a nice ambience?

집안 분위기를 좀 화사하게 바꾸고 싶어서 거실에 꽃을 꽂아 놓았어요.
I placed flowers in the living room because I wanted to liven up the atmosphere of the household.

37
불평하다

[불평하다] 동사 to complain

to not like something and feel that it isn't fitting, to express through actions or words that someone isn't suitable or appropriate

[Usage]

N 을/를 불평하다
N 에 대해서 불평하다
AV / DV 는다고/ㄴ다고/다고 불평하다

[Example]

요즘 아파트에서 애완동물을 키우는 주민들에 대한 불평이 많다면서요?
Is it true that recently there have been a lot of complaints about citizens that raise pets in their apartment?

많은 직원들이 월급이 너무 적다고 불평했지만 그는 아무 말없이 일만 했다.
Though a lot of workers complained that the pay was too low, he just continued to work without saying anything.

38
비밀

[비밀] 명사 secret

something that you cannot tell or hold as a secret from others

[Expression]

비밀을 숨기다 to hide a secret
비밀을 지키다 to keep a secret

[Example]

친구의 비밀을 실수로 다른 사람에게 말해 버렸어요.
I told my friend's secret to someone else by accident.

지난번에 한 이야기는 정말 비밀이니까 꼭 지켜야 돼.
What I told you last time is a secret, so you need to keep it like that.

39
사과하다

[사과하다] 동사 to apologize

to admit one's mistake and ask for forgiveness

[Usage] N 을/를 사과하다
N 에게 N 에 대해서 사과하다
N 에게 AV / DV 는/은/ㄴ 것을 사과하다

[Related Words] 용서하다 to forgive

[Example] 생각해 보니까 제가 잘못한 것 같아서 사과했어요.
After thinking about it, I apologized because I thought I had done something wrong.

다른 사람에게 사과할 때는 진실한 마음으로 해야 합니다.
When apologizing to someone else, one must truly mean it.

40
사교성

[사교썽] 명사 quality of being very social, sociability

[Expression] 사교성이 있다 He is sociable.
사교성이 좋다 He has the quality of sociability.

[Synonym] 붙임성 amiability

[Example] 저는 사교성이 있어서 처음 보는 사람과도 쉽게 사귀는 편이에요.
I make friends very easily with people I meet for the first time because I am very sociable.

요즘에는 성격이 밝고 적극적이면서 사교성이 좋은 남성이 인기가 많아요.
Nowadays, men that are sociable and have active, positive personalities are popular.

41
사이좋다

[사이조타] 형용사 to have a good relationship, to be friendly or amiable with someone

[Usage] N 과/와 사이좋다
사이좋게 AV

[Expression] 사이좋게 지내다 to get along well with someone

[Related Words] 친하다 to be on good terms

[Example] 우리 가족은 이웃집과 사이좋게 지내요.
My family gets along well with the neighbors.

우리 다시 싸우지 말고 전처럼 사이좋게 지내자.
Let's not fight again but rather get along with each other like old times.

42
살짝

[살짝] 부사 1. lightly 2. furtively 3. slightly 4. privately

1. not very heavily, in a light manner

[Example] 그녀는 고개를 살짝 들고 상대편을 쳐다보았다.
She lightly turned her head and stared at the other person.

2. without anyone else knowing or seeing

[Example] 영미 씨는 남자친구와 데이트가 있어서 회식에서 살짝 빠져나갔다.
Yeongmi had a date with her boyfriend so she secretly slipped out of the dinner meeting.

3. not severely but very slightly.

[Example] 시금치는 살짝 데쳐서 준비해 놓으십시오.
Please prepare the spinach by slightly blanching it.

4. very quietly so that no one else can hear.

[Example] 내 단짝 친구는 그 일을 내게만 살짝 알려 주었다.
My best friend only told me in privacy about what happened.

43
상관없다

[상관업따] 형용사 to not matter, to have nothing to do with something

[Usage]
N 이/가 상관없다
N 과/와 상관없다
N 에/에게 상관없다
상관없이 AV / DV

[Synonym] 관계없다 to have no ties

[Antonym] 상관있다 to matter, to have something to do with

[Example] 우리 기숙사는 주말, 주중 상관없이 밤 10시까지 들어 와야 해요.
At my dormitory, regardless of it being weekend or weekday, we have to be back home by 10 PM.

내 친구는 남들이 뭐라고 말하든 상관없이 항상 밝은 모습으로 대한다.
My friend always treats others in a cheerful manner no matter what they say to him.

44
상대방

[상대방] 명사 the opposing party, the other party

[Expression] 상대방의 입장 the view of the opposing party

[Synonym] 상대편 the opposite side

[Example] 상대방이 의견을 말할 때는 잘 들어야 합니다.
You must listen very well when other people say their opinion.

부탁을 하면 상대방에게 부담을 주는 것 같은 기분이 들어요.
If I ask for a favor, I feel like I am burdening the other person.

45
설득하다

[설뜨카다] 동사 to convince, to persuade

to provide a number examples to make the opposing party follow your idea

[Usage]
N 을/를 설득하다
N 에게 AV 도록 설득하다
N 에게 AV 으라고/라고 설득하다

[Example]
경찰은 집 나온 아이들을 설득해서 집으로 돌려보냈다.
The police convinced the kids that came out of their home to go back home.

부모님께서 결혼을 반대하신다면 부모님을 설득하겠어요.
If my parents oppose my marriage, I will convince them not to.

46
소문

[소문] 명사 rumor

[Expression]
헛소문 a false rumor
소문이 돌다 The rumor goes around.
소문이 퍼지다 The rumor spreads.
소문을 내다 to start a rumor
소문으로 듣다 to hear something by rumor

[Example]
영미 씨가 성형수술을 했다는 소문이 있던데 사실인가요?
There is a rumor that says Youngmi had plastic surgery. Do you think it is true?

그 정치인이 뇌물을 받았다는 소문은 근거 없는 헛소문이었다.
The rumor that the politician had taken a bribe is a false rumor without any basis.

47
소용없다

[소용업따] 형용사 to have no effect, to be pointless

[Usage]
N 이/가 소용없다

[Synonym]
쓸데없다 to be useless

[Example]
어머니가 화가 많이 나셔서 빌어도 소용없을 거예요.
My mom is really angry, so even if I beg, it won't make a difference.

지금 5시니까 은행 문을 닫았을 거야. 지금 나가봐야 소용없어.
It's five o'clock now, so the bank probably has already closed. Even if you leave now, to be it's pointless.

48
숙이다

[수기다] 동사 to bow, to incline

to lower something from the front to another side

[Usage] N 을/를 숙이다

[Expression] 고개를 숙이다 to lower one's head
머리를 숙이다 to lower one's head
허리를 숙이다 to bend down at the waist

[Example] 학생들은 선생님을 보자 모두 머리를 숙여 인사했다.
Once the students saw the professor, they all bowed their heads and greeted him.

지하철 안에서 고개를 숙이고 조는 사람들이 많았다.
In the subway, there are a lot of people that lay their heads down and doze off.

49
술자리

[술짜리] 명사 a place where people drink and enjoy themselves or a place where a table with alcohol is set

[Expression] 술자리를 벌이다 to have a drinking party
술자리를 피하다 to avoid drinking places
술자리를 마련하다 to set up a drinking party
술자리에 가다 to go to a bar

[Related Words] 술집 bar, pub

[Example] 술을 좋아하지 않아서 술자리에 잘 가지 않아요.
I don't go too often to bars because I don't like drinking.

술자리 분위기를 좋아해서 친구들과 술을 자주 마시는 편이에요.
Because I like the atmosphere at bars, I tend to go drink there with my friends.

50
신경

[신경] 명사 1. concern, care 2. a nerve in the human body

1. what one feels or thinks about something

[Expression] 신경이 둔하다 to be slow in one's movements, to be insensitive
신경이 날카롭다 to be on edge
신경이 예민하다 to be sensitive/nervous.
신경을 끊다 to not care, to turn off (due to a loss of interest)
신경을 쓰다 to pay attention to, to take an interest in

[Example] 별일 아니니까 신경 쓰지 마세요.
Don't pay attention to it because it is no big deal.

2. nerve ; a structure that is connected like a line that is part of a system where nerve cells are brought together

[Expression] 신경외과 neurosurgery

[Example] 교통사고로 신경을 크게 다쳐서 몸을 전혀 움직이지 못해요.
Due to the accident, I can't move my body at all because I severely damaged some nerves.

51
아무리

[아무리] 부사 1. however, no matter how 2. no matter how

1. even if it is like that

[Example] 아무리 불경기라고 해도 그렇게 많은 직원들이 해고되겠어요?
However bad the recession may be, can so many workers be fired like that?

2. words that describe the serious degree of something.

[Example] 아르바이트를 할 때는 아무리 힘들어도 손님들에게 친절하게 대해야 해요.
When you work a part-time job, no matter how hard it may be, you need to treat the customers kindly.

52
악수

[악쑤] 명사 handshake

the act of two people grabbing hands in order to express a meaning of thanks, greeting, friendship, or reconciliation

[Expression] 악수를 하다 to shake hands
악수를 나누다 to exchange a hand shake
악수를 청하다 to ask for a hand shake

[Example] 보통 남자들은 인사를 나눌 때 악수를 합니다.
Normally, when men greet each other, they shake hands.

오랜만에 만난 두 사람은 서로 악수를 하면서 반갑게 인사했다.
The two people happily greeted each other with a hand shake after not seeing each other for a very long time.

53
안부

[안부] 명사 regards, to inquire about someone's state

[Expression] 안부 인사 a greeting to inquire about someone
안부 전화 a phone call to ask about how someone is doing
안부가 궁금하다 I am curious about how he's doing.
안부를 묻다 to inquire about someone's news
안부를 전하다 to send one's regards

[Example] 미선 씨를 만나거든 안부 전해 주세요.
If you see Miseon, please send her my regards.

오래간만에 고향에 계신 부모님께 안부 전화라도 드려야 겠어요.
I really should check up on my parents that have been living in our hometown for a long time by giving them a phone call.

54
알아듣다

[아라듣따] 동사 to understand

to know the meaning of what others say to you

[Usage] N 을/를 알아듣다

[Expression] 잘 알아듣다 to understand well
못 알아듣다 to not understand
잘못 알아듣다 to not understand well

[Related Words] 알아보다 to recognize, to make out, to identify

[Example] 밍밍 씨의 발음이 부정확해서 알아듣기가 힘들어요.
It is hard to make out what Ming Ming is saying because her pronunciation isn't exact.

할아버지께 전화를 했는데 잘 안 들리셔서 그런지 제 말을 못 알아들으셨어요.
I called up my grandfather, but he wasn't able to understand me because he probably couldn't hear me very well.

55
야유회

[야유회] 명사 excursion, outing, company picnic

[Expression] 야유회에 가다 to go on an excursion
야유회에 참석하다 to participate in an outing

[Example] 스승의 날을 맞이하여 선생님을 모시고 야유회를 가기로 했습니다.
In order to celebrate teacher's day, I decided to take my teacher on an excursion.

지금부터 이번 주말에 갈 야유회 장소와 시간을 결정하도록 합시다.
Let's decide from now the place and time for this weekend's excursion.

56
양보하다

[양보하다] 동사 to yield, to give away

to give a seat, place, or right of way to someone else

[Usage] N 을/를 양보하다

[Expression] 순서를 양보하다 to give up one's spot, to let someone go in front of you
자리를 양보하다 to give up one's seat

[Example] 지하철에서 할머니께 자리를 양보했어요.
I gave up my seat to a grandmother on the subway.

서로 조금씩 양보했더라면 사고가 안 났을 텐데 안타깝네요.
If they had made way for each other, there wouldn't have been an accident. It's quite sad.

57
양해 [양해] 명사 consent, understanding

taking someone else's circumstances into consideration and generously accepting them

[Expression]
양해를 얻다 to obtain consent
양해를 구하다 to seek consent
양해를 바라다 to ask for consideration

[Example]
급한 일이 있으면 사람들한테 양해를 구하고 먼저 가라.
If it is urgent, please ask for people's consent first then go.

집주인에게 집을 구할 때까지 여기에 있게 해 달라고 양해를 구했다.
I asked the house owner for his consent to let me stay here until I find a house.

58
어색하다 [어새카다] 형용사 1. to be awkward 2. to be unfamiliar with

1. to feel out of place and shy

[Usage]
N 이/가 어색하다
AV 기가 어색하다
AV 는 것이 어색하다

[Synonym] 서먹서먹하다 to feel awkward

[Related Words] 쑥스럽다 to feel embarrassed

[Example]
10년 만에 옛날 여자 친구를 만났는데 정말 어색했어요.
It was really awkward meeting my ex-girlfriend after ten years.

2. to not be accustomed with the practices, traditions, or ways and therefore feel unnatural or out of place

[Usage]
N 이/가 어색하다
어색한 N

[Synonym] 서투르다 to be unaccustomed with

[Example]
한국에 와서 오랜만에 운전을 했더니 좀 어색하더군요.
I hadn't driven in a long time until coming to Korea and it felt awkward.

59
여전하다 [여전하다] 형용사 to remain the same, to be unchanged

[Synonym] 그대로이다 to be like before

[Example] 마리아 씨의 테니스 실력은 여전하더군요.
Maria's tennis skills hadn't changed at all.

대학 동창들을 10년 만에 만났는데 다들 여전했어요.
I met my college classmates after ten years without seeing them and they were all just like they had been before.

60
연락처

[열락처] 명사 contact information

a place where someone can leave their contact information

[Expression] 연락처를 적다 to write down one's contact information
연락처를 남기다 to leave one's contact information

[Example] 친구의 연락처를 잊어버렸어요.
I forgot my friend's contact information.

연락처를 남겨 주시면 바로 연락드리겠습니다.
If you leave your contact information, I will get in touch with you right away.

61
예절

[예절] 명사 etiquette

[Expression] 방문 예절 etiquette when making a formal visit
식사 예절 dinner etiquette
예절을 갖추다 to have etiquette
예절을 지키다 to follow etiquette

[Synonym] 예의 manners

[Example] 여러분 나라의 생활 예절은 한국과 어떻게 다릅니까?
How are the everyday manners of your countries different from those of Korea?

다른 사람에게 예절을 지키는 것은 어렸을 때부터 배워야 한다.
One must learn from a young age how to be courteous to others.

62
오랜만

[오랜만] 명사 after a long time

after a long time has passed from the time something had happened

[Synonym] 오래간만 after a long time

[Example] 할머니께서는 오랜만에 우리를 보고 너무 기뻐하셨다.
My grandmother was very happy to see us for the first time in a long time.

오랜만에 갖는 모임이니까 장기 자랑 같은 재미있는 행사가 있으면 좋겠어요.
I think it would be good to have fun events like a talent show since this is the first meeting we are having in a long time.

63
오해

[오해] 동사 to misunderstand

[Expression] 오해하다 to misunderstand
오해를 받다 to be taken as a misunderstanding
오해를 사다 to cause a misunderstanding
오해를 풀다 to solve a misunderstanding

[Example] 영수 씨가 제 말을 오해한 것 같은데 어떻게 하지요?
I think that Youngsoo has misunderstood me. What should I do?

우리 서로 오해를 한 것 같으니까 어디 가서 한잔하면서 오해를 풀어 봅시다.
I think that we have misunderstood each other, so we should go somewhere and try to solve our differences while having a drink.

64
오히려

[오히려] 부사 rather, on the contrary

[Synonym] 도리어 instead

[Related Words] 차라리 rather

[Example] 감기약을 먹고 나서 오히려 몸이 더 안 좋아진 것 같다.
After taking cough medicine, my body didn't feel better. On the contrary, it felt worse.

쓰기 시험이 어려울 줄 알았는데 오히려 말하기 시험이 더 어려웠다.
I was expecting my writing test to be difficult. On the contrary, it was my speaking test that was hard.

65
용서

[용서] 동사 to forgive

[Expression] 용서하다 to forgive
용서를 받다 to be forgiven
용서를 빌다 to pray for forgiveness
용서를 구하다 to seek forgiveness
용서를 바라다 to hope for forgiveness

[Example] 직접 와서 용서를 빈다면 다시 한번 생각해 보겠어.
If he were to come here in person and pray for forgiveness, I would think about it one more time.

다음에는 절대로 약속을 어기지 않을게. 한 번만 용서해 줘.
I swear that I will never break another promise. Please just forgive me this one time.

66
원하다

[원하다] 동사 to desire, to want

[Usage] N 을/를 원하다
AV / DV 기를 원하다

[Synonym] 바라다 to want

[Example] 다른 사람에게 부탁을 할 때 자신이 원하는 것이 무엇인지 분명하게 말해야 한다.
When you ask someone to do you a favor, you need to clearly express what you want.

결혼 정보 회사를 이용하면 본인이 원하는 조건을 갖춘 배우자를 만나기가 쉬워요.
If one uses a marriage agency, it is easy to find a spouse that fulfills the requirements that the individual desires.

67
이해하다

[이해하다] 동사 1. to comprehend, to understand 2. to grasp a concept, idea, or thought

1. to understand

[Usage] N 을/를 이해하다

[Expression] 상황을 이해하다 to comprehend the situation

[Example] 남자 친구가 왜 나에게 거짓말을 했는지 아무리 생각해도 이해할 수가 없다.
No matter how much I think about it, I can't understand why my boyfriend lied to me.

2. to realize and come to know, to accept something due to one's understanding of the situation

[Usage] N 을/를 이해하다

[Expression] 내용을 이해하다 to understand the content

[Example] 읽기는 했지만 무슨 내용인지 너무 어려워서 이해할 수가 없어.
I read it but I can't understand what it means because it is very hard.

68
익숙하다

[익쑤카다] 형용사 1. to be skilled or experienced in 2. to be familiar with

1. to be in a state where one is familiar with something after having done it numerous times

[Usage] 익숙한 N
N 에/에게 익숙하다

[Expression] 익숙한 솜씨 familiar skill

일에 익숙하다 to be experienced in a job

[Synonym] 능숙하다 to be accustomed to

[Antonym] 서투르다 to be unfamiliar with

[Example] 이 공장에서 일한 지 10년 돼서 지금 하는 일에 익숙해요.
I am familiar with the job I am doing at the factory because I have been working here for ten years.

2. to be in a state where one feels like it isn't the first time that they are experiencing or seeing a certain subject

[Usage] N 에/에게 익숙하다
AV 는 데에 익숙하다

[Expression] 한국 생활에 익숙하다 to be familiar with Korean daily life

[Antonym] 낯설다 to be unfamiliar with

[Example] 광고를 보면 우리가 영화나 드라마에서 봤던 익숙한 장면들이 나올 때가 있다.
If you look at an advertisement, there are times where familiar scenes that we have seen before in movies or dramas appear.

69
인상 [인상] 명사 impression

a feeling that is inscribed in one's mind about a certain topic

[Usage] DV 은/ㄴ 인상

[Expression] 첫인상 first impression
인상을 받다 to receive an impression
인상을 주다 to give an impression
인상에 남다 to have an impression of, to be left with an impression

[Example] 새로 오신 사장님의 활짝 웃는 미소가 인상에 남는다.
The bright smile of the new boss left me with a lasting impression.

김 선생님을 처음 만났을 때는 무뚝뚝한 인상을 받았다.
I got a very cold and brusque impression from Mr. Kim when I first met him.

70
잔치 [잔치] 명사 feast, party

an joyful event in which many people come together and prepare food during happy occasions

[Expression] 돌잔치 the first birthday celebration of a baby
회갑잔치 a celebration when one turns 60 years old
생일잔치 birthday feast
잔치를 벌이다 to hold a feast

[Synonym] 파티 party
축제 festival

[Example] 이번 주 토요일에 영수 씨 아들 돌잔치가 있어요.
This Saturday is the first birthday celebration of Youngsoo's baby.

다음 달에 가족과 친지들을 모시고 부모님의 회갑 잔치를 열려고 합니다.
I am planning to gather my family and relatives next month to celebrate the 60th birthday of my parents.

71
전하다

[전하다] 동사 to convey, to send

to let another person know a fact or idea

[Usage] N 을/를 전하다
N 에/에게 전하다

[Expression] 마음을 전하다 to convey one's emotions
소식을 전하다 to send news
안부를 전하다 to send regards

[Example] 고향 친구에게 우리 부모님께 안부를 전해 달라고 부탁했어요.
I asked my friend to send my regards to my parents living in my hometown.

좋아하는 여자에게 마음을 전하고 싶어서 날마다 꽃을 선물해요.
I want to show the girl I like how I feel about her. Therefore, I buy her flowers everyday.

72
참석하다

[참서카다] 동사 to attend a meeting

to take part in an event or meeting

[Usage] N 에 참석하다

[Related Words] 참가하다 to participate
참여하다 to join in

[Example] 내일 신입생을 위한 오리엔테이션이 있으니까 꼭 참석하십시오.
Please attend the orientation tomorrow for the freshman.

바쁘신 중에 제 결혼식에 참석해 주셔서 진심으로 감사드립니다.
I want to truly thank you for taking the time to attend my wedding even while being so busy.

73
쳐다보다

[쳐다보다] 동사 to stare

[Usage] N 을/를 쳐다보다

[Expression] 얼굴을 쳐다보다 to stare at someone's face
힐끔힐끔 쳐다보다 to glance at

[Related Words] 바라보다 to look at

[Example] 기분 나쁘니까 그만 쳐다보세요.
Stop staring at me because you're making me feel bad.

자꾸 저를 힐끔힐끔 쳐다보는 걸 보면 저에게 관심이 있는 게 틀림없어요.
There is no doubt that he is interested in me because he keeps glancing at me.

74
초청장

[초청짱] 명사 invitation card

[Expression] 초청장을 받다 to receive an invitation
초청장을 보내다 to send an invitation
초청장을 발송하다 to send an invitation

[Related Words] 초대장 invitation
청첩장 wedding invitation

[Example] 초청장이 완성됐는데 한번 봐 주실래요?
The invitation card is complete. Could you look at it for me?

파티에 오실 때 초청장을 가지고 오셔야 입장이 가능합니다.
When you come to the party, you must bring the invitation with you in order to enter.

75
추억

[추억] 명사 memories, recollections

[Expression] 옛 추억 old memories
추억하다 to reminisce
추억이 되다 to become a memory
추억을 만들다 to make memories
추억을 떠올리다 to think about a memory

[Related Words] 기억 memory

[Example] 옛날 일을 추억하면 기분이 좋아지지요.
I feel good when I think about old memories.

여행 때 찍은 사진을 보면 아름다운 추억이 떠올라요.
When I look at pictures I took from my trip, beautiful memories come to mind.

76
친근감

[친근감] 명사 a feeling of closeness or friendliness

[Expression] 친근감이 들다 to feel friendly
친근감을 주다 to make one feel friendly

[Related Words] 친밀감 endearment, affinity

[Example] 웨이 씨는 오늘 처음 만난 사람인데도 왠지 친근감이 느껴지더군요.
Even though I met Wei today for the first time, I felt very comfortable around him.

미선이는 웃는 모습이 착해 보여서 누구에게나 친근감을 주는 인상이다.
Since Miseon looks very kind, she gives an impression that makes people feel at ease and close to her.

77
칭찬

[칭찬] 명사 compliment

[Expression]
칭찬하다 to compliment
칭찬을 듣다 to hear compliments
칭찬을 받다 to receive compliments
칭찬을 하다 to give a compliment

[Antonym] 야단 scolding

[Example] 당연히 해야 할 일을 했는데 이렇게 칭찬을 받으니 쑥스러울 뿐입니다.
It was something that I naturally had to do. Therefore, I am just feeling embarrassed that you compliment me like this.

부모끼리 서로 칭찬하는 모습이 아이의 성격에 긍정적인 영향을 미친다고 합니다.
It is said that if parents compliment each other, it has a positive influence on the personality of their child.

78
타이르다

[타이르다] 동사 to reason with, to talk with
to reveal the logic behind a matter so it may be well understood

[Usage]
N 을/를 타이르다
AV 게/도록 타이르다

[Expression]
아이를 타이르다 to reason with a child
잘못을 타이르다 to talk about a mistake
조용히 타이르다 to reason with someone quietly

[Related Words] 설득하다 to persuade

[Example] 아이가 잘못했을 때는 혼내기보다는 좋은 말로 타이르세요.
When a child makes a mistake, in place of scolding him, reason with him using words.

선생님은 학생에게 수업 시간에 핸드폰으로 문자를 하지 말라고 조용히 타이르셨어요.
The teacher talked to the student quietly and told him that he can't send text messages during class.

79
한턱내다

[한턱내다] 동사 to treat someone to a meal or a drink

to invite someone to eat whatever they like

[Usage] N 에게 한턱내다

[Example] 장학금을 받았으니까 한턱내세요.
Please treat us because you were awarded the scholarship.

아들이 좋은 대학교에 합격해서 친구들에게 한턱냈어요.
Since my son got into a good college, I invited my friends out to eat.

80
행동하다

[행동하다] 동사 to act, to behave,

to do something or to moves one's body and take an action

[Usage] N 처럼 행동하다
DV 게 행동하다

[Expression] 침착하게 행동하다 to act calmly

[Example] 내 친구는 우리 집에 오면 주인처럼 행동한다.
When my friend comes to my house, he behaves as if he were the owner.

그런 일일수록 침착하게 행동해야 실수가 없다.
The more that happens, you need to act calmly in order to not make any mistakes.

81
회상

[회상] 명사 recollection

going back and thinking about past actions or the thought of doing so

[Expression] 회상하다 to recall
회상에 잠기다 to be lost in memories

[Example] 한국에서 보낸 지난 1년을 회상해 보니까 후회되는 일이 많네요.
When I reflect on the past year I spent in Korea, there are a lot of things I regret.

아버지는 좋았던 어린 시절을 회상하셨다.
My father counted his own childhood blessings.

82
회식

[회식] 명사 get-together, dinner meeting

the gathering of many people to eat food together (usually people from work)

[Expression] 부서 회식 departmental get-together
회식을 갖다 to hold a get-together
회식을 하다 to have a get-together

[Example] 제 친구 회사는 매주 회식을 한대요.
My friend says that there is an office get-together once a week at her company.
사장님께서 오늘 회식에는 한 사람도 빠지지 말고 참석하라고 하셨어요.
My boss said for no one to miss today's get-together and that we all attend.

83
회원

[회원] 명사 member of a club

[Expression] 정회원 a full-time member
신입 회원 new member
회원 모집 recruitment of new members
회원이 되다 to become a member

[Example] 회원 가입을 하면 10% 할인해 준다고 하니까 먼저 가입부터 하세요.
If you sign up to be a member, they said that they give you a ten percent discount so make sure to sign up.
인터넷 카페에 등록하면 회원들끼리 필요한 정보를 공유할 수 있어서 도움이 돼요.
If you register at the internet café, it is helpful because the members of the club can share necessary information.

84
후회하다

[후회하다] 동사 to regret

[Usage] N 을/를 후회하다
AV 은/ㄴ 것을 후회하다

[Example] 학창 시절에 공부를 열심히 안 한 것을 후회하고 있어요.
I regret the fact that I didn't study very much when I was in school.
회사 생활이 즐겁고 만족스럽기 때문에 이 회사에 취직한 것을 한 번도 후회한 적이 없어요.
I have never regretted getting a job at this company because my daily work life is enjoyable and satisfying.

06 연습문제

[1-16] 다음 단어를 한국어로 바꿔 쓰십시오.

Change the following words into Korean.

1. to be humble ( )
2. to nod ( )
3. conversation ( )
4. to stand up against ( )
5. group date ( )
6. sociability ( )
7. to get along with one another ( )
8. opposing team ( )
9. rumor ( )
10. a place where one drinks ( )
11. hand shake ( )
12. excursion ( )
13. contact information ( )
14. invitation letter ( )
15. sense of closeness ( )
16. get-together ( )

[17-25] [보기]에서 알맞은 단어를 골라 ( ) 안에 쓰십시오.

Choose the appropriate word from the box below and then fill in the parenthesis.

[보기]

도움	미소	아무리	오히려	알아듣다
여전하다	쳐다보다	타이르다	회상하다	

17. 모델 같은 여자가 버스에 타자 버스 안에 있던 모든 사람들이 그 여자를 ( )었다/았다/였다.
18. 어머니는 힘들고 어려운 일이 있어도 항상 얼굴에 ( )을/를 잃지 않으세요.
19. ( ) 친한 친구 사이라고 해도 서로 예의를 지켜야 해요.
20. 한국 친구와 자주 만나서 한국어로 이야기하니까 한국어 말하기에 많이 ( )이/가 되는 것 같아요.
21. 한국 드라마를 자주 봐서 드라마에 나오는 한국말은 들으면 거의 다 ( )을/ㄹ 수 있어요.

22. 식당은 다른 사람들도 있는 곳이니까 시끄럽게 떠들면 안 된다고 아이를 (   )었지만/았지만/였지만 소용없었다.

23. 여자 친구가 약속 시간에 1시간이나 늦게 오고서는 (   ) 저한테 화를 냈어요.

24. 한국어학당을 졸업한 지 10년이 지났는데도 제임스 씨의 한국어 실력은 (   )으시네요/시네요.

25. 지난 토요일에 고등학교 동창들을 만나서 학창 시절을 (   )으며/며 재미있게 얘기했어요.

[26-31] [보기]에서 알맞은 말을 찾아 대화를 완성하십시오.

Complete the conversation with the appropriate word from the box below.

[보기]

예절	말다툼	반하다	오랜만	전하다	용서

26. 가 : 저는 지금까지 남편과 싸운 적이 없어요.

    나 : 부부가 살면서 한 번도 (   )을/를 안 해 봤다는 건 말도 안 되지요.

27. 가 : 어제 소개팅에서 만난 남자한테서 자꾸 만나자고 전화가 와.

    나 : 너한테 첫눈에 (   )었나/았나/였나 봐.

28. 가 : 한국의 식사 (   )을/를 좀 가르쳐 주세요.

    나 : 한국에서는 식사할 때 어른이 식사를 시작한 다음에 아이들이 식사를 해야 하는 것이 예의예요.

29. 가 : 고향에 3년 만에 갔다 오셨다고 들었어요. 가족들은 만나셨어요?

    나 : 네, (   )에 가족들을 만나서 밤새도록 이야기를 했어요.

30. 가 : 자기의 잘못을 알고 진심으로 사과하니까 그만 (   )을/를 해 줘.

    나 : 나도 그러려고 했어.

31. 가 : 오늘 미선 씨를 만나신다면서요? 그때 이 책을 좀 (   )어/아/여 주세요.

    나 : 네, 그럴게요.

[32-36] 다음을 읽고 [보기]에서 알맞은 단어를 골라 쓰십시오.

Read the following definitions and then choose the correct word from the box below.

[보기]

권하다	궁금하다	기대하다	추억하다	후회하다

32. 지나간 일을 생각하다 ······ (　　　　)

33. 관심이 있어 무척 알고 싶어 하다 ······ (　　　　)

34. 어떤 일을 해 보라고 말하다 ······ (　　　　)

35. 어떤 일이 내 생각대로 되기를 바라고 기다리다 ······ (　　　　)

36. 자기가 한 일에 대하여 잘못했다고 생각하다 ······ (　　　　)

[37-39] 다음 밑줄 친 부분과 반대되는 뜻을 가진 것을 고르십시오.

Choose the word that has the opposite meaning from the underlined word.

37. 오늘 부모님이 한국에 오셔서 공항에 <u>마중</u>을 나가야 한다.

❶ 미팅　❷ 회식　❸ 근무　❹ 배웅

38. 입사 초에는 힘들었는데 이제는 회사 생활에 <u>익숙해져서</u> 편하게 지내고 있어요..

❶ 친근하다　❷ 서두르다　❸ 서투르다　❹ 능숙하다

39. 그 사람은 말할 때 좀 <u>잘난 체하는</u> 것 같아요.

❶ 양보하다　❷ 겸손하다　❸ 솔직하다　❹ 까다롭다

[40-46] [보기]에서 알맞은 말을 찾아 대화를 완성하십시오.

Complete the conversation with the appropriate word from the box below.

[보기]

볼일	안부	잔치	대하다	원하다	데려가다	상관없다

40. 가 : 죄송해요. 조금 늦을 것 같아요.

    나 : 조금 늦어도 (   )으니까/니까 너무 서두르지 마세요.

41. 가 : 상담을 받으려면 어떻게 해야 합니까?

    나 : 상담 신청서에 (   )는/은/ㄴ 시간과 상담 내용을 적어서 제출하시면 됩니다.

42. 가 : 유리 씨 하숙집 아주머니가 친절하게 잘 (   )어/아/여 주신다면서요?

    나 : 네, 아주머니가 얼마나 좋으신지 몰라요.

43. 가 : 어제 동대문 시장에 가서 쇼핑했어.

    나 : 나도 동대문 시장에 가고 싶었는데 왜 나한테 얘기 안 했어?
    다음에는 나도 꼭 (   )어/아/여 줘. 알았지?

44. 가 : 지난주에 뭘 했어요?

    나 : 할아버지 회갑 (   )이/가 있어서 할아버지 댁에 다녀왔어요.

45. 가 : 갑자기 급한 (   )이/가 생겨서 모임에 늦을 같아요.

    나 : 얼마나 늦으실 것 같은데요?

46. 가 : 아니, 이게 누구야? 오랜만이구나.

    나 : 선생님께 한동안 연락을 못 드려서 (   ) 전화 드렸어요.

[47-55] [보기]에서 알맞은 단어를 골라 (   ) 안에 쓰십시오.

Choose appropriate word from the box below and then fill in the parenthesis.

[보기]

대화	분위기	숙이다	개인적이다	돌려주다
참석하다	한턱내다	행동하다	이해하다	

47. 봄이 돼서 커튼을 노란색으로 바꿨더니 집안 ( )이/가 달라졌어요.

48. 한국에서는 아랫사람이 웃어른에게 인사를 할 때 고개와 허리를 ( )으며/며 인사해야 해요.

49. 죄송합니다만 지금 사장님은 부장님과 ( )중이시라 전화를 받으실 수 없습니다.

50. 그 인형은 네 것이 아니고 동생 것이니까 동생에게 ( )어라/아라/여라.

51. 목요일 오전 10시에 회의가 있으니까 모두 꼭 ( )어/아/여 주십시오.

52. 부장님이 이번 일을 성공적으로 잘 끝내면 삼겹살집에서 ( )으신다고/신다고 했어요.

53. 어떤 문제가 생기더라도 긴장하지 말고 침착하게 ( )으면/면 실수 없이 문제를 해결할 수 있을 거예요.

54. 외국인들에게 몇 살이냐, 결혼은 했느냐는 등 ( )인 질문을 너무 많이 하는 것은 실례예요.

55. 그 문법은 너무 어려워서 ( )기가 어려워요.

[56-57] **다음 ( )에 공통적으로 들어갈 단어를 쓰십시오.**

Write one word that can commonly fit into the parenthesis below.

56.
❶ 교통사고로 ( )을/를 다쳐서 몸을 전혀 움직일 수가 없어요.
❷ 데이트하러 갈 때는 옷은 물론 머리에도 ( )이/가 많이 쓰여요.
❸ 회사에 문제가 생겨서 ( )을/를 너무 썼더니 머리가 너무 아프네요.

( )

57.
❶ 친구가 퀴즈의 답을 다른 사람들이 모르게 나에게만 ( ) 알려 줬어요.
❷ 맥주 한 잔을 마신 친구의 얼굴이 ( ) 붉어졌다.
❸ 동창회에 갔다가 너무 피곤해서 ( ) 빠져나왔어요.

( )

[58-61] 다음 (　　　)에 공통적으로 들어갈 단어의 기본형을 쓰십시오.
Write the basic form of one word that can commonly fit in the parenthesis below.

58.
❶ 어머니는 케이크를 잘라서 아이들에게 똑같이 (　　　　　)어/아/여 주었다.
❷ 오랜만에 만난 친구랑 밤새도록 긴 이야기를 (　　　　　)었다/았다/였다.
❸ 그 식당 음식은 양이 많아서 삼계탕 하나를 시켜서 친구와 둘이 (　　　　　)어서/아서/여서 먹었어요.

(　　　　　　　　)

59.
❶ 마더 테레사는 평생 아프고 가난한 사람들을 (　　　　　)으면서/면서 살았어요.
❷ 아버지도 연세가 드셨으니까 무리하지 마시고 이제는 건강을 (　　　　　)으셔야/셔야 해요.
❸ 힘들기는 하지만 집안일을 하고 아이들을 (　　　　　)는/은/ㄴ 일은 보람있는 일이에요.

(　　　　　　　　)

60.
❶ 오래간만에 치마를 입으니까 (　　　　　)네요.
❷ 어제 커피숍에서 소개팅을 했는데 할 말이 없어서 무척 (　　　　　)었어요/았어요/였어요.
❸ 친구랑 싸우고 나서 한동안 안 만나다가 어제 오랜만에 만났더니 조금 (　　　　　)었어요/았어요/였어요.

(　　　　　　　　)

61.
❶ 오랫동안 연락이 (　　　　　)었던/았던/였던 친구와 연락이 돼서 너무 반가웠어요.
❷ 부모님과 통화하고 싶어서 고향에 전화를 했는데 계속 연결이 안 되고 자꾸 (　　　　　)네요.
❸ 정치적인 문제로 양국의 관계가 나빠져서 교류가 (　　　　　)으면/면 안 됩니다.

(　　　　　　　　)

[62-70] [보기]에서 알맞은 단어를 골라(　　　) 안에 쓰십시오.

Choose appropriate word from the box below and then fill in the parenthesis.

[보기]

기억	비밀	거짓말	그립다	끼치다
공경하다	무시하다	바라보다	소용없다	

62. 이건 너와 나, 둘만 아는 (　　　　　　　)이야/야. 절대로 다른 사람한테 말하면 안 돼.

63. 친구가 만나자고 전화를 했는데 밖에 나가기 귀찮아서 몸이 좀 아프다고 (　　　　　　　)을/를 했다.

64. 젊은이들은 항상 웃어른에게 (　　　　　　　)는/은/ㄴ 마음을 가져야 한다.

65. 고향 음식을 먹으니까 고향에 있는 가족이 더욱 (　　　　　　　)어지네요/아지네요/여지네요.

66. 그 뮤지컬의 마지막 장면은 인상적이어서 아직까지도 지워지지 않고 제 (　　　　　　　)에 남아 있어요.

67. 건물 공사로 통행하시는 분들께 불편을 (　　　　　　　)어서/아서/여서 죄송합니다.

68. 내가 친구에게 인사를 했는데 친구는 내 인사를 (　　　　　　　)고 그냥 가 버렸다.

69. 어머니께서 내가 밥 먹는 모습을 따뜻한 눈빛으로 (　　　　　　　)으셨다/셨다.

70. 아무리 능력이 많아도 그 능력을 제대로 쓰지 않으면 아무 (　　　　　　　)는다고/ㄴ다고/다고 생각해.

[71-78] 다음 [보기]에서 알맞은 단어를 골라 이야기를 완성하십시오.

Choose the right word from the box below and complete the story.

[보기]

농담	인상	회원	낯설다
모이다	가입하다	고백하다	거절하다

나는 등산을 좋아해서 등산 동호회에 71. (　　　　　　　)었다/았다/였다. 등산

동호회의 72.(   )은/는 총 20명 정도 되는데 지금부터 동호회 친구들을 소개하고자 한다. 먼저 은행에 다니고 있는 민수 씨이다. 처음에 민수 씨를 보고는 무뚝뚝하다는 73.(   )을/를 받았는데 사귀어 보니까 아주 재미있는 사람이었다. 그리고 대학원생인 은영 씨는 처음 만났을 때는 수줍어하고 나를 무척 74.(   )어/아/여 했다. 하지만 지금은 많이 친해져서 잘 웃고 가끔은 재미있는 75.(   )을/를 하기도 한다.

이건 비밀인데 민수 씨는 은영 씨를 혼자 좋아한다. 하지만 민수 씨는 소극적인 성격이라서 아직 은영 씨에게 좋아한다고 76.(   )지 못 했다. 민수 씨는 은영 씨가 데이트 신청을 77.(   )을까/ㄹ까 봐 데이트 신청을 하지 못한다고 한다. 우리는 내일도 등산을 간다. 내일은 아침 7시에 신촌 지하철역 앞에서 78.(   )기로 했다. 즐거운 시간을 보냈으면 좋겠다.

학교와 수업

07

School and Class

07 학교와 수업

01
각자

[각짜] 부사 each, separate

separately or apart

[Related Words] 각각 respectively, each

[Example] 각자 자신의 의견을 말씀해 주십시오.
Please share your own opinion.

오늘 저녁 식사 값은 각자 부담하도록 합시다.
Let's split tonight's dinner bill so that each person pays for your own food.

02
강조하다

[강조하다] 동사 to emphasize

[Usage] N 을/를 강조하다

[Example] 어머니는 아이들에게 저축의 필요성을 늘 강조하신다.
The mother always emphasizes the importance of saving money to her children.

선생님께서 이 문법이 아주 중요하다고 몇 번이나 강조하셨어요.
Our teacher emphasized a number of times that this grammar is very important.

03
거의

[거의] [거이] 부사 almost

[Synonym] 대부분 a large part, mostly

[Example] 민수는 시험만 보면 거의 100점을 맞아요.
Whenener Minsoo takes a test, he almost always gets a perfect score.

세계 여러 나라의 우표를 거의 5,000장 정도 모았어요.
I gathered almost 5000 stamps from various countries around the world.

04
게다가

[게다가] 부사 besides, furthermore

[Synonym] 거기다 moreover
거기다가 furthermore

[Example] 민수는 공부도 잘하고 게다가 성격도 좋아서 인기가 많아요.
Minsoo is popular because he studies hard and also has a nice personality.

어렸을 때는 친구들과 이야기도 나누고 책도 서로 빌려봤다. 게다가 음식도 나누어 먹었다.
When I was younger, my friends and I would talk to each other, share books with each other. and even share food with each other.

05
겨우

[겨우] 부사 1. barely, narrowly 2. only, no more than

1. [Synonym] 가까스로 narrowly
간신히 barely

[Example] 낮에는 아르바이트를 하고 밤에는 학교를 다니면서 겨우 고등학교를 졸업했습니다.
I barely was able to graduate from high school by working a part time job in the mornings and attending school in the evenings.

2. [Synonym] 고작 at most, no more than

[Example] 친구가 너무 바빠서 겨우 전화통화만 할 뿐이에요.
My friend is very busy so he can only speak on the phone.

06
굉장히

[굉장히] 부사 extremely, greatly

[Related Words] 대단히 greatly
매우 extremely
몹시 extremely
무척 quite
아주 very

[Example] 이번 시험이 굉장히 어려웠다고 하더군요.
People were saying that this test was extremely difficult.

이번에 응시한 사람이 굉장히 많아서 합격하기가 어렵다던데요.
It was said that since there were so many people that applied this time, it was very difficult to be accepted.

07
규칙

[규칙] 명사 rule, regulation

[Expression] 규칙을 어기다 to break the rules
규칙을 정하다 to decide the rules
규칙을 지키다 to follow the rules

[Related Words] 규정 stipulation

[Example] 기숙사 규칙을 어기지 않도록 하세요.
Please refrain from breaking the dormitory rules.

교통 규칙을 잘 지켜야지 그렇지 않으면 사고가 나기 쉬워요.
You need to follow the traffic regulations. If not, it is very likely for an accident to occur.

08
그다지

[그다지] 부사 1. not very, much 2. so

1. to a certain degree or amount in negative phrases

[Related Words] 그렇게 like that

그리 so

[Example] 한국어는 그다지 어려운 언어가 아니에요.

Korean isn't that difficult of a language.

2. when describing a certain extent in shock or surprise in interrogative phrases

[Related Words] 그렇게 so

그리 so

[Example] 넌 무슨 걱정이 그다지 많니? 항상 걱정만 하는 것 같아

Why are you worrying so much? It seems like you are always worrying.

09
글

[글] 명사 writing

[Expression] 글씨 handwriting

글자 letters

글재주 writing talent

글을 쓰다 to write a piece of writing

글을 읽다 to read words

[Example] "언어 교환 친구를 구해요." 이 글을 보시고 관심 있는 분들은 연락 주세요.

Please contact me if you are interested in the following: "I'm looking for a language exchange partner."

요즘은 아무리 멀리 있어도 얼굴을 보면서 음성으로 또는 글로 하고 싶은 말을 주고 받을 수 있어요.

Nowadays, no matter how far apart you are, you can share what you have to say through words or sounds while looking at a person's face.

10
깜빡

[깜빡] 부사 1. to flicker, to flash 2. to blink 3. to suddenly forget

1. the sudden brightening and darkening or a light or fire

[Related Words] 깜빡거리다 to flicker

[Example] 무슨 문제가 있는지 전등이 깜빡거렸다.

For some reason the lamp was flickering.

2. to blink one*s eyes

[Related Words] 깜빡거리다 to blink

[Example] 눈에 뭐가 들어갔는지 친구는 계속 눈을 깜빡거렸어요.
My friend kept blinking his eye because he probably had something in it.

3. to suddenly forget

[Expression] 깜빡 잊어버리다 to slip one's mind

[Related Words] 깜빡하다 to suddenly forget

[Example] 아침에 급하게 나오느라고 지갑을 가지고 나오는 것을 깜빡 잊었어요.
I forgot to take my wallet with me because I was in a rush this morning.

11
나날이

[나나리] 부사 day by day

[Example] 과학 기술이 나날이 발전하고 있다.
Science technology is developing day by day.

요즘 언어 교환을 해서 그런지 한국어 실력이 나날이 늘고 있어요.
My Korean language abilities are getting better day by day most likely because of the a language exchange I've been doing nowadays.

12
나머지[1]

[나머지] 명사 remainder

[Expression] 나머지 부분 remaining part

[Related Words] 몫 share

[Example] 7을 2로 나누면 몫이 3이고 나머지가 1이다.
If you divide seven by two, the quotient is three and the remainder is one.

수학에서 나누어서 나머지가 없을 때를 나누어 떨어졌다고 해요.
In math, it is said that when there is no remainder after dividing, it has been divided equally.

13
내용

[내용] 명사 1. content 2. summary of a piece of writing

1. content, meaning

[Expression] 내용이 쉽다 The content is easy.
내용이 좋다 The content is good.
내용이 복잡하다 The content is complicated.
내용을 바꾸다 to change the content

[Antonym] 형식 form

[Related Words] 뜻 meaning

[Example] 아무리 내용이 좋아도 형식이 올바르지 않으면 좋은 평가를 받기 어려워요.
No matter how good the content is, if the form isn't correct, it is difficult to get good reviews.

2. the synopsis or summary of a writing, play, words, or picture

[Expression] 내용 이해 understanding of the content
내용 파악 grasping of the content

[Example] 영화를 보기 전에 내용을 미리 알면 재미가 없지요.
It's no fun knowing the content of a movie in advance before watching it.

14
다행히

[다행히] 부사 fortunately

[Example] 시험 때문에 걱정을 많이 했는데 다행히 시험이 쉬웠어요.
I was really worried about my test, but fortunately it was easy.

늦게 일어났지만 택시를 타고 와서 다행히 제시간에 도착할 수 있었습니다.
I woke up late but since I took a taxi, luckily I was able to arrive on time.

15
떠들다

[떠들다] 동사 to make noise

[Usage] N 이/가 떠들다

[Example] 여러분, 떠들지 말고 모두 조용히 하십시오.
Everyone, please don't make noise and be very quiet.

선생님께서 떠드는 사람의 이름을 칠판에 적으라고 하셨어.
The teacher said to write down the names of people that are making noise on the blackboard.

16
마음대로

[마음대로] 부사 as one desires or wants

[Synonym] 맘대로 as one likes

[Example] 결혼하든 말든 네 마음대로 해라.
It's up to you to decide whether you get married or not.

여기서는 마음대로 행동하면 안 돼요.
Here you can't act as you wish.

17
마치

[마치] 부사 as if

usually followed by the phrases '처럼', '듯', '듯이' and means very similar to or closely resembling

[Usage] 마치 N처럼
마치 AV / DV 는/은/ㄴ 것처럼

[Example] 오늘은 학생들이 마치 약속을 한 것처럼 수업에 늦게 왔어요.
Today the students arrived to class late as if they had all agreed to do so.

하숙집 아주머니가 저를 잘 챙겨 주셔서 마치 고향에 계신 어머니 같아요.
My boarding house lady takes good care of me so it feels as if she were my mom that lives in the countryside.

18
마침내

[마침내] 부사 in the end, finally, at last

[Related Words] 끝내 in the end

[Example] 마침내 교과서를 모두 공부했습니다.
I ended up studying the entire textbook.

옆집 부부가 그렇게 고생하면서 돈을 모으더니 마침내 집을 장만했대요.
The next door neighbors suffered a lot of hardships and after saving up some money, they were finally able to purchase a house.

19
맞다

[맏따] 동사 1. to answer a question correctly 2. to get certain score 3. to welcome, to greet 4. to undergo a bad experience 5. to get a shot

1. to be correct, to be right

[Usage] N 이/가 맞다

[Expression] 답이 맞다 The answer is correct.

[Synonym] 옳다 to be right

[Antonym] 틀리다 to be wrong

[Example] 그 답이 맞는지 더 생각해 보십시오.
Please try thinking if that answer is correct

2. to receive a score

[Usage] N 을/를 맞다

[Expression] 100점을 맞다
to receive a score 100 on a test

[Synonym] 받다 to receive

[Example] 민수는 이번 시험에서도 100점을 맞았대요.
They said that Minsoo also got a 100 on this test.

3. to greet, to welcome

[Usage] N 을/를 맞다

[Expression] 손님을 맞다 to welcome a guest
새해를 맞다 to welcome the new year
명절을 맞다 to celebrate a holiday

[Example] 오전에는 손님 맞을 준비로 정신없이 바빴어요.
I was so busy this morning in preparing to welcome my guest.

4. to suffer a bad event or experience

[Usage] N 을/를 맞다

[Expression] 매를 맞다 to be beaten
야단을 맞다 to be scolded

[Example] 시험을 못 봤다고 부모님한테 야단을 맞은 적이 있습니까?
Have you ever been scolded by your parents for getting a bad grade on a test?

5. to be pricked with a needle when getting a shot

[Usage] N 을/를 맞다

[Expression] 주사를 맞다 to get a shot
침을 맞다 to get acupuncture

[Example] 감기가 너무 심하면 병원에 가서 주사를 맞으세요.
If your cold is very serious, please go to the hospital and get a shot.

20
맞추다[1]

[맏추다] 동사 to check, to compare, to set

[Usage] N 을/를 맞추다

[Expression] 정답을 맞추다 to give the correct answer
일정을 맞추다 to compare schedules

[Example] 시험이 끝나자마자 친구들과 답을 맞춰 보았다.
As soon as the test was over, I checked my answers with my friends.

동료들과의 일정을 맞추어 보고 다음 주 회의 날짜를 정했다.
We compared our schedules with our colleagues and then chose a date for the meeting.

21
미리

[미리] 부사 in advance

[Example] 나가기 전에 미리 상을 차려 놓았어요.
I set the table before going out.

아침에 가방을 챙기지 말고 자기 전에 미리 챙겨 놓도록 해.
Don't pack your bag in the morning. Pack it in advance before going to bed the night before.

22
반드시

[반드시] 부사 without a doubt

[Synonym] 꼭 definitely
틀림없이 surely

[Example] 기숙사에 들어가려면 직원과 학생 모두 반드시 출입증이 있어야 합니다.
If you want to go in the dormitory, all students and employees must have an ID card.

수영 전에는 반드시 준비운동을 해야지 그렇지 않으면 쥐가 날 수가 있습니다.
Before swimming, you definitely need to warm up your body. If not, it's possible that you can get cramps.

23
반복하다

[반보카다] 동사 to repeat

[Usage] N 을/를 반복하다

[Expression] 말을 반복하다 to say the same thing over and over again

[Related Words] 중복하다 to duplicate

[Example] 저는 술만 마시면 같은 말을 계속 반복해요.
When I drink alcohol, I repeat myself a lot.

이해하지 못하는 것 같아서 반복해서 설명을 해 줬어요.
I repeated the explanation one more time because it seemed like he didn't understand me.

24
반장

[반장] 명사 class president

[Related Words] 부반장 class vice-president
회장 club president

[Example] 민수는 중학교 때 반장이었습니다.
Minsoo was the class president in middle school.

내일 반장 모임에 모두 빠짐없이 참석해 주십시오.
Make sure that you all attend the class president meeting tomorrow.

25
밤새다

[밤새다] 동사 to stay up all night

[Usage] N 이/가 밤새다
밤새도록 AV

[Example] 오늘 시험이어서 어제 밤새워서 공부했어요.
I stayed up all night studying yesterday because I had a test today.

오랜만에 친구들을 만나면 밤새도록 이야기하곤 해요.
When I meet up with friends I haven't seen in a while, I usually spend all night talking to them.

26
번역하다

[버녀카다] 동사 to translate

[Usage] N 을/를 번역하다
N 을/를 N 으로/로 번역하다

[Expression] 책을 번역하다 to translate a book
중국어로 번역하다 to translate into Chinese

[Related Words] 통역하다 to interpret

[Example] 한국말 중에는 번역하기 어려운 말이 많습니다.
There are a lot of words that are hard to translate in Korean.

미선 씨가 영어를 잘 하니까 미선 씨에게 번역을 부탁해 보세요.
Please ask Miseon to translate for you because she speaks English well.

27
복사하다

[복싸하다] 동사 to make a photocopy

[Usage] N 을/를 복사하다

[Related Words] 베끼다 to copy

[Example] 이 서류를 복사해서 회의 때 나눠 주세요.
Please make a photocopy of this document and give it out at the meeting.

복사하러 가는데 친구가 부탁해서 친구 것도 복사해다가 줬다.
I was on my way to make a photocopy when my friend asked me to photocopy his paper too, so I did it and gave it to him.

28
불만

[불만] 명사 complaint, dissatisfaction

[Expression] 불만이 생기다 There is a complaint.
불만이 쌓이다 The dissatisfaction builds up.
불만을 가지다 to take grievance
불만에 차다 to be full of dissatisfaction

[Antonym] 만족 satisfaction

[Related Words] 불평 complaint

[Example] 상대방의 의견을 무시하면 점점 불만이 쌓이게 된다.
If you ignore other people's opinions, they may become more and more dissatisfied.

회식 장소를 정할 때 어떻게 해야 사람들의 불만이 없을까요?
When choosing a place for the business meeting, what can we do to make sure there that everyone is satisfied?

29
빠뜨리다

[빠뜨리다] 동사 1.to drop and lose 2. to drop in water 3. to fall into a hard situation

1. to carelessly drop something and lose it

[Usage] N 을/를 빠뜨리다

[Related Words] 흘리다 to drop
잃어버리다 to lose

[Example] 시험 보러 오실 때 수험표를 빠뜨리지 말고 꼭 가지고 오세요.
Please do not lose your test slip when coming to take the test.

2. to drop something into water

[Usage] N 을/를 N 에 빠뜨리다

[Expression] 물에 빠뜨리다 to drop into water

[Related Words] 빠지다 to drop

[Example] 가방을 강물에 빠뜨리고 말았어요.
I dropped my bag into the river.

3. to find oneself in a difficult situation

[Usage] N 을/를 N 에 빠뜨리다

[Example] 경쟁 회사가 우리 회사를 어려움에 빠뜨렸어요.
Our competitors put our company into hardship.

30
빼다

[빼다] 동사 1. to take out 2. to subtract

1. to take out

[Usage] N 을/를 빼다
N 에서 N 을/를 빼다

[Related Words] 뽑다 to pick

[Example] 책꽂이에서 원하시는 책을 빼시면 돼요.
Please take out the book you want from the bookshelf.

2. to subtract

[Usage] N 을/를 빼다
N 에서 N 을/를 빼다

[Related Words] 곱하다 to multiply
나누다 to divide
더하다 to add

[Example] 4에서 3을 빼면 1이 남는다.
If you subtract three from four, the result is one.

31
상담하다

[상담하다] 동사 to advise, to counsel

[Usage] N 이/가 상담하다
N 과/와 상담하다

[Related Words] 상의하다 to consult

[Example] 문제가 생기면 선생님과 먼저 상담하세요.
If a problem arises, please go seek counseling from your professor first.

이 곳은 해외 유학을 전문으로 상담하는 곳입니다.
This is a place that specializes in advising for study abroad.

32
설마

[설마] 부사 don't tell me that, it's not possible that.

this word is used to emphasize a guess or supposition in a negative interrogative statement

[Example] 정직하기로 소문난 김 부장님이 설마 그런 거짓말을 하셨겠어?
Is it true that manager Kim, known for being so honest, really has lied like that?

시험공부를 그렇게 열심히 했는데 설마 떨어진 건 아니겠지요?
You studied so hard for that test. Don't tell me that you failed?

33
성적

[성적] 명사 school grades

[Expression] 성적이 좋다 My grades are good.
성적이 오르다 My grades have gone up.
성적이 떨어지다 My grades have fallen.

[Related Words] 점수 scores

[Example] 기말시험 성적이 지난 중간시험 때보다 많이 올랐네요.
Your final test scores went up a lot from the time of your midterm.

이번 학기에는 공부를 안 해서 성적이 많이 떨어졌어요.
My grades fell a lot this semester because I didn't study that much.

34
스스로

[스스로] 부사 by myself, on my own

[Example] 스스로 할 수 있는 일을 남에게 미루지 마라.
Don't put the responsibility on others for things that you can do yourself.

누구나 스스로 공부하는 습관을 길러야 한다.
Everyone has to develop their own personal studying habits.

35
신청하다

[신청하다] 동사 to apply, to request

[Usage] N 을/를 신청하다

[Example] 동호회에 가입하려면 인터넷 홈페이지에 들어가서 신청하세요.
If you want to join the club, you need to go on the website and apply.

먼저 학교 상담실에 상담을 신청한 후에 약속한 날짜에 상담실에 가서 선생님을 만나면 돼요.
After first applying for a counseling appointment in the school counseling office, please go meet the professor on the indicated date in the office.

36
알맞다

[알맏따] 형용사 to be appropriate, to be suitable, to be proper

[Usage] N 이/가 알맞다

[Related Words] 적당하다 to be appropriate
적합하다 to be suiting

[Example] 빈칸에 알맞은 단어를 찾아 쓰십시오.
Please fill in the blank with the appropriate word.

빈대떡이 알맞게 익었을 때 뒤집어 주세요.
Please flip over the bindaeteok after it is adequately cooked.

37
야단맞다

[야단맏따] 동사 to be scolded

[Usage] N 이/가 N 에/에게 야단맞다

[Synonym] 혼나다 to get in trouble
꾸중듣다 to be reproached

[Antonym] 칭찬받다 to be complimented

[Example] 숙제를 안 해서 선생님께 야단맞았어요.
I was scolded by my professor because I didn't do my homework.

사실대로 말하면 야단맞을까 봐 거짓말을 했습니다.
To be honest, I lied because I was afraid of being scolded.

38
어울리다

[어울리다] 동사 to get along well with, to mingle, to associate with

[Usage] N 과/와 어울리다

[Expression] 친구들과 어울리다 to get along well with one's friends
어울려 놀다 to come together and hang out
어울려 다니다 to go around together

[Example] 저는 대학교 때 동아리 활동을 하면서 선후배들과 자주 어울렸어요.
During college, I often met up with other seniors and juniors while participating in club activities.

제 성격이 지나치게 내성적이라서 친구들과 만나도 잘 어울리지 못해요.
I am an overly introverted person so even though I meet up with my friends, we don't mingle very well together.

39
억양

[어걍] 명사 intonation

[Expression] 억양이 부자연스럽다 The intonation is unnatural.

[Related Words] 발음 pronunciation
어투 manner of speaking

[Example] 그 학생은 발음은 좋은데 억양이 자연스럽지 않은 것이 문제예요.
That student has a good pronunciation but the problem is that his intonation isn't natural.

요즘 독일어를 공부하고 있는데 발음과 억양이 너무 어렵던데요.
Nowadays, I've been studying German but the pronunciation and the intonation have been very difficult for me.

40
언어 교환

[어너 교환] 명사 language exchange

[Expression] 언어 교환을 하다 to do a language exchange

[Example] 중국어를 다시 배우고 싶은데 우리 언어 교환 할까요?
I want to learn Chinese again. Do you want to do a language exchange?

한국 친구와 나는 언어 교환을 통해 서로 말하기 실력이 많이 늘었다.
My Korean friend and I have both improved our language skills through a language exchange.

41
얼른

[얼른] 부사 quickly, swiftly

[Related Words] 곧바로 right away

[Example] 어두워졌으니까 얼른 가자.
Let's go quickly because it's gotten dark.

선생님이 묻는 말에 나는 얼른 대답했다.
I quickly responded to what my teacher asked me.

42
옳다

[올타] 형용사 to be right, to be correct

[Usage] N 이/가 옳다

[Synonym] 바르다 to be proper

[Antonym] 틀리다 to be wrong

[Example] 네 말이 옳았어.
You were right.

제 판단이나 행동이 옳은 것인지 잘 모르겠어요.
I don't know if my judgment or actions are right.

43
외우다

[외우다] 동사 to memorize

[Usage] N 을/를 외우다

[Synonym] 암기하다 to learn by heart

[Related Words] 기억하다 to remember

[Example] 교과서에 있는 대화를 외우십시오.
Please memorize the dialogue in the textbook.

여러분은 외우고 있는 한국 노래가 있습니까?
Are there any Korean songs that you have memorized?

44
의미

[의미] 명사 meaning

[Expression] 의미가 있다 It is meaningful.
의미를 나타내다 to express the meaning
의미를 설명하다 to explain the meaning

[Synonym] 뜻 meaning

[Example] '인생에서 성공했다'는 말은 무슨 의미일까요?
What could "I was successful in life" possibly mean?

정부 투자라는 것은 정부가 공공사업을 위해 지출하는 경비를 의미한다.
Government investing means that the government expends costs for public works.

45
이상

[이상] 명사 being more than or greater than

[Related Words] 이하 less than
초과 surplus, excess
미만 under, less than

[Example] 친구를 1시간 이상 기다리게 한 적이 있어요?
Have you ever made a friend wait for over one hour?

시험에서 60점 이상만 받으면 진급할 수 있어요.
You can only advance to the next level if you receive over a score of 60 on the exam.

46
이유

[이유] 명사 reason

[Expression] 이유가 있다 There is a reason.
이유를 묻다 to ask the reason
이유를 따지다 to inquire about a reason, to ask about a reason

[Related Words] 까닭 reason

[Example] 아이가 잘못했을 때에는 그 이유를 분명히 말해 주고 야단을 쳐야 한다.
When a child makes a mistake, you must clearly tell him the reason and punish him.

영수가 여자들한테 인기가 많은 이유는 잘생긴 데다가 매너도 좋아서이다.
Yeongsoo is very popular with the ladies not only because he is good looking but also because he has good manners.

47
적다

[적따] 동사 to write down

[Usage] N 을/를 적다

[Expression] 답을 적다 to write down an answer
이름을 적다 to write down a name
주소를 적다 to write down an address
전화번호를 적다 to write down a phone number

[Related Words] 쓰다 to write

[Example] 옆에 있는 답안지에 답을 적으세요.
Please write down the answer on the answer sheet next to it.

신청서에 이름과 주소 그리고 전화번호를 적어 주세요.
Please write down your name, address, and phone number on the application form.

48
접수하다

[접쑤하다] 동사 to receive, to accept applications

[Usage] N 을/를 접수하다

[Expression] 원서를 접수하다 to receive an application

[Related Words] 신청하다 to apply
등록하다 to register

[Example] 서류를 다 작성한 후에 창구에서 접수하세요.
After filling out the document, please turn it in at the window.

먼저 입학 원서를 접수하고 입학시험을 봐야 해요.
First, I need to submit the entrance exam paperwork. Then, I must take the test.

49
정도

[정도] 명사 1. to the point that 2. around, about (time)

1. [Example] 이 문제는 중학생도 풀 수 있을 정도로 쉬운 거잖아.
This question so easy that a middle school student could solve it.

2. [Usage] N 정도

[Related Words] 쯤 around, about

[Example] 그곳은 차로 10분 정도 가면 도착할 수 있어요.
You can arrive there if you go about ten minutes in car.

50
정확하다

[정화카다] 형용사 to be exact, to be accurate

[Usage] N 이/가 정확하다

[Antonym] 부정확하다 to be inaccurate

[Example] 계산이 정확한지 확인해 보세요.
Please check to see if the bill is accurate.

우리 반에서 누가 발음이 제일 분명하고 정확하다고 생각합니까?
Who do you think has the most accurate and clear pronunciation out of the students in our class?

51
제목

[제목] 명사 title

[Expression] 제목을 정하다 to decide a title

[Example] 졸업할 때 쓴 논문의 제목이 뭐예요?
What is the title of the thesis that you wrote then you graduated?

지난번에 우리가 같이 봤던 영화 제목이 생각이 안 나.
I don't remember the title of the movie that we saw last time together.

52
종일

[종일] 명사 a whole day

[Expression] 하루 종일 all day long

[Synonym] 온종일 all day long

[Example] 어제는 하루 종일 밀린 숙제를 하느라고 고생했어요.
I went through a lot of trouble yesterday finishing up my homework that had piled up.

병원에 갔다 왔더니 너무 피곤해서 종일 푹 쉬었어요.
After going to the hospital, I was very tired so I rested all day long.

53
주제

[주제] 명사 1. subject, topic 2. theme

1. **[Expression]** 주제 발표 presentation of a topic
주제를 정하다 to choose a topic

[Example] 논문 주제도 정하고 순서도 정했으니까 기본 준비는 끝낸 셈이에요.
Since I have chosen the thesis topic and order, it seems like the basic preparations are done.

2. **[Expression]** 작품의 주제 theme of a piece of art

[Example] 이번 작품의 주제는 사랑입니다.
The theme of this piece of art is love.

54
진학

[진학] 명사 to enter school, to go on to school

[Expression] 진학 상담 consultation about choosing a school to attend
진학 지도 consultation about what school to go to
진학하다 to go on to school

[Example] 대학원에 진학했다면서? 공부는 잘 하고 있지?
I heard that you entered graduate school? You are studying hard, right?

사촌 동생은 집안 형편이 어려워서 대학에 진학하지 못했다.
My younger cousin wasn't able to continue his education by going to college due to hard family circumstances.

55
집중하다

[집쭝하다] 동사 to concentrate

[Usage] N 을/를 집중하다

[Expression] 시선을 집중하다 to focus one's look
주의를 집중하다 to focus one's attention
정신을 집중하다 to focus one's mind

[Example] 취미로 악기를 배우고 있는데 집중해서 연주하다 보면 스트레스가 풀려요.
I am learning how to play an instrument as a hobby. I realized that if I concentrate and play the instrument, I am able to lower my stress.

스트레스가 많은 현대인들에게는 편안한 분위기에서 조용한 음악을 들으며 정신을 집중하는 명상이 도움이 된다.
For the stressed contemporary man, meditation that allows you to concentrate on your mind while listening to music in a calm atmosphere is helpful.

56
최선

[최선] 명사 1. the best 2. one's hardest

1. **[Expression]** 최선이다 to be the best

[Related Words] 최고 the best

[Example] 그 방법이 최선이라고 생각해요.
I think that is the best way.

2. **[Expression]** 최선을 다하다 to do one's best

[Example] 최선을 다했으니만큼 좋은 결과가 나올 거예요.
The results will be good seeing as you tried your best.

57
추천하다

[추천하다] 동사 to recommend

[Usage] N 을/를 추천하다

[Example] 선생님께서 추천해 주신 도서 중에 이미 내가 읽은 책들이 많았다.
There were a lot of books that I already had read from the ones that my teacher had recommended to me.

주말에 할 수 있는 여가 활동을 다른 친구들에게도 추천해 주십시오.
Please recommend some leisure time activities that your friends can also do during the weekend.

58
토론하다

[토론하다] 동사 to debate

[Usage] N 에 대해서 토론하다

[Expression] 찬반 토론을 하다 to split up into pro/con and debate

[Related Words] 토의하다 to discuss

[Example] 오늘 우리는 한국문화에 대해 토론하겠습니다.
Today we will debate about Korean culture.

지금부터 30분 동안 여러분의 생각을 자유롭게 토론해 보시기 바랍니다.
During the next thirty minutes, we want you to freely discuss your thoughts.

59
특히

[트키] 부사 especially

[Related Words] 특별히 especially

[Example] 반 친구들이 모두 좋은 사람들이라서 금방 친해졌어요. 특히 민수 씨는 성격이 참 좋던데요.
I became very close with everyone in my class because they are all nice people. Especially with Minsoo because he has a nice personality.

기숙사는 좋은 점도 있지만 불편한 점도 많은데 특히 두 사람이 같이 방을 쓰는 것이 불편해요.
The dormitory has a lot of good aspects but at the same time there are a lot of inconveniences. It is especially uncomfortable that two people use one room together.

60
틀림없이

[틀리멉씨] 부사 without a doubt, certainly

[Synonym] 꼭 definitely
반드시 for sure

[Example] 이번엔 우리 반이 틀림없이 이길 것이다.
It is without a doubt that our team will win this time.
수업이 9시에 시작되니까 8시 50분까지는 틀림없이 교실에 와야 해.
You must come to the classroom by 8:50 because class begins at 9.

61
풀다

[풀다] 동사 1. to solve 2. to relax 3. to untie, to unfasten

1. to solve or answer a question

[Usage] N 을/를 풀다

[Expression] 문제를 풀다 to solve a problem

[Related Words] 해결하다 to solve

[Example] 문제를 스스로 풀도록 하세요.
Please solve the problem on your own.

2. to release, to relax, to loosen up, to overcome

[Usage] N 을/를 풀다

[Expression] 피로를 풀다 to no longer be tired

[Example] 휴식을 취했더니 피로가 많이 풀렸습니다.
I took a break and therefore no longer felt tired.

3. to take apart by undoing or untying

[Usage] N 을/를 풀다

[Expression] 끈을 풀다 to untie a string

[Antonym] 묶다 to tie
매다 to tie

[Example] 이 끈을 좀 풀어 주세요.
Please untie this string for me.

62
필기하다

[필기하다] 동사 to take notes

[Usage] N 을/를 필기하다

[Related Words] 쓰다 to write

[Example] 선생님의 말씀을 꼼꼼하게 필기하는 습관을 가져야 해.
You need to get into the habit of carefully taking notes of what the teacher says.

지난 수요일 수업 시간에 필기한 노트 좀 빌려줄 수 있어?
Can you lend me the notes from last Wednesday's class?

63
합격하다

[합껴카다] 동사 to pass

[Usage] N 에 합격하다

[Expression] 대학에 합격하다 to be accepted into college
시험에 합격하다 to pass a test

[Synonym] 통과하다 to pass through

[Example] 열심히 노력하셨으니까 꼭 합격하실 거예요.
You will definitely pass because you studied very hard.

어제 연세대학교에 합격했다는 연락을 받았어요.
I received a call yesterday from Yonsei University saying that I have been accepted into their school.

64
행사

[행사] 명사 event

[Expression] 기념행사 commemoratory event
행사 기간 the length of an event
행사가 열리다 to hold an event
행사가 취소되다 The event is cancelled.
행사에 참가하다 to participate in an event

[Example] 한국에는 여러 가지 가족 행사가 있습니다.
There are a lot of events for families in Korea.

행사 일정 및 프로그램은 사정에 따라 변경될 수 있습니다.
The schedule of events and programs are subject to change in accordance with the circumstances.

65
확실하다

[확씰하다] 형용사 to be sure

[Usage]
N 이/가 확실하다
AV 는/은/ㄴ/을/ㄹ 것이 확실하다
확실한 N
확실히 AV
확실하게 AV

[Antonym] 불확실하다 to be unsure

[Related Words] 분명하다 to be obvious

[Example]
이번에는 주희가 반장이 될 것이 확실해요.
I am sure that Juhi will become the class president this time.

오늘 경기에서 연세대 농구팀이 이길 것이 확실하다.
I am sure that Yonsei's basketball team will win in today's competition.

66
훨씬

[훨씬] 부사 much more, by far

[Example]
약속 시간이 훨씬 지났는데도 친구의 모습은 보이지 않았다.
Even though it was much later than our meeting time, my friend still hadn't arrived.

졸업하기 전에는 빨리 졸업하면 좋을 줄 알았는데 졸업하고 보니 학생이었을 때가 훨씬 좋더라.
Before graduating, I thought graduating quickly would be better. However, after graduating I realized that being a student is much better.

07 연습문제

[1-13] 다음 단어를 한국어로 바꿔 쓰십시오.

Change the following vocabulary words to Korean.

1. each ( ) 2. writing ( )

3. content ( ) 4. dissatisfaction ( )

5. grade, mark ( ) 6. to be appropriate ( )

7 intonation ( ) 8. language exchange ( )

9. to be right ( ) 10. meaning ( )

11. title ( ) 12. to concentrate ( )

13. event ( )

[14-26] [보기]에서 알맞은 단어를 골라 ( ) 안에 쓰십시오.

Choose the appropriate word from the box below and then fill in the parenthesis.

[보기]

얼른	종일	미리	특히	적다
다행히	마침내	스스로	반복하다	복사하다
상담하다	접수하다	정확하다		

14. 발표할 내용을 ( ) 준비해 가지고 가면 실수하지 않을 거예요.

15. 학교생활을 하면서 문제가 생기면 보통 담임선생님과 ( )어요/아요/여요.

16. 힘들어도 혼자서 할 수 있는 일이라면 다른 사람의 도움을 받지 않고 ( ) 하는 편이다.

17. 중요한 약속이 있어서 수첩에 약속 장소와 시간을 ( )어/아/여 놓았어요.

18. 국이 식기 전에 ( ) 드세요.

19. 요즘에는 대학 입학 원서를 인터넷으로도 ( )을/ㄹ 수 있어요.

20. 저는 다양한 장르의 영화를 모두 좋아하는데 (　　　　　) 공포 영화를 좋아합니다.

21. 마이클 씨는 한국 사람처럼 한국어 발음이 아주 (　　　　　)어요/아요/여요.

22. 교통사고가 났지만 (　　　　　) 아무도 다치지 않았어요.

23. 오늘 발표할 자료는 사람 수대로 (　　　　　)어서/아서/여서 나눠 주세요.

24. 내 친구는 가수가 되기 위해서 열심히 노력한 결과 (　　　　　) 가수가 되었다.

25. 어려운 발음은 몇 번이고 계속 (　　　　　)어서/아서/여서 연습하는 것이 좋아요.

26. 오늘 날씨가 너무 더워서 하루 (　　　　　) 에어컨을 켰어요.

[27-30] 다음 밑줄 친 부분과 의미가 비슷한 것을 고르십시오.

Choose a word that is similar in meaning to the underlined part of the sentence.

27. 영수 씨는 실력이 있으니까 <u>틀림없이</u> 성공할 거예요.

❶ 하지만　❷ 그러나　❸ 그리고　❹ 반드시

28. 증거를 봐도 그 사람이 범인인 것이 <u>분명하다</u>.

❶ 확장하다　❷ 확실하다　❸ 확대하다　❹ 확인하다

29. 그 호텔은 시설이 좋은 만큼 숙박비가 <u>무척</u> 비쌌어요.

❶ 굉장히　❷ 우연히　❸ 아무리　❹ 어쩐지

30. 이번 쓰기 시험은 외울 단어도 많고 <u>또한</u> 배운 문법도 많아서 공부하는데 시간이 많이 걸릴 것 같다.

❶ 오히려　❷ 반대로　❸ 게다가　❹ 그래도

[31-38] [보기]에서 알맞은 말을 찾아 빈칸에 넣으십시오.

Fill in the empty spaces with the appropriate word from the box below.

[보기]

규칙	반장	나날이	외우다
떠들다	강조하다	마음대로	번역하다

31. 매일 매일 조금씩 ( )

32. 하고 싶은 대로 ( )

33. 특별히 중요한 부분을 강하게 말하다 ( )

34. 어떤 언어로 된 글을 다른 언어의 글로 바꾸다 ( )

35. 말이나 글을 잊지 않고 기억하다 ( )

36. 큰 소리로 시끄럽게 이야기하다 ( )

37. 반을 대표하는 사람 ( )

38. 여러 사람이 지키기로 한 약속 ( )

[39-40] 다음 밑줄 친 부분과 반대되는 뜻을 가진 것을 고르십시오.

Choose the word that has the opposite meaning from the underlined word.

39. 이번 시험을 잘 봤다고 선생님께 칭찬받았어요.

① 야단맞다 ② 조언하다 ③ 상담하다 ④ 토의하다

40. 이 영화는 18세 이하는 관람할 수 없습니다.

① 초과 ② 미만 ③ 이상 ④ 이전

[41-53] [보기]에서 알맞은 단어를 골라 (   ) 안에 쓰십시오.

Coose the appropriate word from the box below and then fill in the parenthesis.

[보기]

거의	마치	이유	설마	진학
깜빡	훨씬	밤새다	신청하다	추천하다
토론하다	필기하다	합격하다		

41. 미선아, 내가 어제 학교에 못 와서 그러는데 수업시간에 (   )는/은/ㄴ 공책 좀 빌려줄 수 있어?

42. 제임스 씨는 노래를 잘해서 (   ) 가수 같아요.

43. 오랜만에 만난 친구와 잠을 자지 않고 (   )도록 이야기를 했어요.

44. 오늘 숙제 공책 가지고 오는 것을 (   ) 잊어버렸어요.

45. 오늘은 사형 제도에 대해서 (   )어/아/여 보도록 하겠습니다.

46. 영화배우 김동건은 유명해서 한국에서 모르는 사람이 (   ) 없을 거예요.

47. 이번에 드디어 운전면허 시험에 (   )었다면서요/았다면서요/였다면서요? 축하드려요.

48. 교통과 통신의 발달로 우리 생활이 (   ) 더 편리해졌다.

49. 선생님께서 이 소설책이 아주 재미있으니까 꼭 읽어보라고 (   )어/아/여 주셨어요.

50. 한국말 연습을 하기 위해서 상담실에 언어 교환을 (   )었어요/았어요/였어요.

51. 대학교를 졸업하면 대학원에 (   )을/를 할 계획이에요.

52. 한국에 왜 왔고 한국어를 공부하는 (   )이/가 무엇인지 이야기해 주십시오.

53. 오늘 중요한 시험이 있는 날인데 (   ) 미선 씨가 오늘도 지각을 하겠어?

[54-59] **다음 (　　　)에 공통적으로 들어갈 단어를 쓰십시오.**

Write one word that can commonly fit into the parenthesis below.

54.
❶ 실력은 부족하지만 저는 (　　　　　)을/를 다 했으니까 후회는 없어요.
❷ 감기가 걸렸을 때는 푹 쉬는 게 (　　　　　)이에요/예요.

(　　　　　　　)

55.
❶ 어제 너무 피곤해서 (　　　　　) 세수만 하고 잤어요.
❷ 아침부터 저녁까지 힘들게 아르바이트를 했는데 (　　　　　) 오천 원을 벌었어?

(　　　　　　　)

56.
❶ 저는 매운 음식을 (　　　　　) 좋아하는 편이 아니에요.
❷ 시험 문제가 생각보다 (　　　　　) 어렵지 않던데요.

(　　　　　　　)

57.
❶ 밥을 먹지 못할 (　　　　　)으로/로 이가 아파요.
❷ 버스 안에 승객들이 한 10명 (　　　　　) 있어요.

(　　　　　　　)

58.
❶ 5를 2로 나누면 몫은 2이고 (　　　　　)은/는 1이 된다.
❷ 오늘 일을 다 못 했는데 (　　　　　) 일은 내일 해도 될까요?

(　　　　　　　)

59.
❶ 오늘 회의의 (　　　　　)이/가 무엇입니까?
❷ 이 소설의 (　　　　　)은/는 어머니의 사랑이다.
❸ '행복'이라는 (　　　　　)을/를 가지고 글을 써 봅시다.

(　　　　　　　)

[60-65] **다음 (　　　)에 공통적으로 들어갈 단어의 기본형을 쓰십시오.**

Write the basic form of one word that can commonly fit in the parenthesis below.

60.

❶ 이 분홍색 원피스가 손님한테 아주 잘 (　　　　　)네요.

❷ 어머니는 저에게 나쁜 친구들과 (　　　　　)지 말라고 늘 말씀하세요.

(　　　　　　　　)

61.

❶ 잘못해서 선글라스를 바닷물에 (　　　　　)었어요/았어요/였어요.

❷ 오늘 중요한 발표가 있는데 서류를 (　　　　　)고 안 가지고 왔어요.

(　　　　　　　　)

62.

❶ 시험이 끝나자마자 친구들과 답을 (　　　　　)어/아/여 보았다.

❷ 저는 보통 사람보다 발이 커서 신발을 (　　　　　)어서/아서/여서 신어야 해요.

(　　　　　　　　)

63.

❶ 숫자 2에서 1을 (　　　　　)으면/면 1이 남습니다.

❷ 사람들 앞에서 이야기할 때는 주머니에서 손을 (　　　　　)고 말씀하세요.

❸ 열심히 운동을 해서 살을 5킬로그램이나 (　　　　　)었어요/았어요/였어요.

(　　　　　　　　)

64.

❶ 난 병원에서 주사를 (　　　　　)는/은/ㄴ 것이 세상에서 제일 싫어요.

❷ 12월 31일이 되면 일출을 보면서 새해를 (　　　　　)는/은/ㄴ 사람들이 많아요.

❸ 제임스 씨가 이번 쓰기 시험에서 또 100점을 (　　　　　)었어요/았어요/였어요.

(　　　　　　　　)

65.

❶ 이 문제는 너무 어려워서 못 (　　　　　)겠어요.

❷ 달리기를 하다가 운동화 끈이 (　　　　　)어졌어요/아졌어요/여졌어요.

❸ 저는 스트레스가 쌓이면 노래방에 가서 노래를 부르면서 스트레스를 (　　　　　)어요/아요/여요.

(　　　　　　　　)

경제

08

Economy

08 경제

01
가난

[가난] 명사 poverty

[Expression] 가난하다 to be poor

[Antonym] 부유 wealth

[Example] 가난에서 벗어나려고 아무리 노력해도 벗어날 수가 없다.
No matter how hard you try to break free from poverty, it is impossible to overcome it.

아프고 가난한 사람들을 돕기 위해서 병원을 세웠습니다.
They established a hospital to help people who are poor and sick.

02
가맹점

[가맹점] 명사 an affiliated store

[Expression] 가맹점 모집 collection/addition of affiliated stores

[Related Words] 본사 main office
본점 headquarters
지점 branch

[Example] 연세 카드를 가지고 가면 가맹점에서 5% 할인 받을 수 있다.
If you bring your Yonsei card with you, you can receive a discount of five percent at affiliated stores.

신용카드 회원이 가맹점에서 받을 수 있는 혜택은 무엇입니까?
What are the benefits I can receive at affiliated stores by applying for a credit card?

03
가짜

[가짜] 명사 fake, false

[Expression] 가짜 서류 fake document
가짜 신분증 fake ID

[Antonym] 진짜 real, true

[Related Words] 짝퉁 fake, imitation
모조품 replica, phony

[Example] 이 물건은 진짜가 아니고 가짜예요.
This object isn't real but fake.

명품 가방의 인기가 높아지면서 가짜를 진짜로 속여서 파는 사람들이 늘고 있다.
As the popularity of designer bags is increasing, the number of people that are tricked into thinking that fake bags are real is also going up.

04
견디다

[견디다] 동사 to withstand, to bear

[Usage] N 을/를 견디다
N 에 견디다

[Expression] 고통을 견디다 to bear a pain
추위에 견디다 to handle the cold

[Synonym] 참다 to deal with
인내하다 to be patient

[Example] 요즘 젊은이들은 힘든 일을 잘 견디지 못하는 것 같다.
Nowadays, it seems like young people can't handle hard situations very well.

이 일에서 성공하려면 온갖 힘든 일을 다 견뎌내야 합니다.
If you want to succeed at this job, you have to bear all the hardships of the job.

05
경우

[경우] 명사 case, circumstances

[Usage] AV / DV 는/은/ㄴ/을/ㄹ 경우

[Expression] 경우에 따라서 according to the circumstances

[Example] 카드로 결제하지 않고 현금으로 결제하실 경우 5% 할인해 드립니다.
In the case that you pay with cash and not credit card, we will give you a five percent discount.

카드로 물건을 구매하는 경우에 몇 개월까지 무이자 할부가 가능한지 꼭 확인해 보세요.
Please check for up to how many months the interest free installment plan is possible when buying an object with credit card.

도움말

<the difference between 경우 and 상황>

상황 expresses the form or circumstance of a work in process and is usually used in active scenes

경우 refers to situations or circumstances that have set standards and is used in suppositional phrases

06
경제적이다

[경제저기다] 형용사 to be economical

[Usage] 경제적인 N
경제적으로 AV

[Expression] 경제적인 투자 economical investment
경제적인 가치 economical value

[Antonym] 비경제적이다 to be uneconomical

[Example] 두 사람은 맞벌이 부부여서 경제적으로 넉넉한 것 같아요.
The couple was economically sufficient since they both had a job.

아이들은 금방 자라니까 책이나 장난감은 대여해서 쓰는 게 경제적이다.
It is economical to borrow and use books or toys for your kids since they grow up very quickly.

07
경험

[경험] 명사 experience

[Expression] 산 경험 life experience
경험하다 to experience
경험이 있다 to have experience
경험이 부족하다 to be lacking experience
경험을 쌓다 to gather experience

[Related Words] 체험 first-hand experience
경력 work experience

[Example] 이 일은 초보자가 하기는 힘든 일인데 경험은 있나요?
This is a difficult job for a beginner. Do you have any experience?

열심히 하겠다는 마음만 있다면 경험이 없어도 그 일을 잘 할 수 있을 거예요.
Even though you don't have any experience, as long as you have the desire to work very hard you can do a good job.

08
고가

[고까] 명사 high price

[Usage] 고가의 N

[Expression] 고가의 물품 an expensive object

[Antonym] 저가 cheap price

[Related Words] 정가 fixed price
특가 special price
중저가 low and middle priced goods
초특가 highly discounted price
할인가 discount price

[Example] 고가의 물건은 신용카드 할부로 사면 좋아요.
It is good to buy expensive goods with an installment program by paying with credit card.

온라인 쇼핑몰에서 고가의 제품을 지나치게 할인해서 판매한다면 조심하는 것이 좋습니다.
When shopping online, it is good to be careful when seeing designer goods being sold for excessively discounted prices.

09
고객

[고객] 명사 customer

[Expression] 우수 고객 preferred customer

[Synonym] 손님 guest

[Related Words] 단골 regular customer

[Example] 고객들의 만족도를 높이기 위해 고객센터를 운영하는 회사가 많다.
There are a lot of companies that run customer services centers in order to raise customer satisfaction.

오늘도 저희 백화점을 이용해 주신 고객 여러분께 진심으로 감사드립니다.
We would like to greatly thank all of our customers that have visited our department store today.

10
고생

[고생] 명사 hardship, trouble

[Expression] 고생하다 to suffer
고생이 심하다 to suffer a lot
고생을 견디다 to deal with hardships

[Example] 겨우 만 원 벌려고 하루 종일 고생을 한 거야?
You mean to tell me you struggled working all day long and only made 10,000 won?

고생을 모르고 자란 사람은 인생의 가치를 잘 모른다.
People who have grown up without troubles don't know the value of life.

11
공짜

[공짜] 명사 free

[Expression] 공짜표 free ticket
공짜로 받다 to get something for free
공짜로 얻다 to obtain for free
공짜로 빌리다 to borrow for free

[Synonym] 무료 free

[Example] 오늘은 어린이들에게 놀이공원 입장료가 공짜입니다.
Today, there is no entrance fee for kids to go into the amusement park.

50만 원짜리 정장을 5만 원에 샀으니 거의 공짜로 산 셈이에요.
I only paid 50,000 won for a suit that cost 500,000 won, so it feels like I bought it for free.

12
관리하다

[괄리하다] 동사 to maintain, to manage

[Usage] N 을/를 관리하다

[Expression] 건물을 관리하다 to maintain a building

[Example] 성공한 사람들은 평소 시간 관리를 효율적으로 한다고 합니다.
They say that successful people effectively manage their time on a daily basis.

저는 목표를 가지고 항상 계획적으로 시간을 관리하는 편입니다.
I tend to manage my time by setting a goal and always working with a plan.

13
광고

[광고] 명사 advertisement

[Expression] 공익 광고 public service announcement
구직 광고 a want ad
상업 광고 business advertisement
광고가 나가다 The advertisement is released.
광고를 내다 to put out an advertisement

[Synonym] 선전 advertisement

[Example] 형은 신문에서 구인 광고를 찾고 있었다.
My older brother is looking for job ads in the newspaper.

신제품을 알리기 위해서 회사들은 광고에 많은 비용을 쓴다.
Companies spend a lot of money in advertising in order to inform about their new products.

14
구매

[구매] 명사 purchase

[Expression] 구매자 purchaser
공동구매 group purchase
충동구매 impulsive buying
구매하다 to purchase

[Synonym] 매입 purchase

[Example] 백화점 세일 때는 충동구매하기가 쉽다.
People very often impulsively buy things during department store sales.

3만원 이상 구매하신 고객들께 사은품을 드립니다.
We will be giving a present to all customers that buy more than 30,000 won worth of merchandise.

15
그만두다

[그만두다] 동사 to quit

[Usage] N 을/를 그만두다

[Expression] 직장을 그만두다 to quit a job
공부를 그만두다 to quit studying

[Synonym] 포기하다 to give up

[Example] 직장 상사 때문에 회사를 그만두고 싶어요.
I want to quit my job because of the boss at my office.

집안 사정이 어려워서 학교를 그만두고 취직하기로 했어요.
I decided to quit school and look for a job because of my family situation.

16
기회

[기회] 명사 opportunity, chance

[Expression] 승진 기회 advancement opportunity (promotion)
기회가 오다 to have an opportunity
기회가 생기다 to have an opportunity
기회를 놓치다 to miss out on an opportunity

[Example] 좋은 기회가 오면 놓치지 말고 꼭 잡도록 하세요.
When a good opportunity comes your way, don't let it slip away.

한국 사람과 말할 수 있는 기회가 많은 일을 해 보고 싶어요.
I want to try doing a job where I have the opportunity to speak with Korean people.

17
긴장

[긴장] 명사 to be nervous, to be tense

[Expression] 긴장하다 to be nervous, to be tense
긴장이 풀리다 to no longer feel nervous, to no longer feel tense
긴장을 풀다 to relax one's nerves

[Example] 처음 하는 일이라서 그런지 너무 긴장을 해서 실수를 많이 했어요.
Since it was my first time doing the job, I made a lot of mistakes because I was so nervous.

사장님을 오늘 처음 뵀는데 너무 긴장을 해서 말을 한 마디도 못 했어요.
Today I met my boss for the first time, and since I was really nervous I couldn't say anything.

18
길이

[기리] 명사 length

[Expression] 길이가 길다 The length is long.
길이가 짧다 The length is short.

길이를 재다 to measure the length
길이를 줄이다 to lessen the length

[Related Words] 밀리미터 (mm) millimeter
센티미터 (cm) centimeter
미터 (m) meter
킬로미터 (km) kilometer
인치 (in) inch
리 (1리 is about 0.393km)

[Example] 소매가 얼마나 긴지 한번 길이를 재 보세요.
Please measure the length of the sleeve to see how long it is.

저는 보통 바지를 사면 길이를 줄여서 입어요.
When I normally buy pants, I shorten the length and then wear them.

19
깊이

[기피] 명사 depth

[Expression] 깊이가 깊다 to be deep
깊이가 얕다 to be shallow
깊이를 재다 to measure the depth

[Example] 해변에서 멀어질수록 바다의 깊이는 점점 더 깊어진다.
The farther away you go from the shore, the deeper the ocean is.

보기에는 깊이가 얕아 보이지만 사실 굉장히 깊은 곳이에요.
Upon first sight, it seemed shallow, but in reality it is a very deep place.

20
나머지[2]

[나머지] 명사 remaining, extra

[Usage] AV 는/은/ㄴ 나머지

[Expression] 나머지 부분 remaining part

[Synonym] 여분 extra

[Example] 오늘 못한 문법 설명의 나머지 부분은 내일 하도록 합시다.
Tomorrow we will finish the remaining grammar explanations that we didn't cover today in grammar.

월급에서 생활비를 제외한 나머지는 모두 은행에 예금해요.
After excluding the money for my everyday purchases from my salary, I deposit the leftover money in the bank.

21
나타나다

[나타나다] 동사 to appear

[Usage] N 이/가 나타나다

[Antonym] 사라지다 to disappear

[Example] 뜻밖에 목격자가 나타나서 범인을 잡을 수 있게 되었어요.
The criminal was caught after a sudden eye-witness appeared.

김영수 씨가 며칠 동안 연락도 없이 사무실에 나타나지 않으니 이상하네요.
It's strange that during the past few days Kim Youngsoo hasn't come by the office without any prior notification.

22
납부

[납뿌] 명사 payment

payments usually referring to taxes or bills

[Expression]
납부금 payment
납부 기한 payment period
납부 고지서 bill, payment notice
납부하다 to pay
등록금을 납부하다 to pay one's tuition

[Example] 웬일인지 아직도 납부 고지서가 안 나왔어요.
For some reason the payment notice still hasn't arrived yet.

공과금을 기한 내에 납부하지 않으면 연체료를 내야 합니다.
You need to pay late fees if you do not pay the bill within the allotted time.

23
낭비하다

[낭비하다] 동사 to waste

[Usage] N 을/를 낭비하다

[Expression]
돈을 낭비하다 to waste money
시간을 낭비하다 to waste time

[Antonym] 절약하다 to conserve

[Example] 쓸데없는 데에 돈을 낭비하지 마.
Don't waste money on useless things.

우리 할머니는 돈을 낭비하지 않으시고 항상 아껴 쓰세요.
My grandmother never wastes money. She always saves it.

24
넓이

[널비] 명사 width

[Expression]
넓이가 넓다 It is wide.
넓이가 좁다 It is narrow.
넓이를 재다 to measure the width

[Related Words]
제곱밀리미터 (㎟) square millimeter
제곱센티미터 (㎠) square centimeter

제곱미터 (㎡) square meter
제곱킬로미터 (㎢) square kilometer
평 (1평 is about 3.3㎡)

[Example] 한국에서는 아파트 넓이를 평으로 나타내기도 합니다.
In Korea, the width of apartments is usually represented in pyong.

넓이가 조금 좁아 보이니까 얼마나 되는지 한번 재 봅시다.
Let's measure the width of the room because it looks a little narrow.

25
높이

[노피] 명사 height

[Expression] 눈높이 the height of one's eyes
키높이 one's height
높이뛰기 high jump

[Example] 바닥에서 천장까지의 높이는 얼마나 됩니까?
How high is the room from the floor to the ceiling?

아이들도 이용할 수 있게 책상의 높이를 낮췄다.
I lowered the height of the desk so that the kids can use it too.

26
늘다

[늘다] 동사 1. to increase 2. to improve

1. to increase or grow in size, length, number or volume

[Usage] N 이/가 늘다

[Expression] 학생 수가 늘다 The number of students increases.
평균 수명이 늘다 The average life expectancy increases.

[Synonym] 증가하다 to increase

[Antonym] 줄다 to decrease

[Example] 날씨가 더워지면서 아이스크림의 판매가 급격히 늘었다.
As the weather is getting hotter, the sales of ice cream has suddenly increased.

2. to improve in one's talent or skill

[Usage] N 이/가 늘다

[Expression] 솜씨가 늘다 My skills improve.
실력이 늘다 My ability improves.

[Synonym] 좋아지다 to become better
나아지다 to get better

[Antonym] 줄다 to get worse

[Example] 나도 모르게 한국어 실력이 많이 늘었다.
My Korean language abilities got better without my even realizing it.

27
단기간

[단기간] 명사 short time period

[Antonym] 장기간 long time period

[Example] 주식 투자로 단기간에 많은 돈을 벌었어요.
I made a lot of money in short term stock investments.

다이어트를 해서 단기간에 10킬로그램이나 살을 뺐다.
I lost ten kilograms in a short time by dieting.

28
대기업

[대기업] 명사 big business, conglomerate

[Expression] 대기업 회장 the president of a big business
대기업 임원 board member of a big business

[Related Words] 중소기업 small and average sized companies

[Example] 요즘 젊은이들은 모두 대기업에 취직하고 싶어해요.
Nowadays, all young kids want to get a job in a big business.

경기가 어려울 때는 대기업보다는 중소기업이 더 힘들어요.
When the economy is tough, it is harder for smaller businesses than big businesses.

29
덜다

[덜다] 동사 1. to lessen, to lighter 2. to take back, to lessen

1. **[Usage]** N 을/를 덜다

[Expression] 고통을 덜다 to ease one's pain
걱정을 덜다 to lessen one's worrying
근심을 덜다 to relieve one's anxiety
수고를 덜다 to lessen one's hardship

[Antonym] 더하다 to add

[Related Words] 줄다 to lessen

[Example] 중요한 회의여서 무척 긴장됐는데 김 과장님이 도와주셔서 제가 걱정을 덜었어요.
I was quite nervous because it was an important meeting. However, I felt less worried because section chief Mr. Kim helped me.

2. **[Usage]** N 을/를 덜다

[Expression] 밥을 덜다 to take food from a plate
짐을 덜다 to lessen the amount of luggage

[Example] 밥이 너무 많은데 좀 덜어 주세요.
There is a lot of rice here, please take some.

30
따지다

[따지다] 동사 1. to calculate, to count, to compute 2. to distinguish

1. to calculate an amount using numbers

[Usage] N 을/를 따지다

[Expression] 가격을 따지다 to calculate a price
날짜를 따지다 to inquire about the weather
비용을 따지다 to analyze an expense

[Related Words] 계산하다 to calculate the bill

[Example] 투자를 하기 전에는 반드시 비용을 따져야 합니다.
Before investing, we must definitely analyze the expenses.

2. to choose between good and wrong, to distinguish between two things

[Usage] N 을/를 따지다
AV / DV 냐고 따지다

[Expression] 잘잘못을 따지다 to distinguish between right and wrong
시시비비를 따지다 to choose between right or wrong

[Related Words] 가리다 to choose

[Example] 사고 원인을 꼼꼼히 따져야 잘못이 되풀이되지 않는다.
You need to carefully study the cause of the accident. If not, you won't be able to solve the problem.

31
맞추다²

[맏추다] 동사 1. to adjust 2. to set, to be fitting 3. to flatter, to humor
4. to custom-make, to tailor

1. to achieve a harmony without going against one another

[Usage] N 을/를 맞추다

[Expression] 마음을 맞추다
to adjust the way one thinks or feels
손발을 맞추다
to work at the same pace, to be on the same page with something
의견을 맞추다
to adjust one's opinion with someone else's

[Example] 회사의 모든 부서들이 서로 손발을 맞춰야 회사가 발전할 수 있지요.
A company can only progress if all departments work together.

2. to match to a standard

[Usage] N 에/에게 맞추다

[Expression] 기준에 맞추다 to standardize

적성에 맞추다 to be fitting to one's aptitude

[Example] 시간에 맞춰서 약을 먹는 것도 꽤 신경이 쓰여요.
A lot of attention is placed on taking your medicine on time.

3. to act in accordance with another person*s attitude or inclination

[Usage] N 을/를 맞추다

[Expression] 기분을 맞추다 to flatter
비위를 맞추다 to humor someone

[Example] 회사에서 상사의 비위를 잘 맞추는 것도 중요한 일 중에 하나다.
One of the important jobs at the office is trying to please your seniors.

4. to order objects to a predetermined set standard or measurement

[Usage] N 을/를 맞추다

[Expression] 옷을 맞추다 to tailor-make closes
신발을 맞추다 to custom make shoes
안경을 맞추다 to get a pair of glasses

[Example] 눈이 너무 나빠져서 안경점에 가서 안경을 맞춰야겠어요.
I need to go the optician and get a pair of eyeglasses because my eyes have gotten much worse.

32
면제

[면제] 명사 exemption

[Expression] 비자 면제 visa exemption
세금 면제 tax exemption
수수료 면제 fee exemption

[Related Words] 면세 tax free

[Example] 그 신용카드는 우수 고객에게 연회비를 면제해 준다.
That credit card company exempts its preferred customers from paying annual fees.

저희 은행 VIP 고객분들께는 환전할 때 수수료를 면제해 드립니다.
The bank exempts its VIP customers from paying fees when exchanging money.

33
무게

[무게] 명사 weight

[Expression] 몸무게 weight
무게가 나가다 to be over one's advised weight
무게를 달다 to weight oneself
무게를 재다 to weight

무게를 줄이다 to lose weight

[Related Words] 밀리그램 (mg) milligram

그램 (g) gram

킬로그램 (kg) kilogram

톤 (t) ton

[Example] 무게에 따라서 운송비도 다릅니다.

The cost of transport is different depending on the weight.

키에 비해서 몸무게가 너무 많이 나갑니다.

He weighs too much for his weight.

34
무이자

[무이자] 명사 interest free

[Expression] 무이자 할부 interest free payment plan

[Example] 인터넷 쇼핑몰에서 10개월 무이자 할부 행사를 하고 있다.

The online shopping mall is running a ten month long interest free payment plan event.

연세 신용카드로 에어컨을 사시면 12개월 무이자 할부로 구입하실 수 있어요.

If you buy the air-conditioner with your Yonsei credit card, you pay using an interest free payment plan for twelve months.

35
문의하다

[무니하다] 동사 to inquire

[Usage] N 에/에게 N 을/를 문의하다

N 으로/로 문의하다

[Expression] 전화로 문의하다 to inquire by phone

[Synonym] 묻다 to ask

질문하다 to ask a question

[Example] 궁금한 사항은 전화나 이메일로 문의하시기 바랍니다.

We ask that you inquire by phone or email if you have any questions.

고장인 것 같으면 서비스 센터에 전화로 문의해 보세요.

Please inquire by calling the service center if you think it is broken.

36
반품

[반품] 명사 to return bought goods or items

[Expression] 반품하다 to return

[Example] 죄송합니다만 이미 설치가 끝난 물건에 대해서는 반품이 안 됩니다.

I regret to inform you that objects whose installation time has passed cannot be returned.

지난주에 소파를 샀는데 집안 분위기와 안 어울려서 반품을 하고 싶어요.
I bought a sofa last week, but it doesn't go along with the atmosphere in my living room so I want to return it.

37
배송

[배송] 명사 to ship, to deliver

[Expression]
배송료 shipping charge
배송비 shipping fee
무료 배송 free shipping

[Example]
5만원 이상 사시면 무료로 배송을 해 드립니다.
If you buy more than 50,000 won in goods, we deliver them for free.

구입한 제품을 교환하시려면 배송료를 따로 지불하셔야 하는데요.
If you want to exchange a product that you purchased, you must pay for the shipping fee separately.

38
보험

[보험] 명사 insurance

[Expression]
보험료 insurance fee
의료 보험 medical insurance
자동차 보험 car insurance
보험을 들다 to buy insurance
보험에 가입하다 to sign up for insurance

[Example]
여행을 떠나기 전에 공항에서 여행자 보험을 들었다.
I bought travelers insurance at the airport before going on vacation.

사고를 낸 트럭은 보험에 가입되어 있지 않아서 보상금을 받는 데 문제가 많을 것 같다.
The truck that caused the accident didn't have insurance so there are going to be a lot of problems when the time comes to receive compensations.

39
부피

[부피] 명사 volume

[Expression]
부피를 재다 to measure the volume
부피를 줄이다 to lessen the volume

[Related Words]
시시 (cc) cubic centimeter
리터 (ℓ) liter
밀리리터 (mℓ) milliliter
세제곱미터 (m^3) cubic meters

[Example] 보낼 물건의 부피가 크면 요금을 조금 더 내셔야 합니다.
If the volume of the object you are going to send is very large, you must pay an extra fee.

부피가 큰 것은 여기에 넣고 부피가 작은 것은 저기에 넣으세요.
Please place the bulky objects over here and the smaller ones over there.

40
살아나다

[사라나다] 동사 1. to recover, to revive 2. to come back to life

1. a weakened energy or force that gathers strength again

[Usage] N 이/가 살아나다

[Expression] 경제가 살아나다 The economy has recovered.
입맛이 살아나다 to have an appetite again

[Example] 경제가 살아나려면 국민 모두가 하나가 되어 열심히 노력해야 합니다.
All citirens must unite and work hard for the econmy to recover.

2. to come back to life

[Usage] N 이/가 살아나다

[Expression] 사람이 살아나다 He comes back to life.
죽다가 살아나다 to come back to life
구사일생으로 살아나다 to barely come back to life

[Example] 교통사고로 거의 죽어가던 친구가 다시 살아났어요.
My friend that had almost died in the car accident came back to life again.

41
상승하다

[상승하다] 동사 to increase, to rise

[Usage] N 이/가 상승하다

[Expression] 물가가 상승하다 The price goes up.

[Antonym] 하락하다 to decrease, to fall

[Example] 환경오염이 심해짐에 따라 지구의 온도도 상승하고 있다.
The temperature of the planet is rising as the state of environmental pollution is worsening.

경제가 조금씩 살아나면서 주가도 조금씩 상승하고 있어요.
The prices of stocks are rising little by little as the economy is recovering.

42
상태

[상태] 명사 state, situation

[Expression] 물건 상태 state of an object
제품 상태 state of a product
건강 상태 state of health

상태가 좋다 He is in a good state.

[Example] 요즘 무리를 해서 건강 상태가 나빠진 것 같아요.
The condition of my health has gotten worse because I have been overexerting myself lately.

기상 상태가 안 좋으면 비행기가 연착하는 수가 있어요.
If the weather condition isn't good, the plane may arrive behind schedule.

43
새롭다

[새롭따] 형용사 to be new

[Usage] N 이/가 새롭다
새로운 N

[Expression] 새로운 경험 new experience
새로운 상품 new product
감회가 새롭다 to be reminded of old memories

[Related Words] 새 new

[Example] 요즘에 새로운 소식이나 중요한 정보가 없어요?
Isn't there any news or important information lately?

새로운 기술의 개발로 생산력이 더 높아질 것으로 예상된다.
It is expected that productivity levels will increase thanks to new technological developments.

44
서명하다

[서명하다] 동사 to sign

[Usage] N 에 서명하다

[Expression] 계약서에 서명하다 to sign a contract

[Synonym] 사인하다 to sign

[Example] 손님, 여기에 서명해 주세요.
Please sign here, sir.

은행에서 돈을 찾을 때 도장이 없으면 서명을 해도 되나요?
If you don't have your seal when taking out money, are you allowed to sign instead?

45
서비스

[서비스] 명사 1. service 2. for free

1. **[Expression]** 서비스 센터 service senter
서비스 정신 service mentality
서비스가 좋다 The service is good.
서비스가 나쁘다 The service is bad.

[Related Words] 에이에스(A/S) after-sales service
애프터서비스(A/S) after-sales service

[Example] 어떤 가게에서는 현금을 쓰면 값을 깎아 주고 서비스도 더 좋아집니다.
In some stores, if you pay with cash they give you a discount and the service is better.

2. **[Usage]** 서비스로 AV

[Synonym] 덤 complimentary
사은품 free gift

[Example] 주유소에서는 주유하는 고객에게 서비스로 물이나 휴지를 줍니다.
At the gas station, they give customers that put gas in their car water or tissue papers for free.

46
서투르다

[서투르다] 형용사 to be clumsy, to be unskilled

[Usage] N 이/가 서투르다
N 에 서투르다

[Expression] 한국말이 서투르다 My Korean is poor.
일에 서투르다 to be unskilled at a job

[Antonym] 능숙하다 to be fluent, to be skilled at

[Example] 이 일을 한 지 6개월밖에 안 돼서 아직 서툴러요.
I'm still unfamiliar with this job because I've only had it for six months.

지금은 서투르지만 계속하다 보면 잘 할 수 있을 거예요.
You may not be very proficient now but if you keep trying, you will be able to do it well someday.

47
선택하다

[선태카다] 동사 to select, to choose

[Usage] N 을/를 선택하다
N 으로/로 선택하다

[Synonym] 고르다 to choose

[Example] 직업을 선택할 때 가장 중요한 것이 무엇입니까?
What is the most important thing when choosing a job?

월급이 많아서 그런지 많은 구직자들이 그 회사를 1지망으로 선택하네요.
Many job seekers choose that company as their dream job probably because the pay is very good.

48
세금

[세금] 명사 tax

[Expression] 세금 납부 tax payment
세금 면제 tax exemption
세금 계산서 tax receipt
세금을 걷다 to collect taxes
세금을 내다 to pay taxes

[Example] 세금이 작년에 비해 올랐다.
The taxes went up in comparison to last year.

매달 월급에서 세금이 빠져 나간다.
Every month, taxes are removed from my paycheck.

49
세다^2

[세다] 동사 to count

[Usage] N 을/를 세다

[Expression] 돈을 세다 to count money
수를 세다 to count an amount

[Example] 돈을 찾은 후에 금액이 맞는지 세어 보세요.
After taking money out, please count to see if the amount is right.

요즘엔 은행에 돈을 세는 기계가 있어서 편리해요.
It's convenient that there are machines that count the money for you in banks.

50
세로

[세로] 명사 vertical

[Usage] 세로로 AV

[Antonym] 가로 horizontal

[Example] 세로로 줄을 그으세요.
Please draw a vertical line.

액자의 크기는 가로 길이가 20cm, 세로 길이가 30cm이다.
The frame is horizontally twenty centimeters wide and vertically thirty centimeters long.

51
소비자

[소비자] 명사 consumer

[Expression] 소비자가 consumer price
소비자 가격 consumer price
소비자 보호 협회 consumer protection association

[Related Words] 과소비 excessive consumption

[Example] 이번 주까지 신제품에 대한 소비자들의 반응을 알아 봅시다.
Let's find out the consumers' reaction about the new product by this week.

제품이 좋으니까 한번 써 본 소비자는 반드시 이 제품을 다시 살 겁니다.
Consumers that have only used the product once will definitely buy it again because it is a good product.

52
손해

[손해] 명사 damage, loss

[Expression]
손해배상 compensation for damage
손해가 나다 to be damaged
손해를 보다 to become damaged
손해를 입다 to become damaged, to suffer from a loss
손해를 끼치다 to cause damage

[Antonym] 이익 profit, benefit

[Example] 계약할 때 잘 살펴봐야 손해를 입지 않습니다.
When signing a contract, you must carefully go through it so that you later don't suffer any losses.

이번 사업 실패로 손해를 본 금액은 약 500억 원 정도에 달할 것으로 예상하고 있다.
I am predicting that the amount of money lost due to the business mistake will come out to be around 50 billion won.

53
수고하다

[수고하다] 동사 to take the trouble to do something, to make an effort
to be difficult and tiresome after doing a certain job for a period of time

[Usage]
N 이/가 수고하다
AV 느라고 수고하다

[Synonym]
애쓰다 to make an effort
힘쓰다 to strive
고생하다 to suffer

[Example] 늦게까지 일하느라고 수고했어요.
I worked very hard until late at night.

지금까지 회사를 위해 수고해 주신 여러분들께 감사하다는 말씀 드리고 싶습니다.
I would like to thank all of you that have worked so hard for our company.

도움말

usually '수고하다' is not said to people that are older or have a higher rank than you.

54
수입

[수입] 명사 import

[Expression] 수입품 import product
직수입 direct import
수입하다 to import
수입을 개방하다 to allow for imports
수입을 규제하다 to regulate imports

[Antonym] 수출 export

[Example] 올해 우리나라는 수출보다 수입을 더 많이 했다.
This year, Korea imported more than it exported.

얼마 전 정부에서 미국산 소고기 수입을 개방했다.
The government allowed for imports of American beef not too long ago.

55
수표

[수표] 명사 check

[Expression] 여행자 수표 traveler's checks

[Related Words] 현금 cash

[Example] 수표를 사용할 때는 수표 뒤에 이름과 연락처를 적어야 해요.
When you want to use a traveler's check, you must write your name and contact information on the back side of the check.

한번에 큰돈을 찾을 때는 현금보다는 수표로 찾는 것이 편해요.
When taking out a large sum of money at once from the bank, it is more convenient to ask for checks than for cash.

56
신용

[시뇽] 명사 credit, credibility, trust

[Expression] 신용 카드 credit card
신용불량자 a person who has poor credit ratings
신용이 없다 to be untrustworthy
신용이 떨어지다 one's credibility has fallen
신용을 잃다 to lose one's credibility

[Synonym] 믿음 trust, faith

[Example] 약속을 안 지키면 신용을 잃는 법입니다.
If you don't keep your promise, you are no longer going to be trustworthy.

제 사촌 동생은 돈을 펑펑 쓰더니 결국 신용불량자가 됐어요.
My younger cousin wasted all of his money and ended up having horrible credit.

57
심각하다

[심가카다] 형용사 to be serious, to be grave

[Usage] N 이/가 심각하다

[Expression] 문제가 심각하다 The problem is serious.
상황이 심각하다 The situation is grave.

[Example] 이 문제는 심각하게 생각해서 결정해야 합니다.
I must make a decision because I believe this is a serious problem.

무슨 일이 있어요? 왜 이렇게 분위기가 심각합니까?
What's the matter? Why is the atmosphere so serious?

58
쌓다

[싸타] 동사 1. to gather 2. to stack, to pile

1. to gather experience, technology, information, or skills

[Usage] N 을/를 쌓다

[Expression] 경험을 쌓다 to gather experience
실력을 쌓다 to build one's skills

[Example] 아르바이트를 하면 다양한 경험을 쌓을 수 있어요.
You can gather a number of experiences by working a part-time job.

2. to place a lot of things on top of each other

[Usage] N 을/를 쌓다

[Expression] 물건을 쌓다 to pile up objects

[Example] 대형 할인 매장에서는 보통 상품을 쌓아 놓고 팔아요.
In large-scale discount stores, they usually stack up the products on top of each other and sell them.

59
얻다

[얻따] 동사 to obtain

[Usage] N 을/를 얻다

[Expression] 정보를 얻다 to obtain information
일자리를 얻다 to secure a job

[Related Words] 구하다 to seek

[Example] 저는 주로 인터넷을 통해서 정보를 얻는 편이에요.
I tend to obtain information through the internet.

요즘은 경기가 좋지 않아서 아르바이트 자리도 얻기 힘들어요.
It is hard to get a part-time job because the economy hasn't been good recently.

60
예금

[예금] 명사 to deposit

[Expression]
예금주 depositor
예금액 total deposit
정기예금 fixed deposit
예금하다 to deposit
예금을 찾다 to withdraw deposited money

[Related Words]
저금 saving small amounts of money over a long period of time
저축 saving money
적금 installment saving
이자 interest

[Example]
목돈이 생겨서 은행에 예금했어요.
I deposited the large sum of money I had recently obtained.

은행 계좌번호는 123-45678-901이고 예금주는 이미선입니다.
The bank account number is 123-45678-901 and the account holder is Miseon Lee.

61
유행

[유행] 명사 trend, fashion

[Expression]
유행하다 to be in style
유행을 따라가다 to follow a trend

[Related Words]
인기 popularity

[Example]
유행이 자주 바뀌니까 유행을 따라 가는 것도 피곤하네요.
It is tiring to follow trends because they change so often.

아무리 온라인 쇼핑몰이 유행한다고 해도 물건을 직접 보고 고르는 재미가 있는 시장이 더 좋아.
I think that even though they say online shopping malls are popular, it is much more fun to go in person to a market and look around at the products there.

62
제공하다

[제공하다] 동사 to offer, to supply, to provide

[Usage]
N 을/를 제공하다

[Expression]
숙식을 제공하다 to provide room and board
정보를 제공하다 to provide information

서비스를 제공하다 to provide a service
할인쿠폰을 제공하다 to offer a discount coupon

[Example] 이 연극은 외국인들을 위해서 자막 서비스를 제공하고 있습니다.
This theater provides subtitles for foreigners.

한국관광공사 홈페이지에서는 관광에 관련된 다양한 정보를 제공해 준다.
The Korean Tourist Service offers diverse information related to tourism on their home page.

63
조건

[조껀] 명사 condition, term

[Expression] 근무 조건 working conditions
계약 조건 terms of a contract
자격 조건 qualifying terms
조건을 갖추다 to be qualified
조건을 제시하다 to suggest terms/conditions

[Synonym] 요건 requirement

[Related Words] 무조건 absolute, unconditional

[Example] 이번 시험은 자격 조건을 갖춘 사람만이 응시할 수 있습니다.
Only individuals that possess the qualifying conditions can register to take this test.

여성들이 생각하는 좋은 직장의 조건을 한번 이야기해 봅시다.
Let's speak about the conditions that women think are good in the workplace.

64
조사하다

[조사하다] 동사 to analyze, to study, to investigate

[Usage] N 을/를 조사하다

[Related Words] 검사하다 to inspect, to examine

[Example] 경찰이 교통사고의 원인을 조사하기 시작했어요.
The police have begun to investigate the causes of the car accident.

윤무식 교수는 오랫동안 우리나라의 새를 조사하고 연구했대요.
It is said that professor Yun Mushik has been studying the birds of Korea for a very long time.

65
중요성

[중요썽] 명사 importance

[Expression] 중요성이 커지다 to become more important
중요성이 강조되다 The importance of this is emphasized.

[Example] 요즘 취업할 때 면접의 중요성이 커지고 있대요.
They say that recently more importance is placed on the interview when applying for a job.

가출 청소년의 수가 증가하면서 가정교육의 중요성이 강조되고 있습니다.
As the number of teenagers that run away from home is increasing, a greater importance is being placed on family education.

66
즉

[즉] 부사 in other words, that is to say

[Synonym] 곧 in other words

[Example] 설날과 추석 때는 제사, 즉 차례를 지냅니다.
During the Korean New Year and Korean harvest festival "jesa," in other words a memorial service for one's ancestors, is held.

24시간, 즉 하루는 짧은 시간이 아니니까 잘 쓰시기 바랍니다.
Twenty-four hours, that is to say one day, is not a short amount of time so I hope you use it well.

67
차이

[차이] 명사 difference, distinction

[Expression] 차이점 a difference
성격 차이 a difference in personality
세대 차이 generational gap
차이가 나다 There is a distinction.
차이가 심하다 The difference is large.

[Related Words] 차별 discrimination

[Example] 사회생활과 학교생활은 차이가 커요.
There is a big difference between being a student and being a working member of society.

청바지를 하나 사려고 백화점과 시장을 비교해 봤는데 가격 차이가 많이 나네요.
I wanted to buy a pair of blue jeans so I compared the prices of a department store and of an open market and I realized that there is a huge difference.

68
창구

[창구] 명사 window, counter

[Expression] 민원 창구 window for civil petitions
수납 창구 receipt window
은행 창구 bank window

[Example] 서류를 다 작성한 후에 창구에서 접수하세요.
After completing the documents, please hand them in at the counter.

먼저 번호표를 뽑은 후에 차례가 되면 창구로 가세요.
After taking a number, please go to the counter when it is your turn.

69
초보자

[초보자] 명사 beginner, novice

[Related Words] 경험자 expert, an person who is experienced in something

[Example] 이번 일은 초보자보다는 경험이 많은 사람한테 맡기는 것이 좋겠습니다.
Rather than giving this job to a beginner, I believe it would be best to assign this job to someone that has a lot of experience.

가격도 비싸지 않고 초보자들도 쉽게 사진을 찍을 수 있는 카메라를 사고 싶습니다.
I want to buy a camera that isn't expensive and is easy for a beginner to use.

70
크기

[크기] 명사 size

[Expression] 글자크기 font size
소리크기 noise level
화면크기 screen size

[Example] 공부를 잘하는 것과 머리의 크기는 상관이 있을까요?
Do you think that the size of your head and how well you do in school are related?

제 방 크기가 이 교실 반만 한데 혼자 쓰기에는 충분해요.
The size of my room is half the size of this classroom. There is plenty of room for me to be living by myself.

71
판매하다

[판매하다] 동사 to sell products

[Usage] N 을/를 판매하다

[Synonym] 팔다 to sell

[Antonym] 사다 to buy
구입하다 to purchase

[Example] 어버이날을 맞아 노인들이 사용하기 편한 휴대폰을 할인 판매하고 있다.
In order to celebrate Parents' Day, they will be selling cell phones that have been modified to be used by the elderly at discounted prices.

업체 간의 심한 경쟁으로 물건을 원가 이하의 가격으로 판매하는 경우가 있다.
As a result of the intense competition between businesses, there are many instances where objects are sold for less than the original price.

72
포기하다

[포기하다] 동사 to give up

[Usage] N 을/를 포기하다

[Synonym] 그만두다 to quit

[Example] 여러 가지 이유로 프랑스 유학을 포기했다.
I gave up on going to study abroad in France for a number of reasons.

저는 아무리 일이 어려워도 쉽게 포기하지 않는 성격이에요.
I am the type of person that doesn't give up on something no matter how hard the job may be.

73
폭

[폭] 명사 breadth, width

[Expression] 폭이 넓다 to be wide
폭이 좁다 to be narrow

[Synonym] 너비 width

[Example] 폭이 넓은 치마가 더 편해요.
A wider skirt is more comfortable.

도로의 폭이 좁아서 차가 다니기 불편해요.
The road is very narrow so it is difficult for cars to circulate easily.

74
폰뱅킹

[폰뱅킹] 명사 telephone banking

a phone service that provides you with a variety of services like checking your account balance, making a deposit, guidance on taking out a loan, and automatic transactions

[Expression] 폰뱅킹을 사용하다 to use telephone banking
폰뱅킹에 가입하다 to register for telephone banking

[Related Words] 인터넷 뱅킹 online banking

[Example] 이번 영화제의 영화표는 폰뱅킹으로도 예매할 수 있습니다.
You can buy movie tickets in advance for the film festival through telephone banking.

저는 폰뱅킹보다는 인터넷 뱅킹을 더 자주 이용하는 편이에요.
I often use online banking more than telephone banking.

75
하자

[하자] 명사 flaw, defect

[Expression] 하자가 많다 to have a lot of defects
하자가 있다 to have a defect

[Synonym] 흠 flaw, crack, chip
문제 problem

[Example] 이렇게 하자가 많아서야 어디 쓸 수 있겠어요?
How am I supposed to use this if it has so many flaws?

제가 3일 전에 그 매장에서 에어컨을 구입했는데 제품에 하자가 있는 것 같아요.
I bought an air conditioner three days ago at that store, but I think that the product is defective.

76
할부

[할부] 명사 monthly installment plan

[Expression] 할부금 installment payments
할부 기간 installment period

[Antonym] 일시불 one-time payment

[Example] 이번에 냉장고를 6개월 할부로 샀어요.
I bought a refrigerator on a six-month payment plan.

할부로 하시겠습니까? 일시불로 하시겠습니까?
Would you like to pay in installments or would you like to pay all at once?

77
할인

[하린] 명사 discount

[Expression] 할인점 discount store
할인 쿠폰 discount coupon
할인 판매 selling at discounted prices
할인 혜택 discount benefits
추가 할인 additional discount

[Related Words] 세일 sale

[Example] 이 제품은 10% 할인해서 270만 원이에요.
After a discount of 10%, this product is 2,700,000 won.

할인 쿠폰을 가지고 오시면 20% 할인을 받으실 수 있습니다.
If you bring a discount coupon with you, you can receive a discount of twenty percent.

78
확대하다

[확때하다] 동사 to enlarge, to expand, to magnify

[Usage] N 을/를 확대하다

[Expression] 고용을 확대하다 to expand employment
사업을 확대하다 to increase business
투자를 확대하다 to expand investments

[Synonym] 늘리다 to increase, to enlarge

[Antonym] 축소하다 to reduce, to shrink

[Related Words] 확장하다 to extend

[Example] 중국 사업에 좀 더 투자를 확대해야 한다고 봅니다.
I believe that we must invest more in Chinese businesses.

올해부터 신입 사원을 대폭 확대하여 모집하기로 했다는 기사를 봤다.
I saw an article that said that from this year on, they have decided to drastically recruit more new employees.

79
환불

[환불] 명사 refund

[Expression] 요금 환불 fee refund
전액 환불 full refund
환불 보증 refundable guarantee
환불하다 to refund
환불이 가능하다 A refund is possible.

[Related Words] 교환 exchange

[Example] 표를 예매한 후에 취소하거나 환불받은 경험이 있어요?
Have you ever cancelled or gotten a refund for a ticket that you bought in advance?

백화점에서는 영수증과 물건을 가지고 오면 14일 안에 교환이나 환불이 가능합니다.
It is possible to exchange or refund a product at the department store if you return it within fourteen days along with the receipt.

08 연습문제

[1-14] **다음 단어를 한국어로 바꿔 쓰십시오.**

Change the following vocabulary words to Korean.

1. gram ( ) 2. length ( )

3. depth ( ) 4. remaining ( )

5. payment ( ) 6. height ( )

7. vertical ( ) 8. check ( )

9. deposit ( ) 10. counter ( )

11. beginner ( ) 12. size ( )

13. width ( ) 14. telephone banking ( )

[15-18] **다음 [보기]에서 알맞은 단어를 찾아 ( )에 맞게 쓰십시오.**

Choose the appropriate words from the following box and write them in the parenthesis.

[보기]

그램(g)	리터(ℓ)	미터(m)	밀리리터(mℓ)
센티미터(cm)	시시(cc)	인치(in)	제곱미터(m²)
제곱센티미터(cm²)	제곱킬로미터(km²)	킬로그램(kg)	톤(t)

15. 길이 : ( ), ( ), ( )

16. 넓이 : ( ), ( ), ( )

17. 무게 : ( ), ( ), ( )

18. 부피 : ( ), ( ), ( )

[19-33] [보기]에서 알맞은 단어를 골라 (   ) 안에 쓰십시오.

Choose the appropriate word from the box below and then fill in the parenthesis.

[보기]

세금	신용	반품	할부	조건
가맹점	단기간	대기업	서투르다	경제적이다
고생하다	관리하다	심각하다	제공하다	포기하다

19. 이번에 새로 바꾼 차는 작지만 기름값이 적게 들어서 (   )이에요/예요.

20. 어머니께서 제 돈을 (   )어/아/여 주시기 때문에 월급을 받으면 모두 어머니께 드려요.

21. 이사한 지 한 달 만에 집값이 많이 올라서 (   )에 돈을 많이 벌었어요.

22. 한국에 온 지 얼마 안 돼서 아직 한국말이 (   )어요/아요/여요.

23. 취직 준비를 하던 아드님이 이번에 유명한 (   )에 취직을 하셨다니 정말 기쁘시겠어요.

24. 면세점은 (   )이/가 면제되어 있는 상품을 판매하는 곳이다.

25. 포장을 뜯어서 사용하신 제품은 (   )이/가 안 되니까 주의해 주십시오.

26. 거래처와의 약속을 그렇게 안 지키다가는 분명 (   )을/를 잃게 될 거예요.

27. 연세 카드 회사에서는 올해부터 고객들에게 고급 식당의 할인 서비스를 (   )기로 했다.

28. 저는 외국인인데 한국 대학교에 입학하고 싶어요. 입학 (   )이/가 어떻게 되나요?

29. 작년에 학원에서 중국어를 배웠는데 어찌나 어려운지 1달 만에 (   )고 말았어요.

30. 이 카드를 백화점, 식당, 커피숍, 놀이동산 같은 여러 (   )에서 사용하시면 할인 혜택을 받으실 수 있습니다.

31. 제 어머니는 혼자 자식 넷을 키우시느라고 평생 (   )으셨어요/셨어요.

32. 자동차나 가구 같이 한꺼번에 결제하기가 힘든 고가품은 (   )으로/로 구매하면 좋아요.

33. 작년에 비해 올해 실업률이 3%나 올라 실업문제가 (   )는/은/ㄴ 것으로 나타났다.

[34-35] 다음 밑줄 친 부분과 의미가 비슷한 것을 고르십시오.

Choose the word that is similar in meaning to the underlined part of the sentence.

34. 저는 백화점에 갔을 때 세일을 하거나 조금 싸게 파는 물건들이 있으면 무조건 사는 습관이 있어요.

① 환불하다 ② 반품하다 ③ 구매하다 ④ 교환하다

35. 신용카드를 처음 사용할 때는 카드 뒷면에 꼭 서명한 후에 사용하세요.

① 사인하다 ② 기록하다 ③ 설치하다 ④ 관리하다

[36-45] 다음 밑줄 친 부분과 반대되는 뜻을 가진 것을 고르십시오.

Choose the word that has the opposite meaning from the underlined word.

36. 이 가방은 유명 상품과 비슷해 보이지만 자세히 보면 가짜라는 것을 금방 알 수 있어요.

① 진짜 ② 공짜 ③ 제품 ④ 유사품

37. 올 여름 무더위가 계속되면서 작년 여름에 비해서 에어컨 판매가 2배나 늘었다.

① 많다 ② 적다 ③ 줄다 ④ 빼다

38. 그 할머니는 돈이 없어 공부를 못하는 가난한 학생들을 위해서 돈을 기부했어요.

① 충분하다 ② 부족하다 ③ 모자라다 ④ 부유하다

39. 열심히 일해서 번 돈을 낭비하면 안 되지요.

① 가난하다 ② 절약하다 ③ 상승하다 ④ 한산하다

40. 항공사들이 항공료를 인상한 이유는 원유 가격이 계속 상승하고 있기 때문이다.

① 올라가다 ② 뛰어나다 ③ 높아지다 ④ 하락하다

41. 주식 투자에 실패해서 손해를 많이 봤어요.

① 이자 ② 예금 ③ 이익 ④ 이상

42. 대한은행에서는 카드 서비스를 확대할 계획입니다.

① 제공하다 ② 축소하다 ③ 수입하다 ④ 선택하다

43. 한국은 원유, 석탄, 석유, 철과 같은 천연 자원을 많이 수입해요.

① 수산 ② 지출 ③ 수표 ④ 수출

44. 명품 가방이나 시계 같은 고가의 수입품을 살 때는 세금을 많이 내야 해요.

① 정가 ② 원가 ③ 저가 ④ 할인가

45. 방금 전까지 여기 있던 고양이가 갑자기 어디론가 사라져 버렸어요.

① 나타나다 ② 없어지다 ③ 넘어지다 ④ 지워지다

[46-60] [보기]에서 알맞은 단어를 골라 (　　) 안에 쓰십시오.

Choose the appropriate word from the box below and then fill in the parenthesis.

[보기]

경험	고객	공짜	광고	배송
상태	차이	하자	무이자	새롭다
견디다	문의하다	선택하다	조사하다	판매하다

46. 이번 세일 기간 동안에는 10만 원 이상 구입하신 (　　　　)분들께 사은품을 드립니다.

47. 오늘 저희 식당에서 식사하시는 모든 분들께 음료수를 (　　　　)으로/로 드립니다.

48. 아이들이 TV (　　　　)에 나오는 물건을 갖고 싶어 하는 것은 당연해요.

49. 올여름 신상품을 카드로 결제하시면 최대 12개월까지 (　　　　) 할부로 구입하실 수 있어요.

50. 제품에 이상이 생기면 먼저 사용 설명서를 읽어 보시고 그래도 해결이 되지 않으면 저희 서비스 센터로 (　　　　)어/아/여 주세요.

51. 인터넷으로 물건을 5만 원 이상 구매하시는 분들께 무료로 (　　　　)을/를 해 드리고 있습니다.

52. 가격이 저렴해서 구입했는데 집에 와서 보니까 제품의 (　　　　)이/가 좋지 않아서 반품했어요.

53. 드디어 그동안 사용해 오셨던 제품과 전혀 다른 (　　　　　)는/은/ㄴ 제품을 만나보실 수 있습니다.

54. 대학교에 다닐 때 등록금을 벌기 위해서 식당에서 아르바이트를 한 (　　　　　)이/가 있어요.

55. 돈이 넉넉하지 않은 소비자들은 고가의 제품보다는 저렴한 제품을 (　　　　　)을/ㄹ 수밖에 없다.

56. 컴퓨터를 사려고 전자제품 상가와 인터넷 쇼핑몰 가격을 비교해 봤더니 가격 (　　　　　)이/가 별로 없던데요.

57. 내일부터 백화점에서 모든 전자제품을 30% 할인해서 (　　　　　)는다고/ㄴ다고/다고 합니다.

58. 지금은 경제 상황이 힘들고 어렵지만 조금만 더 참고 (　　　　　)으면/면 분명 좋은 날이 올 거예요.

59. 물건에 (　　　　　)이/가 있으면 15일 이내에 언제든지 교환이 가능합니다.

60. 한국의 경제 시장을 잘 알기 위해서는 인터넷, 뉴스, 신문 등을 통해서 좀 더 (　　　　　)어야/아야/여야 할 것 같습니다.

[61-66] 다음 (　　　)에 공통적으로 들어갈 단어의 기본형을 쓰십시오.

Write the basic form of the word that can commonly fit into the parenthesis below.

61.
❶ 지금은 누가 잘하고 누가 잘못했는지 잘잘못을 (　　　　　)을/ㄹ 때가 아니다.
❷ 아내는 화가 잔뜩 난 목소리로 남편에게 왜 이렇게 늦었냐고 (　　　　　)었다/았다/였다.
❸ 어머니는 알뜰하셔서 물건을 살 때 항상 가격을 꼼꼼히 (　　　　　)어/아/여 보고 사세요.

(　　　　　　　　)

62.
❶ 올 가을에는 어떤 머리 스타일이 (　　　　　)을까요?/ㄹ 까요?
❷ 요즘 감기가 (　　　　　)는다니까/은다니까/ㄴ다니까 감기에 걸리지 않게 조심하세요.
❸ 친구 생일 선물도 살 겸 요즘 (　　　　　)는/은/ㄴ 옷도 구경할 겸 백화점에 갔다 왔어요.

(　　　　　　　　)

63. ❶ 시험공부를 한다고 책상 위에 책을 잔뜩 (　　　　　)어/아/여 놓기만 하고 공부는 안 했어요.

❷ 영어 공부와 컴퓨터 공부를 하면서 열심히 실력을 (　　　　　)으면/면 곧 좋은 회사에 취직할 수 있을 거예요.

❸ 유학생활은 힘들기는 하지만 그 나라의 언어와 문화를 배울 수 있고 다양한 경험도 (　　　　　)을/ㄹ 수 있어서 좋은 기회라고 생각됩니다.

(　　　　　　　　　　)

64. ❶ 이 약으로 환자의 고통을 좀 (　　　　　)어/아/여 줄 수 있을 거예요.

❷ 어머니께서 큰 접시에 있는 잡채를 제 그릇에 (　　　　　)어/아/여 주셨어요.

❸ 이렇게 미리 자료 준비를 해 줘서 제가 회의 준비하는 데 수고를 (　　　　　)었어요/았어요/였어요.

(　　　　　　　　　　)

65. ❶ 죽어가던 환자가 신속한 응급 조치로 (　　　　　)었어요/았어요/였어요.

❷ 사고로 잃어버렸던 기억들이 이번 일로 서서히 (　　　　　)기 시작했다.

❸ 지금 경제 상황이 안 좋지만 온 국민이 노력하고 있으니까 곧 경제가 (　　　　　)을/ㄹ 거예요.

(　　　　　　　　　　)

66. ❶ 우리 아이는 고집이 너무 (　　　　　)어서/아서/여서 걱정이에요.

❷ 매일 운동하는 민수 씨는 힘이 얼마나 (　　　　　)는지/은지/ㄴ지 몰라요.

❸ 거스름돈을 받은 후에는 금액이 맞는지 잘 (　　　　　)어/아/여 봐야 해요.

(　　　　　　　　　　)

[67-81] 다음 [보기]에서 알맞은 단어를 골라 (　　　) 안에 쓰십시오.

Choose the appropriate word from the box below and then fill in the parenthesis.

[보기]

즉	경우	기회	소비자	보험
할인	긴장	서비스	중요성	얻다
맞추다	그만두다	수고하다	면제되다	환불하다

67. 새로 생긴 그 옷가게는 옷값도 싸고 예쁜 옷들도 많은 데다가 점원들의 (　　　　　　)도 좋아서 자주 가요.

68. 옷이 잘 맞지 않을 (　　　　　　)에는 1주일 안에만 가지고 오시면 교환해 드립니다.

69. 이번 신제품이 (　　　　　　)들에게 좋은 반응을 얻고 있어요.

70. 회사 일이 너무 힘들고 건강도 나빠져서 회사를 (　　　　　　)어야/아야/여야 할 것 같아요.

71. 지금 할인 행사를 하고 있으니 그동안 비용이 부담스러워 구매하지 못하셨던 분들은 이번 (　　　　　　)을/를 절대 놓치지 마세요.

72. 보통 때는 노래를 잘 부르는데 많은 사람들 앞이라 (　　　　　　)을/를 해서 그런지 실수를 많이 했어요.

73. 신발이 작아서 한 치수 더 큰 것으로 교환하려고 왔는데 사이즈가 없다면 그냥 (　　　　　　)어/아/여 주세요.

74. 미선아, 감기에 걸려서 몸도 안 좋은데 밤늦게까지 아르바이트를 하느라고 정말 (　　　　　　)었다/았다/였다.

75. 요즘은 신문이나 잡지뿐만 아니라 인터넷을 통해서도 여러 가지 정보를 (　　　　　　)을/ㄹ 수 있어요.

76. 이번에 수술을 받고 건강의 (　　　　　　)을/를 다시 깨닫게 되었어요.

77. 같은 은행의 계좌로 돈을 보낼 때는 수수료가 (　　　　　　)어요/아요/여요.

78. 자동차를 갖고 계시다면 언제, 어떻게 사고가 날지 모르니까 꼭 자동차 (　　　　　　)에 가입해야 해요.

79. 현금으로 구입하시면 10% (　　　　　　)을/를 해 드립니다.

80. 남는 시간, (　　　　　　) 여가 시간을 잘 활용하는 것이 중요하다.

81. 까다로운 고객들의 기분을 (　　　　　　)기란 쉬운 일이 아니에요.

사회

09

Society

09 사회

01
가능하다

[가능하다] 형용사 to be possible

[Antonym] 불가능하다 to be impossible

[Example] 좀 힘들지만 마음만 먹으면 주말에 시간을 내는 건 가능해요.
Though it may be hard, it is possible for me to make time this weekend as long as I put my mind to it.

구입한 지 3일 안에는 교환이 가능하다고 판매 규정에 써 있습니다.
The store policy is that it is possible to exchange a product within three days of the purchase date.

02
개발하다

[개발하다] 동사 1. to develop 2. to tap into, to exploit

1. to improve the technology, knowledge, or talent of something

[Usage] N 을/를 개발하다

[Example] 자기 개발을 통해 자신의 능력을 좀 더 키울 수 있다.
You can improve your own abilities through self-development.

2. to freely obtain access to natural resources of a land

[Usage] N 을/를 N 으로/로 개발하다

[Related Words] 개척하다 to exploit

[Example] 버려진 땅에 건물을 지어 개발하기로 했어요.
They decided to use the discarded land and erect a building there.

03
거래

[거래] 명사 transaction

[Expression] 거래처 account, client
거래하다 to make a transaction
거래가 활발하다 The transaction is active.
거래가 이루어지다 The transaction is completed.
거래를 트다 to open an account

[Example] 요즘 경기가 좋아서 부동산 거래가 활발하게 이루어지고 있다.
Because the economy is doing well lately, there has been a lot of activity in real estate dealings.

사장님, 거래처에서 연락이 왔는데요. 오늘까지 물건을 보내 달래요.
Boss, the account holder contacted us today. They said to send the item by today.

04
건의하다

[거니하다] 동사 to make a proposal, to make a suggestion

[Usage] N 에/에게 N 을/를 건의하다
N 에/에게 AV 자고 건의하다
N 에/에게 AV 도록 건의하다

[Example] 주민들은 공원을 건립하자고 구청에 건의했다.
The citizens proposed to the district office that they construct a park.

값싸고 품질 좋은 한국 화장품을 해외에 수출하자고 건의했다.
It was suggested that Korea's cheap and high quality makeup be exported abroad.

05
건축가

[건축까] 명사 architect

[Example] 이 건물의 설계는 우리나라 최고의 건축가가 맡았습니다.
The layout of this building was entrusted to Korea's best architect.

어렸을 때부터 건축에 관심이 많았던 아들은 커서 건축가가 되었다.
My son, which had been interested in architecture from the time he was little, grew up to become an architect.

06
검사

[검사] 명사 prosecutor

[Related Words] 판사 judge
변호사 lawyer

[Example] 그 변호사는 검사 출신이다.
He used to be a prosecutor and now works as a lawyer.

법률 관련 다큐멘터리를 본 후에 검사가 되고 싶어졌어요.
I wanted to become a prosecutor after seeing a documentary about law.

07
결과

[결과] 명사 result

[Expression] 결과를 초래하다 to lead to a result

[Related Words] 원인 cause

[Example] 지금 계획을 바꾼다고 해도 결과는 변하지 않을 거예요.
Even if you change your plans now, the results won't be any different.

농구 시합 결과가 궁금해서 수업이 끝나자마자 뛰어왔어요.
I was curious about the results of the basketball game, so I ran to find them out as soon as class finished.

08
결정하다 [결쩡하다] 동사 to decide

[Usage] AV 기로 결정하다

[Synonym] 정하다 to decide

[Example] 이번 세미나 참가 여부를 결정해서 알려 주세요.
Please contact me after you have decided if you are going to attend this seminar.

한국에 유학 가기로 결정하긴 했지만 아직도 걱정이 많아요.
I decided to go to study abroad in Korea but I am still quite worried.

09
경력 [경녁] 명사 work experience

[Expression] 경력자 an experienced worker
경력이 있다 to have work experience
경력이 없다 to have no work experience

[Related Words] 초보 beginner, novice

[Example] 이력서에 지금까지 다닌 학교와 일한 경력을 기록했어요.
I recorded my school information and work experience that I have accumulated until now on my resume.

배달 경력이 없는 초보자도 여기서 아르바이트를 할 수 있어요?
Can a beginner that has no delivery boy experience work here as well?

10
경영하다 [경영하다] 동사 to run a business

[Usage] N 을/를 경영하다

[Expression] 회사를 경영하다 to run a business

[Example] 부모님께서 작은 신발 공장을 경영하고 계세요.
My parents run a small shoe factory.

요즘 같이 경제난이 심할 때 회사를 잘 경영하기란 여간 힘든 일이 아니다.
In difficult times like today, it is extremely difficult to be able to successfully run a business.

11
경쟁 [경쟁] 명사 competition

[Usage] N 이/가 N 과/와 경쟁을 하다

[Expression] 경쟁자 a competitor
경쟁률 competition rate

경쟁이 붙다 to compete against each other
경쟁이 치열하다 The competition is fierce.

[Example] 두 사람은 오래 전부터 선의의 경쟁 관계였다.
There has been a long history of friendly competition between the two of them.

동생은 10대 1의 경쟁을 뚫고 어렵게 대기업에 입사를 했다.
My younger sibling overcame the 10 to 1 rate of competition and secured a job in the corporation.

12
계약

[계약] 명사 contract

[Expression] 계약서 a contract
계약금 contractual fees
계약하다 to make a contract
계약을 깨다 to break a contract

[Example] 방이 마음에 들어서 바로 계약을 하고 싶은데요.
I like the room and I would like to make an agreement right away.

계약을 할 때는 계약서를 꼼꼼히 읽어 봐야 합니다.
When entering a contract, one must carefully go through the contract.

13
고대

[고대] 명사 ancient time

[Related Words] 중세 middle ages
근대 modern times
현대 modern times

[Example] 그리스 아테네는 유명한 고대 도시예요.
Athens was the famous ancient city of Greece.

최 교수님은 요즘 고대 문자를 연구하십니다.
Professor Choi has recently been researching classical letters.

14
공장

[공장] 명사 factory

[Expression] 공장을 짓다 to built a factory
공장을 세우다 to establish a factory
공장에 다니다 to go to the factory
공장에 취직하다 to be employed at a factory

[Example] 아버지는 자동차 공장에서 일하신 지 25년이나 되셨어요.
My father has been working at a car factory for twenty-five years.

우리 회사는 이번에 사업을 확장하면서 시외에 공장을 하나 더 세우려고 해요.
Our company is planning on building another factory outside of the city while expanding its trade.

15
과학자

[과학짜] 명사 scientist

[Example] 아인슈타인은 물리학 분야에서 가장 위대한 과학자라고 할 수 있다.
One could say that Einstein is the greatest scientist in the field of physics.

많은 과학자들의 노력으로 2003년에 사람의 유전자 지도가 완성되었다.
Through the efforts of many scientists, the gene map of man was completed in 2003.

16
국가

[국까] 명사 nation

[Expression] 국가 권력 political power of the nation
국가 기관 national foundation
국가 발전 national development

[Related Words] 국기 national flag
국립 national
국민 national (resident)
국어 language of a country
국토 national territory

[Example] 많은 군인들이 국가를 위해 목숨을 바쳤다.
Many of the soldiers died a martyr to their principles for their country

민주주의 국가에서는 국민의 자유과 권리를 중요하게 생각한다.
In democratic nations, the freedom of its citizens and their rights are considered to be important.

17
국회의원

[구쾨의원] [구쾨이원] 명사 congressman

[Example] 제 꿈은 나라를 위해 열심히 일하는 국회의원입니다.
My dream is to become a congressman that works hard for this country.

5월 29일 토요일은 국회의원 선거일이니까 모두 투표하시기 바랍니다.
Saturday, May 29th is the day of the congressional elections. We hope that everyone comes out to vote.

18
그대로

[그대로] 부사 1. as it is 2. the same

1. without any change in the same form

[Related Words] 변함없이 without change

[Example] 움직이지 말고 그대로 가만히 있어.
Don't move. Stay just the way you are.

2. the same as something

[Related Words] 똑같이 just like

[Example] 그 아이는 정말 아버지를 그대로 닮았네요.
That child really looks just like his father.

19
근로자

[글로자] 명사 laborer, worker

[Related Words] 노동자 worker

[Example] 한국에서 5월 1일은 근로자의 날이다.
May 1st is worker's day in Korea.

그 회사는 이번에 여성 근로자들을 위해 여성 휴게실을 만들었다.
That company built a lounge for its female workers.

20
근무하다

[근무하다] 동사 to work

[Usage] N 에서 근무하다

[Synonym] 일하다 to work

[Example] 어떤 회사에서 근무하고 싶으세요?
In what company would you like to work?

저는 오전 8시부터 오후 6시까지 근무해요.
I work from 8 in the morning until 6 in the evening.

21
능력

[능녁] 명사 ability, skill

[Expression] 능력이 있다 to be skillful
능력이 없다 to have no skill
능력이 뛰어나다 His abilities are excellent.

[Related Words] 실력 capability

[Example] 김 대리님은 능력이 뛰어나서 무슨 일이든지 잘해요.
Deputy Kim can handle any kind of job because he is very capable.

이번 한국어 능력 시험에서 친구는 합격을 했는데 나는 떨어졌어.
My friend passed the Korean proficiency exam but I failed.

22
담당하다

[담당하다] 동사 to be in charge of

[Usage] N 을/를 담당하다

[Synonym] 맡다 to take on

[Example] 이 일을 담당한 지 벌써 2년이 되었네요.
It has already been two years since I have been in charge of this work.

직원 교육을 담당하고 있는 김민수라고 합니다.
My name is Kim Minsu and I am in charge of employee education.

23
대통령

[대통녕] 명사 president

[Related Words] 부통령 vice president

[Example] 대통령께서 6월 말에 중국을 방문하기로 했습니다.
The president has decided to make a formal visit to China at the end of June.

대통령은 월드컵 축구 대표팀 선수들을 직접 만나 격려했다.
The president met the World Cup soccer team players and encouraged them.

24
도전하다

[도전하다] 명사 to challenge

[Usage] N 이/가 N 에 도전하다

[Example] 나는 새로운 일에 도전하는 것을 좋아해.
I like taking on new challenges.

이번에 대학원 시험에 한번 도전해 볼 생각이야.
I am thinking of applying to take the next graduate school exam.

25
디자이너

[디자이너] 명사 designer

[Expression] 헤어 디자이너 hair designer
의상 디자이너 clothes designer, costume designer
인테리어 디자이너 interior designer

[Example] 의상 디자이너들은 예쁘고 실용적인 옷을 만들기 위하여 노력한다.
Clothes designers strive to make practical and pretty clothes.

요즘 젊은 여성들이 가장 좋아하는 전문직 중에 하나가 바로 디자이너 예요.
Nowadays, one of the most liked jobs by women is that of a designer.

26
마치다

[마치다] 동사 to finish, to put an end to

[Synonym] 끝내다 to end

[Example] 이 공사를 마치는데 얼마나 걸릴까요?
How much longer will it take to finish the construction?

일을 마치는 대로 바로 전화해 주세요.
Please contact me as soon as you complete the job.

27
맡다^2

[맏따] 동사 to take on, to be put in charge of

[Usage] N 을/를 맡다

[Expression] 일을 맡다 to take on a job

[Example] 맡은 일은 확실하게 책임지고 끝내겠습니다.
I will fully take the responsibility of the job given to me and will finish it.

이번에 큰 프로젝트를 맡아서 눈 코 뜰 새 없이 바빠요.
I'm very busy because I've taken on this big project.

28
면접시험

[면접시험] 명사 oral interview, test in the form of an interview

[Expression] 면접시험을 보다 to have an interview
면접시험에 붙다 to pass an interview
면접시험에 합격하다 to pass an interview
면접시험에서 떨어지다 to be rejected from an interview, to fail an oral exam

[Related Words] 구술시험 oral test
필기시험 written test

[Example] 면접시험을 볼 때는 자신감을 갖고 대답하세요.
Answer with confidence when you are on interview.

필기시험은 합격했는데 면접시험에서 불합격했어요.
I passed the written test but failed the oral one.

29
목수

[목쑤] 명사 carpenter

[Example] 목수들은 일의 특성상 자주 다친다.
Carpenters often are injured due to the nature of their work.

목수는 목재를 가지고 물건이나 가구를 만드는 사람이에요.
Carpenters are people that take wood and make objects or furniture.

30
목표

[목표] 명사 goal

[Expression] 목표를 위해서 for a goal
목표를 이루다 to achieve one's goal
목표를 향하다 to go towards one's goals
목표를 달성하다 to achieve a goal

[Related Words] 목적 purpose

[Example] 우리 회사 올해 수출 목표는 20억이다.
The company aspires to export 2 billion won in products this year.

라이벌이란 같은 목표를 가진 경쟁자 중에 실력이 비슷한 사람을 말한다.
A rival is someone who has similar skills among a group of competitors with the same goal as you.

31
몰두하다

[몰뚜하다] 동사 to focus

[Usage] N 에 몰두하다

[Synonym] 집중하다 to concentrate

[Example] 김 박사님은 요즘 실험실에서 신약 연구에만 몰두하고 계세요.
Scientist Mr. Kim has been focusing on new medicine research in the laboratory.

그동안 신제품 개발에 몰두한 결과 우리 회사는 이번에 신제품 판매로 10억이 넘는 이익을 얻었다.
As a result of intense new product development, the company has reaped over 1 billion won in new product sales.

32
무렵

[무렵] 명사 around the time

[Usage] N 무렵
AV / DV 을/ㄹ 무렵

[Example] 해가 질 무렵에 아이들이 집으로 돌아왔다.
The kids came home around the time the sun was setting.

전국이 흐리고 저녁 무렵에는 비가 오겠습니다.
The entire country will be cloudy and around the evening time it will rain.

33
무리하다

[무리하다] 동사 to overdo oneself, to overexert oneself

[Usage] N 을/를 무리하다
무리하게 N 을/를 하다

[Example] 몸이 건강해야 뭐든지 할 수 있으니까 무리하지 마세요.
Your body needs to be healthy for you to do anything, so make sure not to overwork yourself.

다리가 다 나은 것은 아니니까 너무 무리하게 운동 하지 마십시오.
Don't do too much exercise because your leg hasn't fully healed yet.

34
무역

[무역] 명사 trade

[Expression] 무역회사 trade company
해외 무역 oversea trade
무역하다 to trade

[Example] 무역회사에서 일해서 해외출장을 많이 가는 편이에요.
I often go abroad on business trips because I work for a trade company.

두 나라의 관계가 가까워짐에 따라 양국 간의 무역이 활발해졌어요.
Since the relationship between the two countries has gotten better, the trade between the two countries has also flourished.

35
문제점

[문제쩜] 명사 problem, drawback

[Expression] 문제점이 있다 There is a problem.
문제점이 없다 There is no problem.
문제점을 발견하다 to discover a problem

[Example] 계획서에 문제점이 많으니까 다시 한 번 검토해 주십시오.
There are a lot of problems in the prospectus, so please edit it one more time.

우리 부서의 가장 큰 문제점은 인원이 부족하다는 것입니다.
The biggest problem in our department is the lack of workers.

36
미래

[미래] 명사 future

[Synonym] 앞날 coming days
장래 future

[Related Words] 과거 past
현재 present

[Example] 밝은 미래를 위해서 열심히 공부하자.
Let's work hard for a brighter future.

부모님들은 자식들의 미래를 위해서 언제나 걱정하십니다.
Parents are always worrying about the future of their kids.

37
반대하다

[반대하다] 동사 to oppose, to go against

[Usage] N 을/를 반대하다
N 에 반대하다

[Antonym] 찬성하다 to agree with, to support

[Example] 이 의견에 반대하시는 분은 손을 들어주십시오.
Please raise your hand if you oppose this opinion.

다행히 부모님께서 우리 두 사람의 결혼을 반대하지 않으셨어요.
Luckily, my parents didn't oppose our marriage.

38
발견하다

[발견하다] 동사 to discover, to uncover

[Usage] N 을/를 발견하다

[Related Words] 발명하다 to invent

[Example] 다른 친구와 여러분의 공통점을 발견해 보세요.
Please discover the similarities between you and your friends.

불씨를 1분만 늦게 발견했어도 큰 화재가 날 뻔했어요.
If we had discovered the fire one minute later, a huge fire would have started.

39
발달하다

[발딸하다] 동사 to develop, to improve

[Usage] N 이/가 발달하다

[Expression] 과학이 발달하다 Science is developed.

[Related Words] 발전하다 to improve

[Example] 최근 연구 결과에 의하면 외우는 능력은 쓰면 쓸수록 발달된다고 합니다.
According to recent research results, the more you use your memorization skills, the more developed they become.

과학이 발달하면서 인간의 생활이 편리해진 점도 있지만 부작용도 생겼어요.
As science becomes more developed, there are a lot more conveniences in the daily life of man. However, this also leads to side effects.

40
번화하다

[번화하다] 형용사 to be busy, to be bustling

[Usage] N 이/가 번화하다

[Related Words] 붐비다 to be crowded

[Example] 도심에는 30층 이상의 고층 건물이 많아서 아주 번화하다.
There are a lot of buildings with over 30 floors in the town center, so it is very busy.

환경이 쾌적하다든가 동네가 번화하다든가 하면 집값이 비싸요.
If the environment is comfortable or the neighborhood is bustling, the prices of houses are very expensive.

41
벌이다

[버리다] 동사 1. to start, to begin 2. to arrange

1. to start or begin

[Usage] N 을/를 벌이다

[Expression] 사업을 벌이다 to start a business
잔치를 벌이다 to start a party

[Synonym] 시작하다 to begin

[Example] 오빠가 이번에 새로운 사업을 벌이려고 해요.
My brother is planning on starting a new business.

2. to put one thing on top of another

[Usage] N 에 N 을/를 벌이다

[Synonym] 늘어놓다 arrange

[Example] 지하철 입구 근처에는 물건을 벌여 놓고 파는 사람들이 많다.
There are a lot of people that arrange goods and sell them near the subway entrances.

42
보고하다

[보고하다] 동사 to report

to inform about the results of an event in written or spoken form

[Usage] N 을/를 N 에/에게 보고하다

[Example] 오늘은 특별히 보고할 사항이 없습니다.
There is no particular matter to report today.

저는 그 문제에 대해서 사장님께 보고하지 않았어요.
I didn't report about that problem to the boss.

43
부담

[부담] 명사 1. responsibility, burden 2. to cover expenses

1. taking responsibility or obligation

[Expression] 부담스럽다 to be burdensome
부담이 없다 to have no burdens
부담이 되다 to become burdensome
부담을 주다 to give a burden to someone else
부담을 느끼다 to feel burdened

[Example] 다행히 의료 보험에 가입되어 있어서 병원비 부담이 적어요.
Luckily, there were few hospital expenses to bear because I was covered by my medical insurance.

2. to cover expenses, to pay

[Expression] 부담하다 to pay

[Synonym] 내다 to pay

[Example] 출장비용은 회사가 부담해야 할 비용이다.
The expenses of the business trip are to be paid by the company.

44
뽑다

[뽑따] 동사 1. to pull out 2. to choose

1. to pull out something that is stuck

[Usage] N 을/를 뽑다

[Expression] 이를 뽑다 to pull out a tooth
풀을 뽑다 to pull out grass
코드를 뽑다 to pull out the cord
번호표를 뽑다 to take a number

[Example] 치과에 일찍 갔으면 이도 안 뽑고 얼마나 좋았겠어요?
How nice would it have been if I had gone to the dentist earlier and not had to pull out a tooth?

2. to pick one thing out of many

[Usage] N 을/를 N 으로/로 뽑다

[Synonym] 선출하다 to elect

[Example] 누구를 동아리 회장으로 뽑을지 결정합시다.
Let's decide whom we are going to choose as our club leader.

45
사정

[사정] 명사 reason, circumstance

[Expression] 개인 사정 personal reason
집안 사정 family reason
회사 사정 company situation
사정이 있다 There is a reason
사정이 생기다 A reason has come up.

[Synonym] 형편 situation

[Example] 요즘 경제 사정이 안 좋아서 취직하기가 정말 힘들어요.
It is really hard to get a job because the economic situation is in a bad state.

올해부터 회사 사정이 좋아졌고 매출액도 눈에 띄게 증가했다.
Starting from this year, my company has been doing much better and there has been a surprising increase in sales.

46
상관

[상관] 명사 superior, boss

[Synonym] 상사 boss

[Related Words] 부하 junior, lower leveled employee

[Example] 내 상관은 항상 친절하고 우리들 일에 하나하나 신경을 써 줘.
My boss is always kind and pays very close attention to all of our work.

신입 사원 때는 제 자신의 능력을 발휘하기보다는 상관이 시키는 일만 하루 종일 해야 했습니다.
When I was a new employee here, I did just as my boss ordered all day long rather than trying to display my own abilities.

47
서류

[서류] 명사 document

[Expression] 서류를 내다 to hand in a document
서류를 작성하다 to write up a document
서류를 제출하다 to submit a document

[Related Words] 문서 papers

[Example] 회의가 곧 시작될 텐데 서류는 다 준비됐나요?
The meeting should be starting soon. Have you prepared all the documents?

쓰레기를 버린다는 것이 그만 중요한 서류를 버렸어요.
Instead of throwing away the garbage, he threw away the important documents.

48
성공하다

[성공하다] 동사 1. to succeed 2. to achieve honor or recognition

1. to achieve one's goals

[Usage] N 에 성공하다
AV 는 데 성공하다

[Antonym] 실패하다 to fail

[Example] 이번 연구에 성공하면 회사를 다시 살릴 수 있을 거예요.
If I succeed at my research this time, I will be able to save the company.

2. to obtain social recognition or honor

[Usage] N 으로/로 성공하다

[Example] 성공하면 돈과 명예를 모두 가질 수 있다고 생각해요.
If you become successful, I think you can obtain both money and fame.

49
세기

[세기] 명사 century

[Example] 15세기는 몇 년부터인가요?
From what year does the 15th century begin?

미술관에 19세기 화가들의 작품이 많이 전시되어 있어요.
Many works of 19th century artists are being displayed at the art museum.

50
세월

[세월] 명사 time, flowing of time, long passage of time

[Expression] 세월이 가다 Time goes by.
세월이 지나다 Time passes.
세월이 흐르다 Time flys by.

[Example] 정말 세월이 빠르게 흐르는 것 같아요.
I think that time really does go by quickly.

지금은 이해하기 힘들겠지만 세월이 흐른 후엔 이해할 수 있을 거야.
I think that it might be hard for you to understand now, but after some time goes by you will be able to.

51
순간

[순간] 명사 1. moment, instant 2. as soon as

1. very short time

[Example] 순간의 실수로 친구에게 오해를 받았다.
There was a misunderstanding between my friend and I due to a sudden mistake.

2. at the time when something happens

[Usage] AV 는/은/ㄴ 순간

[Example] 사진을 보는 순간 옛날 기억이 떠올랐다.
Once I saw the picture, I started to think about the past.

52
승진하다

[승진하다] 동사 to promote

to go up in class or rank in the office

[Usage] N 으로/로 승진하다

[Related Words] 진급하다 to go up in level

[Example] 과장으로 승진하면 한턱낼게요.
I will treat you if you are promoted to chief.

이번에 승진하셨다면서요? 축하드립니다.
I heard that you were promoted? Congratulations.

53
시인

[시인] 명사 poet

[Example] 어렸을 때 제 꿈은 시인이 되는 것이었어요.
When I was young, my dream was to become a poet.

그 시인은 평생 단 한 권의 시집만 냈습니다.
That poet only wrote one book of poems in his entire life.

54
시절

[시절] 명사 time, days

a set time or period of time

[Related Words] 시대 generation

[Example] 아버지께서는 가끔 우리들에게 학창 시절 얘기를 하신다.
My father sometimes tells me about his school days.

대학교에 다닐 때가 인생에서 제일 좋은 시절이었던 것 같다.
I think that the best time in my life was when I attended college.

55
신상품

[신상품] 명사 new products

newly developed products

[Expression] 신상품을 내놓다 to release a new product
신상품을 출시하다 to launch a new product

[Related Words] 신제품 new product

[Example] 이번 신상품이 시장에서 좋은 반응을 얻고 있어요.
The new product has gotten a good reaction in the store.

난 요즘 유행하는 여름 신상품 옷을 너무 사고 싶어.
I really want to buy the new summer clothes that are in style.

56
신형

[신형] 명사 new style, latest model

[Usage] 신형 N

[Expression] 최신형 latest style

[Example] 얼마 전에 신형 냉장고를 구입했어요.
I bought a new styled refrigerator not too long ago.

컴퓨터 사용자들의 대부분이 2년마다 신형 컴퓨터를 구입한대요.
They say that computer users tend to buy the latest computer model every two years.

57
실수하다

[실쑤하다] 동사 to make a mistake

[Synonym] 잘못하다 to make a mistake

[Example] 다시는 실수하지 않도록 주의하겠습니다.
I will be careful as to not make a mistake again.

누구나 실수하기 마련이지요. 완벽한 사람은 없으니까요.
It is natural that we all make mistakes. That is because no one is perfect.

58
아나운서

[아나운서] 명사 announcer, broadcaster

[Example] 오늘은 김영수 아나운서가 축구 중계를 하기로 되어 있습니다.
Today, announcer Kim Youngsoo is going to be televising the soccer match.

딸은 중학교 때 방송반 활동을 하면서부터 아나운서의 꿈을 가지게 되었다.
From middle school, my daughter participated in a lot of broadcasting activities and soon after her dream was to become an announcer.

59
야근

[야근] 명사 late-night shift, working overtime at night

[Expression] 야근 수당 late night work benefits
야근을 하다 to work late nights

[Example] 매일 야근을 해서 건강이 나빠졌어요.
My health got worse after working late at night so often.

출장도 자주 가고 야근도 많던데 건강에는 문제가 없으세요?
You have to go on a lot of business trips and often work late at night. Despite that, is your health okay?

60
어느새

[어느새] 부사 before one knows it, all of a sudden

[Related Words] 벌써 already

[Example] 입학한 지가 어제 같은데 어느새 졸업이다.
It feels just like yesterday that I started school and before you know it I am graduating.

시간이 참 빨라요. 어느새 우리가 만난 지 1년이 다 되었네요.
Times go by so fast. It's already been a year since we have met each other.

61
업무

[엄무] 명사 office work

[Expression] 업무를 맡다 to be given office work

업무를 담당하다 to be in charge of office work
업무를 책임지다 to be responsible for the office work

[Synonym] 일 work

[Example] 저는 수출 업무를 담당하고 있어요.
I am in charge of exports.

다들 업무가 많아서 바쁘니까 회식은 다음 주로 미뤄야 할 것 같습니다.
I know that all of you are busy because of your work here in the office. Therefore, I am going to push back the meeting to next week.

62
여유

[여유] 명사 free time, composure

to have sufficient time to do something, to calmly and rationally think and act in a matter

[Expression] 여유롭다 to be calm and composed
여유가 있다 to have free time
여유가 없다 to have no free time

[Related Words] 여가 leisure

[Example] 시간적인 여유가 있다면 기타를 배워 보고 싶어요.
If I had more free time, I would like to learn how to play the guitar.

자동차를 새로 바꾸고 싶지만 그럴 만한 여유가 없네요.
I would like to change my car again, but I can't afford to buy one.

63
영향

[영향] 명사 influence

[Expression] 영향을 받다 to be influenced
영향을 주다 to influence
영향을 끼치다 to produce an influence

[Example] 인간의 몸은 기후의 영향을 받는다고 합니다.
It is said that the human body is influenced by the weather.

민수 씨의 인생에 가장 큰 영향을 끼치신 분은 누구신가요?
Who do you think is the person that has had the biggest influence in Minsu's life?

64
예전

[예전] 명사 before, in the past

[Synonym] 옛날 a long time ago
이전 before

[Example] 예전에는 이곳이 학교였었어요.
This place was a school in the past.

예전에 나의 꿈은 선생님이 되는 것이었다.
My dream was to become a teacher.

65
예정

[예정] 명사 schedule, plan

expecting to or to planning to do something

[Usage] AV 을/ㄹ 예정이다

[Expression] 예정대로 as expected

[Related Words] 예상 expectation

[Example] 회사일로 다음 주에 러시아로 출국할 예정이에요.
I am expecting to leave to Russia next week on business.

이번 명절에는 비정규직에게도 상여금이 지급될 예정입니다.
We are planning to give a bonus even to the temporary workers this holiday.

66
외교관

[외교관] 명사 foreign diplomat

[Related Words] 대사 ambassador
대사관 embassy

[Example] 서울에 주재하는 각국의 외교관들은 대통령의 초대로 청와대를 방문했다.
The foreign diplomats from every country that are residing in Korea were invited to see the president at "Cheonwadae" (The White House of Korea)

외교관이 되려면 기본적으로 3개 국어를 잘해야 한다고 하던데 정말인가요?
If you want to become a foreign diplomat, they say that you must know at least three foreign languages very well. Do you think that is true?

67
짓다

[짇따] 동사 1. to build, to make 2. to write 3. to prepare medicine

1. to use materials to make food, built a house, or make clothes.

[Usage] N 을/를 짓다

[Expression] 밥을 짓다 to make food
건물을 짓다 to build a building

[Related Words] 세우다 to build
만들다 to make

[Example] 이 건물은 100년 전에 지었어요.
This building was erected 100 years ago.

2. to write a poem, novel, level, song lyrics or any other kind of writing

[Usage] N 을/를 짓다

[Expression] 시를 짓다 to write a poem
이름을 짓다 to write one's name

[Related Words] 쓰다 to write
만들다 to make

[Example] 딸의 이름을 어떻게 지을지 고민 중이에요.
I'm worrying about what to name my daughter.

3. to mix together a lot of materials and prepare a medicine

[Usage] N 을/를 짓다

[Expression] 약을 짓다 to make a medicine

[Related Words] 만들다 to prepare

[Example] 아이가 몸이 약해진 것 같아서 보약을 지어 먹였어요.
I made an herbal remedy for my child because he was feeling weak.

68
최초

[최초] 명사 earliest

[Antonym] 최후 latest

[Example] 최초의 텔레비전은 화면이 흑백이었다.
The earliest television screens were blank and white.

이 제품은 한국에서 세계 최초로 개발한 제품이다.
This product, developed in Korea, was the first one of its kind worldwide.

69
출세

[출쎄] 명사 to rise to a high position, to be successful in life

[Expression] 출세를 하다 to be successful in life

[Example] 열심히 노력해서 유명한 사람이 되었으니까 출세했다고 할 수 있다.
You can say that I have led a successful life because I worked very hard and became a famous person.

부모가 아무리 돈이 많다고 해도 본인이 노력을 안 하면 출세하기 어렵지요.
No matter how much money your parents have, if you don't work hard on your own, it is difficult to be successful in life.

70
탤런트

[탤런트] 명사 an actor or actress that appears on a television drama

[Related Words] 연예인 entertainer

[Example] 탤런트 이영미 씨가 다음 달에 결혼을 한다고 합니다.
People say that television actress Yi Yongmi is getting married next month.

탤런트가 되고 싶어서 요즘 탤런트 학원에 다니고 있어요.
Nowadays, I have been attending television actor's school since I want to become a television personality.

71
파일

[파일] 명사 1. file (office) 2. electronic file (computer)

1. office file

[Expression] 파일을 제출하다 to submit a file
파일에 넣다 to put into a file
파일에 끼우다 to stick into a file

[Synonym] 서류철 file

[Example] 책상 위에 놓아 둔 파일이 어디 갔는지 찾고 있는 중이에요.
I am looking for the file I left on top of the desk.

2. computer file

[Expression] 첨부 파일 attached file
파일을 복사하다 to copy a file
파일을 삭제하다 to delete a file
파일을 첨부하다 to attach a file

[Example] 힘들게 작업한 파일이 모두 지워져 버렸어요.
The file I worked hard on was erased.

72
프로게이머

[프로게이머] 명사 professional computer/online gamer

[Related Words] 게임 game

[Example] 요즘 10대 청소년들에게 가장 인기 있는 직업은 프로게이머라고 해요.
The most popular job among teenagers is to become a progamer.

프로게이머 중에는 돈을 많이 버는 사람도 있지만 대부분 소득이 불안정한 편이에요.
Although there are a few progamers that make a lot money, most of them make little income.

73
한산하다

[한산하다] 형용사 to be dull, to be inactive, to slack off

[Synonym] 한가하다 to rest from work

[Antonym] 붐비다 to be crowded and busy

[Example] 명절이 되면 서울 거리는 오히려 한산해요.
When it's a holiday, the streets of Seoul are rather quiet.

그 한식집은 늘 붐비는 집인데 오늘은 웬일인지 한산하네요.
That Korean restaurant is normally crowded, but for some reason today it is empty.

74
해결하다 [해결하다] 동사 to solve

[Usage] N 을/를 해결하다

[Synonym] 풀다 to solve

[Example] 지구 온난화 문제를 어떻게 해결할 수 있을까요?
How can we possibly solve the problem of global warming?

혼자 해결하기 어려운 문제가 생기면 부모님과 상의합니다.
If a problem that is too hard for me to solve alone arises, I discuss it with my parents.

75
형식적이다 [형식쩌기다] 형용사 to be superficial, to be formal

referring the exterior shape or appearance

[Usage] 형식적인 N
형식적으로 AV

[Example] 두 사람은 깊이 있는 내용 없이 형식적인 대화만 했다.
The two of them were having a superficial conversation that lacked substance.

형식적인 면 보다는 내용적인 면을 더 중요하게 생각해야 한다고 봅니다.
I believe that we must consider the internal aspect more than the external one.

76
획일적이다 [회길쩌기다] 형용사 to be standard, to be uniform

all things being the same in appearance and aspect

[Usage] 획일적인 N
획일적으로 AV

[Example] 그 원칙들은 모든 부서에 걸쳐 획일적으로 적용되었다.
Those rules were applied uniformly across all departments.

요즘엔 획일적인 상품으로는 소비자의 마음을 쉽게 잡을 수 없다.
The standardized products of nowadays can barely grab the attention of the consumer.

77
효율적이다 [효율쩌기다] 형용사 to be efficient

[Usage] 효율적인 N

효율적으로 AV

[Synonym] 능률적이다 efficient

[Antonym] 비효율적이다 ineffective

[Example] 버리는 시간이 없도록 시간을 좀 더 효율적으로 사용해야겠다.
I should use my time more efficiently in order to waste less of it.

예전에는 제품을 손으로 포장하다 보니 일의 속도가 느렸는데 요즘에는 기계로 하니까 훨씬 효율적이다.
Since people wrapped products by hand in the old days, it took too long. Nowadays, it is much more efficient because it is done by a machine.

78
훗날

[훈날] 명사 a future time

some time in the future

[Related Words] 오늘날 these days

[Example] 훗날 우리가 다시 만날 때는 조금 더 성숙해져 있겠지.
When we meet again in the future, we both will be more mature, right?

내일 일도 모르는데 어떻게 훗날의 일을 알 수 있겠니?
We don't know what's going to happen tomorrow. How are we supposed to know what's going to happen in the future?

79
흐르다

[흐르다] 동사 1. to go by 2. to flow

1. the passing by of time

[Usage] N 이/가 흐르다

[Expression] 시간이 흐르다 Time goes by.

[Example] 시간이 흐르면 세상은 변하게 마련이다.
It is expected that the world will change as time goes by.

2. to falling of a substance from a higher place to a lower place as it goes by

[Usage] N 이/가 흐르다

[Expression] 강이 흐르다 The river flows.
땀이 흐르다 Sweat drips.

[Example] 세계에서 도심을 흐르는 강 중에 가장 큰 강이 한강이다.
Out of all the rivers in the world that flow through the city center, the biggest one is the Han River.

09 연습문제

[1-17] 다음 직업을 나타내는 한자 단어를 한국어로 바꿔 쓰십시오.

Change the following words that indicate professions and write them in Korean.

1. prosecutor ( )
2. country, state ( )
3. professor ( )
4. carpenter ( )
5. secretary ( )
6. poet ( )
7. in the old times ( )
8. architect ( )
9. laborer ( )
10. scientist ( )
11. president ( )
12. foreign diplomat ( )
13. entertainer ( )
14. congressman ( )
15. designer ( )
16. broadcaster ( )
17. computer progamer ( )

[18-27] [보기]에서 알맞은 단어를 골라 ( ) 안에 쓰십시오.

Choose the appropriate word from the box below and then fill in the parenthesis.

[보기]

결과	능력	문제점	거래처	계약
경영하다	변화하다	분석하다	실수하다	승진하다

18. 이번에 우리 회사와 같이 일하기로 한 중국의 ( )에서 급하게 연락이 왔어요.
19. 제가 ( )는/은/ㄴ 바람에 많은 사람들이 피해를 입었어요.
20. 올 상반기 제품 판매량이 작년보다 10% 늘어난 것은 모두 우리 직원들이 열심히 일한 ( ) 입니다.
21. 우리 아버지는 부산에서 작은 중소기업을 ( )고 계신다.
22. 두 회사의 발전에 도움이 될 수 있는 아주 좋은 조건으로 ( )을/를 했다.

23. 고객센터 직원이 고객님의 질문에 직접 답변해 드리고 제품의 (   )도 해결해 드릴 것입니다.

24. 이번에 과장에서 부장으로 (   )으신/신 거 진심으로 축하드려요.

25. 인간은 태어날 때부터 언어 학습 (   )을/를 가지고 태어난다.

26. 실패했을 때는 왜 실패했는지 그 원인을 자세히 (   )어야/아야/여야 한다.

27. 저는 조용한 곳보다 사람들이 많고 상가들도 많은 (   )는/은/ㄴ 곳을 좋아해서 시내 중심가에 집을 구했어요.

[28-34] 다음 밑줄 친 부분과 의미가 비슷한 것을 고르십시오.

Choose a word that is similar in meaning to the underlined part of the sentence.

28. 오늘은 생각보다 회사 일을 비교적 짧은 시간에 마쳤다.

❶ 끝내다 ❷ 준비하다 ❸ 분석하다 ❹ 시도하다

29. 이번 회식은 연세 호프에서 할 예정이니까 시간이 있는 분들은 참석하시기 바랍니다.

❶ 예약하다 ❷ 예매하다 ❸ 계획이다 ❹ 유행이다

30. 이번 일이 무척 어렵다는 것은 알지만 한번 도전해 보고 싶어요.

❶ 가능하다 ❷ 성공하다 ❸ 수고하다 ❹ 시도하다

31. 지금은 여행을 갔으니까 한 4일 후에 돌아올 거예요.

❶ 사흘 ❷ 나흘 ❸ 열흘 ❹ 보름

32. 신입 사원 시절 실수를 했을 때 과장님께서 잘 할 수 있을 거라고 용기를 주셨던 기억이 있다.

❶ 신뢰하다 ❷ 격려하다 ❸ 설득하다 ❹ 대화하다

33. 저는 회사에 취직하기보다는 사업을 해서 돈도 많이 벌고 유명한 사람이 되고 싶습니다

❶ 신청하다 ❷ 추천하다 ❸ 출세하다 ❹ 결심하다

34. 영수 씨는 현재 미국 뉴욕 지사에서 일하고 있어요.

❶ 취직하다 ❷ 이사하다 ❸ 출장가다 ❹ 근무하다

[35-44] [보기]에서 알맞은 단어를 골라 (   ) 안에 쓰십시오.

Choose the appropriate word from the box below and then fill in the parenthesis.

[보기]

몰두하다	신상품	공장	사정	순간
가능하다	메모하다	신형	영향	야근

35. 집안 형편이 어려워서 누나는 중학교를 졸업하자마자 돈을 벌기 위해 인형을 만드는 (   )에 취직했다.

36. 직장 스트레스는 일에만 너무 (   )는/은/ㄴ 사람들에게 생기는 정신적인 병이다.

37. 신입 사원 시절에 사장님께서 해 주신 말씀이 회사 생활을 하는데 많은 (   )을/를 미쳤다.

38. 항상 카메라를 가지고 다니면 놓치고 싶지 않은 (   )을/를 찍을 수 있어요.

39. 고객센터에서는 상표를 떼지 않았기 때문에 환불이 (   )는다고/ㄴ다고/다고 했다.

40. 중요한 일은 수첩에 (   )어/아/여 놓아야지 그렇지 않으면 잊어버리기 쉽다.

41. 이번에 새로 개발한 우리 회사의 (   )이/가 시장에서 좋은 반응을 얻었다.

42. 회사 일이 많아서 요즘 늦게까지 (   )을/를 자주 했더니 무척 피곤하네요.

43. 회사 (   )이/가 안 좋아져서 직원들에게 월급을 못 주고 있습니다.

44. 그 회사는 내년에 (   ) 스포츠카를 판매할 것이다.

[45-47] 다음 밑줄 친 부분과 반대되는 뜻을 가진 것을 고르십시오.

Choose the word that has the opposite meaning from the underlined word.

45. 회사 내에 감시 카메라를 설치한다는 계획에 직원들이 모두 반대했다.

❶ 신청하다 ❷ 찬성하다 ❸ 해결하다 ❹ 경험하다

46. 1년 전에 회사를 차렸는데 갑자기 경제가 어려워져서 결국 크게 <u>실패했다</u>.

❶ 고생하다 ❷ 후회하다 ❸ 당황하다 ❹ 성공하다

47. 점심시간보다 좀 늦게 와서 그런지 오늘은 회사 식당이 <u>한산하네요</u>.

❶ 붐비다 ❷ 여유롭다 ❸ 조용하다 ❹ 한가하다

[48-50] 다음 (　　)에 가장 알맞은 단어를 고르십시오.

Choose the most appropriate word and fill in the parenthesis.

48. 사무실에서 친근한 말투를 사용하면 다정한 분위기가 돼서 사무적이고 (　　　　) 느낌을 없애준다.

❶ 대표적인 ❷ 초보적인 ❸ 개방적인 ❹ 형식적인

49. 계획을 세우면 정해진 일을 좀 더 (　　　　) 빨리 할 수 있다.

❶ 사회적으로 ❷ 과학적으로 ❸ 효율적으로 ❹ 획일적으로

50. 김영수 씨는 수출 업무를 (　　　　)고 있어요.

❶ 담당하다 ❷ 선택하다 ❸ 부담하다 ❹ 반대하다

[51-56] 다음 [보기]에서 알맞은 단어를 골라 이야기를 완성하십시오.

Choose the appropriate word from the box and complete the story.

[보기]

취직하다	면접시험	무역	능통하다	서류	경력자

내일은 회사 51.(　　　　　　)이/가 있다. 2주 전에 이력서와 자기 소개서와 같은 여러 가지 52.(　　　　　　)과/와 입사원서를 회사에 제출했다. 지난주에 있었던 필기 시험은 무사히 잘 봤는데 이번 시험은 좀 긴장이 된다. 이 회사는 일본과 53.(　　　　　　)을/를 하는 회사라서 일본어에 54.(　　　　　　)는/은/ㄴ 직

원을 뽑는다고 한다. 대학시절에 미리 일본어를 배워두기를 잘 한 것 같다. 초보자도 상관이 없다고 했지만 55.(   )은/는 특별히 우대를 해 준다고 한다. 시험을 잘 봐서 이 회사에 꼭 56.(   )었으면/았으면/였으면 좋겠다.

[57] **다음 (   )에 공통적으로 들어갈 단어를 쓰십시오.**

Write one word that can commonly fit into the parenthesis below.

57.
❶ 오늘 식사는 각자 (   )을/를 하도록 합시다.
❷ 회사에서 너무 중요한 일을 맡아서 (   )이/가 돼요.
❸ 제가 무리한 부탁을 해서 영수 씨에게 (   )을/를 드린 것 같아 죄송하네요.

(   )

[58-62] **다음 (   )에 공통적으로 들어갈 단어의 기본형을 쓰십시오.**

Write the basic form of one word that can commonly fit in the parenthesis below.

58.
❶ 옆에 (   )고 있는 건물은 기숙사예요.
❷ 아들의 이름을 '민준' 이라고 (   )었어요/았어요/였어요.
❸ 몸살이 심해서 약을 (   )어다가/아다가/여다가 먹어야 겠어요.

(   )

59.
❶ 날씨가 너무 더워서 땀이 비 오듯이 (   )어요/아요/여요.
❷ 우리 동네를 지나가는 시냇물은 바로 강 하류로 (   )고 있어요.
❸ 시간이 많이 (   )었지만/았지만/였지만 선생님 모습은 여전하셨다.

(   )

60.
❶ 회사 기숙사에서 자고 식사는 회사 식당을 이용하니까 숙식은 쉽게 (   )을/ㄹ 수 있어요.

② 이번 문제는 김영수 씨가 거래처 담당자를 직접 만나 (　　　　　)는다고/ㄴ다고/다고 합니다.

③ 24시간 외국어 안내 서비스를 이용하면 외국인이나 관광객에게 어려움이나 문제가 생겼을 때 쉽게 (　　　　　)어/아/여 준다.

(　　　　　　　　)

61. ① 결혼식을 하는 가정은 잔치를 (　　　　　)어서/아서/여서 주위 사람들을 초대해 함께 기쁨을 나눕니다.

② 민수 씨는 전 재산을 걸고 무리하게 사업을 (　　　　　)었다가/았다가/였다가 결국 사업에 실패하고 말았다.

③ 봉사 단체에서는 외롭게 혼자 사는 노인들이나 가난하게 사는 사람들을 위해 불우이웃 돕기 사업을 (　　　　　)고 있다.

(　　　　　　　　)

62. ① 은행에 가면 제일 먼저 번호표를 (　　　　　)어요/아요/여요.

② 흰머리를 (　　　　　)어도/아도/여도 계속 그 자리에 흰머리가 나는 것 같아요.

③ 다음 주에 연극 대회 반장 모임이 있으니까 오늘 반장을 (　　　　　)도록 합시다.

(　　　　　　　　)

[63-74] 다음 〈보기〉에서 알맞은 단어를 골라 (　　　　) 안에 쓰십시오.

Complete the sentence with the appropriate word from the box below.

[보기]

파일	여유	목표	무리하다
그대로	어느새	건의하다	개발하다
결정하다	발견하다	발달하다	보고하다

63. 각 부서별로 계획서를 작성하여 이번 회의 때 (　　　　　　)어/아/여 주세요.

64. 과학과 인터넷이 (　　　　　　)으면서/면서 우리의 생활은 점점 편리해지고 있다.

65. 이메일에 이번 계약과 관련된 (　　　　　　)을/를 첨부해서 보냈으니까 확인해 보세요.

66. 지금은 부족한 것이 많은 신입사원이지만 미래의 제 (　　　　　　　)은/는 이 회사의 사장이 되는 것이에요.

67. 요즘 회사 일로 며칠 동안 일하느라고 (　　　　　　　)어서/아서/여서 그런지 몸살이 났어요.

68. 한국에 온 지가 바로 엊그제 같은데 (　　　　　　　) 10년이 흘렀어요.

69. 이번 회식 자리에 사장님도 참석하시니까 요구 사항을 사장님께 직접 (　　　　　　　)어/아/여 보세요.

70. 대학교를 졸업한 후에 취직할지 계속 공부할지 아직 (　　　　　　　)지 못했어요.

71. 국내에서 세계 최초로 (　　　　　　　)는/은/ㄴ 물걸레 청소 로봇이 소비자들에게 큰 인기를 얻고 있습니다.

72. 회사 생활에 적응이 됐는지 이제는 (　　　　　　　)이/가 있어 보여요.

73. 책상 정리를 하다가 우연히 10년 전에 쓴 일기장을 (　　　　　　　)었다/았다/였다.

74. 세월은 흘렀지만 집안의 모든 물건들이 변함없이 그 자리에 (　　　　　　　) 있었다.

[75] **다음 [보기]에서 알맞은 말을 골라 빈 칸에 쓰고 문장을 완성하십시오.**

Choose the appropriate words from the box below and fill in the blanks and complete the sentences.

[보기]

미루다	세월	시대	현대	경력	출세
옛날	시절	현재	세기	미래	무리
세대	고대	경쟁	훗날	무렵	

① 미	루	다				⑤	
			②		④		
		③					
⑥					⑦		
		⑨					
	⑧				⑩	⑪	

[가로]

① 계획을 세우지 않는다면 오늘 해야 할 일을 내일로 (　　미루　　)게 될 수 있다.

③ 오늘의 감동적인 이 일은 (　　　　　　) 여러 사람에게 기억될 것이다.

④ 원시 시대와 중세 시대 사이의 시대를 (　　　　　　)이라고/라고 한다.

⑤ (　　　　　　) 상태에 만족하지 말고 더 나아지도록 노력하세요.

⑥ 병원에서 의사 선생님이 건강이 안 좋으니까 한동안 (　　　　　　)을/를 하지 말라고 했어요.

⑦ 작은 아들은 욕심이 많아서 항상 큰 아들한테 이기려고 (　　　　　　)을/를 해요.

⑧ 부모와 자식 간에 의견을 주고받다 보면 서로 (　　　　　　) 차이를 느낀다.

⑨ 힘들었던 (　　　　　　)을/를 생각하면 지금도 눈물이 나요.

⑩ 부모의 재력으로 (　　　　　　)을/를 하는 것을 보면 세상은 공평한 것 같지 않다.

[세로]

① 지금은 경제적으로 어려울 수 있지만 행복한 (　　　　　　)을/를 위해서 조금씩 은행에 저금을 하고 있다.

② 경복궁은 (　　　　　　)에 왕이 살던 곳인데 오래된 건물들이 아주 멋있다고 한다.

⑤ 바쁘고 복잡한 (　　　　　　) 사회는 개인을 더욱 외롭게 만든다.

⑥ 해 질 (　　　　　　)의 동해 바다의 모습은 정말 인상적이었다.

⑦ 이력서에 학력과 지금까지 일한 (　　　　　　)을/를 적어 오세요.

⑧ 조카가 벌써 대학생이 되었다. 정말 (　　　　　　)이/가 빨리 흐르는 것 같다.

⑨ 경주에는 신라 (　　　　　　)의 유적지가 많아요.

⑪ 2001년 1월 1일부터 2100년 12월 31일까지를 21(　　　　　　)이라고/라고 한다.

문화

10

Culture

10 문화

01
가면극

[가면극] 명사 a mask dance performance

a play where masks are worn

[Related Words] 인형극 puppet play

탈춤 mask dance

[Example] 지난 주말에 가면극 공연을 보고 왔어요.

I saw a mask dance performance last weekend.

오늘 학교 극장에서 가면극 공연과 유명 가수의 축하 공연이 있을 예정입니다.

Today at the school theater a mask dance performance and a congratulatory performance from a famous singer are scheduled to be shown.

02
가이드

[가이드] 명사 guide

a person that brings you around tourist places

[Expression] 여행 가이드 travel guide

[Synonym] 안내자 guide

[Example] 친구가 서울에 여행을 오면 제가 가이드를 해 주기로 했어요.

I have decided to guide my friends around Seoul when they come here on vacation.

이번 여행에서 친절한 가이드를 만난 덕분에 즐겁게 보낼 수 있었어요.

I enjoyed my vacation thanks to the kind guide that I met there.

03
감동하다

[감동하다] 동사 to be moved, to be emotionally touched

[Usage] N 에/에게 감동하다

[Example] 친구의 따뜻한 마음에 감동했다.

I was moved by my friend's kind heart.

주인을 위해서 죽은 개의 이야기를 듣고 많이 감동했어요.

I was really touched after hearing the story of the dog that had died for his owner.

04
강강술래

[강강술래] 명사 traditional full moon dance

traditional Korean circle dance performed by women under the full moon

[Expression] 강강술래를 하다
to perform the kangkangsulae

[Example] 강강술래 노래를 들어 본 적이 있어요?
Have you ever heard the traditional full moon dance song?

강강술래는 춤과 노래를 함께 하는 놀이입니다.
The kangkangsulae is a performance that involves both dance and song.

도움말

씨름
traditional Korean wrestling

널뛰기
traditional Korean jumping game on a see-saw

그네뛰기
traditional Korean swinging game

줄다리기
Korean tug-of-war

05
개봉하다

[개봉하다] 동사 to premiere

to show a new movie for the first time

[Usage] N 을/를 개봉하다

[Expression] 영화를 개봉하다 to premiere a movie

[Related Words] 상영하다 to show a movie

[Example] 어제 개봉한 영화 '영원한 사랑'이 볼 만하던데요.
The movie "Eternal Love" that premiered yesterday is worth seeing.

매우 보고 싶었던 영화 '무서운 사람들'이 다음 주에 개봉한대요.
The movie I really wanted to see, "Scary People," will be released new week.

06
결승전

[결씅전] 명사 final match

the final face-off in a sports competition

[Expression] 준결승전 semi-finals
결승전에 나가다 to go to the finals
결승전에 오르다 to make it to the finals

[Related Words] 예선전 qualifiers

[Example] 2006년 독일 월드컵에서 독일과 이탈리아가 결승전에 올라갔어요.
In the 2006 Germany world cup match, Italy and Germany made it to the finals.

우리나라 축구 대표팀이 올림픽 결승전에 나간다면 얼마나 좋을까?
How great would it be if Korea's national soccer team made it to the finals at the Olympics?

07
경조사비

[경조사비] 명사 expenses that are incurred upon mourning or celebrating an event

[Expression] 경조사비를 내다 to pay celebratory or mourning expenses

[Example] 우리나라 국민의 대부분이 경조사비를 부담스러워한다.
Almost all Korean citizens must pay celebratory or mourning expenses.

이번 달에는 친구 결혼식도 있었고 부장님 아버님도 돌아가셔서 경조사비 지출이 많았어요.
This month I had to attend both the wedding of my friend and the death of my boss's father, which means I had to pay a lot of celebratory and mourning expenses.

08
공연

[공연] 명사 performance

a music, dance, or play performed in front of many people

[Expression] 공연장 theater, venue
공연 날짜 performance date
공연 시간 performance time
공연 일시 performance date and time
공연 장소 performance place

[Example] 주말에는 네 시와 일곱 시에 공연을 합니다.
On the weekend, there are performances at 4 and at 7 o'clock.

정해진 좌석에 앉아서 공연을 관람해 주시기 바랍니다.
We ask you to please sit in your assigned seat and enjoy the show.

09
관객

[관객] 명사 spectator, audience

[Expression] 관객석 seats of the audience

[Synonym] 관람객 spectator

[Example] 그 공연을 관람한 관객들의 평이 좋아요.
The reviews of the spectator that went to see the show were very good.
영화 '태극기 휘날리며'는 관객이 천만 명을 넘었어요.
There were over ten million visitors that came to see the movie 'The Korean Flag flutters'.

10
관람

[괄람] 명사 visiting, watching

seeing a play, movie, movement, competition, or art exhibition

[Expression] 관람료 admission fee
관람석 seats of the audience
관람 연령 visiting age
관람하다 to watch, to see

[Related Words] 구경 to see, to watch

[Example] 주말에는 미리 예약하지 않으면 관람하기가 힘들어요.
It is hard to go see a show on the weekend if you don't book it in advance.
이 영화는 관람 연령이 7세 이상이니까 가족이 모두 함께 볼 수 있어요.
My entire family can watch this movie because the age requirement to see it is seven and above.

11
교류

[교류] 명사 exchange

exchange of culture or ideas

[Expression] 문화 교류 cultural exchange
교류하다 to exchange

[Example] 남북한 교류가 활발해졌다던데 언제쯤 통일이 될까요?
I heard that the interaction between North and South Korea has gotten better. I wonder when they are going to unite again?

두 나라의 교류가 활발해짐에 따라 유학생 수가 급증하고 있습니다.
The number of study abroad students is suddenly increasing due to the improved relations between the two countries.

12
교포

[교포] 명사 a Korean national living abroad, a child of a Korean living abroad

[Expression] 재독 교포 a Korean that resides in Germany
재미 교포 a Korean that resides in America
재일 교포 a Korean that resides in Japan

[Related Words] 동포 compatriot, countryman

[Example] 나는 미국에서 온 교포이다.
I am a Korean that has come from the United States.

마이클 씨는 재미 교포인데 사고방식이 한국 사람하고는 달라서 외국 사람이나 다름없어요.
Michael is a Korean-American. Since his way of thinking is different from that of a Korean, there is no difference between him and any other foreigner.

13
귀성

[귀성] 명사 going home from the holidays, returning to the country for the holidays
returning to one's hometown in order to visit parents

[Expression]
귀성객 a person that returns home for the holidays
귀성길 the path that a person takes to return home for the holidays
귀성 차량 the cars of people that are returning home for the holidays
귀성 행렬 the line of people that are returning home for the holidays

[Example] 추석 이틀 전부터 서울역은 귀성을 하려는 사람들로 복잡해진다.
Seoul Station gets very crowded starting from two days before the harvest festival due to the people that are getting ready to return home for the holidays.

명절만 되면 귀성을 하는 차량들로 고속도로는 주차장으로 변한다.
As soon as the holidays arrive, the highways turn into parking lots because of the cars from people returning home.

14
기도

[기도] 명사 prayer

[Expression]
기도하다 to pray
기도를 올리다 to offer a prayer

[Example] 제발 이번 시험에는 꼭 합격할 수 있도록 기도를 했어요.
I prayed so that I could pass the test.

교회에 가면 두 손 모아 기도를 하는 사람들을 많이 볼 수 있어요.
If you go to church, you can see many people putting their hands together to pray.

15
기독교

[기독꾜] 명사 christianity

[Expression]
기독교인 christian
기독교 신자 believer in christianity
기독교를 믿다 to believe in christianity

[Related Words]
교회 church
목사 priest

[Example] 저는 기독교 신자예요.
I am of the Christian faith.

기독교는 여러 종교 중에 하나예요.
Christianity is one of many religions.

16
다양하다

[다양하다] 형용사 to be diverse, to be varied

[Usage] N 이/가 다양하다
다양한 N

[Expression] 무늬가 다양하다 The pattern is diverse.
다양한 색상 diverse color

[Example] 한국 음식은 참 다양해요.
Korean food is quite diverse.

이렇게 다양한 기능을 가진 로봇이 나오다니 세상이 참 좋아졌어요.
Upon hearing that a robot with a lot of diverse functions is being released, I thought that the world has become a much better place.

17
다큐멘터리

[다큐멘터리] 명사 documentary

a movie, radio, or television drama or novel that factually represents the events of a certain incident.

[Expression] 다큐멘터리를 찍다 to film a documentary

[Example] 다큐멘터리 영화는 각본은 없고 편집만 있다고 해요.
The documentary film only has an edited version. There is no screenplay.

나는 드라마든 뉴스든 가리지 않고 보는데 보통 다큐멘터리를 자주 봐.
I watch either dramas or the news. However, I normally watch documentaries.

18
대단하다

[대단하다] 형용사 1. to be very serious 2. to be amazing 3. to be important 4. to be numerous or large

1. to be very serious

[Usage] N 이/가 대단하다

[Expression] 고집이 대단하다 to be very stubborn
추위가 대단하다 to be extremely cold

[Synonym] 심하다 to be serious

[Example] 작년 겨울에 추위가 정말 대단했다.
It was extremely cold last winter.

2. to be amazing or outstanding

[Usage] N 이/가 대단하다

[Expression] 실력이 대단하다 one's abilities are amazing
솜씨가 대단하다 one's skills are amazing

[Synonym] 뛰어나다 to be outstanding

[Example] 공부와 일을 함께 하기란 쉽지 않은데 둘 다 잘하니 정말 대단하지요?
It is quite difficult to work and study at the same time. Isn't it quite amazing that you do both at the same time?

3. to be very important

[Usage] 대단한 N

[Expression] 대단한 일 an important business

[Synonym] 중요하다 to be important

[Example] 대단한 문제가 아니니까 크게 걱정하지 않아도 된다.
There is no need to greatly worry about it because it isn't a serious problem.

4. to be a lot in number or size

[Usage] N 이/가 대단하다

[Expression] 기대가 대단하다 to have high hopes
욕심이 대단하다 to be very greedy

[Synonym] 많다 to be a lot

[Example] 해외에서 배우 이영아의 인기가 대단하대요.
They say that the actress Younga Lee is very popular abroad.

19
대사

[대사] 명사 lines, dialogue

the words in a movie or play that an actor recites

[Expression] 대사가 길다 The lines are long.
대사를 하다 to recite one's lines

[Related Words] 대본 script

[Example] 연극 대사가 길어서 배우들이 많이 힘들어했어요.
The actors had a hard time because their lines were very long.

목소리가 멋질 뿐만 아니라 연기도 훌륭했어요. 대사도 재미있었고요.
Not only did he have a nice movie but his acting was also spectacular. The lines were also really fun.

20
대중문화

[대중문화] 명사 popular culture

[Expression] 대중문화를 이끌다 to lead popular culture
대중문화에 영향을 주다 to influence mainstream culture

[Example] 많은 연예인들이 대중문화에 큰 영향을 준다.
A lot of entertainers greatly influence popular culture.
텔레비전은 현대 대중문화를 이끈다고 할 수 있어요.
One can say that the television has driven contemporary popular culture.

21
대회

[대회] 명사 rally, competition, large meeting

a large meeting in which people compete their skills or technology

[Expression] 웅변대회 oratorical speech contest
체육대회 sports competition
장기 자랑 대회 talent show
대회를 열다 to hold a competition
대회에 참가하다 to participate in a competition

[Synonym] 경기 competition

[Example] 이번 마라톤 대회에 참가하는 모든 사람들에게 기념품을 증정합니다.
All participants in this marathon will receive a souvenir.
외국인 노래 자랑 대회에는 외국인이라면 누구나 참가할 수 있습니다.
In a singing competition for foreigners, as long as you are a foreigner, you are allowed to participate.

22
돌

[돌] 명사 first birthday of a baby

[Expression] 돌잔치 first birthday feast
돌 반지 first birthday ring
돌 선물 first birthday present

[Related Words] 생일 birthday

[Example] 요즘 금값이 비싸니까 돌 선물로 다른 것을 삽시다.
The price of gold is expensive nowadays, so let's buy something else for the boby,s first birthday present.
아이의 한 살 생일에는 돌 반지를 선물하는 풍습이 있다.
On a baby's first birthday, it is custom to buy a ring as a present.

23
동기

[동기] 명사 motive, reason

[Expression] 동기가 있다 to have a motive
동기가 없다 to have no motive

[Synonym] 계기 opportunity

[Example] 작품을 쓰게 된 동기는 바로 제 친구의 부탁 때문이었습니다.
The reason I ended up writing the picec of work was just because my friend requested me to do so.

이번 연극에 출현하게 된 것은 특별한 동기가 있어서가 아니라 단지 제가 하고 싶어서일 뿐입니다.
I didn't have any special reason for appearing in this play. I am doing it just because I felt like it.

24
따다

[따다] 동사 1. to pluck, to pick 2. to win a prize 3. to receive a score

1. to pick off something that is attached

[Usage] N 을/를 따다

[Expression] 꽃을 따다 to pick a flower
과일을 따다 to pluck a fruit

[Example] 과수원에서 과일을 딴 후에 바로 먹으면 시장에서 사 먹는 것보다 더 맛있어.
If you eat a fruit right after plucking it at an orchard, it tastes much better than the ones you buy at the market.

2. to obtain a prize in a competition or game or to win money.

[Usage] N 을/를 따다

[Expression] 돈을 따다 to win money
금메달을 따다 to obtain a gold medal

[Example] 올림픽에서 금메달을 딴 선수가 귀국할 때 대단한 환영을 받지요.
The player that won the gold medal at the Olympics received a huge welcoming when coming home.

3. to get a score or certificate.

[Usage] N 을/를 따다

[Expression] 학위를 따다 to obtain a degree
면허증을 따다 to get a driver's license

[Related Words] 취득하다 to acquire

[Example] 혼자 열심히 공부해서 요리사 자격증을 땄습니다.
I obtained my chef's license by studying very hard on my own.

25
마술

[마술] 명사 magic

[Expression] 마술사 magician
마술을 부리다 to do magic

[Related Words] 마녀 witch
요술 sorcery

[Example] 마술사가 아무것도 없는 모자 속에서 토끼를 꺼냈다.
The magician pulled a rabbit out of his empty hat.

오늘 파티에서는 간단한 마술행사도 있을 예정이니까 기대하셔도 좋을 것 같습니다.
At today's party there will be a simple magic show. We hope you are looking forward to the show.

26
매진되다

[매진되다] 동사 to be sold out

[Usage] N 이/가 매진되다

[Expression] 표가 매진되다 The tickets are sold out.

[Example] 영화를 보러 갔다가 매진돼서 그냥 왔어요.
I went to see the movie, but after arriving I saw it was sold out so I just came back.

표를 판 지 하루밖에 안 되었는데 벌써 표가 매진되었다니 정말 인기있는 공연인가 봐요.
They have only been selling the tickets for a day and they have already sold out. It must be quite a popular performance.

27
머무르다

[머무르다] 동사 to stay

to stop in one's travels or to lodge in a certain place for a period of time

[Usage] N 에/에서 머무르다

[Expression] 호텔에 머무르다 to stay at a hotel
친구 집에 머무르다 to stay at a friend's house

[Synonym] 지내다 to spend time

[Example] 제주도 여행을 갔을 때 친구 집에서 일주일 동안 머물렀어요.
When I went on vacation to Jeju Island, I stay at my friend's house for one week.

일이 있어서 더 이상 머무를 수가 없네요. 먼저 가 보겠습니다.
I can't stay anymore because I have some business to attend to. I'll be heading out now.

28
무용 [무용] 명사 dance

an art that expresses an emotion through movement as one dances to music

[Expression] 무용단 dance team
무용수 dancer
고전 무용 classical music
한국 무용 Korean dance
현대 무용 contemporary dance

[Synonym] 춤 dance

[Example] 저는 대학 때 무용을 전공했어요.
I majored in dance when I was in college.

요즘은 복싱 같은 스포츠부터 고전무용까지 다양한 취미를 가진 주부들이 늘고 있다.
Nowadays, there are more housewives that have diverse hobbies, including boxing to classical dance.

29
문화유산 [문화유산] 명사 cultural asset, cultural property

a cultural product of a society or people that holds a value worth preserving so that future generations or youth can appreciate it. It often refers to art, science, habits, or customs.

[Expression] 세계 문화유산 World Heritage
문화유산을 지키다 to preserve cultural heritage assets
문화유산을 보존하다 to conserve a cultural heritage asset
문화유산을 보호하다 to protect a cultural heritage asset

[Example] 스페인, 이탈리아, 중국은 세계 문화유산 3대 보유국이다.
Spain, Italy, and China are three countries that possess World Heritage sites.

한국의 세계 문화유산으로는 불국사와 창덕궁 등이 있다.
Some of Korea's World Heritage sites include Bulguksa and Changduk Palace.

30
뮤지컬 [뮤지컬] 명사 musical

one of the styles of modern music performances developed in America. a combination of music, dance, and singing

[Related Words] 오페라 opera

[Example] 방학때 어린이들을 위한 뮤지컬 공연이 많아요.
During the vacation, there are a lot of musical performances for kids.

뮤지컬 '춘향전'이 아주 감동적이라고 하던데 보셨어요?
I heard many people thought that the musical "Chun Hyang Jeon" was very moving. Have you seen it?

31
미담 [미담] 명사 a beautiful story, an inspiring story

a story that has a beautiful storyline that can emotionally move people

[Expression] 미담이 전해지다 The inspiring story is passed down.

[Example] 우리의 마음을 따뜻하게 해주는 미담이 있어서 여러분에게 소개할까 합니다.
I want to tell you all an inspiring story that will warm up your hearts.

저는 제 아들을 구해준 분이 너무 고마워 어떻게든 이러한 미담을 세상에 알리고 싶었습니다.
I wanted to let the whole world know about the touching story of the person that saved the life of my son.

32
미디어 [미디어] 명사 media

[Expression] 뉴미디어 new media
멀티미디어 multimedia

[Related Words] 채팅 chatting
네티즌 netizen
동영상 video
블로그 blog
홈페이지 home page
인터넷 사이트 internet site

[Example] 요즘은 정보 통신 미디어가 급속히 발전하고 있다.
Nowadays, communication media is quickly developing.

미디어의 발달로 사람들은 좀 더 다양한 방법으로 정보를 얻을 수 있게 되었습니다.
Thanks to the developments in media, people can now obtain information in a number of ways.

33
민간신앙 [민간시낭] 명사 beliefs that have been handed down from traditions of people.

[Example] 옛날부터 전해 내려오는 민간신앙에는 어떤 것들이 있습니까?
What are some traditional beliefs that have been handed down from antiquity?

한국에서는 오래 전부터 태몽이 태아의 성별이나 미래 운명을 예시한다고 믿어 왔으며, 그 꿈을 풀이하는 태몽점은 민간신앙의 하나가 되어 있다.
From a long time ago, Koreans have believed that when one dreams of their future child, it is possible to predict the gender of the embryo or its fate. The psychics that analyze these dreams are cosidered to be part of the folk culture of Korea.

34
믿다

[믿따] 동사 to believe

to think that a fact or statement will turn out a certain way.

[Usage] N 을/를 믿다

[Expression] 신을 믿다 to believe in a god
친구를 믿다 to believe a friend

[Synonym] 신뢰하다 to trust

[Antonym] 의심하다 to suspect

[Example] 솔직해야 서로를 믿을 수 있지요.
The only way to believe each other is by being honest.

믿을 수 있는 사람은 너밖에 없어.
You are the only person I can trust.

35
박수

[박쑤] 명사 applaud

clapping one's hands to follow a rhythm or to express happiness, agreement, or welcome

[Expression] 박수를 치다 to applaud

[Related Words] 손뼉 clap

[Example] 어찌나 박수를 열심히 쳤는지 손바닥이 다 아팠어요.
The palm of my hands were hurting because I had clapped my hands so hard.

가수의 멋진 무대가 끝나자 관중들이 모두 일어나서 뜨거운 박수를 보냈어요.
As soon as the singer's performance ended, all the spectators stood up and madly clapped their hands.

36
배경

[배경] 명사 1. background 2. scene

1. the back part of a side.

[Expression] 아름다운 배경 beautiful background
배경이 예쁘다 The background is pretty.

[Example] 공원에 산책을 갔다가 아름다운 봄꽃을 배경으로 사진 한 장을 찍었어요.
After going to the park for a walk, I took a picture of the beautiful spring flowers in the background.

2. a sight that surrounds the events or actions of a happening.

[Expression] 배경 음악 background music

[Example] 아일랜드를 배경으로 한 이 영화는 거리의 음악가와 가난한 소녀의 사랑 이야기이다.
This movie, that is set on an island, is the love story of a street musician and a poor young girl.

37
벅차다

[벅차다] 형용사 1. to be beyond one's power 2. to be too full for

1. hard to deal with or handle

[Usage] N 이/가 벅차다
AV 기가 벅차다

[Synonym] 힘겹다 to be beyond one's strength

[Example] 혼자서 20인분의 음식을 준비하기가 너무 벅차요.
It is almost impossible for me to make food for twenty people all by myself.

2. to be full to the point of overflowing with emotion, hope, or happiness

[Usage] N 이/가 벅차다

[Expression] 가슴이 벅차다 I am full of emotions.

[Example] 합격 소식을 듣고 가슴이 너무 벅찼다.
I felt full of emotions when I received the news that I passed.

38
보호하다

[보호하다] 동사 1. to protect, to conserve 2. to safeguard, to shield

1. to protect something to keep it in its original form

[Usage] N 을/를 보호하다

[Expression] 자연을 보호하다 to protect nature
환경을 보호하다 to protect the environment
문화재를 보호하다 to protect a cultural asset

[Synonym] 지키다 to protect

[Example] 자연을 보호하기 위해 일회용품 사용을 줄여야 해요.
We must use less single-use products in order to protect nature.

2. to take of someone so that they do not fall into danger or confusion

[Usage] N 을/를 보호하다

[Expression] 몸을 보호하다 to protect one's body

아이를 보호하다 to protect a child

[Synonym] 돌보다 to take care of

[Example] 체력이 떨어진 아이들에게는 몸을 보호하고 튼튼하게 하는 영양제를 먹이는 것이 좋다.

It is good to give nutritional supplements to children whose physical strength has fallen in order to protect their bodies and make them strong.

39
복

[복] 명사 blessing

fortune that leads to happiness.

[Expression]
행복 happiness
복이 많다 to be fortunate
복이 없다 to have no fortune
복을 받다 to receive blessings
복을 빌다 to pray for blessings

[Related Words] 벌 punishment

[Example] 새해 복 많이 받으십시오.

I hope you have a lot of new year blessings(Happy New Year).

착하게 살면 누구나 복을 받게 마련이지요.

If you are kind in your life, you will be rewarded with blessings.

40
불교

[불교] 명사 Buddhism

[Expression]
불교 신자 a believer of Buddhism
불교를 믿다 to believe in Buddhism

[Related Words]
절 Buddhist temple
스님 Buddhist monk

[Example] 우리 어머니는 독실한 불교 신자예요.

My mother is a very fervent believer of Buddhism.

부처님 오신 날은 부처님이 태어나신 날로 불교의 가장 큰 명절이라고 할 수 있어요.

The day that Buddha was born is known to be one of the important holidays.

41
빌다

[빌다] 동사 1. to pray, to hope 2. to ask a person's pardon, apologize

1. to beg a god or man or any other individual for something to happen

[Usage]
N 을/를 빌다
N 에/에게 빌다

[Expression] 소원을 빌다 to pray for a wish
신에게 빌다 to pray to a god

[Example] 이번 일이 잘 해결되기를 마음속으로 빌었어요.
I prayed inside of my heart that everything would turn out okay.

2. to beg for forgiveness

[Usage] N 을/를 빌다
N 에/에게 빌다

[Expression] 용서를 빌다 to beg for forgiveness
잘못을 빌다 to ask for forgiveness for one's mistake

[Example] 그 사람에게 잘못을 사과하고 용서를 빌어라.
Go apologize to that person and beg for forgiveness

42
사고방식

[사고방식] 명사 manner of thinking, way of thinking

the way in which one regards an issue

[Expression] 사고방식의 차이 difference in a way of thinking
사고방식을 이해하다 to understand a person's way of thinking

[Example] 오해는 사고방식의 차이에서 시작된다.
Misunderstandings start from differences in ways of thinking.

신세대들의 결혼관을 보면 그들의 사고방식을 알 수 있어요.
You can understand the thinking patterns of the younger generation by looking at their value system towards marriage.

43
사물놀이

[사물노리] 명사 Korean traditional percussion quartet, folk music accompanied by four percussion instruments including the 꽹과리, 징, 장구, and 북

[Expression] 사물놀이를 하다 to do samoulnori

[Example] 사물놀이 연주자는 보통 4명이 기본입니다.
The basic number of performers in a samulnori is four people.

얼마 전에 사물놀이 공연을 봤는데 정말 볼 만하더라.
I saw a samulnori performance not too long ago. It was really nice!

44
사실적이다

[사실쩌기다] 형용사 to be factual

representing something exactly as it is

[Usage] 사실적인 N
사실적으로 AV

[Related Words] 현실적이다 to be real or actual

[Example] 뉴스 보도는 사실적이며 편견이 없어야 한다.
A news report needs to stick to the facts and not be prejudiced.

그 연극은 현대를 사는 우리들의 모습을 사실적으로 표현하려고 노력했다.
That play tried to factually express the conditions that contemporary people live in.

45
사주

[사주] 명사 four pillars for the year, month, day, and hour of one's birth that has an influence upon one's fortune

[Expression] 사주팔자 a fortune teller
사주가 좋다 to have good fortune
사주를 보다 to have your fortune read

[Example] 사주는 시대에 뒤떨어진 미신이다.
Saju is a superstition that is lagging behind the times.

비과학적이고 시대에 뒤떨어진다고 해도 사주를 보는 사람은 여전히 많다.
Even though they say that saju is unscientific and behind the times, there still are a lot of people that go and get their fortune read.

46
사투리

[사투리] 명사 provincialism, dialect, or accent

the language or accent used only in one region and that refers to non-standard Korean

[Expression] 사투리를 쓰다 to speak a dialect
사투리로 말하다 to speak using a dialect

[Synonym] 방언 dialect

[Example] 한국 사람이라도 제주도 사투리를 쓰는 사람과는 의사소통이 쉽지 않아요.
Even Korean people have difficulties in communicating with Koreans from Jeju island that speak in their provincial accent.

제 친구는 부산 사람이라서 말을 할 때마다 부산 억양이 느껴지고 사투리도 많이 씁니다.
Since my friend is from Busan, whenever he speaks I can feel his Busan intonation and accent.

47
상쾌하다

[상쾌하다] 형용사 to be refreshing, to be crisp

to feel cool and nice

[Usage] N 이/가 상쾌하다
상쾌한 N

[Expression] 바람이 상쾌하다 The wind is invigorating.
상쾌한 공기 crisp air
상쾌한 아침 refreshing morning

[Related Words] 불쾌하다 to be ruddy

[Example] 아침 공기가 상쾌해요 The morning air is no freshing.

오랜만에 산에 오르니까 몸과 마음이 상쾌해지는 것 같아요.
After climbing up the mountain after a long time, both my body and mind felt refreshed.

48
성묘

[성묘] 명사 to visit one's ancestral graves usually on lunar new year or harvest festival.

[Expression] 성묘객 a person that visits their ancestral graves
성묘를 가다 to go pay respects to one's ancestral graves
성묘를 하다 to pay respects to one's ancestral graves

[Related Words] 제사 memorial services for one's ancestors
차례 memorial service (conducted on Chuseok)

[Example] 추석을 맞아 할아버지 산소에 성묘하러 갔어요.
I went to pay respects to my grandfather's grave on Chuseok.

아버지 산소에 성묘를 다녀왔는데 산소에 풀이 많이 자랐더라고요.
I went to visit my father's grave and noticed that a lot of grass had grown on top of his grave.

49
성직자

[성직짜] 명사 cleric, clergy, ordained religious leader

[Related Words] 스님 monk
목사님 pastor
신부님 catholic priest
수녀님 nun

[Example] 존경하는 성직자가 있나요?
Are there any religious leaders that you respect?

그는 성직자로서 일생을 교회에서 보냈다.
He spent his whole life in the church as a cleric.

50
세배

[세배] 명사 New Year's bow

[Expression] 세배를 하다 to do a New Year's bow
세배를 드리다 to bow down to an elder on New Year's

[Related Words] 절 bow
세뱃돈 money received after completing a New Year's bow

[Example] 세뱃돈은 세배를 받은 어른이 세배한 아랫사람에게 주는 돈입니다.
Sae bae money is the money that is given to a younger person that has just bowed down to an adult.

차례를 지낸 후에 어른들께 세배를 드리는데 이때 어른들은 새해에 더 잘 되기를 바라는 마음에서 덕담을 해 주신다.
After paying respect to your ancestors, you bow down to your elders. At this time, your elders then sincerely wish that you have a good year .

51
소원

[소원] 명사 wish, hope

[Expression] 소원을 빌다 to pray for a wish
소원을 이루다 to fulfill a wish

[Synonym] 소망 hope

[Example] 영화배우를 한번 만나보는 게 제 소원이에요.
My wish is to meet a movie actor.

제 소원은 죽기 전에 이집트에 한번 가 보는 것이에요.
My wish is to go to Egypt at least once before I die.

52
속담

[속땀] 명사 proverb, saying

[Related Words] 격언 maxim, proverb

[Example] 한국에는 말과 관련된 속담이 많습니다.
In Korea, there are a lot of proverbs related to words.

여러분 나라에도 '세월이 약이다'라는 한국 속담과 비슷한 뜻을 가진 속담이 있습니까?
Is there a saying in your countries that has a similar meaning to the Korean phrase "세월이 약이다" (Time cures everything)

53
쇼

[쑈] 명사 show

[Expression] 패션쇼 fashion show
쇼를 하다 to hold a show

[Example] 그 쇼는 환상적인 분위기로 사람들에게 인기가 높았다.
That show was very popular among people because of its fantastic atmosphere.

이번 여행의 마지막 날 저녁에는 태국의 유명한 쇼를 구경할 수 있습니다.
On the last day of this trip, you can watch a famous Thai show during the evening.

54
수상

[수상] 명사 being awarded a prize

having been awarded a prize

[Expression] 수상자 a recipient of a prize
수상 소감 one's reaction or feeling to having been given a prize
수상하다 to award someone with a prize

[Related Words] 입상 to win a prize

[Example] 그 배우의 수상 소감이 아주 감동적이어서 기억에 남아요.
I still remember that actor's reaction to being given an award because it was so touching.

이 영화는 신촌 영화제에서 작품상 수상 이후 그 인기가 높아지고 있다.
This movie has become more popular after being awarded a price in the Shin chon film festival.

55
숙소

[숙쏘] 명사 lodging, accommodations

a place where one stays for a short period of time after leaving their house

[Expression] 숙소를 잡다 to set up accommodations
숙소를 옮기다 to change accommodations
숙소를 정하다 to arrange accommodations

[Example] 가이드는 저녁 시간이 되자 나를 숙소로 안내해 주었다.
As soon as it became night time, the guide led me back to my accommodations.

훈련이 끝난 후에 우리는 모두 숙소에 모여서 휴식을 취했어요.
After the training ended, we all went back to the lodging and rested.

56
신

[신] 명사 god

[Expression] 신을 믿다 to believe in a god
신에게 빌다 to pray to a god

[Example] 영수 씨는 신이 없다고 믿는 무신론자예요.
Youngsoo is an atheist that believes there is no god.

옛날 사람들은 신이 아주 많다고 생각했어요.
In the old days, people thought that there were many gods.

57
신기록

[신기록] 명사 new record

a new record that goes beyond the existing one

[Expression] 세계 신기록 a world record
한국 신기록 new record in Korea
신기록이 나오다 There is a new record.
신기록을 세우다 to establish a new record

[Example] 기네스북은 세계 신기록을 모은 책입니다.
The Guinness Book is a book that compiles all the world records.

이번 올림픽에서 수영 경기에서만 신기록이 5개나 나왔다.
There were five new records only in the swimming competition of the Olympics.

58
신나다

[신나다] 형용사 to be excited

to feel moved or interested by something and therefore feel very good

[Usage] N 이/가 신나다
신나는 N

[Expression] 신나는 일 exciting event
신나는 이야기 exciting story

[Related Words] 즐겁다 to enjoy
흥겹다 to be interested

[Example] 영화의 마지막 장면의 노래는 정말 신났어요.
The song in the last scene of the movie was really exciting.

저는 지난 주말에 사물놀이 공연을 보고 왔는데 정말 신나는 공연이었습니다.
Last week I saw a samulnori performance. It was a really exciting performance.

59
역사적이다 [역싸저기다] 형용사 to be historical or related to history

[Usage] 역사적인 N
역사적으로 AV

[Example] 이번 일은 역사적으로 큰 의미를 가지고 있다.
This happening has an important historical meaning.

이 드라마는 진짜 있었던 역사적인 사건을 바탕으로 만들었대요.
They say that this drama is based on real historical incidents.

60
역시 [역씨] 부사 1. as expected 2. more, also 3. just as before

1. as one expected or imagined

[Example] 그 아이가 열심히 공부하더니 역시 수석을 차지했군요.
That child studies very hard so I wasn't surprised to find out he was top of his class.

2. more, in addition to

[Synonym] 또한 also

[Example] 네가 좋다면 나도 역시 좋다.
If you are happy, I am also happy.

3. just like in the past

[Example] 나는 오늘도 역시 7시에 버스를 탔다.
I took the bus at 7 o'clock today just like I always do.

61
역할 [여칼] 명사 1. role, part 2. role, part, function

1. the part an actor is given in a movie or play

[Expression] 역할을 맡다 to be given a part

[Synonym] 역 role
배역 part

[Example] 연극 연습을 해야 하는데 중요한 역할을 맡은 친구가 안 왔어요.
I need to practice for the play, but my friend that has an important role hasn't arrived yet.

2. a responsibility or obligation one has received and needs to complete properly

[Expression] 역할을 하다 to have a role

[Synonym] 임무 duty, assignment

[Example] 영수 씨는 차남이지만 형이 외국에 나가 있어서 집안의 맏아들 역할을 하고 있다.
Though Youngsoo is the second oldest son, since his older brother is abroad he has assumed the role of eldest son in the household.

62
연기

[연기] 명사 acting

an actors expression of lines through feeling and movement

[Expression] 연기력 acting ability
연기자 actor
연기하다 to act

[Example] 배우들의 연기뿐만 아니라 노래, 춤 모두가 너무 좋았어.
Not only was their acting great, but their dancing and singing were as well.

요즘 연기는 못하면서 인기가 많은 배우들이 많은 것 같아요.
Nowadays, I think there are a lot of actors that don't act very well but are still popular.

63
연장하다

[연장하다] 동사 to extend

[Usage] N 을/를 연장하다

[Expression] 기간을 연장하다 to extend a time period
비자를 연장하다 to extend one's visa

[Related Words] 연기하다 to delay

[Example] 집주인이 전세 계약 기간을 연장하자고 했어요.
The house owner suggested that I extend my lease.

여권 기간을 연장하려고 출입국관리사무소에 갔어요.
I went to the Immigration office in order to extend my passport.

64
열리다

[열리다] 동사 to be held, to commence

for a meeting or discussion to be held

[Usage] N 이/가 열리다

[Expression] 회의가 열리다 The meeting begins.

[Related Words] 열다 to open

[Example] 박물관이나 미술관에서는 새로운 전시회가 자주 열려요.
New exhibitions are opened very often at museums and art galleries.

한국에서는 명절 때마다 축제가 열리는데 단오제도 그 중의 하나이다.
Festivals are held during holidays in Korea. One of those is the Dano Festival.

65
예술

[예술] 명사 arts

a piece of work or movement of man whose goal is the appreciation of beauty through various materials or technique

[Expression] 예술가 artist
예술품 piece of art
예술 작품 a piece of art

[Related Words] 미술 fine art

[Example] 인생은 짧고 예술은 길다.
Life is short but art is long.

지난주 금요일에 예술의 전당으로 공연을 보러 갔었습니다.
Last Friday I went to see a performance in an art hall.

66
올림픽

[올림픽] 명사 Olympic Games

[Expression] 올림픽이 열리다 The Olympics are held.
올림픽을 개최하다 to initiate the Olympics
올림픽에 나가다 to be a part of the Olympics
올림픽에 참가하다 to participate in the Olympics

[Example] 올림픽이나 월드컵 때는 자원 봉사자들의 도움이 많이 필요하다.
The help of volunteers is greatly needed during the Olympic Games or the World Cup.

이번에 이겼으면 올림픽에 나갈 수 있었는데 우리 팀이 져서 너무 아쉬웠어요.
If we had won this time, we would have been able to go to the Olympics, but I was very disappointed because our team lost.

67
옮기다

[옮기다] 동사 1. to move 2. to execute, to carry out

1. to move an object from one place to another and change its location

[Usage] N 을/를 옮기다

[Expression] 가구를 옮기다 to move furniture
회사를 옮기다 to change companies

[Example] 일이 적성에 안 맞아서 회사를 옮길까 해요.
I am thinking about changing companies because it doesn't fit my aptitude.

2. to progress to the next level or stage of something

[Usage] N 에 옮기다
N 으로/로 옮기다

[Expression] 실천에 옮기다 to put into practice
행동으로 옮기다 to put into action, to take an action

[Example] 계획을 하기는 쉬운데 실천에 옮기기란 아주 어렵다.
Making a plan is easy, but the difficult part is actually putting it into practice.

68
우승하다

[우승하다] 동사 to be victorious

to win and hold first place in a competition or event

[Usage] N 이/가 우승하다
N 에/에서 우승하다

[Expression] 경기에서 우승하다 to win first place in a competition
올림픽에서 우승하다 to be victorious at the Olympics

[Example] 우리 학교 축구 대표팀은 정신력이 좋으니까 체력만 뒷받침되면 우승도 가능할 겁니다.
Our school's soccer team has good willpower, so if their physical power was up to par, they could have a chance at winning.

이번 경기에 세계적으로 유명한 선수들이 모두 참가한다고 하니까 우승하기가 쉽지 않겠어요.
It is not going to be easy to win first place at this competition because they say that all the world famous players are going to be participating.

69
운

[운] 명사 luck, fortune

a predestined luck that man cannot change with his own powers.

[Expression] 불운 misfortune
행운 luck
운이 좋다 to be lucky
운이 나쁘다 to be unlucky

[Example] 운이 좋게 잃어버린 지갑을 금방 찾았다.
Luckily enough, I found the wallet that I had lost right away.

제임스가 이번에 시험도 보지 않고 대학에 들어갔다고? 정말 운 좋은 사람이야.
You said that James didn't take the test and still got into college? He is a really lucky guy.

70
인기

[인끼] 명사 popularity

[Expression] 인기 가수 popular singer
인기가 많다 to be very popular

인기가 있다 to be popular
인기를 잃다 to lose popularity
인기를 얻다 to gain popularity

[Example] 다양한 기능들을 갖춘 제품이 젊은이들에게 인기가 많아요.
The product that has a wide range of functions is very popular among the younger generations.

김태호 선수가 올림픽에서 금메달을 딴 후에 인기가 많아졌다지요?
I heard that the athlete Kim Taeho became more popular after winning the gold medal in the Olympics. Is that true?

71
전통

[전통] 명사 tradition

[Expression] 전통문화 traditional culture
전통악기 traditional instruments
전통의상 traditional outfit
전통을 따르다 to follow traditions
전통을 지키다 to keep a tradition alive

[Example] 저는 해외여행을 가면 꼭 그 나라의 전통의상을 입고 사진을 찍어요.
When I travel abroad, I always wear the traditional outfit of the country I travel to and take a picture of myself wearing it.

전통은 지금 생활하고 맞지 않는 것이 많으니까 꼭 따를 필요는 없다고 봐요.
As for tradition, since there are so many of them that match up with our daily lives, I believe it isn't necessary to definitely follow them.

72
종교

[종교] 명사 religion

[Expression] 종교단체 a religious organization
종교를 갖다 to have a religion
종교를 믿다 to believe in religion
종교가 있다 to have a religion

[Related Words] 불교 Buddhism
기독교 Christianity
천주교 Catholicism
힌두교 Hinduism
이슬람교 Islam

[Example] 무슨 종교를 믿으세요?
What is your religion?

저는 종교는 없지만 힘들 때는 하느님께 기도해요.
Even though I don't have a religion, when things get tough I pray to God.

73
좌석

[좌석] 명사 seat

[Expression] 좌석표 ticket with a seat number
극장 좌석 theater seat
좌석을 잡다 to take a seat
좌석을 양보하다 to give up one's seat

[Synonym] 자리 place

[Example] 비행기에서 제 옆 좌석에 유명한 배우가 앉았어요.
A famous actor was sitting in the seat in front of me on the airplane.

인터넷 예매를 하면 앉고 싶은 좌석을 정할 수 있어서 좋아요.
I like the fact that if I buy my tickets in advance online, I can choose the seat I want to sit in.

74
주인공

[주인공] 명사 protagonist

[Expression] 남자 주인공 male protagonist
여자 주인공 female protagonist
주인공이 바뀌다 to change protagonists
주인공을 맡다 to have the part of protagonist

[Related Words] 조연 supporting actor

[Example] 이번 연극의 주인공은 6살짜리 소녀예요.
The play's protagonist is a six-year-old girl.

주인공을 하던 배우가 감기에 걸려서 주인공이 바뀌었대요.
The actor that was doing the role of the protagonist caught a cold, so they said that there has been a change in actor.

75
지다

[지다] 동사 to lose

to succumb to the competition after using your strength and skill in a fight, match, or game.

[Usage] N 이/가 지다
N 에/에서 지다

[Expression] 경쟁에 지다 to lose in a competition
경기에서 지다 to lose in a match

[Related Words] 패배하다 to lose

[Example] 어제 야구 경기에서 5:2로 이겼어요.
They won 5 to 2 yesterday in the baseball match.

이번 경기에서 지면 4강에 올라갈 수 없어요.
If we lose this match, we cannot go to the semifinals.

76
짐

[짐] 명사 suitcase, luggage

[Expression] 짐이 많다 to have a lot of luggage
짐을 싸다 to pack a suitcase
짐을 나르다 to carry a suitcase
짐을 옮기다 to move a suitcase
짐을 정리하다 to organize a suitcase

[Example] 혹시 내일 짐 싸는 것 좀 도와줄 수 있어?
Could you help me pack my suitcase tomorrow?

짐이 너무 무거워서 다른 사람과 같이 들어야겠어요.
My luggage is too heavy so I need to pick it up with someone else.

77
차다

[차다] 동사 1. to be full 2. to be full of an emotion

1. be to maximum capacity to the point that nothing else can enter

[Usage] N 이/가 차다
N 으로/로 차다

[Expression] 가득 차다 to be full

[Synonym] 가득하다 to be full

[Example] 광장은 월드컵을 응원하기 위해 나온 사람들로 가득 찼다.
The plaza was full of people that had come out to cheer for the world cup game.

2. to be full of a certain emotion or feeling

[Usage] N 으로/로 차다

[Expression] 자신감으로 차다 to be overly confident

[Synonym] 가득하다 to be full of

[Example] 김현아 선수는 자신감으로 가득 찬 목소리로 이번 대회에서 반드시 우승하겠다고 말했다.
The athlete Kim Hyuna said in a confident voice that she would take first place without a doubt in the upcoming competition.

78
참가하다

[참가하다] 동사 to participate in

to be a part of a meeting or event

[Usage] N 에 참가하다

[Expression]
경기에 참가하다 to participate in a sports competition
대회에 참가하다 to participate in a contest
올림픽에 참가하다 to participate in the Olympics

[Related Words]
참석하다 to attend
참여하다 to join in

[Example]
다음 주까지 '서울시 외국인 장기 자랑 대회'에 참가할 학생들을 모집한다.
We are recruiting students up until next week to participate in the "Seoul City Foreigner Talent Contest."

'자전거 문화 유적 체험 투어'에 참가하는 사람들은 본인의 자전거를 가지고 가야 한다.
People that are participating in the "Bicycle Tour Around Cultural Ruins" must bring their own bicycle.

79
천사

[천사] 명사 1. angel 2. angel

1. angel

[Antonym] 악마 devil

[Example]
인간의 마음속에는 천사와 악마가 늘 같이 있으면서 싸우는 것 같다.
In the heart of man, it seems like there is an angel and a devil that are constantly together and fighting inside of us.

2. to metaphorically describe a sweet and angelic person

[Expression]
수호천사 guardian angel
백의의 천사 white-robed angel

[Example]
아이의 자고 있는 모습이 마치 천사같아요.
The sleeping baby almost looks like an angel.

80
천주교

[천주교] 명사 Catholicism

[Expression]
천주교 신자 a believer of Catholicism
천주교를 믿다 to be catholic, to believe in Catholicism

[Synonym] 가톨릭교 Catholicism

[Related Words]
성당 catholic church
신부 priest
수녀 nun

[Example] 천주교에서는 낙태를 반대해요.
The catholic church opposes abortion.

천주교 신자들은 성당에 가고, 기독교 신자들은 교회에 가요.
Catholics go to catholic church and Christians go to Christian church.

81
체육

[체육] 명사 physical training

an act that strengthens one's body through consistent working out

[Expression] 체육관 gym
체육 대회 athletic meet
체육 시간 gym time, physical education
체육 시설 physical training facilities

[Example] 전 운동을 못해서 체육 시간이 싫어요.
I hate physical education because I am not good at working out.

내일 체육 대회가 있는데 비가 너무 많이 와서 걱정입니다.
Tomorrow there will be an athletic meet. I am very worried because it is raining a lot.

82
축제

[축쩨] 명사 festival, feast

[Expression] 축제 분위기 festive atmosphere
불꽃놀이 축제 fireworks festival
축제에 참가하다 to attend a festival

[Example] 월드컵 경기로 유럽은 물론 한국도 축제 분위기입니다.
Europe and Korea both are in festive moods because of the world cup competition.

저는 며칠 전 보령 머드 축제에 다녀왔는데 참 좋았어요.
A few days ago I went to the mud festival at Boreong. It was really nice.

83
출연하다

[추련하다] 동사 to come out in a movie, show, performance, or novel

[Usage] N 이/가 출연하다
N 에 출연하다

[Expression] 영화에 출연하다 to appear in a movie

[Example] 이 영화에 출연하려고 거의 1년 정도 무술 연습을 했어요.
He did over one year of martial arts training in order to appear in that movie.

이번 자선 행사에는 유명 가수와 배우들이 많이 출연한다고 해요.
They say that in this charity event famous singers and actors are going to make an appearance.

84
출전하다

[출쩐하다] 동사 to compete

to take part in a competition

[Usage] N 에 출전하다

[Expression] 경기에 출전하다 to compete in a competition
대회에 출전하다 to compete in a contest

[Related Words] 나가다 to appear, to take part in

[Example] 그의 꿈은 올림픽에 출전하는 것이다.
His dream is to compete in the Olympics.

이번 대회에 부상 때문에 출전하지 못한 선수가 있었다고 해요.
They said that there was an athlete that wasn't able to compete in the competition because of an injury.

85
포스터

[포스터] 명사 poster

[Expression] 영화 포스터 movie poster
포스터 광고 poster advertisement
포스터를 붙이다 to stick up a poster

[Example] 그 연극 포스터를 봤는데 그 공연을 꼭 보고 싶어요.
I saw a poster for that play. I really want to see that performance.

포스터가 없다니? 어제만 해도 여기에 붙어 있었는데.
You said there is no poster? Just yesterday it was hung up here.

86
포함하다

[포함하다] 동사 to include

[Usage] N 을/를 포함하다

[Example] 교통비, 숙박료, 입장료를 모두 포함해서 총 여행 비용은 30만 원입니다.
After including all the transportation, lodging, and entrance fees, the total cost of the trip is 300,000 won.

전기세, 난방비는 관리비에 포함되어 있으니까 따로 내실 필요가 없어요.
Since the heat and maintenance fees are included in the monthly rent, there is no need to pay anything extra.

87
표현하다

[표현하다] 동사 to express

to show one's feeling or thought

[Usage] N 을/를 표현하다
N 으로/로 표현하다

[Expression] 마음을 표현하다 to express one's feelings
말로 표현하다 to express with words

[Synonym] 나타내다 to illustrate

[Example] 너무 감동적이어서 말로 표현할 수가 없어요.
It is so touching that I cannot express myself by words.

자신의 감정을 직접 표현하지 않으면 다른 사람들은 알 수가 없지요.
If you cannot express your own feelings, there is no way other people can understand them.

88
현지인

[현지인] 명사 local, native

[Example] 배낭여행을 하면 현지인들에게 이런저런 도움을 받는 경우가 많아요.
If you go backpacking, there are many cases that you will get all kinds of help from the locals.

언어교환을 하면 현지인에게 직접 언어를 배울 수 있기 때문에 외국인을 만났을 때 느끼는 두려움도 덜 수 있다.
If you do a language exchange, you can lessen the fear that you have when meeting a foreigner because you directly learn the language from them.

89
화려하다

[화려하다] 형용사 1. to be magnificent, to be splendid 2. to be impressive

1. to be shiny and beautiful

[Usage] N 이/가 화려하다
화려한 N
화려하게 AV

[Expression] 화려한 무대 magnificent performance
화려하게 입다 to wear something flashy

[Antonym] 수수하다 to be ordinary

[Example] 파티에 갈 때 사람들은 화려한 옷을 입어요.
People wear flashy clothes when going to a party.

2. to be impressive

[Usage] 화려한 N

[Expression] 화려한 경력 impressive work experience

[Example] 영화배우들의 생활이 겉으로 보기에는 화려해 보인다.
The life of an actor seems very impressive on the outside.

90
환갑

[환갑] 명사 60th birthday

[Expression] 환갑 잔치 60th birthday party celebration
환갑이 지나다 to pass one's 60th birthday

[Synonym] 회갑 60th birthday

[Related Words] 칠순 the age of seventy
팔순 the age of eighty

[Example] 우리 할아버지는 환갑이 지나셨는데도 아직도 정정하세요.
Although my grandfather is over 60 years old, he is still very vigorous and healthy.

지난주에 할머니 회갑 잔치가 있어서 할아버지 댁에 다녀왔어요.
I went to my grandparents' house last week because my grandmother held her 60 year old birthday party.

91
환상적이다

[환상저기다] 형용사 1. to be fantastic and imaginary 2. to be amazing

1. to be beyond fact, to be in the realm of imagination

[Usage] 환상적인 N
환상적으로 AV

[Expression] 환상적인 장면 fantastic scene

[Example] 그 영화에는 환상적인 장면이 많아요.
There are a lot of fantastic scenes in that movie.

2. to be amazing and admirable

[Usage] 환상적인 N
환상적으로 AV

[Expression] 환상적인 연주 amazing musical performance

[Example] 어제 들은 바이올린 연주는 정말 환상적이었어.
The violin performance I heard yesterday was amazing.

92
훌륭하다

[훌륭하다] 형용사 to be admirable, to be amazing

to be so good that you cannot scold or find flaw in something

[Usage] 훌륭한 N
훌륭하게 AV

[Expression] 훌륭한 일 excellent thing
훌륭하게 연주하다 to perform spectacularly

[Synonym] 대단하다 to be great

[Example] 연극 내용도 좋았지만 배우들의 연기가 정말 훌륭했어요.
The content of the play was nice but the acting was really amazing.

평소 남모르게 봉사활동을 많이 하신다니 정말 훌륭하세요.
It is really great that you do a lot of volunteer work without others knowing.

93
흥겹다

[흥겹따] 형용사 to be cheerful and exciting, to be interesting

[Usage] 흥겨운 **N**

[Expression]
흥겨운 노래 exciting song
흥겨운 리듬 exciting rhythm
흥겨운 음악 exciting music
흥겨운 연주 exciting performance

[Related Words] 신나다 to be excited

[Example] 어제 공연때 흥겨운 장단에 맞춰 춤을 추는 사람도 있었다.
At yesterday's performance, there were people that were dancing to the exciting rhythm.

저는 사물놀이가 지루할 줄 알았는데 생각외로 정말 흥겹고 재미있었어요.
I expected the samulnori performance to be boring, but it was exciting and fun.

10 연습문제

[1-11] **다음 단어를 한국어로 바꿔 쓰십시오.**

Change the following vocabulary words to Korean

1. show ( )
2. luggage ( )
3. exchange ( )
4. magic ( )
5. physical education ( )
6. festival ( )
7. media ( )
8. factual ( )
9. poster ( )
10. expenses for celebrations ( )
11. popular culture ( )

[12-23] **[보기]에서 알맞은 말을 찾아 빈칸에 넣으십시오.**

Fill the empty spaces with the appropriate word from the box below.

[보기]

개봉	공연	관객	관람	대사	무용
연기	예술	가면극	뮤지컬	주인공	다큐멘터리

12. 새 영화를 처음으로 극장에서 상영하는 것.

( )

13. 자연이나 사람들의 있는 그대로의 모습을 사실대로 찍어서 보여 주는 영화나 드라마.

( )

14. 음악, 무용, 연극을 많은 사람 앞에서 보여주는 것.

( )

15. 운동 경기, 공연, 영화를 보거나 듣는 사람.

( )

16. 연극, 영화, 운동 경기, 그림을 구경하는 것.

( )

17. 가면을 쓰고 하는 연극.

( )

18. 부채춤, 탈춤, 발레 등과 같은 춤.

( )

19. 연극 안에 음악과 노래, 춤이 모두 있는 것.

( )

20. 연극이나 영화 따위에서 배우가 하는 말.

( )

21. 배우가 배역의 인물, 성격, 행동 등을 표현하는 것.

( )

22 작가, 음악가, 화가가 아름다움을 표현하기 위해 하는 활동과 그 작품.

( )

23. 연극, 영화, 소설에서 가장 중심이 되는 사람.

( )

[24-34] **[보기]에서 알맞은 단어를 골라 (　　　) 안에 쓰십시오.**

Choose the appropriate word from the box below and then fill in the parenthesis.

[보기]

복	동기	박수	인기	결승전	열리다
감동하다	민간신앙	수상하다	출전하다	표현하다	

24. 이 연극을 만들게 된 (　　　　　　)은/는 많은 어린이들에게 즐거움을 주기 위해서입니다.
25. 어머니는 내가 직접 만든 영화를 보시고는 (　　　　　　)으셨는지/셨는지 눈물을 흘리셨다.
26. 국제 영화제에서 영화배우 김도연이 여우주연상을 (　　　　　　)었대요/았대요/였대요.
27. 배우들의 연기뿐만 아니라 노래, 춤 모두 훌륭해서 많은 관객들이 오랫동안 (　　　　　　)을/를 보냈다.
28. 매년 가을 부산에서 국제 영화제가 (　　　　　　)는다고/ㄴ다고/다고 합니다.
29. 그 영화는 요즘 (　　　　　　)이/가 있어서 일주일 전에 예약해야 볼 수 있어요.
30. 지금 아주 행복해서 말로 (　　　　　　)을/ㄹ 수가 없다.
31. 옛날 사람들은 돌, 나무 같은 자연이나 동물을 신으로 생각하고 믿는 (　　　　　　)을/를 가지고 있었다.
32. 이번 올림픽 농구 경기에서 스페인과 네덜란드가 마지막 (　　　　　　)까지 올라갔는데 결국 스페인이 우승을 했어요.
33. 1948년 런던 올림픽은 한국이 최초로 (　　　　　　)는/은/ㄴ 올림픽입니다.
34. 친구가 평소에 다른 사람들을 잘 도와주더니 복권에 당첨됐어. 역시 착한 일을 하면 (　　　　　　)을/를 받는 것 같아.

[35-43] **단어의 설명을 읽고 [보기]에서 알맞은 단어를 골라 쓰십시오.**

Read the explanation of the following vocabulary words and then choose the appropriate word from the box below and fill in.

[보기]

돌	귀성	성묘	세배	속담
환갑	사투리	사물놀이	강강술래	

35. 정월 대보름날이나 8월 한가윗날에 여자들이 서로 손을 잡고 노래를 부르며 도는 놀이 ······ (   )

36. 아기의 첫 번째 생일 ······ (   )

37. 예전부터 전해져 내려오는 조상들의 지혜가 담긴 말 ······ (   )

38. 북, 장구, 징, 꽹과리 네 가지 악기로 연주되는 음악 ······ (   )

39. 만 60세의 생일을 축하하는 날. 회갑이라고도 함 ······ (   )

40. 설날이나 추석 등에 조상의 무덤을 찾아감 ······ (   )

41. 새해에 웃어른께 인사로 하는 절 ······ (   )

42. 서울이 아닌 다른 지역에서 쓰는 말 ······ (   )

43. 명절에 고향에 가는 것 ······ (   )

[44-45] **다음 밑줄 친 부분과 반대되는 뜻을 가진 것을 고르십시오.**

Choose the appropriate word from the box below and then fill in the parenthesis.

44. 오늘 본 뮤지컬은 배우들의 무대 의상이 보통과 다르게 <u>수수했어요</u>.

❶ 어색하다   ❷ 화창하다   ❸ 화려하다   ❹ 변화하다

45. 제 친구는 정말 <u>천사</u>같이 착한 마음을 가졌어요.

❶ 목사   ❷ 승려   ❸ 신부   ❹ 악마

[46-56] **[보기]에서 알맞은 단어를 골라 (   ) 안에 쓰십시오.**

Choose the appropriate word from the box below and then fill in the parenthesis.

[보기]

운	대회	사주	숙소	지다	가이드
신기록	머무르다	사고방식	상쾌하다	우승하다	

46. 생년월일과 태어난 시간으로 운명을 점치는 (   )을/를 믿는 사람들이 있다.

47. 오늘은 정말 (　　　　　　　)이/가 좋은 날이네요. 시험을 봤는데 제가 공부한 부분에서 시험 문제가 많이 나왔어요.
48. 마리아 씨는 작년에 노래 자랑 (　　　　　　　)에 나가서 1등을 했어요.
49. 이번 올림픽에서 김현아 선수가 최고의 점수를 받아 세계 (　　　　　　　)을/를 세웠어요.
50. 이번 월드컵에서는 어느 나라가 (　　　　　　　)을/ㄹ 것 같아요?
51. 우리 대학교 축구 동아리가 한국대학교 축구 동아리와 축구 경기를 했는데 2:3으로 안타깝게 (　　　　　　　)었어요/았어요/였어요.
52. 남자 친구가 외국 사람인데 문화와 (　　　　　　　)이/가 달라서 가끔 싸울 때가 있어요.
53. 운동을 한 후에 샤워를 하면 기분이 (　　　　　　　)어요/아요/여요.
54. 저는 한국어 공부를 열심히 해서 한국 관광객들을 안내하는 (　　　　　　　)이/가 되고 싶어요.
55. 내가 작년 제주도 여행 때 사흘 동안 (　　　　　　　)었던/았던/였던 펜션을 소개해 줄게.
56. 밤이 늦었으니까 이제 구경은 그만하고 오늘 밤에 묵을 (　　　　　　　)을/를 정합시다.

[57-59] **다음 (　　　)에 공통적으로 들어갈 단어를 쓰십시오.**

Write one word that can commonly fit into the parenthesis below.

57.
❶ 뒤에 있는 한라산을 (　　　　　　)으로/로 해서 사진 한 장 찍읍시다.
❷ 그 소설가는 자신의 고향인 강원도 춘천을 (　　　　　　)으로/로 소설 작품을 썼다.

(　　　　　　　　)

58.
❶ 자녀들을 올바르게 기르는 데에는 부모의 (　　　　　　)이/가 제일 중요하다.
❷ 사실 저는 아직 미혼인데 이번 연극에서 아버지 (　　　　　　)을/를 맡아서 좀 부담이 돼요.

(　　　　　　　　)

59.
❶ 그 쇼는 현실에서는 볼 수 없는 (　　　　　　)인 분위기로 사람들에게 인기가 높았다.
❷ 어제 본 뮤지컬은 그동안 제가 본 뮤지컬 중에서 가장 훌륭했어요. 배우들의 연기도 정말 (　　　　　　)이었고요/였고요.

(　　　　　　　　)

[60-66] **다음 (　　　)에 공통적으로 들어갈 단어의 기본형을 쓰십시오.**

Write the basic form of one word that can commonly fit in the parenthesis below.

60. ❶ 회사에서 중요한 일을 맡았는데 신입사원인 제가 혼자 하기에는 좀 (　　　　　)네요.
❷ 그동안 열심히 준비해 오던 연극을 드디어 내일 공연하게 돼서 가슴이 (　　　　　)어요/아요/여요.

(　　　　　　　)

61. ❶ 생일 케이크의 초를 끄고 소원을 (　　　　　)었어요/았어요/였어요.
❷ 동생을 때려서 잘못했다고 엄마한테 (　　　　　)었어요/았어요/였어요.

(　　　　　　　)

62. ❶ 선글라스를 쓰면 햇빛으로부터 눈도 (　　　　　)을/ㄹ 수 있고 멋도 있다.
❷ 환경을 (　　　　　)기 위해서 쓰레기는 재활용되는 것과 그렇지 않은 것으로 분리해서 따로 버려야 한다.

(　　　　　　　)

63. ❶ 이사 준비는 다 끝났고 이제 짐을 (　　　　　)기만 하면 돼요.
❷ 하숙집이 학교에서 너무 멀어서 하숙집을 (　　　　　)었어요/았어요/였어요.
❸ 담배를 끊겠다고는 했는데 행동으로 (　　　　　)기는 것은 쉬운 일이 아니네요.

(　　　　　　　)

64. ❶ 이태환 선수가 올림픽 대회 수영 종목에서 금메달을 (　　　　　)었어요/았어요/였어요.
❷ 제주도 감귤 농장에 가면 직접 감귤을 (　　　　　)어서/아서/여서 먹을 수도 있어요.
❸ 할머니께서 운전 면허 시험을 열 번이나 보신 후에 겨우 운전면허증을(　　　　　)으셨어요/셨어요.

(　　　　　　　)

65.
❶ 마리나 씨, 러시아에서는 겨울에 추위가 (　　　　　　)는다면서요/ㄴ다면서요/다면서요?
❷ 세계적인 연주자라서 그런지 피아노 연주 실력이 (　　　　　　)던데요.
❸ 외국에서도 그 배우를 만나려고 오는 걸 보니까 그 배우의 인기가 (　　　　　　)는/은/ㄴ 모양이에요.

(　　　　　　　　)

66.
❶ 아직 1월이라서 그런지 겨울 바람이 무척 (　　　　　　)네요.
❷ 출퇴근 시간에는 직장인들로 지하철이 가득 (　　　　　　)어서/아서/여서 앉을 자리가 없어요.
❸ 우리나라 선수들이 그동안 열심히 연습을 해서인지 자신감이 가득 (　　　　　　)는/은/ㄴ 모습이었어요.

(　　　　　　　　)

[67-77] **[보기]에서 알맞은 단어를 골라 (　　　) 안에 쓰십시오.**

Choose the appropriate word from the box below and then fill in the parenthesis.

[보기]

기도	교포	역시	연장하다	전통	역사적이다
올림픽	현지인	문화유산	참가하다	포함되다	

67. 중국에는 만리장성, 자금성 같은 세계적인 (　　　　　　)이/가 많아요.

68. 길이 많이 막히네. (　　　　　　) 엄마 말씀이 맞았어. 엄마가 월요일이라서 길이 막히니까 일찍 나가라고 하셨는데.

69. 경주는 신라의 수도였기 때문에 지금도 경주에는 (　　　　　　)인 유물과 유적이 많이 남아 있어요.

70. 나의 하루는 한국의 (　　　　　　) 무술인 태권도와 함께 시작된다.

71. 호텔 요금에 조식 가격도 (　　　　　　)어/아/여 있는 건가요?

72. 비자 기간이 이번 달에 끝나서 내일은 출입국 관리 사무소에 가서 비자를 (　　　　　　)어야겠어요/아야겠어요/여야겠어요.

73. 해외여행을 갔을 때는 그 곳에 사는 (　　　　　　)의 안내를 받는 것이 더 좋은 것 같아요.

74. 노래 대회에 (　　　　　　)고 싶기는 하지만 노래를 잘 할 자신이 없어요.

75. 올해에도 우리 가족 모두 건강하고 행복하게 살게 해 달라고 하나님께 (　　　　　　)을/를 드렸어요.

76. 사실 저는 재미 (　　　　　　)이에요/예요. 부모님은 한국 사람이시지만 저는 미국에서 태어났어요.

77. 4년마다 개최하는 국제 스포츠 대회인 (　　　　　　)이/가 베이징에서 2008년에 열렸어요.

[78-84] **다음 밑줄 친 부분과 의미가 비슷한 것을 고르십시오.**

Choose a word that is similar in meaning to the underlined part of the sentence.

78. 20년 동안 불쌍한 이웃을 도와온 김연순 할머님의 <u>아름다운 이야기</u>를 신문에서 읽었다.

❶ 미담　❷ 미인　❸ 미소　❹ 미술

79. <u>신나는</u> 리듬에 맞춰 사람들이 하나 둘씩 춤을 추기 시작했다.

❶ 재밌다　❷ 흥겹다　❸ 기쁘다　❹ 흥미롭다

80. 출근 시간이어서 버스에 빈 <u>자리</u>가 없었다.

❶ 승객　❷ 책상　❸ 동전　❹ 좌석

81. 영화를 보러 갔다가 <u>표가 다 팔려서</u> 그냥 왔어요.

❶ 예약되다　❷ 예매하다　❸ 매진되다　❹ 확인하다

82. 이번 콘서트에 어떤 가수들이 나오는지 알면 가르쳐 주세요.

❶ 지각하다 ❷ 출연하다 ❸ 출석하다 ❹ 결석하다

83. 이 식당의 음식은 여러 가지 종류가 있어요.

❶ 다양하다 ❷ 다정하다 ❸ 복잡하다 ❹ 지루하다

84. 오늘 본 뮤지컬 공연은 배우들의 연기도 좋았을 뿐만 아니라 무대도 아름다웠어요. 공연이 정말 대단했어요.

❶ 서투르다 ❷ 감동하다 ❸ 표현하다 ❹ 훌륭하다

[85-90] **다음 [보기]에서 알맞은 단어를 골라 이야기를 완성하십시오.**

Choose the right word from the box below and complete the story.

[보기]

신	불교	소원	기독교	성직자	천주교

현대 사회의 종교는 정말 다양하다. 대표적인 종교로는 '가톨릭교'라고도 불리우는 85.(　　　　　　), 예수를 믿는 86.(　　　　　　), 석가모니를 믿는 87.(　　　　　　) 그리고 그 이외에 이슬람교나 힌두교와 같은 종교도 있다. 또한 신부, 목사, 승려와 같은 종교인을 88.(　　　　　　)이라고/라고 한다. 그러나 평소에 예수나 석가모니같은 89.(　　　　　　)을/를 믿지 않는 무신론자도 자신이 해결할 수 없는 문제나 어려운 일이 있을 때는 기도를 하거나 몹시 바라는 일이 생길 때는 90.(　　　　　　)을/를 비는 사람들도 있다.

속담, 관용어, 한자성어, 의태어, 의성어

11

Proverbs, Idioms, Chinese character phrases, Mimetic words, Onomatopoeias

11-1 속담

01
가는 날이 장날

This saying is used when someone is trying to do a certain action and suddenly something unexpected occurred.

[Example] 가는 날이 장날이라더니 공부를 하려고 도서관에 갔는데 휴관일이었어요.

As the expression "가는 날이 장날" goes, I was on my way to the library when suddenly I arrived and saw that it was closed.

02
가는 말이 고와야 오는 말이 곱다

This saying means that you must speak and act nicely towards someone so that you will be treated nicely.

[Example] 네가 친구에게 먼저 바보라고 놀려서 친구도 너에게 돼지라고 놀린 거야. 가는 말이 고와야 오는 말이 고운 거란다.

Since you first made fun of your friend calling him an idiot, he called you a pig in the same way. Just as the expression goes, "가는 말이 고와야 오는 말이 곱다".

03
갈수록 태산

As time goes by, a problem can become more and more difficult.

[Example] 세탁기가 잘 작동하지 않아서 걱정하고 있었는데 갈수록 태산이라고 이제는 아예 세탁기가 켜지지도 않아요.

I was worried because my dryer wasn't running well. You know how people say that "갈수록 태산", now the dryer doesn't even turn on anymore.

04
고래 싸움에 새우 등 터진다

In the midsts of a fight, an uninvolved person ends up getting damaged or harmed.

[Example] 김 부장님이 어제 이 부장님하고 싸우고 나서 잘못한 것도 없는 나한테 화를 내더라. 고래 싸움에 새우 등 터진다더니 그 말이 맞는 것 같아.

After superintendent Kim fought yesterday with superintendent Lee, Mr. Kim was angry at me even though I did nothing wrong. I guess what they say about "고래 싸움에 새우 등 터진다 is true".

05
고생 끝에 낙이 온다

After enduring a hard or difficult job, this saying means that a good and enjoyable outcome is sure to come.

[Example] 고생 끝에 낙이 온다고 지금은 고생스럽지만 곧 좋은 결과가 있을 테니까 걱정하지 마세요.

As they say that "고생 끝에 낙이 온다", though it may be challenging now, don't worry too much because a good result is sure to come.

06
금강산도 식후경

No matter how fun an event can be, you can only enjoy it if you feel full. If you are hungry, you can't do anything.

[Example] 금강산도 식후경이라는데 우리 밥부터 먹고 제주도 여행을 시작하자.
As the saying "금강산도 식후경" goes, let's eat first and then start traveling around Jeju island.

07
꼬리가 길면 밟힌다

Even if others don't find out about the bad things you have done, if you let some time go by and continue to do the same act over and over again, you will end up getting caught.

[Example] 꼬리가 길면 밟힌다고 너 계속 공부 안 하고 컴퓨터 게임만 하면 부모님께 들킬 지도 모르니까 조심해.
Just like they say, "꼬리가 길면 밟힌다", if you don't study and just play computer games, sooner or later your parents are going to catch you. Be careful.

08
꿩 대신 닭

When you don't have the most suitable or fitting choice available, you replace it with something that is similar to what you are looking for.

[Example] 꿩 대신 닭이라고 오렌지가 없으면 그냥 귤을 삽시다.
As the saying "꿩 대신 닭" goes, if they don't have oranges, let's just buy mandarins.

09
누워서 침 뱉기

While trying to do something bad to someone else, in the process you end up causing damage to yourself.

[Example] 나른 사람들 앞에서 자기 부모님에 대해서 나쁘게 말하는 건 정말 누워서 침 뱉기나 다름없어요.
Speaking badly about your parents in front of other people is no different than just "누워서 침 뱉기".

10
돌다리도 두들겨 보고 건너라

No matter how well you can do something or how sure something may seem, you must be careful and take time your time when doing it.

[Example] 돌다리도 두들겨 보고 건너라고 시험 문제를 다 풀었어도 다시 한번 꼼꼼하게 확인해 보세요.
Just like they say "돌다리고 두들겨 보고 건너라", even though you solved all the test questions, take the time to carefully go through them once again.

11
땅 짚고 헤엄치기

This saying refers to a job that is extremely easy to do.

[Example] 미선 씨 영어 실력은 대단해요. 이 정도의 문장을 번역하는 건 미선 씨에게 땅 짚고 헤어치기죠.

Miseon speaks English very well. Translating a sentence of this level should be "땅 짚고 헤엄치기" for her.

12
떡 줄 사람은 꿈도 안 꾸는데 김칫국부터 마신다

This saying refers to a person acting as if a goal or job were already completed or done without taking into consideration the absence of another person needed to do so.

[Example] 영희는 너하고 결혼할 생각이 없는데 너만 혼자 결혼고백을 하려고 반지를 산 건 아니야? 야, 떡 줄 사람은 꿈도 안 꾸는데 김칫국부터 마시지 마.

Younghee doesn't intend on marrying you. You went and bought a ring so that you can confess your desire to marry her? Hey! Don't even do that because "떡 줄 사람은 꿈도 안 꾸는데 김칫국부터 마시지 마".

13
말 한마디에 천 냥 빚도 갚는다

This saying means that words can help solve or patch up any problems.

[Example] 말 한마디에 천 냥 빚도 갚는다고 하던데 네가 실수를 했으니까 먼저 잘못을 했다고 사과를 하면 용서해주지 않을까?

They say that "말 한마디에 천 냥 빚도 갚는다", so don't you think she will forgive you if you go and apologize saying that you made a mistake?

14
믿는 도끼에 발등 찍힌다

When believing that something will turn out well and unexpectedly it doesn't because the person you trusted betrayed you and in the process harmed you.

[Example] 믿는 도끼에 발등 찍힌다고 믿었던 친구에게 비밀을 얘기했는데 그 친구가 글쎄 다른 사람들에게 모두 말해 버렸어요.

Just like the saying "믿는 도끼에 발등 찍힌다" goes, I told a secret to a friend that I trusted, but that friend later told it to other people behind my back.

15
밑 빠진 독에 물 붓기

No matter hard you try, a job destined to fail can only end in failure.

[Example] 회생 가능성이 없는 회사에 자금을 계속 대출해 주는 것은 밑 빠진 독에 물 붓기예요.

Constantly loaning funds to a company that has no possibility to recover is nothing more than a "밑 빠진 독에 물 붓기".

16
바늘 도둑이 소 도둑 된다

This saying literally means that a thief that starts off robbing small objects like needles will end up robbing something big and valuable like a cow. In other words, if a person continues to commit a small crime, as time goes on they will end up committing a much bigger one.

[Example] 작은 잘못이라도 그냥 눈감아 주지 마시고 혼내세요. 바늘 도둑이 소 도둑 된다고 나중에 더 큰 잘못을 할 수도 있으니까요.

Even though it is a small mistake, don't just ignore it but punish him. Just like they say, "바늘 도둑이 소 도둑이 된다", later on he will end up making much bigger mistakes.

17
발 없는 말이 천 리 간다

A saying that means that we must be careful before speaking because rumors and news spread very fast.

[Example] 확실하지도 않은 남의 이야기를 함부로 하지 마. 발 없는 말이 천 리 간다잖아.

Don't thoughtlessly talk about other people if you are not sure about what you are saying. Don't you know that "발 없는 말이 천리 간다".

18
배보다 배꼽이 더 크다

A saying used when an additional fee or cost is larger or most expensive than the original one.

[Example] 차 값보다 수리비가 더 들다니 배보다 배꼽이 더 큰 셈이다.

After hearing that the repair fees cost more than the car itself, it seems that "배보다 배꼽이 더 크다".

19
백문이 불여일견

Seeing something in person is much better than hearing about it over one hundred times.

[Example] 제주도가 아름답다는 말은 많이 들었지만 직접 가서 보니까 제주도 경치가 정말 아름답더군요. 역시 백문이 불여일견이라는 말이 맞는 것 같아요.

Even though I heard that Jeju island was beautiful, after going in person, I really saw how beautiful the scenery was. What they say about "백문이 불여일견" is definitely true.

20
빈 수레가 요란하다

People that lack substance on the inside need to be louder on the outside by screaming and making noise.

[Example] 빈 수레가 요란하다는 말이 맞긴 맞나 봐. 민수 씨가 이번 승진 시험에 자신 있다고 큰소리치더니 떨어졌대요.

I think what they say about "빈 수레가 요란하다" is true. Minsoo screamed that he was confident about passing the promotion exam but in the end they say that he failed.

21
산 넘어 산이다 (= 산 넘어 산)

This means that the more you suffer, the more intense and serious it gets.

[Example] 회사에 일이 생겨서 겨우 해결하고 집에 돌아오니까 어머니께서 쓰러지셔서 병원에 입원하셨다는 연락이 왔다. 사는 게 정말이지 산 넘어 산이다.
I barely solved the problem that arose at work and then after going home, I received a call that my mother had passed out and had to be hospitalized. What they say about life is true. It's just "산 넘어 산이다".

22
세 살 적 버릇이 여든까지 간다

The bad habits you have as a child get worse and follow you all throughout life.

[Example] 세 살 적 버릇이 여든까지 간다고 나쁜 버릇은 일찍 고쳐야 한다.
Since they say that "세 살 적 버릇이 여든까지 간다", you must fix all your bad habits early on.

23
소 잃고 외양간 고친다

This saying means that it is meaningless to try to address a problem very late into a job after it has already failed or is about to fail.

[Example] 소 잃고 외양간 고친다더니 미리 불조심을 했으면 좋았을 텐데 산불이 난 후에 산불 예방을 하면 무슨 소용이 있겠어요?
After remembering the saying "소 잃고 외양간 고친다", I thought how nice it would have been if they had been more careful about forest fires. After a fire breaks out, what good will it do if you try to prevent the next one?

24
쇠귀에 경 읽기

If you read a script directly into the ears of a cow, he won't understand anything. In the same way, no matter how hard you try to teach or inform someone about something, it's pointless because they won't understand you.

[Example] 아들에게 공부 좀 하라고 여러 번 얘기했는데 말을 듣지 않고 놀기만 해요. 쇠귀에 경 읽기예요.
I told my son to study a number of times, but he doesn't listen to me and just plays around. It is like "쇠귀에 경 읽기".

25
시작이 반이다 (= 시작이 반)

Starting is always the hardest part of any job. Once you start something, finishing it isn't as difficult.

[Example] 시작이 반이라는 말이 있으니까 영어 공부가 어렵다고만 생각하지 말고 내일부터라도 영어 공부를 시작해라.
Just like they say "시작이 반이다", stop complaining that studying English is difficult and start studying already.

26
싼 것이 비지떡 (= 싼 게 비지떡)

The quality of a cheap product is just as bad as its price is cheap.

[Example] 휴대전화를 싼 값에 사서 좋아했는데 일주일도 안 돼서 고장났어요. 역시 싼 게 비지떡이라는 말이 맞는 것 같아요.

I was happy because I had bought the phone for a cheap price. However, it broke just after one week. What they say about "싼 게 비지떡" is true.

27
아니 땐 굴뚝에 연기 나랴

If there is no cause, there is also no result. In other words, there needs to be a reason for a rumor to spread.

[Example] 미선 씨랑 영수 씨 두 사람이 정말 사귄다고 하던데 정말일까요? 두 사람은 아니라고 하지만 아니 땐 굴뚝에 연기 나겠어요?

People are saying that Miseon and Youngsoo are dating. Is it really true? Even if the two of them deny it, "아니 땐 굴뚝에 연기 나겠어요"?

28
우물 안 개구리

To believe that one knows a lot even though they know very little or to be a person that knows nothing about the circumstances of the world.

[Example] 우물 안 개구리가 되지 않기 위해서는 많은 사람들을 만나서 이야기하거나 다양한 경험을 많이 쌓는 것도 중요하다.

In order to not become a "우물 안 개구리", it is important to meet a lot of different people and try to have diverse experiences in life.

29
원숭이도 나무에서 떨어진다

This saying means that even though you are familiar and skilled at doing something, there are times that you make mistakes.

[Example] 원숭이도 나무에서 떨어질 때가 있다고 날마다 시험에서 100점만 받던 친구가 실수로 한 개 틀렸다.

Like they say that "원숭이도 나무에서 떨어진다", my friend that used to get a perfect score on all of his tests made a mistake and got one wrong.

30
윗물이 맑아야 아랫물이 맑다

If an older person does something well, the younger person will follow their elder and end up doing well as well. (The apple doesn't fall too far from the tree)

[Example] 윗물이 맑아야 아랫물이 맑다고 저 집은 부모가 책을 안 읽으니 아이들도 전혀 책을 안 읽는다.

As they say, "윗물이 맑아야 아랫물이 맑다", the parents that live over there don't read books and their kids now don't read them either.

31
콩 심은 데 콩 나고 팥 심은 데 팥 난다

The results of all actions are proportional to their causes. In other words, a tree will grow just as you plant it. The saying literally means that if you plan a bean, a bean will grow and if you plan a red bean, a red bean will grow.

[Example] 콩 심은 데 콩 나고 팥 심은 데 팥 난다고 저 사람은 놀기만 하더니 결국 시험에서 떨어졌다.

Just like people say that "콩 심은 데 콩 나고 팥 심은 데 팥 난다", that person only fooled around and never studied so he ended up failing the test.

32
티끌 모아 태산

No matter how small an object is, if you continue to gather it, later on it will turn into a big lump.

[Example] 티끌 모아 태산이라고 100원짜리 동전을 모아 840만 원의 장학금을 모았다고 한다.

As the saying "티끌 모아 태산" goes, after saving up 100 won coins, they say he gathered 8,400,000 won in money.

33
호랑이도 제 말 하면 온다

This saying means that after speaking of a person, he or she appears in the moment and place where his or her name was mentioned.

[Example] 호랑이도 제 말 하면 온다더니 영수 이야기를 하고 있었는데 마침 영수가 들어왔다.

Like the saying "호랑이도 제 말 하면 온다" goes, I was talking about Youngsoo and he later walked in.

11-1 연습문제 (속담)

[1-9] **다음 [보기]에서 알맞은 속담을 찾아 대화를 완성하십시오.**

Find the appropriate saying in the box below and complete the conversation.

[보기]

믿는 도끼에 발등 찍히다	금강산도 식후경
가는 날이 장날	배보다 배꼽이 크다
고래 싸움에 새우등 터진다	세 살 적 버릇 여든까지 간다
아닌 땐 굴뚝에 연기 날까	원숭이도 나무에서 떨어질 때가 있다
떡 줄 사람은 꿈도 안 꾸는데 김칫국부터 마신다	

1. 가 : 너는 날마다 그렇게 늦잠만 자서 어떡하니? 나중에 커서 회사에 취직한 후에도 늦잠 잘래?

   나 : 그 때 가면 안 그렇겠죠, 뭐.

   가 : ______________________ 는다고/ㄴ다고/다고 내일부터 조금씩 일찍 일어나는 연습 좀 해.

2. 가 : 어서 점심 먹으러 가자.

   나 : 오늘 입학했는데 학교 구경부터 하고 먹자.

   가 : ______________________ 이라고/라고 밥부터 먹어야 제대로 구경하지.

3. 가 : 컴퓨터 전문가이신 김 선생님이 큰 실수를 하셨어요.

   나 : ______________________ 는다고/ㄴ다고/다고 그럴 수도 있지요.

4. 가 : 어제 남대문 시장에 갔다가 가방이 너무 싸서 친구 생일 선물로 미국에 부쳤어요. 그런데 가방은 3만 원짜리인데 소포 값이 5만 원 들었어요.

   나 : ______________________ 는군요/군요.

5. 가 : 올해는 월급이 오르지 않는다고 하던데 사실이에요?

   나 : 그럴 리가요? 연초에 사장님이 직원들 앞에서 월급을 올려주기로 약속했잖아요.

   가 : ______________________ 겠어요? 직원들도 벌써 다 알고 있던데요.

6. 가 : 다음 주말에 친구들과 동해안 여행을 가기로 했어. 물론 언니 자동차를 가지고.

   나 : 얘는, ______________________ 는다고/ㄴ다고/다고 언제 내가 차를 빌려준다고 했니?

7. 가 : 영수 엄마가 옆집에 사는 아줌마와 친하게 지내서 큰돈을 빌려 줬는데, 그 아줌마가 돈을 가지고 도망갔대.

   나 : ______________________ 었네/았네/였네.

8. 가 : 어제 백화점에서 남자 친구 선물을 샀어요?

   나 : 아니요, 못 샀어요. ______________________ 이라고/라고 어제 백화점에 가니까 휴점일이더라고요.

9. 가 : 엄마가 아빠하고 싸움을 크게 하신 후로 나한테 용돈을 안 주셔.

   나 : 그래? 완전히 ______________________ 는/은/ㄴ 거네.

[10-18] **다음 [보기]에서 알맞은 속담을 찾아 대화를 완성하십시오.**

Find the appropriate saying in the box below and complete the conversation.

[보기]

소 잃고 외양간 고친다	빈 수레가 요란하다
누워서 침 뱉기	바늘 도둑이 소 도둑 된다
돌다리도 두들겨 보고 건너라	호랑이도 제 말 하면 온다
윗물이 맑아야 아랫물이 맑다	꼬리가 길면 밟힌다
콩 심은 데 콩 나고 팥 심은데 팥 난다	

10. 가 : 민수 씨는 자동차 전문가도 아니면서 전문가들보다 더 아는 척을 해요.

    나 : ______________________ 는다더니/ㄴ다더니/다더니 아는 것이 없는 사람들이 더 떠들며 자랑하는군요.

11. 가 : 편의점 도둑이 잡혔대요. 벌써 3번이나 같은 방법으로 도둑질을 했대요.

    나 : ______________________ 는다더니/ㄴ다더니/다더니 결국 잡혔군요.

12. 가 : 남편이 너무 게으르고 책임감도 없어. 이웃집 사람들과 얘기해 보니 다른 집 남편들은 안 그렇다던데……

나 : ________________ 이라고/라고 어떻게 다른 사람들한테 자기 남편을 그렇게 말할 수 있니?

13. 가 : 어제 보니까 영수 씨가 친구들과 뭔가 심각한 표정으로 얘기를 하던데 무슨 일이 있는 걸까요?

나 : ________________ 는다더니/ㄴ다더니/다더니 마침 저기 영수 씨가 오네요.

14. 가 : 서류를 완성했어요. 어제 두 번이나 확인했으니까 바로 사장님께 드리는 게 어때요?

나 : ________________ 으라고/라고 실수가 있을지 모르니까 다시 한번 확인해 봅시다.

15. 가 : 예전부터 사람들이 자동차를 수리해야 한다고 말했는데 고치지 않아서 사고가 났다면서?

나 : 음, 그래서 어제 자동차 수리 센터에 맡겼어.

________________ 는다고/ㄴ다고/다고 진작 고쳤으면 사고도 안 났을 텐데……

16. 가 : 아이가 편의점에서 자꾸 과자를 말도 없이 가져 와요.

나 : 별 생각 없이 그랬겠지요. 하지만 ________________ 는다고/ㄴ다고/다고 더 잘못되기 전에 가르쳐야 할 것 같은데요.

17. 가 : 저 아이는 어른들한테 인사를 안 해요. 말도 함부로 하고요.

나 : ________________ 는다고/ㄴ다고/다고 저 아이 부모들도 사람들한테 인사도 잘 안 하고 예의도 없다던데……

18. 가 : 한국어 능력 시험 결과가 나왔는데 친구는 합격을 했지만 나는 떨어졌어.

나 : ________________ 는다고/ㄴ다고/다고 친구는 열심히 공부했는데 너는 이번 학기에 놀기만 했잖아.

11-2 관용어

01
귀(를) 기울이다

to pay attention to someone else's conversation or to take interest in their opinion

[Example] 그의 장점은 다른 사람이 말을 할 때 항상 귀를 기울인다는 것이다.
His strong point is that when someone else is speaking, he always takes an interest in his or her opinion.

02
귀에 못이 박이다

to get sick of hearing the same words over and over again

[Example] 어렸을 때부터 공부하라는 얘기를 귀에 목이 박이도록 들었어요.
I was told to study over and over again from when I was little and I'm just sick of hearing it now.

03
그림의 떡

No matter how much you like something, you cannot obtain it.

[Example] 그 자동차는 너무 비싸서 우리 같은 보통 사람들에게는 그림의 떡이에요.
That car is very expensive, so ordinary people like us can only dream of buying it.

04
금(이) 가다

a phrase that means that the relationship between two people has gotten worse

[Example] 별로 중요하지 않은 일로 우리 사이에 금이 가서야 되겠니?
How can we let out relationship get so bad because of an unimportant issue?

05
길눈(이) 어둡다

to be unable to remember how to get somewhere even though you have gone down the same road a number of times to have a bed sense of direction

[Example] 저는 길눈이 어두워서 여러 번 갔던 식당도 잘 못 찾아가요.
I can't find the restaurant that I have been to a number of times because I have a bad sense of direction.

06
낯을 가리다

to hate greeting unknown people or to treat people that you aren't close with in a different manner to become very shy or bashful

[Example] 아기가 낯을 많이 가려서 모르는 사람이 안으면 울어요.
The baby is very shy so he cries if an unknown person holds him.

07
낯(이) 두껍다

Even though one makes a mistake, one doesn't understand the concept of shame or humiliation.

[Example] 큰 죄를 짓고도 아무렇지도 않게 사람들 앞에 나서다니 정말 낯이 두껍다.

After coming out in front of everyone as if the huge mistake he had made was no big deal, I realized how shameless he could be.

08
누워서 떡 먹기

to be extremely easy

[Example] 이건 초등학교 1학년 때 배운 문제니까 저에게는 누워서 떡먹기예요.

This question is a piece of cake because it is something that I learned how to solve in the first grade.

09
눈 감아 주다

to make believe to ignore or not know of someone else's mistake even though you are fully aware of it

[Example] 교통 규칙을 위반한 초보 운전자가 교통경찰에게 한 번만 눈 감아 달라고 부탁했지만 소용없었다.

The novice driver that broke the traffic regulation begged the traffic officer to excuse him but it was no use.

10
눈 코 뜰 새가 없다 (= 눈코 뜰 사이 없다)

to be so busy to the point that you cannot focus or concentrate

[Example] 요즘 새 학기가 시작되어서 눈 코 뜰 새가 없이 바쁘게 지내고 있다.

I have been so busy lately since the new semester has started.

11
눈에 안경 (= 제 눈에 안경)

No matter how useless or worthless of an object, if it is something that you like, everything related to that object looks good to you.

[Example] 내가 보기에는 영수 씨 여자 친구가 못생겼는데 영수 씨는 예쁘다고 하니 제 눈에 안경이지 뭐야.

In my opinion, Youngsoo's girlfriend is ugly, but since Youngsu thinks she is pretty, I guess beauty really is in the eye of the beholder.

12
눈이 높다

to have very high standards

[Example] 영수 씨는 눈이 높은 편이어서 평범한 여자는 마음에 안 들어한다.

Since Youngsoo tends to have high standards, he doesn't like ordinary women.

13
맛이 가다

a phrase used to describe a taste that has gone bad or lost it's flavor

[Example] 날씨가 더워져서 그런지 음식이 쉽게 맛이 간다.
The food lost its flavor probably because the weather got hot.

14
발을 끊다

to give up or stop doing something

[Example] 나는 올해부터 술집에 발을 끊고 가족들과 많은 시간을 보내기로 마음먹었다.
I decided that I am not going to step foot again in a bar starting this year and instead I'm going to spend more time with my family

15
발이 넓다

to be very sociable and know people across all fields

[Example] 김 기자님은 발이 넓으니까 연예계 쪽에 아는 사람이 많을 거예요.
Reporter Kim is very social and well-know, so he has a lot of friends in the entertainment world.

16
손을 떼다

to quit a job that you were doing

[Example] 회장님께서는 이미 오래전에 회사 경영에서 손을 떼셨어요. 지금은 아드님이 회사를 경영하고 있어요.
The president gave up running the company a long time ago. Now, his son is running the company.

17
손을 잡다

to combine forces and work together

[Example] 연세 병원은 독일의 유명한 제약 회사와 손을 잡고 신약을 개발했다.
Yonsei hospital and a famous German medicine company joined forces and developed new medicines.

18
손이 크다

to be generous with money, to give a large portion or size

[Example] 하숙집 아주머니는 손이 크셔서 음식을 한번에 많이 하세요.
The boarding house lady is generous with her money and makes a lot of food at one time.

19
식은 죽 먹기

for something to be just as easy as one expects it to be

[Example] 영수 씨는 영어를 잘 하니까 그 정도 번역은 식은 죽 먹기일 거예요.
Youngsoo already speaks English that well, so translating a text of that level will be easy.

20
어깨가 무겁다

to feel the stress and pressure after taking on a huge responsibility

[Example] 회사에서 중요한 일을 맡아서 어깨가 무거워요.
I feel like I've taking on a huge responsibility because I was given an important job at work.

21
엎어지면 코 닿을 데

to be very close to somewhere

[Example] 엎어지면 코 닿을 데에 집이 있는데 왜 매일 지각을 해요?
Your house is so close by. How is it that you arrive late everyday?

22
옷이 날개다

If your clothes are nice and pretty, you will look special and stick out more.

[Example] 옷이 날개라더니 영수가 정장을 입으니 정말 멋있어 보인다.
Just as they say that the clothes make the man, Youngsoo looked really good after putting on a suit.

23
입이 무겁다

a person who doesn't speak very much or can keep a secret

[Example] 그는 입이 무거운 사람이니까 비밀을 꼭 지켜 줄 거예요.
He won't tell your secret to anyone because he is a trustworthy guy.

24
입이 짧다

to be a picky eater or to eat very little

[Example] 우리 아이는 입이 짧아서 입맛을 맞추기가 어려워요.
It is hard to cook food that my child likes to eat because he is a picky eater.

25
하늘의 별 따기

to be very difficult to achieve or obtain something

[Example] 그 회사에 취직하는 것은 하늘의 별 따기라고 하던데요.
They were all saying that it is almost impossible to get a job at that company.

11-2 연습문제 (관용어)

[1-11] **다음 [보기]에서 알맞은 표현을 찾아 대화를 완성하십시오.**

Find the appropriate expression in the box below and complete the conversation.

[보기]

하늘의 별 따기	눈을 감다	손을 잡다	손을 떼다
길눈이 어둡다	발이 넓다	발을 끊다	손이 크다
옷이 날개다	눈이 높다	제 눈에 안경	

1. 가 : 이번에 UN에서 세계 환경 문제에 대한 회의가 있었지요?

   나 : 네, 이번 회의에서 각국 정부가 ________________고 환경 문제를 해결하기로 했답니다.

2. 가 : 그 회사는 취직하기가 그렇게 어렵다면서?

   나 : 응, 그 회사는 지원자가 많아서 취직 시험에 합격하는 게 ________________이야/야.

3. 가 : 민수는 아직도 컴퓨터 게임을 많이 한다면서?

   나 : 아니, 이제 완전히 컴퓨터 게임에서 ________________었다던데/았다던데/였다던데.

4. 가 : 우리 집이 어디 있는지 몰라요? 지난번에도 우리 집에 놀러 왔었잖아요?

   나 : 제가 좀 ________________어서/아서/여서 길을 잘 못 찾아요.

5. 가 : 수진 씨 생일 선물로 이 스카프가 어떨까?

   나 : 수진 씨는 ________________어서/아서/여서 색상이나 디자인을 까다롭게 보는 편이니까 좀 더 좋은 제품이 있는지 찾아보자.

6. 가 : 민수가 술을 완전히 끊었다던데 사실이야?

   나 : 응, 평소에 그렇게 잘 가던 단골 술집에도 ________________었대/았대/였대.

7. 가 : 우와, 어머니께서 김치를 100포기나 담그셨어요?

나 : 네, 우리 엄마가 워낙 ________________으셔서/셔서 음식을 많이 하시는 편이에요.

8. 가 : 마리아 씨가 평소엔 청바지만 입더니 오늘 드레스를 입었네요.

   나 : ________________고 평소와 달라 보여요. 정말 여성스럽고 예쁘지요?

9. 가 : 아침에 배가 아파서 잠깐 약국 앞에 주차했다가 주차 단속에 걸리고 말았어.

   나 : 저런, 벌금을 냈어?

   가 : 아니, 급한 사정을 얘기했더니 다행히 경찰관이 ________________어/아/여 줬어.

10. 가 : 논문에 필요한 설문지를 돌리고 싶은데 아는 사람이 별로 없어.

    나 : 영수한테 부탁해 봐. 영수는 ________________어서/아서/여서 아는 사람이 많던데?

11. 가 : 윗집 아주머니는 항상 자기 아이가 예쁘고 똑똑하다고 자랑만 해.

    나 : ________________이라고/라고 아주머니 눈에는 자기 아이가 예쁘게만 보이는 거야.

[12-22] **다음 [보기]에서 알맞은 표현을 찾아 대화를 완성하십시오.**

Find the appropriate expression in the box below and complete the conversation.

[보기]

엎어지면 코 닿다	금이 가다	어깨가 무겁다
눈 코 뜰 새가 없다	낯을 가리다	맛이 가다
귀를 기울이다	입이 무겁다	낯이 두껍다
귀에 못이 박이다	누워서 떡 먹기	

12. 가 : 요즘 우리 어머니가 나한테 공부하라고 ________________도록 말씀하셔서 괴로워

    나 : 하루에 몇 번이나 말씀하시는데?

    가 : 나하고 눈 마주칠 때마다.

13. 가 : 저는 학교에서 걸어서 5분밖에 안 걸리는 하숙집에 살고 있어요.

    나 : ________________을/ㄹ 데에 사시는군요.

14. 가 : 김 선생님께 이번 일에 대해 이야기해도 될까요?

    나 : 김 선생님은 ______________________는/은/ㄴ 분이니까 이야기해도 비밀을 지켜줄 거예요.

15. 가 : 이번에 부장님으로 승진되셔서 기쁘시겠어요.

    나 : 기쁘기는 합니다만 자리가 자리이니만큼 ______________________네요.

16. 가 : 아기가 아주 귀엽네요.

    나 : 그런데 ______________________어서/아서/여서 낯선 사람만 보면 울어요.

17. 가 : 이 우유 맛이 왜 이래?

    나 : 어머, 어제 깜빡하고 냉장고에 안 넣어서 ______________________었나/았나/였나 봐.

18. 가 : 요즘 어떻게 지내세요?

    나 : 대학원 수업이며 회사일이며 집안일이며 할 일이 많아서 ______________________어요/아요/여요.

19. 가 : 어떤 정치가가 훌륭한 정치가일까요?

    나 : 국민들 말에 ______________________을/ㄹ 줄 아는 사람이 훌륭한 정치가지요.

20. 가 : 다들 줄 서서 기다리고 있는데 저 사람은 차례를 지키지 않는군요. 창피하지도 않을까요?

    나 : 그러게요, 정말 ______________________네요.

21. 가 : 정희 씨가 남자 친구하고 헤어졌나 보지? 요즘엔 같이 붙어 다니는 모습을 못 봤어.

    나 : 집안 문제로 두 사람 사이에 ______________________는/은/ㄴ 지 오래 됐어.

22. 가 : 미영 씨가 이것을 한국말로 번역할 수 있을까요?

    나 : 물론이죠. 미영 씨는 일본에서 오래 산 데다가 경험도 많으니까 이런 일은 미영 씨에게 ______________________일 거예요.

11-3 한자성어

01
고집불통 [고집뿔통]

a person who only focuses on themselves and is very stubborn

[Example] 아이가 고집불통이라고 걱정을 하는 부모들이 요즘 점점 많아지고 있다.
There are more and more parents that are worrying about their children who are "고집불통".

02
과소평가 [과소평까]

to be evaluated or judged as less or weaker than stated

[Example] 자신을 다른 사람과 비교하면서 과소평가하지 마십시오.
Don't "과소평가" yourself when comparing yourself to others.

03
다다익선 [다다익썬]

the more the better

[Example] 다다익선이라는 말처럼 친구는 많으면 많을수록 좋다.
As the phrase "다다익선" says, the more friends you have, the better.

04
대기만성 [대기만성]

Just as it takes a long time to make a big bowl, one doesn't become an important person in life overnight.

[Example] 대기만성이라는 말처럼 영수 씨는 오랜 시간이 지나서야 사회적으로 크게 성공할 수 있었다.
Just like the phrase "대기만성", Youngsoo was only able to become greatly successful after a long time went by.

05
동문서답 [동문서답]

when asking for the east and getting the west as a response in other words, to give a random answer that is incorrect to a certain question

[Example] 이름이 뭐냐고 물었는데 20살이라고 동문서답을 했어요.
I asked him what his name was, and he answered that he was 20 years old in a "동문서답" manner.

06
막상막하 [막쌍마카]

for there to be very little difference to the point that it is difficult to say which is better or worse

[Example] 두 사람 모두 잘 달리는군요. 두 사람의 달리기 실력이 막상막하예요.
Both of them run very well. It looks like both of your running skills are "막상막하".

07
부전자전 [부전자전]

Meaning that a father inherits what he has to his son, a father passes on his traditions or ways to his son.

[Example] 부전자전이라더니 노래를 잘하시던 민수 아버지처럼 민수도 노래를 잘 한다.

Just like they say that "부전자전", Minsu sings just as well as his father does.

08
상부상조 [상부상조]

to help one another

[Example] 사람은 어려울 때일수록 상부상조해야 한다.

When times are hard, people must "상부상조".

09
설상가상 [설쌍가상]

literally meaning "when frost falls on top of snow", this expression refers to unfortunate events that occur one another one.

[Example] 태풍으로 큰 피해를 입은 남부지방에 설상가상으로 또 다시 큰 비가 내리면서 주민들의 걱정이 늘고 있다.

People are worrying even more in the southern region that was greatly damaged by the typoon because it has begun to rain heavily again. It is "설상가상".

10
용두사미 [용두사미]

The phrase literally means to have a head of a dragon and the tail of a snake. In other words, the start of something is admirable and the end is worthless.

[Example] 목표를 크게 세워 놓으면 용두사미로 끝날 수 있어요.

If you set very high goals, they could turn out being "용두사미".

11
우왕좌왕 [우왕좌왕]

to run from right to left in other words, to run around without knowing what to do or where to go

[Example] 여행 안내원이 갑자기 없어져서 관광객들은 우왕좌왕했어요.

When the travel guide suddenly disappeared, the tourists began to "우왕좌왕".

12
유명무실 [유명무실]

Though something has a meaningful and important name, it has no internal substance.

[Example] 장애인을 위해 도입된 장애인 해피 콜택시 서비스가 유명무실하게 운영되고 있다.

The Happy Call Taxi service, established to help the disabled, has been running in a very "유명무실" manner.

13
유비무환 [유비무환]

When something is planned properly from the start, there is no need to worry about any future problems

[Example] 유비무환이란 말처럼 건물을 튼튼하게 짓는다면 지진이나 사고가 발생해도 큰 피해를 입지 않을 것이다.

Just like the "유비무환" saying goes, if you build a building strongly, even if there is an accident or an earthquake, it won't be damaged.

14
유언비어 [유언비어]

a rumor that has spread far and wide without any basis

[Example] 인터넷에서 떠도는 유언비어를 그대로 믿는 사람들이 많다.

There are lot of people that still believe the "유언비어" that is spreading around on the internet.

15
이심전심 [이심전심]

without using words or writing, a transferring of meaning from one mind to another

[Example] 이심전심이라는 말처럼 친구와 나는 말을 하지 않아도 서로의 마음을 잘 안다.

As the expression "이심전심" goes, my friend and I can read each other's mind without having to speak.

16
이열치열 [이열치열]

to kill fire with fire. In other words, on hot days, the best way to beat the heat is to drink hot tea.

[Example] 이열치열이라고 이렇게 더운 날에는 뜨거운 삼계탕을 먹어야 기운이 나지요.

Like they say "이열치열", on hot days like these, you feel energetic only if you eat hot samkye tang.

17
일석이조 [일써기조]

to kill two birds with one stone

[Example] 지금 이 컴퓨터를 사시면 값이 30% 할인되고 선물도 받을 수 있으니까 일석이조입니다.

If you buy this computer now, you will receive a 30 pecent discount and a free present, so it is "일석이조".

18
작심삼일 [작씸사밀]

Just like a person that makes up their mind only can hold on for three days, this expression refers to a decision that lasts a very short time.

[Example] 운동을 시작했는데 며칠을 가지 못해서 그만두고 말았다. 정말 작심삼일이다.

I started working out. However, I couldn't make it past a few days and quit. It is really "작심삼일".

19
팔방미인 [팔방미인]

No matter how you look at someone, you still find him or her beautiful. Or a person that is talented in all fields.

[Example] 제임스 씨는 그림도 잘 그리고 외국어도 잘 하고 못 하는 것이 없는 팔방미인이다.

James draws well and is good at speaking foreign languages. He is just a "팔방미인".

20
횡설수설 [횡성수설]/[휑설수설]

to speak thoughtlessly and illogically

[Example] 오늘 발표 시간에 너무 긴장해서 횡설수설한 것 같아요.

At today's presentation, I was a little nervous so I spoke very "횡설수설".

11-3 연습문제 (한자성어)

[1-10] 서로 뜻이 같은 것을 찾아 연결하십시오.

Find and connect the two phrases that have similar meanings.

1. 고집불통 •		• ㉠ 사실보다 작거나 약하게 평가하다
2. 과소평가 •		• ㉡ 서로 서로 돕다
3. 다다익선 •		• ㉢ 아버지가 아들에게 전하다
4. 대기만성 •		• ㉣ 차이가 별로 없다
5. 동문서답 •		• ㉤ 크게 될 사람은 갑자기 이루어지지 않다
6. 막상막하 •		• ㉥ 고집이 너무 세고 자기주장만 내세우다
7. 부전자전 •		• ㉦ 일의 시작은 훌륭하나 끝은 좋지 않다
8. 상부상조 •		• ㉧ 불행한 일이 계속 일어나다
9. 설상가상 •		• ㉨ 많으면 많을수록 더욱 좋다
10. 용두사미 •		• ㉩ 질문에 맞지 않는 이상한 대답을 하다

[11-20] 서로 뜻이 같은 것을 찾아 연결하십시오.

Find and connect the two phrases that have similar meanings.

11. 우왕좌왕 •		• ㉠ 돌 한 개를 던져서 새 두 마리를 잡다
12. 유명무실 •		• ㉡ 여러 방면에 능통한 사람
13. 유비무환 •		• ㉢ 결심한 일이 오래가지 못하다
14. 유언비어 •		• ㉣ 조리가 없이 되는 대로 함부로 말하다
15. 이심전심 •		• ㉤ 어디로 갈지, 무엇을 할지 헤매다
16. 이열치열 •		• ㉥ 근거 없이 널리 퍼진 소문
17. 일석이조 •		• ㉦ 이름만 그럴듯하고 실속은 없다
18. 작심삼일 •		• ㉧ 마음에서 마음으로 전하다
19. 팔방미인 •		• ㉨ 열을 열로 다스리다
20. 횡설수설 •		• ㉩ 미리 준비를 잘 하면 걱정할 일이 없다

[21-30] **다음 [보기]에서 알맞은 한자성어를 찾아 빈칸에 쓰십시오.**

Find the appropriate Chinese character phrase in the following box and then fill in the blank.

[보기]

일석이조	막상막하	동문서답	작심삼일	대기만성
유언비어	다다익선	팔방미인	고집불통	이심전심

21. 가 : 너 왜 이렇게 늦게 다니니? 솔직히 말해. 너 요즘 연애하는 거지?

나 : 너무 덥네요. 에어컨이 어디 있지?

가 : 내가 묻는 말에 대답하지 않고 웬 ________________ 이야/야?

22. 가 : 오늘은 왜 이렇게 공부하기 싫지?

나 : ________________ 이네/네. 나도 공부하기 싫어서 너한테 밖으로 놀러가자고 이야기할 참이었어.

23. 가 : 그 여자는 예쁘고 예의도 바른 것 같아요.

나 : 그 뿐만이 아니에요. 노래도 잘 부르고 그림도 얼마나 잘 그린다고요.

가 : ________________ 이군요/군요.

24. 가 : 주영 씨가 담배를 끊는다고 하더니 오늘 보니까 다시 피우고 있던데요.

나 : 그래요? ________________ 이라는/라는 말이 맞군요. 며칠 지나지 않아 다시 피우는 걸 보니……

25. 가 : 영수야! 너 연희랑 결혼한다면서?

나 : 뭐야? 누가 그런 ________________ 을/를 퍼뜨렸지? 영희와 몇 번 만나지도 않았는데 말이야.

26. 가 : 지금 어느 팀이 이기고 있어? 아까 전반전에서는 한국과 일본이 1:1로 동점이었는데……

나 : 한국이 한 골을 넣어서 2:1이 됐어. 그런데 방금 일본이 또 한 골을 넣어서 다시 2:2로 동점이 됐어. 정말 두 나라 실력이 ________________ 이야/야.

27. 가 : 엄마! 이 장난감 사 줘.

나 : 나중에 사줄게.

가 : 싫어, 싫어. 이 장난감 사 주지 않으면 여기서 조금도 움직이지 않을 거야.

나 : 너 정말 ____________________이구나/구나.

28. 가 : 아버지, 다음 주에 친구들과 여행을 가기로 했는데 용돈 좀 주세요.

나 : 얼마나 필요하니?

가 : ____________________이지요/지요. 많으면 많을수록 좋은 거 아니에요?

29. 가 : 영희는 너랑 비슷한 시기에 바이올린을 시작했는데도 연주를 잘하는데 넌 왜 그렇게 못 켜니?

나 : 아버지, ________________이란/란 말도 모르세요? 큰 그릇은 늦게 되는 법이에요.

30. 가 : 내일부터 미선 씨 집에 가서 동생에게 영어를 가르쳐 주기로 했어.

나 : 그것 참 잘 됐구나. 네가 좋아하는 미선 씨도 볼 수 있고 돈도 벌 수 있으니까 ________________이네/네.

[31-40] **다음 [보기]에서 알맞은 한자성어를 찾아 빈칸에 쓰십시오.**

Find the appropriate Chinese character phrase in the following box and fill in the blank.

[보기]

횡설수설	우왕좌왕	유명무실	이열치열	용두사미
과소평가	설상가상	상부상조	부전자전	유비무환

31. 가 : 여행은 어떠셨어요?

나 : 여기저기 볼 게 너무 많아서 ________________하다가 시간만 낭비했어요.

가 : 계획을 잘 세우셨어야지요.

32. 가 : 아니, 이 더운 날에 땀을 뻘뻘 흘리면서 삼계탕을 먹어요?

나 : ____________________이라고/라고 더위는 뜨거운 음식을 먹으면 이길 수 있는 법이에요.

33. 가 : 난 왜 이렇게 못생겼지? 게다가 잘하는 것도 하나도 없고……

나 : 그렇지 않아. 자신을 너무 ____________________하지 마. 넌 누구보다도 고운 마음씨를 가졌잖아.

34. 가 : 영수 엄마! 접시 좀 빌려줄 수 있어요? 손님이 많이 오는데 접시가 모자라서요.

나 : 그럼요. 들어오셔서 마음에 드는 것을 골라 보세요.

가 : 너무 감사해요.

나 : 뭘요. 이웃끼리 ____________________하면서 살아야지요.

35. 가 : 다니던 회사를 그만두셨다면서요? 집에 무슨 일이라도 있으세요?

나 : 그런 게 아니라 아이 때문에 그래요. 돌봐줄 사람이 없으니까 회사를 그만둘 수밖에 없지요.

가 : 법에 따르면 직장 여성을 위해 각 회사마다 탁아소를 만들어야 하잖아요.

나 : 그럼 뭘 해요? 법대로 탁아소를 만드는 회사가 없으니 그 법은 ______________할 뿐이에요.

36. 가 : 옆집 아이는 정말 공부를 잘 하는 것 같아.

나 : 아버지가 교수라고 들었는데 아이도 공부를 잘하네. ____________________이구나/구나.

37. 가 : 일이 계획대로 잘 돼요?

나 : ____________________이/가 되지 않게 끝까지 열심히 해야지요.

가 : 처음처럼 끝까지 열심히 하시면 꼭 성공하실 거예요.

38. 가 : 친구 집에 불이 난 데다가 어머니께서 병으로 병원에 입원하셨대요.

나 : 저런, ____________________이로구나/로구나.

39. 가 : 이상하다. 점심 때 먹으려고 만든 샌드위치를 냉장고 안에 넣어 두었는데 어디 있지? 영수야,

너 혹시 못 봤니?

나 : 아, 그거? 영희 누나가 먹었나? 아니, 숙희 누나가 먹었어.

가 : 뭐? 둘 다 학교에서 아직 안 왔는데?

나 : 아, 그럼, 엄마가 잡수셨어.

가 : 너 ____________________ 하는 걸 보니까 네가 먹었구나!

40. 가 : 감기 예방주사 맞으러 가자.

나 : 아버지, 저는 주사 맞는 거 너무 싫어요.

가 : 이 녀석아! 주사 맞기 싫다고 안 맞으면 어떡해? 넌 ____________________ 도 몰라? 미리 예방을 해 둬야 독감에 안 걸리지.

11-4 의태어

01
꽉

to push or pull with a lot of strength

[Example] 흔들리는 버스 안에서는 넘어지지 않게 손잡이를 꽉 잡으십시오.
I "꽉" grabbed on to the handle inside of the shacking bus as to not fall.

02
꾸벅꾸벅

the state of lowering one's head or body forward and then back again over and over

[Example] 봄이라서 그런지 사무실에는 꾸벅꾸벅 조는 사람들이 많다.
There are a lot of people that are "꾸벅꾸벅" dozing off in the office probably because it is springtime.

03
반짝반짝

sparkling, shinning

[Example] 밤하늘의 별들이 반짝반짝 빛나는 모습이 정말 아름답다.
The "반짝반짝" shinning stars of the night sky are really beautiful.

04
방실방실

to slightly open one's mouth and laugh without making a sound

[Example] 내 동생은 귀엽고 사랑스럽게 방실방실 웃는다.
My younger sibling "방실방실" smiles.

05
뻘뻘

the state of sweating profusely

[Example] 한낮의 무더운 날씨에 사람들이 땀을 뻘뻘 흘리면서 일을 하고 있다.
In the humid noon weather, people are "뻘뻘" sweating while working.

06
살금살금

to be cautious as to not be found out or seen by someone else and approach little by little

[Example] 아이들이 나비를 잡으려고 살금살금 다가간다.
The child approaches the butterfly "살금살금" in order to catch it.

07
주룩주룩

the sound that a stream or raindrops make as they quickly and consistently flow

[Example] 늦가을 밤늦도록 멈추지 않고 주룩주룩 내리는 비를 보면서 왠지 모를 외로움을 느낀다.

In late fall, I feel an unknown loneliess as I watch it "주룩주룩" rain all night long.

08
줄줄

the sound or state of sweat, water, or anything else that continues to smoothly flow by

[Example] 영화가 너무 슬퍼서 영화를 보는 내내 눈물이 줄줄 흘러 내렸다.

The movie was so sad that she "줄줄" cried while watching it.

09
텅

the state of a large object's inside that is empty

[Example] 명절에는 서울 거리에 가게들도 문을 닫고 차도 거의 없어 거리가 텅 빈 것 같다.

During holidays in Seoul, all the stores are closed and there are almost no cars in the street. The streets are "텅" empty.

10
활짝

the form of a flower, wing, or door that is completely open

[Example] 개나리와 진달래가 활짝 핀 걸 보니 이제 완전한 봄이군요.

After seeing the forsythias and azaleas in that have "활짝" bloomed, I thought that spring was finally here.

11-4 연습문제 (의태어)

[1-10] **다음 [보기]에서 알맞은 말을 골라 빈칸에 쓰십시오. 단어는 한 번만 쓰십시오.**

Choose the appropriate word from the box below and fill in the blank. Use each word only once.

[보기]

뻘뻘	줄줄	꽉	살금살금	텅
꾸벅꾸벅	주룩주룩	반짝반짝	활짝	방실방실

1. 울던 아이가 엄마를 보더니 다시 ____________ 웃어요.
2. 수업이 끝나고 학생들이 다 나간 후 ____________ 빈 교실에 혼자 앉아 있었다.
3. 그 아이의 눈은 다른 사람들보다 훨씬 ____________ 빛나요.
4. 너무 더워서 가만히 있어도 등 뒤로 땀이 ____________ 흘러요.
5. 장마철이라서 하루 종일 비가 ____________ 내린다.
6. 표정이 너무 굳어 있어요. ____________ 웃으세요. 이제 사진 찍습니다!
7. 이 옷은 몸에 너무 ____________ 끼는데요. 좀 큰 사이즈로 주세요.
8. 공장에서 아버지가 땀을 ____________ 흘리시면서 일하는 모습을 보고 눈물이 나왔어요.
9. 영수 씨가 어제 잠을 못 잤는지 오늘 수업 시간에 계속 ____________ 졸아요.
10. 어제 밤 12시에 하숙집에 들어갔는데 다른 사람들이 깰까 봐 ____________ 들어갔다.

11-5 의성어

01
꼬르륵

the sound that your stomach makes when you are hungry (grumbling)

[Example] 오늘 저녁을 안 먹었더니 뱃속에서 꼬르륵 소리가 난다.
My stomach was "꼬르륵" grumbling because I hadn't eaten dinner today.

02
덜컹덜컹

the sound that a car or any other object makes as it shakes

[Example] 차가 시골길을 가면서 덜컹덜컹 소리를 냈다.
The car was making a "덜컹덜컹" rattling noise as it was going down the country road.

03
딸랑딸랑

the sound a paper or metal bell makes when rung (ding ding)

[Example] 문에 종을 매달았더니 문이 열릴 때마다 딸랑딸랑 소리가 난다.
After putting a bell on the door, every time it opens it makes a "딸랑딸랑" sound.

04
똑딱똑딱

the sound a watch or motor makes when it is running (tick tock)

[Example] 시계가 똑딱똑딱 잘도 간다.
The watch goes "똑딱똑딱".

05
보글보글

the sound stew or soup makes as it is boiling.

[Example] 보글보글 끓는 찌개가 맛있어 보인다.
The "보글보글" bubbling stew looked delicious.

06
앵

the sound that a small insect or bug makes as it flies around (buzz)

[Example] 귓가에서 앵 하는 소리가 들리더니 모기가 팔을 물었다.
After hearing the "앵" buzzing sound of a mosquito in my ear, it bit my arm.

07
쿨쿨

the sound a person makes when they are deep asleep (zzz)

[Example] 그 사람이 너무 깊게 쿨쿨 자고 있어서 깨우지 않았다.
I didn't wake him up because he was "쿨쿨" asleep.

08
펑

the sound that an object makes when it explodes (boom)

[Example] 폭탄이 날아오더니 펑 터졌다.
The bomb went flying and "펑" exploded.

09
풍덩

the sound a heavy object makes as it falls into water (splash)

[Example] 무거운 돌이 강물 속으로 풍덩 빠졌다.
A heavy rock "풍덩" splashed as it fell into the water.

10
훅

the sound of blowing strongly out of one's mouth

[Example] 종이를 입으로 훅 불었더니 종이가 날아가 버렸다.
After "훅" blowing on the piece of paper with my mouth, it went flying away.

11-5 연습문제 (의성어)

[1-10] **다음 [보기]에서 알맞은 말을 골라 빈칸에 쓰십시오.**

Choose the appropriate word from the box below and fill in the blank.

[보기]

꼬르륵	덜컹덜컹	딸랑딸랑	보글보글	앵
펑	풍덩	훅	똑딱똑딱	쿨쿨

1. 된장찌개가 불 위에서 ______________ 끓고 있습니다.
2. 내가 대문 안으로 들어서니까 강아지가 ______________ 방울 소리를 내며 뛰어 왔다.
3. 지난 밤 11시 쯤 가스 공장에서 ______________ 소리와 함께 불이 났습니다.
4. 시간이 없어서 아침을 못 먹은 날은 11시만 돼도 뱃속에서 ______________ 소리가 나요.
5. 버스 안에는 아기를 안고 있는 아주머니, 책을 읽고 있는 학생, ______________ 자고 있는 아저씨, 그리고 나 이렇게 네 명 뿐이었다.
6. 돌다리를 건너가던 아저씨가 미끄러져서 물속으로 ______________ 하고 빠지고 말았다.
7. 나는 촛불 앞에서 소원을 빌고 나서 촛불을 한번에 ______________ 불어서 다 껐다.
8. 모기가 ______________ 소리를 내며 날아다닌다.
9. 오늘 따라 ______________ 하는 시계 소리가 무척 크게 들린다.
10. 내 자동차는 너무 낡아서 조금 험한 길을 갈 때면 ______________ 소리가 나요.

정답 · 색인

Correct Answer
Index

01 정답

01 · 사람

1. 엄살
2. 개인
3. 용기
4. 표정
5. 고집
6. 참을성
7. 바르다
8. 순수하다
9. 너그럽다
10. 씩씩하다
11. 얌전하다
12. 평범하다
13. 완벽하다
14. 단순하다
15. 무표정하다
16. 비관적이다
17. 느끼는
18. 떨리
19. 감정을
20. 겁이
21. 짜증이
22. 미워요
23. 부러웠다
24. 이상하
25. 사랑스러워요
26. 심술궂
27. 쑥스럽습니다
28. 우울해
29. ❹
30. ❷
31. ❶
32. ❹
33. ❸
34. ❷
35. ❶
36. 소심하다
37. 무뚝뚝하다
38. 성격이 급하다
39. 변덕스럽다
40. 꼼꼼하다
41. 솔직하다
42. 겁이 많아서
43. 엄살이 심하
44. 짜증이 났을
45. 욕심이 많은
46. 용기는 내
47. 고집이 세
48. 당황했어요
49. 사생활
50. 자신
51. 특징
52. 매력을
53. 불쌍한
54. 고민하
55. 자유롭
56. 상상해
57. 주장하
58. 판단하
59. 버릇이
60. 심리
61. 태도
62. 오직
63. ❸
64. ❷
65. ❹
66. ❸
67. ❶
68. 개성적이다
69. 소극적이다
70. 활발하다
71. 가식적이다
72. 덜렁거리다
73. 독립적이다
74. 상하다
75. 까다롭다
76. 답답하다
77.

		①불	안	하	다		③감		④고	민
		행				②표	정		려	
	⑤심	하	다						하	
⑥떨	리	다			⑧내		⑨부	럽	다	
			⑦참	을	성		끄			
	⑩욕				적		럽		⑫개	인
⑪소	심	하	다				다		성	
									적	
⑬이	⑭상	하	다							
	상									

02 · 일상생활

1. 모습
2. 무조건
3. 묶다
4. 밀다
5. 정거장
6. 차례
7. 특기
8. 펴다
9. 활용하다
10. 흔히
11. 어쩌면
12. 줍다
13. 괜히
14. 맞벌이를
15. 이용한다고
16. 깜짝
17. 만족해
18. 변해
19. 충고했어요
20. 푹
21. 향기
22. 외출하
23. 비교해
24. ❷
25. ❶
26. ❹
27. ❸
28. ❷
29. ❹
30. ❹
31. 변경해야
32. 또한
33. 주웠어요
34. 어쩐지
35. 넘어져서
36. 들러서
37. 방금
38. 아무래도
39. 마침
40. 자르
41. ❶
42. ❷
43. ❸
44. ❶
45. ❹
46. ❷
47. ❶
48. 가만히

49. 가까이
50. 잔뜩
51. 그냥
52. 결국
53. 떨어뜨렸어요
54. 밟
55. 방문할
56. 봉사하
57. 서늘해진
58. 알려
59. 우연히
60. 가득
61. 모으
62. 평소
63. 이르다
64. 짜다
65. 꺼내다
66. 낫다
67. 진하다
68. 다듬다
69. 고치다
70. 묻다
71. 타다
72. 즐기다
73. 떠오르다

03 · 건강

1. 뇌
2. 뺨
3. 턱
4. 폐
5. 간
6. 장
7. 주먹
8. 손등
9. 손목
10. 근육
11. 긴급
12. 눈곱
13. 눈썹
14. 늙다
15. 뜨다
16. 병들다
17. 숨
18. 장
19. 털
20. 혀
21. 혈관
22. 혈압
23. 떨
24. 민간요법으로
25. 움직이셔야
26. 규칙적
27. 기운이
28. 보약을
29. 비결이
30. 비위생적
31. 소모해야
32. 숙면을
33. 식사량
34. 약해서
35. 소식
36. 건강식
37. 육식
38. 과식
39. 채식
40. 편식
41. ❸
42. ❷
43. ❶
44. ❷
45. 영양이
46. 식습관은
47. 식욕을
48. 피로가
49. 구급차
50. 참
51. 부상을
52. 치과
53. 당뇨병
54. 부작용이
55. 지쳤어요
56. 동맥경화
57. 암
58. 심장병
59. 성인병
60. 전염병
61. 불면증
62. 우울증
63. 합병증
64. 소화불량
65. 염증
66. ❹
67. ❸
68. ❷
69. ❸
70. ❶
71. ❹
72. 신장
73. 막
74. 취하다
75. 붓다
76. 낳다
77. 옮은
78. 비만이
79. 효과가
80. 비상약을
81. 앓았더니
82. 응급실
83. 사망했습니다
84. 치매
85. 어리
86. 항암제를
87. 하품이

04 · 음식

1. 꿀
2. 무
3. 팥
4. 껌
5. 레몬
6. 배추
7. 버섯
8. 생강
9. 버터
10. 달걀
11. 땅콩
12. 인삼
13. 식빵
14. 가지
15. 후추
16. 식초
17. 소시지
18. 콩나물
19. 옥수수
20. 고구마
21. 빈대떡
22. 식용유
23. 포도주
24. ❹
25. ❸
26. ❶
27. ❷
28. ❸
29. ❸
30. ❹
31. ❷
32. 김장하려고
33. 차려
34. 껍질을
35. 전혀
36. 미지근한
37. 흘리
38. 식
39. 집어서
40. 씹어서
41. 재료
42. 도시락을
43. 특별히
44. 송편은
45. 번거로운
46. 넘치다
47. 썩다
48. 남다
49. 깎다
50. 담그다
51. 부드럽다
52. 쏟다
53. 싸다
54. 맡다

55. 담아
56. 갈아서
57. 섞으면
58. 솜씨가
59. 밥맛이
60. 뒤집어
61. 벗겨
62. 데치세요
63. 밀가루
64. 국물이
65. 억지로
66. 포도주
67. ❷
68. ❹
69. ❸
70. ❶
71. ❶
72. ❷
73. ❸
74. 느끼하
75. 비린
76. 떫은
77. 달콤해서
78. 고소하

05 · 가정

1. 빗
2. 가구
3. 오븐
4. 지붕
5. 침실
6. 베개
7. 도구
8. 바늘
9. 대문
10. 밥솥
11. 렌즈
12. 담요
13. 유리
14. 벨트
15. 가스
16. 신문지
17. 라이터
18. 테이프
19. 손윗사람
20. 알뜰해서
21. 닮아
22. 외동딸로
23. 동네
24. 용돈을
25. 자식을
26. 심부름을
27. 치워야겠어요
28. 배터리를
29. 비닐봉지
30. 공과금을
31. 남매
32. 며느리
33. 배우자
34. 손자(손주)
35. 시부모
36. 신랑
37. 신혼부부
38. 장남
39. 막내
40. 형님
41. 형부
42. 아버님
43. 세입자는
44. 보증금
45. 설치해
46. 화분을
47. 플라스틱은
48. 꾸몄어요
49. 목욕탕
50. 전기
51. 바구니
52. 서랍
53. 손잡이를
54. 식구
55. 안방
56. ❷
57. ❸
58. ❷
59. ❶
60. ❹
61. ❶
62. ❸
63. 당신
64. 수도
65. 치우다
66. 모시다
67. 깨다
68. 달다
69. 들다
70. 산더미
71. 현관
72. 먼지가
73. 바닥
74. 털
75. 쓰레기통
76. 쓸

06 · 인간관계

1. 겸손하다
2. 끄덕이다
3. 대화
4. 맞서다
5. 미팅
6. 사교성
7. 사이좋다
8. 상대방
9. 소문
10. 술자리
11. 악수
12. 야유회
13. 연락처
14. 초청장
15. 친근감
16. 회식
17. 쳐다봤다
18. 미소를
19. 아무리
20. 도움이
21. 알아들을
22. 타일렀지만
23. 오히려
24. 여전하시네요
25. 회상하며
26. 말다툼을
27. 반했나
28. 예절을
29. 오랜만
30. 용서를
31. 전해
32. 추억하다
33. 궁금하다
34. 권하다
35. 기대하다
36. 후회하다
37. ❹
38. ❸
39. ❷
40. 상관없으니까
41. 원하는
42. 대해
43. 데려가
44. 잔치가
45. 볼일이
46. 안부
47. 분위기가
48. 숙이며
49. 대화
50. 돌려줘라
51. 참석해
52. 한턱내신다고
53. 행동하면
54. 개인적
55. 이해하
56. 신경
57. 살짝
58. 나누다
59. 돌보다
60. 어색하다
61. 끊어지다
62. 비밀이야

63. 거짓말을
64. 공경하는
65. 그리워지네요
66. 기억
67. 끼쳐서
68. 무시하
69. 바라보셨다
70. 소용없다고
71. 가입했다
72. 회원은
73. 인상을
74. 낯설어
75. 농담을
76. 고백하
77. 거절할까
78. 모이

07 학교와 수업

1. 각자
2. 글
3. 내용
4. 불만
5. 성적
6. 알맞다
7. 억양
8. 언어 교환
9. 옳다
10. 의미
11. 제목
12. 집중하다
13. 행사
14. 미리
15. 상담해요
16. 스스로
17. 적어
18. 얼른
19. 접수할
20. 특히
21. 정확해요
22. 다행히
23. 복사해서
24. 마침내
25. 반복해서
26. 종일
27. ❹
28. ❷
29. ❶
30. ❸
31. 나날이
32. 마음대로
33. 강조하다
34. 번역하다
35. 외우다
36. 떠들다
37. 반장
38. 규칙
39. ❶
40. ❸
41. 필기한
42. 마치
43. 밤새
44. 깜빡
45. 토론해
46. 거의
47. 합격했다면서요
48. 훨씬
49. 추천해
50. 신청했어요
51. 진학을
52. 이유가
53. 설마
54. 최선
55. 겨우
56. 그다지
57. 정도
58. 나머지
59. 주제
60. 어울리다
61. 빠뜨리다
62. 맞추다
63. 빼다
64. 맞다
65. 풀다

08 · 경제

1. 그램
2. 길이
3. 깊이
4. 나머지
5. 납부
6. 높이
7. 세로
8. 수표
9. 예금
10. 창구
11. 초보자
12. 크기
13. 폭
14. 폰뱅킹
15. 센티미터(cm), 미터(m), 인치(in)
16. 제곱센티미터(cm^2), 제곱미터(m^2), 제곱킬로미터(km^2)
17. 그램(g), 킬로그램(kg), 톤(t)
18. 밀리리터(mℓ), 리터(ℓ), 시시(cc)
19. 경제적이에요
20. 관리해
21. 단기간
22. 서툴러요
23. 대기업
24. 세금이
25. 반품이
26. 신용을
27. 제공하
28. 조건이
29. 포기하
30. 가맹점
31. 고생하셨어요
32. 함부로
33. 심각한
34. ❸
35. ❶
36. ❶
37. ❸
38. ❹
39. ❷
40. ❹
41. ❸
42. ❷
43. ❹
44. ❸
45. ❶
46. 고객
47. 공짜로
48. 광고
49. 무이자
50. 문의해
51. 배송을
52. 상태가
53. 새로운
54. 경험이
55. 선택할
56. 차이가
57. 판매한다고
58. 견디면
59. 하자가
60. 조사해야
61. 따지다
62. 유행하다
63. 쌓다
64. 덜다
65. 살아나다
66. 세다
67. 서비스
68. 경우
69. 소비자
70. 그만두어야
71. 기회를
72. 긴장을

73. 환불해
74. 수고했다
75. 얻을
76. 중요성을
77. 면제돼요
78. 보험
79. 할인을
80. 즉
81. 맞추

09 · 사회

1. 검사
2. 국가
3. 교수
4. 목수
5. 비서
6. 시인
7. 예전
8. 건축가
9. 근로자
10. 과학자
11. 대통령
12. 외교관
13. 탤런트
14. 국회의원
15. 디자이너
16. 아나운서
17. 프로게이머
18. 거래처
19. 실수하는
20. 결과
21. 경영하
22. 계약을
23. 문제점
24. 승진하신
25. 능력을
26. 분석해야
27. 번화한
28. ❶
29. ❸
30. ❹
31. ❷
32. ❷
33. ❸
34. ❹
35. 공장
36. 몰두하는
37. 영향을
38. 순간을
39. 가능하다고
40. 메모해
41. 신상품이
42. 야근을
43. 사정이
44. 신형
45. ❷
46. ❹
47. ❶
48. ❹
49. ❸
50. ❶
51. 면접시험이
52. 서류와
53. 무역을
54. 능통한
55. 경력자는
56. 취직했으면
57. 부담
58. 짓다
59. 흐르다
60. 해결하다
61. 벌이다
62. 뽑다
63. 보고해
64. 발달하면서
65. 파일을
66. 목표는
67. 무리해서
68. 어느새
69. 건의해
70. 결정하
71. 개발한
72. 여유가
73. 발견했다
74. 그대로
75.

①미	루	다				⑤현	재
래			②옛		④고	대	
		③훗	날				
⑥무	리				⑦경	쟁	
렵					력		
		⑨시	절				
	⑧세	대			⑩출	⑪세	
	월					기	

10 · 문화

1. 쇼
2. 짐
3. 교류
4. 마술
5. 체육
6. 축제
7. 미디어
8. 사실적
9. 포스터
10. 경조사비
11. 대중문화
12. 개봉
13. 다큐멘터리
14. 공연
15. 관객
16. 관람
17. 가면극
18. 무용
19. 뮤지컬
20. 대사
21. 연기
22. 예술
23. 주인공
24. 동기는
25. 감동하셨는지
26. 수상했대요
27. 박수를
28. 열린다고
29. 인기가
30. 표현할
31. 민간신앙을
32. 결승전
33. 출전한
34. 복을
35. 강강술래
36. 돌
37. 속담
38. 사물놀이
39. 환갑
40. 성묘
41. 세배
42. 사투리
43. 귀성
44. ❸
45. ❹
46. 사주를
47. 운이
48. 대회
49. 신기록을
50. 우승할

51. 졌어요
52. 사고방식이
53. 상쾌해요
54. 가이드가
55. 머물렀던
56. 숙소를
57. 배경
58. 역할
59. 환상적
60. 벅차다
61. 빌다
62. 보호하다
63. 옮기다
64. 따다
65. 대단하다
66. 차다
67. 문화유산이
68. 역시
69. 역사적
70. 전통
71. 포함되어
72. 연장해야겠어요
73. 현지인
74. 참가하
75. 기도를
76. 교포예요
77. 올림픽이
78. ❶
79. ❷
80. ❹
81. ❸
82. ❷
83. ❶
84. ❹
85. 천주교
86. 기독교
87. 불교
88. 성직자라고
89. 신을
90. 소원을

11 속담, 관용어, 한자성어, 의태어, 의성어

11-1 속담

1. 세 살 적 버릇 여든까지 간다고
2. 금강산도 식후경이라고
3. 원숭이도 나무에서 떨어질 때가 있다고
4. 배보다 배꼽이 크군요.
5. 아닌 땐 굴뚝에 연기나
6. 떡 줄 사람은 꿈도 안 꾸는데 김칫국부터 마신다고
7. 믿는 도끼에 발등 찍혔네
8. 가는 날이 장날이라고
9. 고래 싸움에 새우등 터진
10. 빈 수레가 요란하다더니
11. 꼬리가 길면 밟힌다더니
12. 누워서 침 뱉기라고
13. 호랑이도 제 말 하면 온다더니
14. 돌다리도 두들겨 보고 건너라고
15. 소 잃고 외양간 고친다고
16. 바늘 도둑이 소 도둑 된다고
17. 윗물이 맑아야 아랫물이 맑다고
18. 콩 심은 데 콩 나고 팥 심은데 팥 난다고

11-2 관용어

1. 손을 잡
2. 하늘의 별 따기야
3. 손을 뗐다던데
4. 길눈이 어두워서
5. 눈이 높아서
6. 발을 끊었대
7. 손이 크셔서
8. 옷이 날개라고
9. 눈을 감아
10. 발이 넓어서
11. 제 눈에 안경이라고
12. 귀에 못이 박이도록
13. 엎어지면 코 닿을
14. 입이 무거운
15. 어깨가 무겁
16. 낯을 가려서
17. 맛이 갔나
18. 눈 코 뜰 새가 없어요
19. 귀를 기울일
20. 낯이 두껍
21. 금이 간
22. 누워서 떡 먹기

11-3 한자성어

1. ㉥
2. ㉠
3. ㉨
4. ㉤
5. ㉩
6. ㉣
7. ㉢
8. ㉡
9. ㉦
10. ㉧
11. ㉤
12. ㉧
13. ㉩
14. ㉥
15. ㉦
16. ㉨
17. ㉠
18. ㉢
19. ㉡
20. ㉣
21. 동문서답이야
22. 이심전심이네
23. 팔방미인이군요
24. 작심삼일이라는
25. 유언비어를
26. 막상막하야
27. 고집불통이구나
28. 다다익선이지요
29. 대기만성이란
30. 일석이조네
31. 우왕좌왕
32. 이열치열이라고
33. 과소평가
34. 상부상조
35. 유명무실
36. 부전자전이구나
37. 용두사미가
38. 설상가상이로구나
39. 횡설수설
40. 유비무환

11-4 의태어

1. 방실방실
2. 텅
3. 반짝반짝
4. 줄줄
5. 주룩주룩
6. 활짝
7. 꽉
8. 뻘뻘
9. 꾸벅꾸벅
10. 살금살금

11-5 의성어

1. 보글보글
2. 딸랑딸랑
3. 펑
4. 꼬르륵
5. 쿨쿨
6. 풍덩
7. 훅
8. 앵
9. 똑딱똑딱
10. 덜컹덜컹

02 색인

표: 표제어(headwords), 유: 유의어(synonyms), 반: 반의어(antonyms), 관: 관련어(related words)

외국인을 위한

한국어 어휘 연습 (중급)

영어판

편저자 연세대학교 한국어학당 교재편찬위원회
집필진 전나영 · 오경은 · 김종인 · 김민지
펴낸곳 연세대학교 대학출판문화원

주소 서울시 서대문구 연세로 50
전화 2123-3380~2
팩스 2123-8673
ysup@yonsei. ac. kr
http://www. yonsei. ac. kr/press
등록 1955년 10월 13일 제9-60호
인쇄 (주)동국문화

2011년 11월 2일 1판 1쇄 2024년 11월 25일 1판 9쇄
ISBN 978-89-7141-966-3(03710)

값 25,000원